THE INDISSOLUBILITY OF MARRIAGE & THE COUNCIL OF TRENT

E. CHRISTIAN BRUGGER

THE INDISSOLUBILITY OF MARRIAGE & THE COUNCIL OF TRENT

THE CATHOLIC UNIVERSITY OF AMERICA PRESS

WASHINGTON, D.C.

Copyright © 2017
The Catholic University of America Press

All rights reserved

Library of Congress Cataloging-in-Publication Data
Names: Brugger, E. Christian, (Eugene Christian), 1964– author.
Title: The indissolubility of marriage and the Council of Trent /
E. Christian Brugger.
Description: Washington, D.C. : The Catholic University of America Press, 2017. |
Includes bibliographical references and index.
Identifiers: LCCN 2016055811 | ISBN 9780813237862 (pbk)
Subjects: LCSH: Marriage—Religious aspects—Catholic Church—History—
16th century. | Council of Trent (1545–1563 : Trento, Italy) |
Catholic Church—Doctrines.
Classification: LCC BX2250 .B78 2017 | DDC 234/.165088282—dc23
LC record available at https://lccn.loc.gov/2016055811

CONTENTS

List of Tables in Appendix B   vii
Preface   ix
List of Abbreviations   xiii

Introduction   1

1. The *Errores* of the Reformers   21
2. The *Ritus* of the Greeks   34
3. Indissolubility and the 1547 Bologna Sessions   50
4. Discussions at Trent on Marriage (1563)   90
5. Trent's Teaching on Indissolubility   125

Appendix A. Authorities Referenced at Trent   149
Appendix B. Recorded Statements of the General Congregation on Indissolubility from 1563   200
Appendix C. Schedule of the Council of Trent   272
Selected Bibliography   275
Index   283

TABLES IN APPENDIX B

TABLE B-1. Remarks of General Congregation on the First Formulation of the Canons on Matrimony (July 24–31, 1513) — 208

TABLE B-2. First Formulation of the Canon on Adultery (Canon 6) Using a Direct Formulation — 220

TABLE B-3. Remarks of the General Congregation on the Second Formulation (August 7–23) — 228

TABLE B-4. Second Formulation of Canon 7 — 237

TABLE B-5. Remarks of the General Congregation on the Third Formulation (September 7–10, 1563) — 240

TABLE B-6. Third Formulation of Canon 7 — 250

TABLE B-7. Remarks of the General Congregation on the Fourth Formulation (October 26–27, 1563) — 254

TABLE B-8. Fourth Formulation of Canon 7 — 262

TABLE B-9. Final *Vota* of the Council Fathers on the Final Formulation (November 11, 1563) — 265

PREFACE

In speaking about marriage, Aquinas introduces the concept of *coniunctio* (joining together). He says marriage is the *coniunctio* of a husband and wife for the sake of establishing a common life in family affairs.[1] For this reason, he continues, marriage is referred to as the "conjugal union."[2] Some might render "conjugal" simply as *sexual*, holding that any persons engaged in sexual behavior for the sake of establishing a common life can form a conjugal union. But Aquinas means the term in a very specific sense. He means a joining together of *complementary* persons, that is, a "coniunctio corporum vel animorum" (a joining together of bodies and souls) for the sake of begetting and raising the children who are the fruits of their *coniunctio*.[3] This joining makes the couple so one that the bond it brings into existence is "indissoluble."[4]

Aquinas, like Augustine before him and the Councils of Trent and Vatican II after him, held this truth about the indissolubility of the conjugal union to be *de fide* (i.e., a truth of divine revelation). But many Catholics today not only deny its revealed status; they think that the view is false. In 2004, Kenneth Himes and James Coriden published a forceful denial of the indissolubility of marriage in *Theological Studies*.[5] The authors asserted that the church's teaching that all consummated, sacramental marriages are absolutely indissoluble "is unrealistic, incoherent, and injurious"; the teaching, they state, "is neither *de fide* nor definitive doctrine." And they

---

1. "*Vita communis* in rebus domesticis"; Aquinas, *Summa Theologiae* [hereafter "ST"] Supp., q. 44, a. 3, co. Note that Aquinas himself did not write the supplement to the ST from which I am citing; it was compiled from his commentary on the *Sentences* of Peter Lombard by his students after his death.
2. ST, Supp., q. 44, a. 2, co.: "coniugium."
3. ST, Supp., q. 44, a. 1, co.
4. ST, Supp., q. 44, a. 3, co.: "indissolubilis."
5. Kenneth R. Himes, OFM, and James A. Coriden, "The Indissolubility of Marriage: Reasons to Reconsider," *Theological Studies* 65, no. 3 (2004): 453-99.

argue that their essay adequately demonstrates the teaching's falsity: "we maintain that the evidence marshaled in this article constitutes a substantial case against the present teaching on indissolubility."[6] Included in their "evidence" was an argument that the Council of Trent's teaching on marital indissolubility does not constitute a dogma of faith, a conclusion which they believed justified them in arguing for a reform in the substance of the ancient Catholic teaching.

In 2011, the moral theologian Germain Grisez and his colleague Peter F. Ryan, SJ, published a reply to Himes and Coriden in the same journal.[7] Their research brought them into contact with Trent's teaching on marriage, especially with disputed questions—dealt with in this book—over the formulation of canon 7 on adultery in the Council's treatise on the sacrament of matrimony. They also became acquainted with the interpretation of the Council's teaching on indissolubility by the Flemish Jesuit theologian, Piet Fransen, upon whom Himes and Coriden relied. Although Fransen's treatment appeared to be learned and was far and away the most influential account on Trent and indissolubility published in the twentieth century, Grisez and Ryan observed that at multiple points the author seemed to assert conclusions that were not supported by the historical record as set down in the Council's *Acta*. "Fransen," Grisez said to me, "seems simply to help himself to his conclusions." I began to read my way into the Conciliar proceedings, as well as into the writings of Piet Fransen. I eventually decided to undertake a substantial research project on the very narrow topic of the meaning and scope of the Council of Trent's teaching on the indissolubility of marriage.

Pope Benedict XVI was reigning at the time. He resigned in February 2013, and a month later Jorge Bergoglio was elected as his successor, taking the name Francis. Almost a year after Benedict's resignation, Cardinal Walter Kasper, at the invitation of Pope Francis, delivered a controversial address to a gathering of cardinals in Rome defending the permissibility and advisability of admitting some divorced and civilly remarried Catholics to the sacraments without having received annulments.[8] Cardinal Kasper claimed that what was in question was not the doctrinal principle of marital indissolubility, but only the traditional ecclesial practice of ex-

---

6. Ibid., 499.

7. Peter F. Ryan, SJ, and Germain Grisez, "Indissoluble Marriage: A Reply to Kenneth Himes and James Coriden," *Theological Studies* 72 (2011): 369-415.

8. The address, delivered on February 20, 2014, was published in English under the title *The Gospel of the Family* (Mahwah, N.J.: Paulist Press, 2014).

cluding the divorced and civilly remarried from receiving the eucharist. He proposed a "path of conversion and penance" in which divorced and civilly remarried individuals approach the church on a "case by case" basis. The church's pastoral minister, taking into consideration the "uniqueness of every person and every situation," would accompany the petitioners on a pathway that would result in their return to the sacrament of penance and communion "after a period of reorientation."⁹ That "reorientation" need not include as a condition for reconciliation and return to the sacraments that the individuals resolve to live consistent with the church's ancient interpretation of Jesus' teaching on marriage in scripture, which, practically, has always required the separation of those in the second union, or, at least, their resolution to "live in complete continence."¹⁰

My very narrow topic suddenly became pressingly current. For despite Kasper's claim, the proverbial elephant in the room is the substantive question of the nature and authority of the church's teaching on indissolubility. The logic of the ancient practice of excluding those who are in sexually active second unions from participation in the eucharist while their first spouses still live is tightly bound to the content of the teaching on the absolute indissolubility of a consummated sacramental marriage. An alteration in the practice will almost certainly require in time a reconsideration of the truth of the ancient doctrine. So the question of the content and scope of Trent's teaching on indissolubility has everything to do with whether Kasper's proposal can be adopted by the Catholic church.

I offer my research and conclusions as a contribution to this important debate. I offer them as a theologian, not a historian. The historical examination tracing the debates of the Council fathers on marriage, especially the successive formulations of the canons on indissolubility, is set forward with one purpose in mind: to determine what the Council intended to teach on the question of indissolubility and with what authority it intended to teach it.

I received invaluable assistance and support in completing this work. I wish to thank in the first place Prof. Grisez, who both inspired the project and read and commented on the entire manuscript in draft. I thank also John M. Finnis, Peter F. Ryan, SJ, Elizabeth Shaw, Robert P. George, Patrick Lee, Ryan Anderson, Sherif Girgis, Wolfgang Mann, Marianne Kantert, and Rose L. Brugger. I thank as well the penultimate rector of St. John

9. Ibid., 26, 32, 46.
10. Pope John Paul II, *Familiaris Consortio*, Apostolic Exhortation, November 22, 1981, par. 84, in *Acta Apostolicae Sedis* [hereafter "AAS"] 74 (1982): 185-86.

Vianney Theological Seminary, Msgr. Michael Glenn, and its present rector, Rev. Scott Traynor, for granting me a sabbatical in 2014-15 to advance the project, as well as John and Carol Saeman, who funded the J. Cardinal Stafford Chair in Moral Theology, which I hold and which assisted me with research expenses. I thank also my seminary colleagues in theology, Alan Fimister and Joel Barstad, and the seminary's intrepid Latinist, Philip Banning, who endured on my behalf many hours of Latin proofreading. Thanks are also due to the director of the Cardinal Stafford Library, Steven Sweeney, and his chief librarian, Tamara Conley, for many hours of assistance in hunting down texts. Finally, I wish to thank my wife, Melissa, who supported me during this project in untold ways, some of which are known only to our Father in heaven.

ABBREVIATIONS

AAS — *Acta Apostolicae Sedis*
CIC — *Corpus Iuris Canonici*
CT — *Concilium Tridentinum: diariorum, ectorum, epistularum tractatuum*
DEC — *Decrees of the Ecumenical Councils* (ed. Tanner)
Denz. — *Enchiridion Symbolorum* (ed. Denzinger)
FOTC — Fathers of the Church series (The Catholic University of America Press)
GS — *Gaudium et Spes* (Vatican Council II)
Mansi — *Sacrorum Conciliorum Nova et Amplissima Collectio* (Mansi)
NPNF-I — Nicene and Post-Nicene Fathers, First Series (ed. Schaff)
NPNF-II — Nicene and Post-Nicene Fathers, Second Series (eds. Schaff and Wace)
PG — Patrologiae Cursus Completus, Series Graeca (ed. Migne)
PL — Patrologiae Cursus Completus, Series Latina (ed. Migne)
RSV — Revised Standard Version (Holy Bible)
ST — *Summa Theologiae* (Thomas Aquinas)
VUL — *Biblia Sacra Iuxta Vulgatam Versionem*

THE INDISSOLUBILITY OF MARRIAGE & THE COUNCIL OF TRENT

INTRODUCTION

I, ____, take you, ____, to be my lawfully wedded husband/wife, to have and to hold, from this day forward, for better, for worse, for richer, for poorer, in sickness and in health, until death do us part.

Even today, when marriage is the subject of many bitter disputes, the power and attraction of these words can be recognized. The solemn promise of a couple to love one another until death represents the highest ideal of a human relationship, one in which two people unrelated by blood resolve to enter a union stronger than blood, a union that transcends the instabilities of other friendships, where the giving of oneself and receiving of another are marked by totality and permanence.

Among the great world religions, the permanence of marriage is still held today—indeed only held today—by the Catholic church. The source of its teaching are the words of Jesus, whose discourses on marriage recorded in the synoptic Gospels transformed the history of the institution. Jesus said that from the beginning, God made human beings male and female, and "for this reason a man shall leave his father and mother and be joined to his wife, and the two shall become one flesh." This was familiar to his disciples, who knew well the words he was quoting from Genesis 2. But then Jesus adds something entirely new, something that no teacher in Israel had ever taught, something that, as John P. Meier says, "seems to come out of nowhere in Judaism and to go nowhere in Judaism."[1] This is that when two unite in marriage and consummate their union, God too does something. God joins the spouses in such a way that the resulting union—the marriage—not only must not but cannot be broken: "What therefore God has joined together, let not man put asunder."[2] This teaching of Jesus is the

---

1. John P. Meier, "The Historical Jesus and the Historical Law: Some Problems within the Problem," *Catholic Biblical Quarterly* 65 (2003): 52–79, at 79.
2. Mt 19:5–6, from the Revised Standard Version, in *The New Oxford Annotated Bible with*

origin and substance of the Catholic church's doctrine of the *indissolubility* of marriage.³

The Second Vatican Council in 1965 repeated the teaching when it stated that the giving of oneself and receiving of the other that takes place in and through marital consent and consummation results in a relationship that by God's *ordinatio* (arrangement) is "stable and lasting."⁴ Marriage, the council taught, is an "*indissoluble* covenant between persons," a "sharing and communion for the *whole* of life."⁵ Married love is "*indissolubly* faithful physically and mentally in prosperity and adversity" and so is "inconsistent with all adultery and divorce;" it is made "especially *inviolable* by the sacrament."⁶ Even if children are not able to come forth from the union, the marriage still "retains its goodness and *indissolubility*."⁷ To emphasize that God is the guarantor of this permanence, the Council referred to the *vinculum* (marriage bond) as "sacred," something consecrated, a holy thing.⁸ More than five hundred years earlier, the Council of Florence taught that this indissolubility "signifies the indivisible union of Christ and the Church," and adds, "the bond of a legitimately contracted marriage is *perpetual*."⁹ In the words of Vatican II, it "does not depend on human decision."¹⁰

Despite the lax divorce practices of the Empire into which Christianity was born and periodic toleration of divorce by some local churches in the early Middle Ages, the Catholic church from the apostolic period down to

---

the Apocrypha, eds. Herbert G. May and Bruce M. Metzger (New York: Oxford University Press, 1962), 1196. Unless stated otherwise, all scriptural translations below are drawn from the RSV.

3. See also Mt 5:32, Mk 10:11–12, Lk 16:18, Rom 7:2–3, 1 Cor 7:10–11.

4. "Intima communitas vitae et amoris coniugalis, a creatore condita suisque legibus instructa, foedere coniugii seu irrevocabili consensu personali instauratur. Ita actu humano, quo coniuges sese mutuo tradunt atque accipiunt, institutum ordinatione divina firmum oritur." Vatican Council II, *Gaudium et Spes*, December 7, 1965, no. 48 [hereafter, GS], in *Decrees of the Ecumenical Councils*, ed. Norman P. Tanner (Washington, D.C.: Georgetown University Press, 1990), 2:1100 [hereafter, DEC].

5. GS, no. 50: "foederis inter personas indissolubilis" (DEC, 2:1103). Ibid.: "totius vitae consuetudo et communio" (emphasis added).

6. GS, no. 49: "inter prospera et adversa corpore ac mente indissolubiliter fidelis est, et proinde ab omni adulterio et divortio alienus remanet" (DEC, 2:1102; emphasis added). Ibid.: "potissimum sacramento Christi sancitus" (emphasis added).

7. Ibid.: "valorem atque indissolubilitatem servat" (emphasis added).

8. GS, no. 48: "hoc vinculum sacrum" (DEC, 2:1100).

9. Council of Florence, "Bull of Union with the Armenians" (1439): "significat indivisibilem coniunctionem Christi et ecclesie" (DEC, 1:550). Ibid.: "matrimonii vinculum legitime contracti perpetuum sit" (emphasis added).

10. Ibid.: "non ex humano arbitrio pendet."

today has taught and teaches the absolute indissolubility of Christian marriage.[11] Most scholars agree that indissolubility was taken to be exceptionless by all Christian writers, East and West, during the first five centuries of the Christian era.[12] As a textual tradition of canon law developed within Byzantine Christianity starting in the sixth century, the Eastern ("Greek") church began to fall under the influence of the more permissive views of divorce found in the civil laws of the Eastern emperors.[13] By the high Middle Ages, the Greek church officially permitted divorce and remarriage for more than a dozen reasons. Similarly, Protestant Christians believed that Jesus made an exception to the rule of indissolubility in cases of adultery. Within the first fifteen years of Luther's public ministry, he defended divorce and remarriage multiple times, not only for adultery—which using an analogy with death, he argued was like the death of a spouse—but also for spousal conflict and the denial of conjugal right, which he said were forms of spiritual death.

But the Western church maintained throughout its strict position. It was especially influenced by Augustine, who argued that if remarried divorcees are guilty of adultery while their first spouse remained alive, then something of the first marriage must remain in existence after the other

---

11. Roman law permitted divorce and remarriage for a variety of reasons. Even after the conversion of Constantine, permissive divorce laws in the Roman Empire continued. In addition, according to Joyce, the Frankish church in the eighth century, under the influence of permissive penitential manuals, began to tolerate divorce in certain circles; but the practice was an anomaly. George Hayward Joyce, SJ, *Christian Marriage: An Historical and Doctrinal Study* (London: Sheed and Ward, 1933), 334.

12. With the exception of the fourth-century biblical commentator referred to as Ambrosiaster, no Patristic author, East or West, and no decree of a pope or council ever taught the permissibility or even possibility of divorce and remarriage, including in cases of adultery. See Joyce, *Christian Marriage*, 359; Henri Crouzel, *L'Église primitive face au divorce: Du premier au cinquième siècle* (Paris: Beauchesne, 1971); John P. Beal, "Commentary on Art. 1, Ch. IX, Title VII: Marriage," in *New Commentary on the Code of Canon Law*, eds. John P. Beal, James A. Coriden, and Thomas J. Green (New York: Paulist Press, 2000), 1359; John Rist, "Divorce and Remarriage in the Early Church: Some Historical and Cultural Reflections," in *Remaining in the Truth of Christ: Marriage and Communion in the Catholic Church*, ed. Robert Dodaro, OSA (San Francisco: Ignatius, 2014), 64–92, esp. 81–83. The claim holds true "despite those rare texts that are open to ambiguous interpretations or that signal the admission of a certain rational comprehension and eventual pastoral tolerance of isolated cases of divorce and remarriage in contradiction to the gospel" (Archbishop Cyril Vasil', SJ, "Separation, Divorce, Dissolution of the Bond, and Remarriage: Theological and Practical Approaches of the Orthodox Churches," in *Remaining in the Truth of Christ*, ed. Dodaro, 93–128, at 98–99). The most influential of these "rare texts" are considered in appendix B.

13. Clarence Gallagher, *Church Law and Church Order in Rome and Byzantium: A Comparative Study* (Cornwall: Ashgate, 2002), 32.

parts of the union have broken down. He refers to it variously as the "marital covenant," the "marriage bond," and the "nuptial bond."[14] Its substance (*res*), he says, is inseparability.[15] The bond only dissolves at the death of one of the spouses.[16] The dissolution of political unity in the Western part of the Empire from the sixth century left the Latin church much less encumbered by imperial interference. Consequently, the Latin bishops had greater freedom to maintain fidelity to the teachings of scripture on marriage. By the time of the Council of Trent in the sixteenth century, the permissive practices of the Greeks and strict practices of the Romans were firmly established in their respective theological and canonical traditions.

This is not to say the doctrine of indissolubility was born in a fully developed form. Interpretive questions had to be addressed, such as to how to understand the so-called exceptive clause in the Gospel of Matthew—"And I say to you: whoever divorces his wife, *except for unchastity* [Greek *porneia*; Latin *fornicationem*; interpreted as "adultery" at Trent], and marries another, commits adultery" (19:9). The tradition in the Western church was that Jesus was referring to a *separation of spouses* in cases of adultery, not divorce and remarriage ("separation of bed, not bond").

Development also took place in the church's understanding of the scope of the doctrine of indissolubility. When Jesus taught that Moses permitted divorce for Israel's "hardness of heart," but that "from the beginning" marriage was indissoluble (Mt 19:8), he indicates that by its very nature marriage is indissoluble. But the passage from Paul (1 Cor 7) permitting a Christian convert to separate from an unbelieving spouse if the latter was unwilling to live peaceably with the Christian spouse seemed to single out a class of natural marriages susceptible to dissolution.[17] This "Pauline

---

14. *De Bono Conjugali*, 7 (Patrologiae Cursus Completus, Series Latina, ed. J.-P. Migne [Paris, 1841–55]): "confoederatio nuptialis," 40:378 [hereafter, PL]. Ibid., 15 (PL 40:385): "vinculum nuptiarum." Ibid., 24 (PL 40:394): "vinculum nuptiale."

15. *De Nuptiis et Concupiscentia* I, 11 (PL 44:420): "huius procul dubio sacramenti res est, ut mas et femina connubio copulati quamdiu vivunt inseparabiliter perseverant."

16. "When a wife is divorced for committing adultery, the bond of marriage union remains in her, and she does not lose that bond even if she is never reconciled with her husband. She will lose it, however if her husband dies." *De Adulterinis Conjugiis ad Pollentium* II, 4–5; English translation from "On Adulterous Marriages," in *Marriage and Virginity* (*Works of St. Augustine: A Translation for the 21st Century*), ed. John Rotelle, OSA (Hyde Park, N.Y.: New City, 2000), 168.

17. "To the married I give charge, not I but the Lord, that the wife should not separate from her husband... and that the husband should not divorce his wife. To the rest I say, not the Lord, that if any brother has a wife who is an unbeliever, and she consents to live with him, he should not divorce her. If any woman has a husband who is an unbeliever, and he consents to live wither, she should not divorce him .... But if the unbelieving partner desires to separate,

Privilege" became enshrined in Western canon law in the Middle Ages.[18] It permitted the dissolution of a marriage between two non-baptized persons in the case that one (but not both) of the partners seeks baptism and converts to Christianity and the other partner "departs" the marriage (i.e., is unwilling to live peacefully within the marriage).[19] In response to the missionary growth in the New World in the sixteenth century, the popes began to extend the Pauline Privilege to polygamous unions that missionaries in the Americas encountered.[20] As mixed cult marriages became more common in the modern period, the logic of the Pauline exception was applied to marriages between a *baptized* and a *non-baptized person*. Known as the Petrine Privilege, this type of union—a valid natural marriage between a baptized and a non-baptized person—admitted of dissolution by the pope, and him alone thus permitting both to remarry. The petitioner had to be one of the parties in the marriage to be dissolved. And the dissolution had to be for one of the parties to remarry in the church—necessary for salvation. Thus it came to be called the "privilege of the faith" or dissolution "in favor of the faith."[21]

How could these forms of dissolution be reconciled with the teaching of Jesus on the indissolubility of natural and not merely sacramental marriage? To conceptually distinguish classes of marriages susceptible to dissolution from those that were not, traditional authors came to differentiate between "intrinsic" and "extrinsic" indissolubility.[22] Intrinsic indissolubility refers to a property of marriage against which spousal action—that is, action taken by those who contract the marriage—cannot dissolve the union.

---

let it be so; in such a case the brother or sister is not bound. For God has called us to peace" (1 Cor 7:10–15).

18. See the writings of Pope Innocent III, in *Decretals of Gregory IX*, §§ 7–8, *de divortiis* iv. 19. The Council fathers at Trent were familiar with the Pauline Privilege; see *Concilium Tridentinum: diariorum, ectorum, epistularum tractatuum nova collectio*, Societas Goerresiana, Tomus IX (Freiburg im Breisgau: Herder, 1965), 404.21–23 [hereafter, CT, followed by volume number in Roman numerals]. But their knowledge of this exception to the indissolubility of natural marriage had no effect on their final teaching on the indissolubility of Christian marriages.

19. See 1983 Code of Canon Law, c. 1143, §1 and §2, for a modern explanation of the conditions for this type of dissolution.

20. See c. 1148, §1; also John Beal, "Commentary on Art. 1, Ch. IX, Title VII: Marriage," in *New Commentary on the Code of Canon Law*, ed. Beal, 1361.

21. See Beal's commentary on "Dissolution of a Non-sacramental Marriage 'In Favor of the Faith,'" in *New Commentary on the Code of Canon Law*, ed. Beal, 1372–73; and c. 1150.

22. See, for example, Dominico Palmieri, *Tractatus de Matrimonio Christiano*, cap. III, § II, thesis XVI (Rome, 1880), 125–40; Felix Cappello, *De Sacramentis*, vol. V: *De Matrimonio (Tractatus Canonico-Moralis)* (Rome: Marietti, 1961), no. 45.

It does not imply that an extrinsic authority, such as the church, cannot dissolve it. This is contrasted with "extrinsic indissolubility" which means that nothing but death can dissolve the marriage. The church came to hold that all valid natural marriages are intrinsically indissoluble. Only consummated sacramental marriages are extrinsically or absolutely indissoluble.[23]

SHOULD THE CHURCH CHANGE ITS TEACHING?

Theologians today debate whether the Catholic church can and should moderate its strict teaching on the absolute indissolubility of a ratified and consummated marriage (*ratum et consummatum*) to bring it into conformity with what one theologian referred to as the "tolerant tradition" of the Orthodox churches.[24] Some answer that it both can and should be changed, others that it can be changed but that there are good reasons for preserving the traditional teaching in pastoral practice, and still others that the teaching constitutes an irreformable part of the Catholic moral tradition.[25] Each answer relies among other things on an examination of the status of the doctrine in Catholic teaching, in particular, answering whether marital indissolubility constitutes an irreformable "dogma" of faith.[26]

---

23. "A marriage that is *ratum et consummatum* can be dissolved by no human power and by no cause, except death" (c. 1141).

24. Regarding "ratified" and "consummated" marriages, c. 1061, §1, states: "A valid marriage between the baptized is called *ratum tantum* [i.e., ratified only] if it has not been consummated; it is called *ratum et consummatum* if the spouses have performed between themselves in a human way a conjugal act which is suitable in itself for the procreation of offspring, to which marriage is ordered by its nature and by which the spouses become one flesh." (Matrimonium inter baptizatos validum dicitur ratum tantum, si non est consummatum; ratum et consummatum, si coniuges inter se humano modo posuerunt coniugalem actum per se aptum ad prolis generationem, ad quem natura sua ordinatur matrimonium, et quo coniuges fiunt una caro.) On the "tolerant tradition," see Giancarlo Pani, SJ, "Matrimonio E 'Seconde Nozze' Al Concilio Di Trento" (Matrimony and 'Second Marriages' at the Council of Trent), *La Civiltà Cattolica*, IV, no. 1 (2014): 3–104.

25. See Himes and Coriden, "Indissolubility of Marriage"; Walter Kasper, *Theology of Christian Marriage* (New York: Crossroad, 1981), originally published as *Zur Theologie der christlichen Ehe* (Mainz: Matthias-Grünwald-Verlag, 1977), 59–62; and Joyce, *Christian Marriage*, 395, respectively.

26. "Dogma" refers to a teaching proposed by the Catholic church in a solemn judgment as a matter to be believed as divinely revealed. See Vatican Council I, *Dei Filius*, 1870, no. 8; Sacred Congregation for the Doctrine of the Faith, "Declaration in Defense of the Catholic Doctrine on the Church Against Certain Errors of the Present Day" (*Mysterium Ecclesia*) (1973), chap. 3. "Dogma" also refers to teachings infallibly proposed by the Ordinary and Universal Magisterium (bishops teaching throughout the world that some proposition of faith or morals is to be held definitively: on this see also Vatican Council II, *Lumen Gentium*, November 21, 1964, no. 25), in DEC, 2:869.

IMPORTANCE OF THE COUNCIL OF TRENT (1545–63)

At the beginning of the sixteenth century the Catholic doctrine of the absolute indissolubility of a consummated Christian marriage was taken for granted.[27] When the Council of Trent opened in 1545, Martin Luther's most influential criticism of the doctrine, from his *De captivitate babylonica*, had already been in print for twenty-five years.[28] Trent replied to Luther's (and Calvin's) challenge to the doctrine in its teaching on the sacrament of matrimony. The account still stands today as the Catholic church's most authoritative teaching on the subject.

On November 11, 1563, at the start of session 24, Trent published twelve canons on marriage preceded by a doctrinal introduction. The canons were published as solemn anathemas, a fact generally but not universally accepted by theologians as giving them the weight of dogmatic definitions. Two bear directly on the question of indissolubility: canons 5 and 7. Canon 5

---

27. A statement of Pope Adrian VI (1522–23) in a work on the sacrament of marriage illustrates the common Catholic doctrine at the beginning of the sixteenth century: "The bond of matrimony is itself the tying of a husband to his wife and vice versa .... If the marriage is between Christians and consummated, then the bond is dissolved only by the natural death of one of the spouses." (Vinculum matrimoniale est ipsa obligatio viri ad mulierem et e converso ... solvitur sola morte naturali alterius coniugum, si est consummatio inter fideles.) Adrian VI, *De Sacramentis* (Rome, 1522), 188. See also the influential Louvain theologian, Ruard Tapper (1487–1559): "Matrimonium contractum et consummatum inter christianos est indissolubile, qualiscumque fiat alter coniugum, sive adulter, sive sterilis, sive haereticus." (A contracted and consummated marriage between Christians is indissoluble, whatsoever be (the condition of) one of the spouses, whether an adulterer, or sterile, or a heretic.) Tapper, *Opera* (Cologne, 1582), *De matr.*, art. 18, sec. II, p. 272. Domingo de Soto (1494–1560) refers the doctrine to *all* marriages, not just to those of Christians: "A consummated marriage is temporally dissolved only through the death of one of the spouses." (Matrimonium consummatum per solum temporalem obitum alterius coniugum dissolvitur.) Soto, *In quartum Sententiarum* (Venice, 1584), 2:116. This is not to say that the doctrine did not have its influential opponents. Erasmus (1469–1536), Cardinal Cajetan (1469–1534), and Ambrogio Catharinus, bishop of Minor (1484–1555), each considered the possibility of the dissolution of marriage on account of adultery. But these appeared, as Bressan notes, "as innovators, outside the mainstream of Catholic thinking; although they were not excommunicated, they had no followers; and Cardinal Cajetan even acknowledged that he had a torrent of doctors (*torrens doctorum*) against him." See Bressan's in-depth consideration of the three authors at Luigi Bressan, *Il Canone Tridentino Sul Divorzio Per Adulterio e L'interpretazione Degli Autori* (Rome: Università Gregoriana Editrice, 1973), 30–48, at 38.

28. *On the Babylonian Captivity of the Church* was first published in 1520. In English it can be found at *Luther's Works*, ed. Abdel R. Wentz (Philadelphia: Fortress Press, 1959), 36:11–126; Luther's argument on divorce and remarriage is at 36:105–6. In Latin, see *Luthers Werke: kritische Gesammtausgabe* VI (Weimar: Hermann Böhlau, 1888), 559–60.

is a straightforward condemnation of anyone who says that the bond of marriage can be dissolved on the grounds of heresy, spousal conflict, or the willful desertion of a spouse.[29] Canon 7 is less straightforward. It addresses the ground of adultery, but does so indirectly.

During session 23 (see appendix C), the canon underwent four revisions. The second formulation was proposed in August 1563. It condemned directly the proposition that marriage can be dissolved on account of adultery:

> If anyone says, that on account of the adultery of one of the spouses a marriage can be dissolved, and that it is licit for both spouses, or at least the innocent spouse who gave no cause for adultery, to remarry while the other spouse is living, and that he does not commit adultery who dismisses an adulteress and marries another, nor she commit adultery who dismisses an adulterer and marries another, let him be anathema.[30]

Had this formulation been promulgated, the question of the status of the Catholic doctrine of indissolubility would be clearer today. Canon 7, however, was not published in this form. It underwent a notable revision as a result of a petition to speak on the formulation made to the Council by a political delegation from the Republic of Venice. The legates explained that in certain territories under Venice's political jurisdiction, the majority of inhabitants, who were Greek Christians, live in singular but fragile unity with the Roman church. The Venetian government permits the Greek archpriests to exercise limited rule over Greek clergy and liturgy, while the Greek inhabitants submit to the loosely defined jurisdiction of the territories' Rome-appointed bishops and periodically profess acknowledgement of the authority of Rome. And while subject and obedient to Roman authority, the Greeks maintain a "most ancient *ritus* of their fathers" which permits them to dismiss an adulterous wife and marry another, a tradition known to and tolerated by the Roman church. Publishing an anathema now would burden the Greeks, confuse them, and incite their rebellion against Rome. The delegation entreated the Council to moderate the language of the canon to relieve the Greeks of the burden of falling under an anathema.

---

29. CT, IX, 967: "Si quis dixerit propter haeresim, aut molestam cohabitationem, aut affectatam absentiam a coniuge dissolve posse matrimonii vinculum, anathema sit."

30. CT, IX, 682.21–24: "Si quis dixerit, propter adulterium alterius coniugum posse matrimonium dissolvi, et utrique coniugum vel saltem innocenti, qui causam adulterio non dederit, licere, altero coniuge vivente, aliud matrimonium contrahere, neque moechari eum, qui dimissa adultera aliam duxerit, neque eum, quae dimisso adultero alii nupserit: anathema sit."

In response the Council adopted a revised formulation for canon 7. It reads:

> If anyone says the church errs, when she has taught and teaches, in accordance with the evangelical and apostolic doctrine, that the bond of marriage cannot be dissolved on account of the adultery of a spouse, and that neither spouse, even one who is innocent and gave no cause for adultery, can contract another marriage while the other spouse is living, and that he commits adultery who dismisses an adulterous wife and marries another, and she commits adultery who dismisses an adulterous husband and marries another: let him be anathema.[31]

We see that Trent adopted an indirect formulation for the canon. Whereas the prior formulation condemned anyone who says that marriage can be dissolved on account of adultery, the revised formula condemns anyone who says "the church errs" when it taught and teaches that marriage can be dissolved on account of adultery. Although the Council adopted in canon 5 a direct formulation for its teaching on indissolubility in the cases of heresy, spousal conflict, and spousal absence, it adopted this rare indirect approach for its teaching on divorce in cases of adultery. That decision has generated a 450-year debate over the meaning and scope of canon 7.

CONTROVERSY OVER INTERPRETATION

The debate began about fifty years after the closing of the Council of Trent. The Servite father Paolo Sarpi (1552–1623), a Venetian canonist, published the first history of the Council in 1619: *Istoria del Concilio Tridentino*.[32] Sarpi had been at odds with the papacy since Pope Paul V had placed the Republic of Venice under an ecclesiastical interdict in 1606. Sarpi energetically defended the Republic with strong polemical writings against papal and curial authority. The polemic continued in his *Istoria*, where he argued that the Council did not intend to define the doctrine of indissolubility, but to leave open the question of whether remarriage in cases of adultery was legitimate.[33]

---

31. "Si quis dixerit, ecclesiam errare, cum docuit et docet, iuxta evangelicam et apostolicam doctrinam, propter adulterium alterius coniugum matrimonii vinculum non posse dissolvi, et utrumque, vel etiam innocentem, qui causam adulterio non dedit, non posse, altero coniuge vivente, aliud matrimonium contrahere, moecharique eum, qui dimissa adultera aliam duxerit, et eam, quae dimisso adultero alii nupserit: anathema sit." CT, IX, 967.31–35.

32. London, 1619; he published it under the pseudonym Pietro Soave. An English translation was published later that century: *History of the Council of Trent* (London, 1676).

33. His antipapalist approach appealed to many Protestants who adopted his account of the Council's teaching on indissolubility. The biased *Istoria*—which "quivers with fierce ha-

In 1651, Pope Innocent X commissioned Italian Jesuit theologian and historian Pietro Sforza Pallavicino (1607–67), later made cardinal (1657), to finish the work on a comprehensive history of the Council of Trent begun two decades earlier by his confrere Terenzio Alciato, SJ. The work was meant as a definitive refutation of Sarpi's anti-Roman work.[34] Pallavicino—who had at his disposal some eighty volumes compiled by Alciato, additional manuscripts, and all the volumes of conciliar acts compiled by the Council secretary Angelo Masarelli—argued that Sarpi's account attributes to the Council not only an alteration in the wording of canon 7, which is beyond doubt, but also, erroneously, a change in the canon's fundamental meaning, "as if the Council embraced a change out of thin air and effected an empty benefit."[35] Although a majority of Council fathers, he said, accepted the proposal to change the canon from a direct to an indirect formulation, most saw no substantive difference in meaning between the two forms.

The seventeenth-century French historian and theologian Jean de Launoy (1603–78) added to the Sarpi interpretation. Since the Council deliberately avoided condemning the Greek practice, he argued, canon 7 should be counted among Trent's "disciplinary" canons. And the church has the power to change the discipline enacted in the canon to suit the needs of

---

tred for the Curia"—has long been recognized as an historically untrustworthy anti-Roman polemic: "the arbitrary way in which he uses his sources in cases where we are in a position to check his statements makes it impossible to rely on the information he supplies and deprives it of all value." Hubert Jedin, *A History of the Council of Trent* (St. Louis, Mo.: B. Herder, 1961), 520. See also L. F. Bungener, *History of the Council of Trent* (New York: Harper and Brothers, 1855), xix–xx. Bossuet wrote of Sarpi: "He was a Protestant under a religious habit, who said Mass without believing in it, and who remained in a Church which he considered idolatrous." Quoted in Bertrand L. Conway, CSP, "Original Diaries of the Council of Trent," *Studies in Church History*, 2nd ed. (London: Herder, 1916), 119–37, at 120.

34. Pallavicino's *Istoria del Concilio di Trento* (History of the Council of Trent) was published in two parts in 1656 and 1657 respectively; it was published again in three volumes in 1664. See Johann Peter Kirsch, "Pietro Sforza Pallavicino," *The Catholic Encyclopedia*, vol. 11 (New York: Robert Appleton, 1911). Pallavicino's *Istoria* is also more a work of apologetics than of history, as the author himself admits: "My history is in great part apologetic in tone. In fact it is more of a book of polemics than a history properly so-called. I aim at refuting my adversary [Sarpi] by showing his ignorance and deceit, and hope to win the confidence of my readers by proving to them that I am well informed. I would have them highly esteem both the rulers of the Church and those who presided over the Council." From a personal letter dated June 2, 1667, to Marchese Durazzo, in *littere del Pallavicino* (Venice, 1669), 71, quoted in Conway, *Original Diaries*, 120.

35. Jedin, *A History of the Council of Trent*, 2:520. P. S. Pallavicino, *History of the Council of Trent* (1666), lib. XXII, cap. IV, nos. 49–50: "quasi complexum mutationem aeream, et utilitatis effectusque vacuam."

the time.[36] About seventy-five years later another French theologian, Pierre François Le Courayer, translator of Sarpi's work into French, followed de Launoy in arguing that the question of indissolubility addressed in canon 7 should be understood as pertaining to the disciplinary and not dogmatic teaching of the church.[37]

This view was rejected by the nineteenth-century Italian Jesuit theologian Giovanni Perrone in his influential work, *De Matrimonio Christiano*. Perrone argued that "the first intention of the fathers was to define *directly* [*directe*] the indissolubility of the bond of marriage." After accepting the petition to change the formulation of canon 7, the fathers "*defined* the same thing *indirectly* [*indirecte*]."[38] Although the Council fathers obviously had in view the Protestants "who not only taught contrary doctrine, but also in this way attacked the teaching of the Catholic Church and accused her of tyranny and error," they "did not spare the [divorce] practice of the Greeks, which was certainly known to them, but exposed it as contrary to the evangelical and apostolic teaching."[39] Perrone argued that since the Greeks had never obstinately argued for their error against the church of Rome, there was no need to strike them with an anathema, as there was to strike the Protestants. In this, he says, we can see the reason for the change from the first to the second formulation: the direct formulation struck not only the Protestants, but also the Greeks with an anathema. The indirect formulation struck only the Protestants, while "guaranteeing the same perma-

---

36. Johannes Launoy, *Regia in Matrimonium Potestas* (Paris: Edmundi Martini, 1674), tom. I, part II, 825–58: "ita ut in Ecclesiae potestate sit disciplinam hoc in canone sancitam pro ratione temporis immutare."

37. Pierre François Le Courayer, *Histoire du Concile de Trente* (Amsterdam, 1750), tom. III, 92. The opinion that the content of canon 7 should be counted merely among the disciplinary precepts of the church and not as a truth of divine revelation seems to be dominant in the eighteenth and early nineteenth centuries. Examples include: J. Adamus Braun ("nonnisi disciplinarem esse"), *Dissertatio utrum matrimonii vinculum, et in casu adulterii alterius conjugum, juxta Tridentini can: VII. sess: XXIV jure divino an solum ecclesiastico insolubile sit* (Moguntiae, 1787), in Bintherim, *Collectio dissert. sing. de matrimonio* (Dusseldorf, 1807), 83, quoted in Johannes Perrone, *De Matrimonio Christiano* (Liege: Dessain, 1861), 3:381; the anonymous author of *De potestate Ecclesiae in matrimonium et de indissolubilitate matrimonii* (1791) ("the view is erroneous that holds that the Church in Canon 7 taught a defined doctrine"), quoted in Augustinus de Roskovány, *De Matrimonio in Ecclesia Catholica* (On the Indissolubility of Marriage), vol. II (Augsburg: Charles Hollmann, 1840), 344; Johann Joseph Batz ("nicht strenge eine dogmatische Entscheidung, sondern nur eine Disciplinar-Anordnung"), *Harmonie der neuesten Baierischen Ehescheidungs-Gesetze mit Schrift und Tradition* (Bamberg: Joseph Anton Goebhardt, 1809), 103.

38. Perrone, *De Matrimonio*, 3:379.

39. Ibid., 380.

nent doctrine of the church."[40] Against Sarpi, de Launoy, and Le Courayer, Perrone argued that since canon 7 "asserts the infallibility of the Church as teacher" on this matter and has "for its object a teaching of the Gospel and the apostles," it should be understood as constituting a dogmatic definition.[41] Perrone's view seems to have been dominant in the second half of the nineteenth and early twentieth century, followed in substance by such noteworthy scholars as the Italian theologian Domenico Palmieri, SJ, as well as by the scholarly priest-editor of the eminent *Dictionnaire de théologie catholique,* Alfred Vacant.[42]

It can be argued that a fully informed judgment on the question was not possible before Pope Leo XIII opened the Vatican Archives to scholarly research in 1881, making accessible original documents of the Council of Trent that not even Pallavicino had seen. We owe a great debt to the scholars of the German Görres-Gesellschaft (Goerres Society) for undertaking the monumental task of publishing all documents related to the Council. The thirteen volumes of *Concilium Tridentinum* treat in a single series the diaries of Council participants (vols. 1–3), the *Acta* of the Council (vols. 4–9), its epistles (vols. 10–11), and its theological and canonical treatises ("Tractates") (vols. 12–13), along with copious critical notes.[43] The first volume was published in 1900.[44]

Despite these advantages, scholars in the twentieth century continued to disagree over the proper interpretation of canon 7. Jesuit theologian George H. Joyce, in his work *Christian Marriage* (1933), argued, "the char-

---

40. Ibid.

41. Ibid.: "Patet non solum canonem hunc esse dogmaticum, quatenus infallibilitatem Ecclesiae docentis adstruit, sed praeterea etiam dogmaticum esse, quatenus pro obiecto habet doctrinam evangelicam et apostolicam."

42. Dominico Palmieri, *Tractatus de Matrimonio Christiano* (Rome, 1880), 142: "Canonem esse *doctrinalem* nemo negare potest. Asseritur enim indissolubilitatem matrimonii esse doctrinam Ecclesiae, doctrinam juxta evangelicam et apostolicam doctrinam, h.e. revelatam, Ecclesiam in hac doctrina tradenda infallibilem esse, et haereticos esse eos qui id negant. Porro canon proponens doctrinam revelatam et ab Ecclesia infallibiter assertam, est certe doctrinalis. Immo et *dogmaticus* est, astruens scilicet fidei dogma ab omnibus credendum: cujus tamen objectum directum est inerrantia Ecclesiae in ea re docenda; indirectum vero ipsa res seu indissolubilitas conjugalii." A. Vacant, s.v., "Divorce," *Dictionnaire de théologie catholique* (1908), vol. XII, cols. 498–505. The conclusion is also followed by Francis E. Gigot, *Christ's Teaching Concerning Divorce in the New Testament: An Exegetical Study* (New York: Benziger, 1912), 5.

43. See Conway, "Original Diaries of the Council of Trent," 470.

44. The collection was compiled and edited under the leadership of the indomitable Sebastian Merkle, who held the chair in church history, the history of dogma, and archaeology at Würzburg's katholishe Fakultät from 1898 to 1935. He spent over three decades editing nearly three thousand pages of documentation from Trent, along with providing commentary.

acter of the canon [7] admits of no question. It is a dogmatic definition of the indissolubility of marriage."[45] On the contrary, Victor Pospishil, a Ukrainian priest-canonist, writing two years after the Second Vatican Council, argued that the canon "could not have excluded the possibility of a hypothetical granting of divorce by the Catholic Church herself."[46] Theodore Mackin, SJ, writing nearly two decades later, is among those who agreed with Pospishil.[47]

Noteworthy is the account of German theologian and Catholic cardinal, Walter Kasper. As early as 1977, he argued that the doctrine of the indissolubility of marriage taught in canon 7 "is not simply a question of church discipline," but nor is it "an ultimately obligatory dogma." It is a teaching "justified by and based on the revelation of Christ," but not identical with it.[48] The formulation in canon 7 was a compromise. The Council intended to respond distinctly to the challenges of the Reformers, while avoiding a condemnation of the divorce practice of the Greeks. It clearly did not intend to settle the question of the status of the doctrine of indissolubility in Catholic teaching.[49] It therefore offers us little by way of responding to contemporary pastoral problems: "All that the council has done to further the solution of these problems in an obligatory way is to provide us with a number of essential points of view."[50]

---

45. Joyce, *Christian Marriage*, 395.

46. Victor J. Pospishil, *Divorce and Remarriage* (New York: Herder and Herder, 1967), 70; he argues misleadingly that "the majority of the [Council] Fathers opposed the condemnation of the Greeks for one or the other reason" (66). The most that can be said is that a majority of the fathers opposed alienating the Greeks and so consented to an indirect formulation for canon 7. There is no indication that more than a very small number were opposed to condemning the Greek practice of divorce and remarriage.

47. "Canon 7 ... was intended to anathematize Luther's position but spare the Orthodox." Theodore Mackin, SJ, *Divorce and Remarriage* (New York: Paulist Press, 1984), 388.

48. "The conciliar text speaks not of an identity between the evangelical doctrine and the teaching and practice of the Church, but only an 'accordance.'" Kasper, *Theology of Christian Marriage*, 61–62.

49. Kapser, *Theology of Christian Marriage*, 62.

50. Ibid. Proposing his own resolution to contemporary pastoral problems, Kasper attempts an unsuccessful compromise between doctrine and praxis. He says on the one hand that Catholic tradition maintains an "unconditional faithfulness to Jesus' teaching" (55). On the other, he says the concrete situation of marriage in a fallen world requires "tolerance" and "leniency": "the validity of Jesus' words could not be restricted, but Christians placed in such situations could not be condemned" (56). He favors the Eastern church's practice of allowing divorce and remarriage in accordance with the principle of *economia*: "this practice does not violate the principle of indissolubility as such. What it does in fact is to provide the Christian who is ready to do penance, on the basis of God's mercy, with a new possibility of a human and Christian life within the Church in certain difficult situations" (56–57). (Kasper defended

The permissive reading of Trent on marriage is developed by the Flemish Jesuit theologian Piet F. Fransen (1913–83), who spent his final years as a professor of dogmatic theology at the Catholic University of Leuven. Fransen's 1947 dissertation at the Gregorian University was entitled: "On the indissolubility of Christian marriage in the case of adultery: On Canon Seven, Session 24 of the Council of Trent (Jul.–Nov. 1563)."[51] He later published his account in five influential essays in the 1950s in the journal *Scholastik*.[52] The account has influenced a generation of scholarship. Theologians such as Karl Lehmann, Walter Kasper, the young Joseph Ratzinger, the Jesuit professor Francis Sullivan, and the members of the 1978 International Theological Commission follow Fransen in arguing that Trent did not intend to define the indissolubility of marriage as a truth of faith.[53]

---

more fully the Orthodox principle of *economia* in a lecture to the extraordinary Consistory of Cardinals delivered at Rome on February 20–21, 2014, in *Gospel of the Family*, 50–51, also 37–38, 46.) His view has unacceptable implications for the doctrine of indissolubility. If a divorced person living in a sexually active partnership with someone other than his or her divorced spouse, while that spouse still lives, can be in full communion with the Catholic church (i.e., can be considered not to be living in a *de facto* adulterous union), it implies either that the first marriage never came into existence, or it has been dissolved. Without due diligence on the part of the church to verify there was no first marriage, permitting remarriage *implies*, in those cases where the first marriage was in fact valid, that either the church can approve of adulterous unions, or that the marriage has somehow subsequently dissolved.

51. Piet Fransen, *De indissolubilitate Matrimonii christiani in casu fornicationis. De canone septimo Sessionis XXIV Concilii Tridentini* (Jul.–Nov. 1563) (Rome: Pont. Univ. Gregoriana, 1947).

52. They are reprinted as chaps. 1–5 in a collection of Fransen's essays entitled *Hermeneutics of the Councils and Other Studies*, eds. H. E. Mertens and F. de Graeve (Leuven: Leuven University Press, 1985). Two additional articles on Trent's teaching are also published as chaps. 6 and 7 respectively: "Réflexions sur l'anathème au Concile de Trente (Bologne, 10–24 septembre 1547)" (Reflections on the anathema used at the Council of Trent: Bologna Session, September 10–24, 1547) originally published in *Ephemerides Theologicae Louvanienses* 29 (1953): 657–72; and "The Sacramental Character at the Council of Trent (17 January–3 March 1547)," originally published in *Bijdragen* 32 (1971): 2–33; an additional essay published in Dutch, which I was not able to find, is "Echtscheiding na echtbreuk van een van de gehuwden. Het kerkrechterlijk dossier van Trente (1563)" (Divorce after the adultery of one of the spouses. The canonical [or canonists'] dossier at Trent), in *Bijdragen* 14 (1953): 363–87. For those interested in a summary in English of Fransen's account of Trent on divorce and remarriage, see P. Fransen, "Divorce on the Ground of Adultery—The Council of Trent (1563)," printed in a special edition of the journal *Concilium*, entitled *The Future of Marriage as Institution*, ed. Franz Böckle (New York: Herder and Herder, 1970), 89–100.

53. Karl Lehmann, *Gegenwart des Glaubens* (Mainz: Matthias-Grünwald-Verlag, 1974), 285–86. See Kasper, *Theology of Christian Marriage*, 98n87. Joseph Ratzinger, "Zur Frage nach der Unauflöslichkeit der Ehe: Bemerkungen zum dogmengeschichtlichen Befund und zu seiner gegenwärtigen Bedeutung," in *Ehe und Ehescheidung: Diskussion Unter Christen*, eds. Franz Henrich and Volker Eid (München: Kösel, 1972), 35–56; see also 47–49. Later, however, as Prefect of the Congregation for the Doctrine of the Faith, Ratzinger, in a personal corre-

THE INDISSOLUBILITY THESIS

Thus, beginning with Paulo Sarpi, an impressive list of authorities denies what I call the "indissolubility thesis," that is, that Trent defined the absolute indissolubility of Christian marriage as dogma of faith. Yet a careful examination of the evidence throws the judgment of these authorities into serious doubt. From the first discussions of the Council on marriage in spring 1547 through the second formulation presented to the General Congregation of bishops in August 1563, and indeed right through to November 1563, when Trent published its definitive teaching, a majority of Council fathers defend the absolute indissolubility of marriage. Nothing, they argue, not even adultery, can dissolve the bond of a Christian marriage. About this they entertain no serious doubts. Their chief concern is to formulate it clearly. The apparently conflicting opinions of certain Church Fathers do not cause them any serious hesitation, nor do they fret over the permissive divorce practices of Greek Christians. They believe that Jesus taught the absolute indissolubility of marriage and they interpret the so-called exceptive clause in Matthew mentioned above—"Every one who divorces his wife, *except in cases of adultery* and marries another, commits adultery" (5:32)—to mean that a separation of bed is possible and permissible in cases of adultery, but not the dissolution of the bond (*vinculum*).[54]

LIMITED PURPOSE OF THIS BOOK

The purpose of this book is limited. It provides a detailed reading and interpretation of Trent's teaching on indissolubility, primarily (but not exclusively) through the lens of canon 7. There are other pressing questions pertaining to marriage that it does not take up. It does not attempt

---

spondence with Charles Curran, stated that Trent "defined" the indissolubility of a sacramental and consummated marriage; the correspondence was published in Charles E. Curran, *Faithful Dissent* (London: Sheed and Ward, 1986), 269. Francis A. Sullivan, *Creative Fidelity: Weighing and Interpreting Documents of the Magisterium* (New York: Paulist Press, 1996), 131–34. International Theological Commission, "Propositions on the Doctrine of Christian Marriage," *Origins* 8 (1978): 235–39. The ITC does not reference Fransen, but the influence of Fransen is reasonable to infer. Himes and Coriden write: "In its interpretation of Trent the ITC was in accord with ... Piet Fransen." See "The Indissolubility of Marriage: Reasons to Reconsider," 463–64.

54. The biblical Greek of "except in cases of adultery" is "parektos logou porneias," in the Latin Vulgate, with which the Council fathers were familiar, "excepta fornicationis causa." At the time of Trent, *fornicatio* (*porneia*) in this passage was understood by all Council fathers to mean adultery.

to address the problems raised in the Catholic church's doctrine of marriage by the various privileges of the papacy and church in dissolving non-consummated and non-sacramental marriages. It neither defends nor criticizes the canonical process of granting annulments. It makes no practical recommendations for addressing the pastoral catastrophe of large numbers of Catholics excluded from the sacraments on account of the irregularity of their unions. And it offers no recommendations on how the church of the twenty-first century should undertake marriage preparation.

This is not to say that its conclusions have no relevance to these questions. Up until the past half-century, Trent's teaching on marital indissolubility within Catholic theology was essentially a speculative matter with few practical implications. Whatever "side" of the question one defended, the pastoral practice and accompanying firm teaching of the church was to exclude remarriage after divorce as an alternative for separated Christian couples while one of the spouses was still living.

The question today is no longer merely speculative. The rate of civil divorce among baptized Catholics is high. This, along with frequent entry into a second civil marriage during the lifetime of the civilly divorced spouse, has given rise to widespread pastoral problems.[55] The problems have prompted some Catholics to ask whether the church's judgment that it has no authority to dissolve validly celebrated and physically consummated marriages can be revised.[56] The church takes for granted, presumably, that its answer must be consistent with what it judges to be the content of the "single sacred deposit of the word of God," that is, with a proper understanding of divine revelation.[57] The most important task of a universal council is to make known and certain that deposit's intelligible content, where it has come into dispute (especially among Catholics or former Catholics) through its acts of teaching. Therefore a properly theological (and so pastoral) answer to this marriage question must, as it were, go *through* Trent's teaching on marriage.

---

55. The pastoral problems are compounded by confusions engendered by the apparent teaching of Pope Francis, "Amoris Laetitia," Post-Synodal Apostolic Exhortation, March 19, 2016, especially chap. 8, which treats the question of sacramental participation for divorced and civilly remarried Catholics. For a critical reading of chap. 8, see C. Brugger, "Five Serious Problems with Chapter 8 of *Amoris Laetitia*," Catholic World Report, April 22, 2016; available at http://www.catholicworldreport.com/Item/4740/five_serious_problems_with_chapter_8_of_iamoris_laetitiai.aspx.

56. See c. 1141, which teaches: "A marriage that is *ratum et consummatum* can be dissolved by no human power and by no cause, except death."

57. Vatican Council II, *Dei Verbum*, November 18, 1965, no. 10, in DEC, 2:975: "unum verbi Dei sacrum depositum."

The question in the background is whether Jesus taught that marriage is absolutely indissoluble. No one can responsibly deny that a majority of Council members at Trent believed he did. But did they also intend to teach it as a truth of faith? Since Trent is the only universal council to publish dogmatic canons on the sacrament of marriage, if Trent did not define marital indissolubility, the doctrine has not been defined by any extraordinary act of the church.[58] Cardinal Kasper claims that the historical argument "by its very nature, [can] never be regarded as absolutely certain and will always be disputed in the questions we are considering here."[59] He is only half correct. Although absolute certitude on anything can never be achieved through the scholarly process, Trent's teaching need not remain indefinitely in dispute. Responsible scholarship can settle the question in a way that excludes serious doubt.

In 1986, Cardinal Ratzinger, then Prefect of the Congregation for the Doctrine of the Faith, wrote to Charles E. Curran saying: "The Church's position on the indissolubility of sacramental and consummated marriage, which you claim ought to be changed, was in fact defined at the Council of Trent and so belongs to the patrimony of the Faith."[60] Disagreeing with the Cardinal, Curran replied: "All Catholic theologians recognize the teaching of the Council of Trent does not exclude as contrary to faith the [divorce] practice of *'economia'* in the Greek church."[61] Our brief review of the debate since Trent suggests the falsity of Curran's claim. But it is true that

---

58. Even if it has not been defined by an extraordinary act of a pope or universal council, this does not mean it is not an irreformable doctrine of the Christian faith. The Ordinary and Universal Magisterium also exercises the charism of infallibility when "though dispersed throughout the world, but maintaining the bond of communion among themselves and with the successor of Peter, when in teaching authentically matters concerning faith and morals they agree about a judgment as one that has to be definitively held"; see *Lumen Gentium*, no. 25 (DEC, 2:869). Interestingly, John Paul II clearly suggests that the conditions for this third mode of infallibility have been fulfilled in relation to the doctrine that papal authority does not extend to the dissolution of consummated Christian marriages: "It seems quite clear then that the non-extension of the Roman Pontiff's power to ratified and consummated sacramental marriages is taught by the Church's Magisterium as a doctrine to be held definitively, even if it has not been solemnly declared by a defining act. This doctrine, in fact, has been explicitly proposed by the Roman Pontiffs in categorical terms, in a constant way and over a sufficiently long period of time. It was made their own and taught by all the Bishops in communion with the See of Peter, with the knowledge that it must always be held and accepted by the faithful." John Paul II, *Address to the Tribunal of the Roman* Rota, January 21, 2000, no. 8; available at www.vatican.va.

59. Kasper, *Theology of Christian Marriage*, 58.

60. The letters exchanged between the CDF and Fr. Curran during the 1980s are published in *Faithful Dissent*; quotation from 269.

61. Curran, *Faithful Dissent*, 272.

many theologians remain uncertain about the proper meaning and status of the Council of Trent's teaching. The purpose of this book is to dispel this uncertainty.

To do this, historically authenticated premises must be provided to four common objections to the indissolubility thesis. For if any is true, then the truth of the thesis itself is doubtful. They are the reasons most often found in the literature, individually or together, by opponents of the indissolubility thesis beginning with Sarpi.[62] They are set forth here and replied to throughout the book.

First, in addressing the challenges posed by the teachings of the Reformers, Trent was mainly concerned with Luther's denial of papal prerogative and not with substantive issues concerning and raised by the nature of marriage.

Second, because of questions raised by the "exceptive clause" in the Gospel of Matthew, the bishops at Trent were doubtful as to whether absolute indissolubility was a truth of divine and Catholic faith. They thus grounded their teaching on the indissolubility of marriage on the firm and ancient *legal* tradition in the Western church prohibiting divorce and remarriage. Given that the common meaning of "dogma" at the time of Trent included truths not pertaining to divine revelation but contained merely in ecclesiastical law, the Council used the formula *anathema sit* to define indissolubility as a disciplinary doctrine (along with other disciplinary doctrines denied by the Protestants)—without the intent to define it properly as a *de fide* truth.

Third, because certain Church Fathers, especially Pseudo-Ambrose, apparently believed that divorce and remarriage after adultery was not always excluded to the innocent party, the Council feared that if its teaching anathematized the proposition that marriage can be dissolved on account of adultery these Fathers would be subject to condemnation (which effectively meant excommunication). The Council was not willing to do this.

Fourth, the bishops were aware that any anathema directly condemning divorce and remarriage would fall too upon Greek Christians. The Council moderated its teaching on marriage so as to include within its scope the errors of the Protestants, but to exempt the divorce practices of the Greeks.

---

62. Since Piet Fransen elaborates the four objections most thoroughly throughout his writings, I frequently reference his works. He summarizes the four objections in Fransen, "Divorce on the Ground of Adultery," 90–92.

METHODOLOGY

The positive aim of this book is to interpret correctly the Council of Trent's teaching on marital indissolubility. Such an interpretation would make possible a sustained and grounded reply to those four common objections. In ordinary human discourse, when we want to understand people's intended meaning for some written communication, we first clarify what problem or question they are replying to. We then look at what they asserted, the context in which they asserted it, other things they said relevant to what they asserted, and relevant discussions they had that preceded their assertion. In our interpretation of canon 7, we will follow this inferential line of inquiry. What precise problems related to the indissolubility of marriage was Trent replying to? What did the Council say by way of reply—that is, what did it assert? What was the context for the assertions: the historical context of the question at hand, the theological context for the terms it chose, and the social and political context in which the teaching was proposed? Other than canon 7, what did Trent say relevant to the doctrine of indissolubility? We will see that immediately preceding the twelve dogmatic canons, the Council published a 360-word doctrinal preface that also addresses indissolubility. It also published canon 5. Which interpretation of canon 7 is most plausible and satisfactory when read in the light of these other statements? Finally, what can we conclude about the meaning of canon 7 from the preliminary discussions on the sacrament of marriage by the conciliar theologians and, more importantly, the voting prelates over the course of the Council? What questions did they believe were most important? What truths needed defending and errors condemning? At what stage of the Council do these become clear? How firm did the fathers' judgments remain over the course of the Council? What status did they believe the truths held in Catholic teaching? With what type of formulation did they think the truths should be taught?

Reading canon 7 in continuity with the preliminary discussions of the Council members will require us to wade neck-deep in the Council's *Acta* and other writings immediately related to the Council. Though, as already remarked, we are indeed indebted to the editors of the *Concilium Tridentinum* for making this a living possibility, the present task is undeniably a tedious one, and readers, particularly of the third and fourth chapters, will need fortitude to persevere. The effort should be worthwhile. Hasty summaries and unsubstantiated assertions of what the Council did or did not do and say are common but inadequate, as are the simple multiplication of authorities for one conclusion or another. A thorough examination of the Council's discussions on divorce and remarriage is necessary to see the whole picture.

Chapters 1 and 2 establish a very important context for the Conciliar discussions on marriage that took place at Bologna in 1547 and later at Trent in 1563. The chapters ask what the Council participants knew or were very likely to have known about the beliefs, teachings, and practices on divorce and remarriage of (chap. 1) the Protestant Reformers, chiefly Luther and Calvin, who publicly denied the Catholic church's teaching on indissolubility, as well as (chap. 2) the Greek churches, whose beliefs and practices on divorce and remarriage were in some respects contrary to the Catholic church's. They examine published statements and trace historical events in order to formulate a picture of what the Council fathers at Trent knew of these two communities' beliefs and practices. This will help us to understand the nature of the doctrinal and pastoral problems to which the council participants believed they were responding, and the gravity of the threats to Catholic faith and practice that they believed the problems posed.

Chapter 3 considers the statements of the Conciliar theologians and Council fathers on indissolubility that took place from April 21 to November 7, 1547, during what are referred to as the "Bologna Sessions." Chapter 4 then examines the debates and discussions surrounding the four formulations of the canons on marriage proposed during the three formal meetings of the General Congregation that ran from July 24–31, August 7–23, and October 26–27 (respectively), all during session 23 of the Council.

Chapter 5 is the heart of the text. It consolidates the materials examined and conclusions reached in chapters 1–4, and in their light provides a scholarly interpretation of the final promulgations of Trent on divorce, remarriage, and indissolubility, particularly as found in the doctrinal preface (the *doctrina*) as well as canons 5 and 7, each of which were published on November 11, 1563, during session 24. Readers only interested in these conclusions may happily skip chapters 3–4.

CHAPTER 1

THE *ERRORES* OF THE REFORMERS

When Trent's decree on marriage was published on November 11, 1563, both Protestant and Orthodox Christians defended and practiced divorce and remarriage for multiple reasons. The Conciliar *Acta* show that the Council fathers were aware of this fact, and Trent's final teaching illustrates the Council intended to reply to it.

This chapter is meant to be read in tandem with chapter two. Together their aim is to clarify what the Council fathers knew, or were most likely to have known, about the Protestant and Greek beliefs on marriage at the time of the Council. Understanding the regnant positions of these two communities will help us reply to at least two of the four objections to the indissolubility thesis formulated in the introduction (see above). The first asserts that in its teaching on marriage Trent was chiefly concerned with rejecting Luther's denial of Roman authority over the marriages of Christians, and therefore was not really interested or only tangentially interested in the substantive question of the nature of marriage itself. This chapter, therefore, will show that by the beginning of the debates on marriage in 1547, Luther had already published multiple essays clearly illustrating his support for divorce and remarriage for several reasons; and that by the time the final teaching was promulgated by the Council in 1563, his denials of indissolubility had been in print for nearly thirty years. Moreover, the testimony of episcopal opinion at Trent demonstrates that the Council fathers were indeed aware of Luther's settled judgment on the legitimacy of divorce and remarriage, that they intended to condemn that judgment as false and contrary to divine revelation, and to do so in canons that were entirely separate from the canons addressing his denial of Roman jurisdiction in matters of marriage.

The second and more serious objection is that the Council, in adopting an indirect formulation for canon 7, intended to exempt from the scope of its teaching on indissolubility the divorce practices of the Greeks. Chapter two will show that by the middle of the sixteenth century the Greek churches had officially permitted divorce and remarriage, not only for adultery but for multiple other reasons, for over six hundred years. All the council fathers knew this, and no more than the smallest number intended for the Catholic church to overlook or approve the practice. Though the Orthodox churches have never elaborated a systematic doctrine of indissolubility, a common belief can be identified among Greek authorities, namely, that the Gospel of Matthew permits remarriage in cases of adultery. Consequently, they claim the Greek practice is founded on the teaching of Jesus.[1] But the fathers at Trent knew well that the Greek *ritus* was grounded on any and all "just reasons" for divorce accepted as such by the Greek churches. If the view was truly based upon the words of Jesus, then only adultery (*porneia* from Matthew 5:32 and 19:9) could be set forward as justifying divorce and remarriage, since the other teachings of Jesus and St. Paul on the matter are unambiguously absolute.[2] But the Orthodox churches have never limited their practical approval of divorce and remarriage to adultery. The permissibility therefore did and does not rest exclusively on any appaent biblical exception, but rather on the belief—which was perhaps originally rationalized on the basis of Matthew—that marriage is not indissoluble.

PROTESTANT BELIEFS AND PRACTICES ON MARRIAGE IN THE SIXTEENTH CENTURY

Commentators have argued that in addressing the sacrament of marriage, the Council was principally concerned with Luther's treatment of marriage in *Babylonian Captivity*, published in 1520. Since Luther's position on divorce and remarriage, they claim, was not yet definitive in that text, the Council fathers concerned themselves more with his clearly formulated opinion that the issue of divorce could not be decided by the pope or

---

1. See the treatment of this question by Archbishop Vasil' in "Separation, Divorce," 120–26.
2. See, e.g., Mk 10:11–12, Lk 16:18, Rom 7:2–3, 1 Cor 7:10–11.

bishops.³ Luther inveighed against Roman authority at every opportunity, accusing it of tyranny and exceeding its competence whenever it ruled on the nature and validity of marriage. So when the Council in canon 7, the argument continues, used the formulation "Si quis dixerit ecclesiam errare" (If anyone says that the church errs), it guaranteed that the anathema rested squarely on the shoulders of Luther, condemning narrowly his opinion that the church exceeds its competence whenever it grants a divorce for reasons other than adultery.⁴ *Errare*, therefore, must be understood to refer to the Catholic church exceeding its competence and not to an error in doctrine.⁵

The only part of this argument supported by the Council's proceedings is that the fathers in publishing canon 7 (*and* canon 5) intended specifically to strike Luther and Calvin with anathemas. The two other parts—that the Council was not concerned with defining marriage and that *errare* refers only to the Roman belief that the church rightly exercises authority over the sacrament—are false. There are strong reasons for holding that *errare* does in fact refer also to a doctrinal error in the content of the church's teaching on marriage, and for denying that the Council's final teaching on marriage was chiefly concerned with Luther's treatment in *Babylonian Captivity*.

Luther's Writings on Indissolubility (1520–32)

If we take for argument's sake that Luther's ideas on divorce and remarriage in cases of adultery are not clearly expressed in 1520 in *Babylonian Captivity*, his ideas could certainly be said to have crystallized two years later in his *Estate of Marriage*. Commenting on the exceptive clause in Matthew 19, he writes: "Here you see that in the cause of adultery Christ permits the divorce of husband and wife, so that the innocent person may remarry. For in saying that he commits adultery who marries another after divorcing his wife, 'except for unchastity,' Christ is making it quite clear that he who divorces his wife on account of unchastity and then marries another does not commit adultery."⁶ After addressing the problem of private divorces for clandestine adultery, Luther writes: "But a public divorce, whereby [the innocent party] is enabled to remarry, must take place through the investigation and

---

3. Fransen, "Divorce on the Ground of Adultery," 90.
4. Ibid., 92.
5. Ibid., 94.
6. Luther, "Estate of Marriage" (1522), *Luther's Works*, ed. Walther I. Brandt (Philadelphia: Muhlenberg Press, 1962), 45:17–49, at 30–31.

decision of the civil authority so that the adultery may be manifest to all."[7] Asking what should become of the adulterous spouse, he recommends the death penalty, "for whoever commits adultery has in fact himself already departed and is considered as one dead." The innocent party "may remarry just as though his spouse had died."[8] Note well Luther's move here, because we will see it repeated in his other defenses of divorce and remarriage. Adultery is *like* death. If a spouse truly dies, no one can deny that the marriage dissolves and remarriage is permissible. In cases of adultery, the guilty spouse is *like* one who has died. Consequently, the innocent spouse may remarry.

With no less forthrightness, Luther recommends remarriage for the wronged spouse in unions where the wife has deprived her husband of the marriage debt: "here it is time for the husband to say, 'If you will not, another will; the maid will come if the wife will not.'" Again, Luther justifies dissolution using an analogy with death. Since in marriage a wife has freely bestowed her body upon her husband, to withhold her body is to rob her husband of what is his. This is, in a sense, to slay herself: as if "his wife has been stolen away and slain by robbers." If he himself were slain, we would certainly accept the dissolution of the marriage: "Why then should we not also accept it if a wife steals herself away from her husband"?[9] Implied here is that a husband cannot be expected to live peacefully chaste when deprived by his wife of conjugal rights; some concession needs to be made for his inability, and this is found in his rightful pursuit of "another [who] will."

In Luther's *Commentary on 1 Corinthians 7*, sometimes referred to as the "Epithalamium," published a year later in 1523, he again uses the analogy with death to justify divorce and remarriage, this time on the grounds of enmity between the spouses.[10] If a husband and wife are at odds, and one party is unwilling to be reconciled with the other, and the other is unable to live celibately, may the other remarry? Luther replies: "Yes, without doubt." A spouse in this situation "does not have the grace" to live chastely; and "God will not demand the impossible because of the disobedience of the other." The incontinent spouse "should then act as though his spouse

---

7. Ibid., 32. Cf. Luther, "On Marriage Matters," in *Luther's Works*, ed. Robert C. Schultz (Philadelphia: Fortress Press, 1967), 46:311.

8. Ibid., 32. If, however, civil authority is unwilling to put the adulterer to death, the adulterous spouse, if he cannot remain continent, too may remarry, presuming he first "betake himself to a far country."

9. Ibid., 33-34.

10. He first defends divorce and remarriage for non-Christians and for "crude, false Christians," but then also for Christians. Luther, "Commentary on 1 Corinthians 7," in *Luther's Works*, ed. Hilton C. Oswald (St. Louis, Mo.: Concordia, 1973), 28:1-56, at 32.

were dead."[11] Here we see most clearly the concession to human weakness as a ground for the dissolution of marriage.

After the Diet of Spires (Speyer) in 1526, the Protestant princes in the German realms began to organize territorial churches. To offer them instruction, Luther addressed himself to practical problems of marriage formerly regulated by canon law. In 1530 he published *On Marriage Matters*. Here he argues that since adultery was punished with death in the Law of Moses, "it is certain that adultery also dissolves a marriage."[12] This is confirmed by Christ's words prohibiting divorce except for the cause of adultery (Mt 19:9), and again by the example of Joseph who, thinking Mary was an adulteress, resolved to divorce her, and was praised by the evangelist as a righteous man. Luther then says: "Accordingly I cannot and may not deny that where one spouse commits adultery and it can be publicly proven, the other partner is free and can obtain a divorce and marry another man."[13] Luther adds that the remarriage should not be undertaken with haste: "he should wait at least a year or six months."[14]

Between 1530 and 1532, Luther delivered a series of Wednesday sermons on the Gospel of Matthew at the city church in Wittenberg. In his commentary on the *Sermon on the Mount* (1532), drawn from these sermons, Luther defends divorce and remarriage not only for adultery, but also for abandonment and prolonged absence.[15] Commenting on Matthew 5:32, he asks: "What is the proper procedure for us nowadays in matters of marriage and divorce?"[16] He denies that the governance of marriage is the domain of the church; marriage is not a sacrament but "a secular and outward thing." Its governance is the domain of the "lawyers" and "secular government." "Therefore we should not tamper with what the government and

---

11. Ibid. In the next chapter, Luther commends divorce and remarriage for one whose spouse has encouraged him to commit adultery or other grave evil: "This," he says, "explains why adultery brings on divorce and permits a change in status." Ibid., 34. The context of the chapter is marriages between Christians and non-Christians, but these comments seem to extend to all.

12. Luther, "On Marriage Matters," in *Luther's Works*, 46:311.

13. Ibid.

14. Ibid.

15. Because some details surrounding the original editing of the *Sermon* are obscure, Jaroslav Pelikan recommends "a certain amount of caution" in referring to the text as a source for understanding Luther. At the same time, he rejects "the extreme skepticism of certain scholars regarding the reliability" of the text (21:xxi).

16. Luther, "The Sermon on the Mount," *Luther's Works*, ed. Jaroslav Pelikan (St. Louis, Mo.: Concordia, 1956), 21:3–284, at 93.

wise men decide and prescribe with regard to these questions on the basis of the laws and of reason."[17]

He asks whether there exists any legitimate ground for divorce and remarriage. He says that Christ in Matthew 5 and 19 authorizes one and only one ground—adultery. Jesus, he says, draws his teaching from the Law of Moses (Lv 20:10). Luther again skillfully reasons to divorce and remarriage from an analogy between adultery and death:

> Since it is only death that can dissolve a marriage and set you free, an adulterer has already been divorced, not by men but by God Himself, and separated not only from his wife but from this very life. By his adultery he has divorced himself from his wife and has dissolved his marriage.... Before God he is already dead.... Because it is God that is doing the divorcing here, the other partner is set completely free and is not obliged, unless he chooses to do so, to keep the spouse that has broken the marriage vow. We neither commend nor forbid such divorces, but leave it to the government to act here; and we submit to whatever the secular law prescribes in this matter.[18]

He adds "abandonment" and "prolonged absence" as additional causes of divorce, and says that if after a summons the guilty party refuses to return, "the other partner should be left completely free."[19] These clear formulations of the Reformer's position on divorce and remarriage were published between 1522 and 1532, fifteen years before the Council at Bologna began its initial discussions on the sacrament of marriage.

We said above that "for the sake of argument" we would presume that Luther's ideas were not yet clearly formulated in his seminal text, *Babylonian Captivity* (1520). But even if they are not plainly and explicitly stated, they are strongly suggested. Commenting on Christ's teaching in Matthew 5:32, Luther writes: "Christ, then, permits divorce, but only on the ground of unchastity.... Yet it is still a greater wonder to me, why they [i.e., Roman Catholics] compel a man to remain unmarried after being separated from his wife by divorce, and why they will not permit him to remarry."[20] For since Christ permits divorce on account of adultery and compels no one to choose continence for the sake of the kingdom, and since Paul teaches that it is better to marry than to burn, Christ "certainly seems to permit a man to marry another woman in the place of the one who has been put away."[21] Luther expresses

---

17. Ibid., 93.
18. Ibid., 96.
19. Ibid., 97.
20. Luther, *Babylonian Captivity*, 105.
21. Ibid., 105–6.

a desire for greater clarity so he can give more confident advice to those "who, without any fault of their own, are nowadays compelled to remain unmarried." If Paul permits a Christian spouse to put away an unbelieving spouse and remarry, "why should not the same hold true when a believer ... deserts his wife, especially if he intends never to return. I certainly can see no difference between the two."[22] He ends, as if to guard himself from the watching eye of informers, saying:

> Nevertheless, in these matters I decide nothing ... I would have nothing decided here on the mere authority of the pope and the bishops; but if two learned and good men agreed in the name of Christ and published their opinion in the spirit of Christ, I should prefer their judgment even to such councils as are assembled nowadays, famous only for numbers and authority, not for scholarship and saintliness.[23]

John Calvin (1509–64)

Luther's challenges to Catholic doctrine on marriage were not the Council's only concern. We know this because in August 1563, during session 22 of Trent, one of the Council's most influential prelates, Charles de Guise—the cardinal of Lorraine, who was familiar with Calvin's theology—proposed that a new canon should be formulated condemning three heretical propositions attributed to the Swiss Reformer: marriage is dissolved on account of disparity of cult, disharmony between the spouses, and prolonged absence.[24] We also know that the Council ultimately published a slightly revised version of Lorraine's formulation in canon 5 the following November.

Calvin published his most influential defenses of divorce and remarriage in his *Institutes of the Christian Religion* (1536) and *Commentary on a Harmony of the Evangelists* (1558).[25] Both argue from the Matthean ex-

---

22. Ibid., 106.
23. Ibid.
24. Lotharingus, in CT, IX, 642.25–28.
25. Calvin condemns the Catholic church for enacting "that a husband who has repudiated an adulteress may not marry again." John Calvin, *Institutes of the Christian Religion*, trans. Henry Beveridge (Grand Rapids, Mich.: Eerdmans, 2001), book IV, ch. 19, par. 37 (649). In his discussion of the Precept of the Decalogue prohibiting adultery, Calvin does not mention the issue of indissolubility; book II, chap. 8, pars. 41–44 (348–50). Calvin's treatment in the *Commentary* is considerably longer. In his commentary on Mt 5:31, he argues simply that the exceptive clause establishes an "exception" to the prohibition against divorce and remarriage for adultery, but only mentions the liberties of the husband: "for the woman, who has basely violated the marriage-vow, is justly cast off; because it was by her fault that the tie was broken, and the husband set at liberty." Calvin, "Commentary on Matthew 5:31," in *Commentary on a Harmony of the Evangelists, Matthew, Mark, and Luke*, trans. William Pringle (Edinburgh: The Calvin

ceptive clause that the case of adultery constitutes an exception to the rule against divorce and remarriage. But he expands the exceptions in other writings. One example is his "Ecclesiastical Ordinances," an expansive set of rules governing church discipline, first published in 1541 and approved as law for the Reformed church in Geneva in 1542. In his first edition of the *Ordinances*, Calvin gave authority to the ruling church consistory to hear divorce suits *only* in cases of alleged adultery.[26] But in his revised *Ordinances* of 1561, he includes an enlarged section on norms for marriage.[27] In addition to adultery, he approves divorce and remarriage in cases of prolonged abandonment and irksome cohabitation.[28] Finally, in his *Commentary on 1 Corinthians* published in 1546, Calvin adds disparity of cult to his list of exceptions.[29] These correspond to the three grounds for the dissolution of marriage condemned in the cardinal of Lorraine's proposal: disparity of cult, marital conflict, and prolonged absence.[30]

Translation Society, 1845), 1:293. His commentary on Mt 19 is more developed. He states that the liberty of the innocent spouse to remarry belongs also to the wife, and says—similarly to Luther—that when either husbands or wives commit adultery, they have "dissolved the marriage" (2:384). But he insists that the *only* cause of dissolution is adultery. To those who say leprosy is also a ground, who argue that one who divorces a leprous wife needs a "remedy" to be protected from the weaknesses of the flesh, Calvin replies, "what is sought in opposition to the word of God is not a remedy" (2:383). Calvin also hints at a comparison between adultery and death. He says the "exception" of Christ for adultery seems to be superfluous: "for if the adulteress deserve to be punished with death, what purpose does it serve to talk of divorces?" But since the community is not always willing to put her to death, so long as the husband "convicts her of uncleanness," he is "freed by Christ from the bond" (2:384). He ridicules the idea that when Jesus says "whoever marries a divorced woman commits adultery," the Lord meant to teach that celibacy is required after divorce; when Christ calls the man who marries a divorced woman an adulterer, his words are "undoubtedly restricted to unlawful and frivolous divorces" (2:383-84).

26. Robert M. Kingdon, *Adultery and Divorce in Calvin's Geneva* (Cambridge, Mass.: Harvard University Press, 1995), esp. chaps. 2-3. In the widely publicized divorce cases of Pierre and Benoite Ameaux (the "first Calvinist divorce") and Antoine Calvin (John's brother) and Anne Le Fert, the final resolution of divorce with permission to remarry for the man (in 1545 and 1557 respectively) was approved by the church but ordered by the secular government.

27. John Calvin, "Les Ordonnances Ecclesiastiques De 1561," in *Opera Quae Supersunt Omnia*, eds. Guilielmus Baum, Eduardus Cumtz, and Eduardüs Reüss (Brunsvigae: C. A. Sohwetsohke and Son, 1871), 10.1:91-124; on marriage, 105-14. Calvin introduced his revised ordinances on marriage in 1545-46, and they governed most questions on marriage in Geneva from that time, but were not formally enacted until 1561. See John Witte, Jr., and Robert M. Kingdon, *Sex, Marriage, and Family in John Calvin's Geneva*, vol. 1, *Courtship, Engagement, and Marriage* (Grand Rapids, Mich.: Eerdmans, 2005), 40.

28. Ibid., 110-12; cf. David L. Snuth, "Divorce and Remarriage from the Early Church to John Wesley," *Trinity Journal* 11, no. 2 (Fall 1990): 131-42, esp. 138.

29. John Calvin, *Commentary on St. Paul's First Epistle to the Corinthians*, trans. John King (Altenmünster: Jazzybee Verlag, 2012), 1:196-203.

30. CT, IX, 642.26-28: "dirimatur matrimonium propter disparitatem cultus, propter non convenientiam in conversatione et propter longam absentiam."

The Testimony of Episcopal Opinion at Trent

By considering the direct and sustained interest the Council fathers took in the question of the permanence of marriage, we are also warranted in rejecting the argument that canon 7 was directed only to Luther's challenge of papal authority and not also to the question of the substantive nature of marriage. The three most serious Protestant *errores* confronted by the Council fathers were: (1) that matrimony does not constitute a true sacrament of the New Law of the Gospel; (2) that the pope, and the church more generally, does not exercise legitimate authority over marriage; and (3) that Christian marriage is not indissoluble. Each of these is noted in the earliest recorded statements on marriage at the Council, and each statement is followed by a reference to Luther, usually his *Babylonian Captivity*.[31] These early articles were used to develop the "articles of heresy" presented by Massarelli to the *congregatio theologorum* on April 26, 1547, as the basis of that congregation's first formal discussion on marriage. Three of these latter articles address directly the legitimacy of remarriage after divorce, two referring to cases of adultery.[32] They are worth repeating:

Art. 3: "A married woman who has committed adultery [*sui fecit copiam*] has ceased to be a wife, so that it is licit for both spouses, or at least the one (who gave no cause for divorce), to take another wife or to marry another."[33]

Art. 4: "He does not commit adultery who has married another after dismissing an adulterous wife."[34]

---

31. In April 1547, the Council Secretary, Angelo Massarelli, delivered fifteen propositions on matrimony to the Council theologians: two articles directly deny the sacramentality of marriage (nos. 1, 4); two others indirectly deny it (nos. 2, 3). Six deny papal and church authority over marriage, five in a variety of different expressions: papal authority to rule on clandestine marriages (no. 5); church authority to establish what grades of affinity and consanguinity constitute impediments to marriage (no. 6); church authority to establish impediments to marriage (no. 7); papal authority to rule on legitimate grounds for separation (no. 8); the exclusive authority of ordained priests to witness a marriage (no. 9); and the sixth by asserting that marriage cases should be resolved by secular rulers (no. 15). One article denies the indissolubility of marriage (no. 10) and two place the doctrine in jeopardy by asserting that Christians may have many wives (no. 11), and that Paul does not prohibit bigamy (no. 14). They are recorded at CT, VI, 92–93.

32. The other three articles concern clandestine marriages, polygamy, and grades of consanguinity and affinity.

33. CT, VI, 98.17–19: "Mulier, quae alteri viro sui fecit copiam, adeo uxor esse desiit, ut utrique aut alteri saltem coniugum, (qui causam non dedit divortio), liceat (novare coniugium, hoc est) aliam uxorem ducere vel alteri nubere."

34. CT, VI, 98.21: "Non moechatur, qui dimissa adultera aliam duxerit."

Art. 5: "Divorce annuls marriage; wherefore after a divorce has been lawfully performed, it is licit for both spouses to remarry."[35]

None of these makes any reference to papal or church authority. Each is interested in whether adultery or divorce dissolves marriage and whether remarriage after divorce is ever licit. Interestingly, in the *Acta* all three reference Luther's *Babylonian Captivity*. There is no indication that the Council believed that Luther's position on divorce and remarriage was undeveloped. And the substantive question about the nature of marriage is clearly distinct from the question of church authority.

When canons on marriage are first recorded in spring 1547, canons 4, 5, and 6 single out for condemnation the heretical propositions asserted in articles 3, 4, and 5 just cited, again without reference to papal authority.[36] When the General Congregation of prelate members is first presented on August 29 with two articles of heresy for discussion, article 2, combining propositions from canons 4 and 5, once again addresses directly divorce and remarriage in cases of adultery with no reference to church authority.[37] When Massarelli on September 6 summarizes the opinions of the fathers on article 2, he says: "the vast majority agreed that adultery *cannot* dissolve a marriage; that one who takes another wife while his first wife is living commits adultery; and that for no reason can they be separated except as far as the bed."[38] This same sort of direct treatment of the problem of divorce and remarriage without reference to church authority is continued in

---

35. CT, VI, 99.1-2: "Divortium dirimit matrimonium, unde ab illo rite celebrato licet repudianti et repudiatae reiterare coniugium."

36. CT, VI, 129.12-14: "Can. 4: If anyone says that a married woman who has committed adultery has ceased to be a wife, so that it is licit for both spouses, or at least the one who gave no cause for divorce, to marry whom he or she will, let him be anathema." (Si quis d[ixerit] mulierem, quae alteri viro sui fecit copiam, adeo desinere esse uxorem, ut utrique coniugum aut saltem innocenti, qui scilicet causam non dedit divortio, liceat cui velit nubere, a. s. [anathema sit].) CT, VI, 129.15: "Can. 5: If anyone says that a man who after dismissing an adulterous wife has married another does not commit adultery, let him be anathema." (Si quis d[ixerit] non mechari, qui dimissa adultera aliam duxerit a. s.) CT, VI, 129.16-17: "Can. 6: If anyone says divorce annuls marriage, wherefore after a divorce has been lawfully performed, it is licit for either spouse to contract a marriage with another person, let him be anathema." (Si quis d[ixerit] divortium dirimere matrimonium, ideoque ab illo rite celebrato licere utrique cum alia persona contrahere, a. s.)

37. CT, VI, 402.19-21: "A married woman who has committed adultery has ceased to be a wife, so that it is licit for both spouses, or at least the innocent one who gave no cause for the divorce, to marry whom he or she will. And a man who after dismissing an adulterous wife has married another does not commit adultery." (Mulier, quae alteri viro sui fecit copiam, adeo uxor esse desiit, ut utrique coniugum aut saltem innocenti, qui scilicet causam non dedit divortio, liceat cui velit nubere. Neque mechari eum, qui dimissa adultera aliam duxerit.)

38. CT, VI, 434.28-30 (emphasis added): "longe maior pars confirmavit matrimonium ob

the final two formulations of the canon on indissolubility published, during the Bologna sessions, respectively on October 18 and November 7. Both directly condemn anyone who denies that according to the law of God the bond of marriage is indissoluble and that divorce and remarriage even in cases of adultery is always wrongful.[39] These provide the basis for the "first reform" of the canon on indissolubility at Trent in the summer of 1563.

If the Council in formulating its teaching on indissolubility were only interested in Luther's attack on papal authority, we would expect the fathers and theologians to make this plain by frequent reference to it. But as I have shown from the first formulations of heretical articles on divorce and remarriage in early 1547 until the Venetian intervention in August 1563, no reference whatsoever is made to the church in any formulation addressing indissolubility. They singularly and persistently interest themselves in the doctrinal question of the nature of marriage and the possibility of dissolution, especially in cases of adultery.

When the Council published its definitive teaching on marriage in November 1563, the three "most serious" *errores* noted above are each distinctly addressed. Canon 1 condemns anyone who denies that marriage is a true sacrament of the law of the Gospel. Canons 3, 4, 8, 11, and 12 address the authority of the church in matters of marriage.[40] And canons 5 and 7 address the indissolubility of marriage. The issues are clearly distinguished. And the formulations correspond to years of discussion and debate.

It might also be noted that unlike Luther, Calvin defends a robust role for ecclesial authority in divorce proceedings and so does not concern himself with rejecting the role of church authority in divorce.[41] When Trent

---

fornicationem dissolvi non posse, mecharique eum, qui vivente uxore aliam duxerit, nullamque separationem fieri posse nisi quoad thorum."

39. The November 7 formulation reads: "[Canon 3] If anyone says that the bond of marriage between legitimately contracted persons is not indissoluble according to divine law, and consequently that on account of adultery it is licit for both spouses or the spouse who gave no cause of adultery, not only to have a separation of bed, but to contract another marriage, let him be anathema." (Si quis dixerit matrimonii inter legitimas personas contracti vinculum non esse iure divino indissolubile, ac proinde ex causa fornicationis licere utrique aut alteri coniugum, qui fornicationis causam non dedit, non solum thori separationem facere, sed aliud contrahere matrimonium, a.s.) CT, VI, 578.7–10.

40. C. 3 teaches that the church has the authority to establish grades of affinity and consanguinity as impediments to marriage and can dispense from those impediments as well; c. 4 teaches that the church has the authority to establish diriment impediments (a "diriment impediment" is a circumstance that results in the invalidity of an attempted marriage); c. 8 teaches that the church has the authority to decide that a separation between spouses may take place; c. 11 teaches that the church has the authority to prohibit the celebration of marriage during certain seasons of the year; c. 12 teaches that marriage cases are the affairs of ecclesiastical judges.

41. Calvin's ecclesiastical ordinances of 1541, drafted by the Reformer himself, which cre-

condemns Calvin's errors in canon 5, it rejects them precisely as errors pertaining to the nature of the marriage bond. And that condemnation constitutes a solemn definition of the indissolubility of marriage with respect to the issues of heresy, injury and desertion.[42]

CONCLUSION

We have shown that Luther's judgment that the marriages of Christians were not absolutely indissoluble was firm and publicly articulated by the Council during the Bologna sessions in 1547. By the middle of the 1530s, Luther had already defended multiple times divorce and remarriage in the case of adultery. He believed his conclusion was consistent with Christ's teaching in the Gospel of Matthew. Attempting to maintain some continuity with the ancient Christian view that only death dissolves a marriage, he drew an analogy between adultery (as well as spousal conflict and the denial of conjugal right) and death, concluding that in God's eyes adultery (etc.) was a kind of death; and just as bodily death dissolves a marriage, so too the spiritual death caused by adultery (etc.) dissolves a marriage. Consequently, the innocent party at least, and when not subject to the death penalty even the guilty party, should be free to remarry. In addition to Luther's arguments, we see that Calvin published denials of the Catholic doctrine of indissolubility between 1536 and 1561, and we know these were evident to the Council fathers by their final discussions on marriage in summer 1563. To suggest that the only clear threat from Luther's teaching against Catholic doctrine known at Trent was his denial of church authority over Christian marriage is erroneous.

---

ated a constitution for the canton of Geneva, made provision for the creation of a council of church ministers called the "Consistory." It was responsible for controlling the behavior of Genevans and because adultery was one of the behaviors brought before the council, and adultery was a ground recognized as justifying divorce, the Consistory naturally began hearing divorce cases. It issued its first legal divorce in Geneva in January 1545, with a subsequent order in June granting the male petitioner permission to remarry. See Kingdon, *Adultery and Divorce in Calvin's Geneva*, chaps. 1–2, esp. 11, 21, 60–62.

42. Fransen in one place seems to concede that the Council intended its teaching solemnly to define absolute indissolubility and not merely to target Luther's view of papal authority. Although he believes that the church's doctrine was not derived from scripture but rather from canonical tradition, he says nevertheless that the frequent repetition of the tradition by early councils, in the *Decretum Gratiani*, and in later papal decretals gave rise to "a firm legal tradition in the West which *rejected any breaking of the marriage bond*," and he refers the type of act that Trent was willing to undertake in teaching this as "defining the faith" (definire fidem). Fransen, "Divorce on the Ground of Adultery," 90.

It is true that the early articles of heresy on marriage formulated in April 1547 draw upon Luther's *Babylonian Captivity*. But no procedure was established—and hence none was followed—referencing Luther or formulating future articles in accord with his antecedent wording. Once the basic errors had been articulated, the effort to follow Luther's formulations was set aside in favor of doctrinal precision.

We have also replied to the claim that in addressing indissolubility Trent was mainly concerned with Luther's denial of papal authority over marriage and not the substantive issue of the nature of marriage itself. Trent was indeed well aware of Luther's denial of papal prerogative. But this in no way minimized the Council fathers' simultaneous concern with clarifying the doctrinal issue of indissolubility. From its first recordings of articles of heresy and discussions of canons relating to the sacrament of marriage in March/April 1547 through the consensus formulation of canon 3 in November of the same year, a large majority of theologians and fathers agree that adultery does not dissolve the bond of marriage, that this is taught in divine revelation and is consistent with the Matthean "exceptive clause" rightly interpreted, and that divorce and remarriage even in the case of adultery is illicit.

Our review demonstrates that all the developed ideas of the two great Reformers on divorce and remarriage were published before the Council promulgated its treatise on marriage in November 1563, and several were published decades before. The argument that in their considerations the Council fathers were limited to Luther's undeveloped ideas on divorce and remarriage in *Babylonian Captivity* is patently false. As we shall see in chapter three, not only *Babylonian Captivity*, but several other texts of Luther are referenced as sources of erroneous Protestant ideas on marriage; and the articles of heresy (*articuli haereticorum*) drawn from Luther's writings include not only attacks on Roman authority, but propositions asserting the dissolubility of marriage and permissibility of remarriage; and that *when discussing indissolubility*, the Council, from its first considerations in 1547 to its final discussions in fall 1563, expresses almost no interest at all in Luther's denial of Roman authority and great and sustained interest in the nature of the marriage bond and implications of that nature for the questions of marital dissolubility, divorce, and remarriage.

CHAPTER 2

THE *RITUS* OF THE GREEKS

The Council fathers knew well that Greek Orthodox Christians ("Graecos") had practiced the custom, or *ritus*, of divorce and remarriage. It was mentioned several times during the discussions, and some even thought that because of it the Council should withhold formulating canon 7 with an anathema.[1] After the intervention of the Venetian delegation in August 1563, explained in chapter four, all the Council fathers were familiar with the opinion that canon 7 had implications for the social and political balance between Latin and Greek Christians living in territories under Venice's authority.[2] The support for the indirect formulation tells us that the fathers wished to teach indissolubility with as little disruption as possible to Greek-Latin relations.

In the introduction we have discussed the objection to the indissolubility thesis that Trent's teaching exempts the divorce practices of the Greeks.[3] The view is so common that it prompted Charles E. Curran to proclaim: "All Catholic theologians recognize the teaching of the Council of Trent does not exclude as contrary to the faith the practice of *'economia'* in the

---

1. See the remarks of Naxiensis (CT, VI, 449.8–10) and Aciensis (CT, VI, 450.22–23), as well as Cretensis on the first reform of canon 6 in July 1563: "non placet quia ferit Graecos et Ambrosium" (CT, IX, 644.2).

2. The oration is recorded at CT, IX, 686.3–37. For an English translation, see appendix B, part A.

3. A few examples of the argument include: Mackin, *Divorce and Remarriage*, 388; Fransen, "Divorce on the Ground of Adultery," 98–99; Pospishil, *Divorce and Remarriage*, 70; Lehmann, *Gegenwart des Glaubens*, 285–86; Pani, "Matrimonio"; Himes and Coriden, "Indissolubility of Marriage," 473.

Greek church."[4] The question is obviously of importance for the Catholic church's doctrine of marriage. For if the Council meant to exclude from the scope of its teaching on indissolubility the sacramental marriages of some Christians, then it did not define the absolute indissolubility of Christian marriage as a truth of faith. We know that canon 5 taught the impossibility of divorce and remarriage in cases of heresy, irksome cohabitation, and willful abandonment. But Trent's adoption of an indirect formulation for canon 7 has left doubts as to whether it meant to do the same with adultery.

This chapter considers the divorce practices of the Greek church as the Council fathers probably knew them. Its argument is simple. In November 1563, Trent published its *doctrina* and twelve canons on marriage condemning "haereticos eorumque errores" (the heretics and their errors). Since some of the beliefs underlying the Greek divorce practices were identical to the "errores" of the Protestants, we have a good reason for concluding that the Council did not intend to exempt the errors and correlative practices from the scope of its teaching.[5]

What Did the Greeks Believe?

The *Acta* do not tell us much about what the Council fathers knew of the precise beliefs of the Greeks on divorce and remarriage. They knew they followed the "antiquissimum ritum suorum patrum" (most ancient rite of their fathers).[6] And some Council fathers cited Eastern Patristic writers such as Basil, Chrysostom, and Origen in support of the custom. But each writer cited in support is referenced elsewhere as a witness to the tradition of strict indissolubility.[7] And so these relatively few references do not tell us much about what the Council fathers understood the Greeks to believe.

---

4. Charles E. Curran, *Faithful Dissent*, 272. The views on this question of Pallavicino, Perrone, Palmieri, Vacant, Joyce, and Ratzinger (summarized in the introduction to this book) demonstrate the falsity of Curran's claim.

5. CT, IX, 967.15. For the doctrinal preface in Latin and English, see appendix B.

6. From the Venetian delegation's intervention of August 11; see CT, IX, 686.19.

7. For example, Legionensis argues, contrary to the Greeks, that Basil does not support remarriage in cases of adultery (CT, IX, 721.2–4). Segovia however argues that Basil thinks the scriptures permit not only separation of bed, but of bond; he names Ambrose and Origen as defenders of this position (656.42–43, 657.1); but Virdunensis contradicts Segobiensis saying both Ambrose and Origen argue that remarriage constitutes adultery (657.26–29). Ilerdensis says Basil and Chrysostom contradict the Roman position (722.27–33); Aliphanus adds Origen (734.9–11), but Cassinensis adduces the authority of Basil to defend the strict formulation of the canon on adultery (678.17–18).

The Council fathers did know of the negotiations for reunion between the Roman Church and Armenian Orthodox Christians at the Council of Florence (1439).[8] And they knew that that Council's *Bulla unionis Armenorum* (Decree of Union with the Armenians) taught that the bond of a Christian marriage is absolutely indissoluble.[9] It is true there was no anathema to back up that teaching. But "this was no wonder," as the bishop of Corosopitanus stated at Trent, since Florence did not use anathemas.[10] So we cannot infer from the absence of an anathema at Florence that the Council fathers (at Florence) were opposed to a formal definition of the doctrine.[11] Greeks and Latins were equally represented at Florence seeking ecclesial union in the face of increasing threats from the Turks. Mackin argues that because the Council did not address the issue of divorce and remarriage in its negotiations for union with the Greeks, this suggests both Latins and Greeks "were quietly willing to allow the other its position."[12] Mackin's vague statement should not be taken to mean that Florence judged the Greek practice to be acceptable. Joyce recounts how after the union was effected, Pope Eugenius IV "summoned the Greek bishops, who were still in the city and informed them that divorce was one of the points in Greek practice which must be corrected."[13] This makes evident that the pope believed the practice was wrongful. The fact that Florence did not require conformity with the Roman position as a condition for reunion

---

8. References to Florence at Trent were numerous: e.g., Conciliar theologians Vincent Placentia (CT, VI, 110.4), Antonius Demochares (CT, IX, 411.28), Matthew Guera (CT, IX, 418.24–26); Cardinal Seripando (CT, VI, 480.10–11); Bishops Materanus (CT, VI, 420.2–4 and n1) and Corosopitanus (CT, IX, 672.28–30).

9. In the Decree with Armenians, Florence teaches that the good of "the indissolubility [indivisibilitas] of marriage ... signifies the indivisible union of Christ and the church"; therefore "although a separation of bed is licit on account of adultery, it is not licit to contract another marriage [non tamen aliud matrimonium contrahere fas est], since the bond of a legitimately contracted marriage is perpetual." DEC, 1:550.

10. See comments of Corosopitanus: "nec mirum, quod in Florentino concilio non adducitur anathema, quia illud concilium nullibi utitur anathemate" (CT, IX, 672.28–30). More precisely, Florence published no canons using the formula ending *anathema sit*, but in its bull of union with the Copts (*Cantate Domino*, February 4, 1442), it declares that "it anathematizes" certain heretical groups and heresiarchs who teach contrary to the doctrine of the Trinity, especially the Manicheans. See DEC, 1:567–82, esp. 572–74.

11. The Latin in the phrase "non tamen aliud matrimonium contrahere fas est" (nevertheless it is not licit to contract another marriage), as Walter Brandmüller notes, signifies more than moral impermissibility, "it denotes 'sacrilege.'" Brandmüller, "Unity and Indissolubility of Marriage: From the Middle Ages to the Council of Trent," in *Remaining in the Truth of Christ*, ed. Dodaro, 140.

12. Mackin, *Divorce and Remarriage*, 376.

13. Joyce, *Christian Marriage*, 387.

should be taken to mean no more than that the church of Rome was willing to tolerate a practice it believed to be contrary to the teaching of divine revelation in order to realize what unity was possible with the Greeks in the hopes that through it a more perfect communion with the Greeks might later be realized.

Roman Law and Greco-Christian Marriage Legislation

Adultery was the one ground for divorce and remarriage that caused any doubt in the minds of the Council fathers. When the fathers reference the "practices of the Greeks" and "opinions of the holy fathers" as witnesses to a permissive tradition on divorce and remarriage, the doubt is almost always traceable to the exceptive clause in Matthew.[14] So the fathers at Trent knew that the Greeks practiced their *ritus* at least in cases of adultery. The fathers knew too that the Greeks justified the practice at least on the ground that Matthew establishes a real exception to indissolubility for adultery. Were there other grounds defended by the *Graecos* at the time of Trent?

From the sixth to the ninth century the Greek church came under the increasing influence of Byzantine civil law on marriage issues. Roman law permitted divorce and remarriage for a variety of reasons. There is debate over whether a tradition of toleration existed *within* the Christian church in the first five centuries. There is almost no positive evidence for such a tradition, but scholars disagree on how this lack of evidence should be interpreted. Joyce argues that because the evidence is so meager as to be practically non-existent, no such tradition of toleration for divorce and remarriage existed in the early church; Eastern Christians began to permit the practice because "the Greek episcopate simply ceased to insist" that indissolubility be upheld for Christian marriages.[15] Gallagher and Meyendorff, however, put forward an *argumentum silentio*. If the church were opposed in principle to remarriage after divorce, they argue, the Greek Fathers

---

14. For the fathers' references, see, e.g., appendix table B-6, column 4.

15. Joyce, *Christian Marriage*, 359. Earlier he writes: "The result of our enquiry may be stated in few words. During the first five centuries of our era there is not to be found a single utterance of any Christian teacher nor a single decree of any council which furnishes support to the view that the marriage-tie can under any circumstances be severed.... The statement often made that there is a twofold tradition regarding divorce, our Lord's words being interpreted with less strictness in the East than in the West, is destitute of foundation. There is evidence that many nominal Christians disregarded the Church's law and availed themselves of civil divorce. But the Church, alike in her assemblies and by the mouth of her acknowledged spokesmen, never failed to proclaim the indissolubility of marriage" (327–28).

would have protested the permissive divorce legislation of the Eastern emperors. But since we find few such protests among the Eastern Fathers, we should conclude that there was no widespread opposition to divorce and remarriage in the East.[16]

Henri Crouzel strongly disagrees. At the end of his magisterial work on divorce and remarriage in the first five centuries of Christianity, Crouzel states he found widespread evidence in the writings of both Eastern and Western authorities that remarriage after dismissal for adultery (or anything else) was prohibited either to both or to one or other of the spouses; and he names the following sources: Shepherd of Hermas, Justin Martyr, Athenagoras, Theophilus of Antioch, Irenaeus, Ptolemy, Clement of Alexandria, Origen, Tertullian, the Councils of Elvira and Arles, Basil of Ancyra, Basil of Caesarea, Gregory Nazianzus, Apollinaris of Laodicea, Theodore of Mopsuestia, John Chrysostom, Theodoret of Cyr, Epiphanes, Ambrose, Innocent, Pelagius, Jerome, the Arian author of the *Opus Imperfecum*, Leo the Great, Augustine, and even his Manichaean opponent, Faustus.[17] He notes that modern interpreters claim that some of these sources implicitly allow remarriage. He rejects these interpretations as "forced." If some Patristic author mentions a "rupture" or "dissolution" of a marriage, these interpreters anachronistically project onto the expressions the meaning of modern canonists, or they simply presume the authority is being lenient towards remarriage. Cruzel is especially severe towards accounts that appeal to the *argumentum silentio*: "abusing the argument from silence, clinging to detail and ignoring the context, [these interpretations] disfigure the profound intention of the passage."[18] This debate is certainly not irrelevant to our investigations, but an examination of the opinions of

---

16. Gallagher, *Church Law*, 77; John Meyendorff, *Byzantine Theology: Historical Trends and Doctrinal Themes* (New York: Fordham University Press, 1979), 197–98. Gallagher writes: "There is no convincing evidence to show that the Church formally and expressly prohibited divorce and re-marriage from the very beginning, and many Christians continued to regard marriage as dissoluble" (33).

17. "Nous avons trouvé des témoignages semblables refusant, soit le remariage après répudiation en général; soit plus précisément le remariage après répudiation pour adultère, des témoignages concernant soit tous, soit l'une ou l'autre des personnes intéressées, dans Hermas, Justin, Athénagore, Théophile d'Antioche, Irénée, Ptolémée, Clément d'Alexandrie, Origène, Tertullien, Concile d'Elvire, Concile d'Arles, Basile d'Ancyre, Basile de Césarée, Grégoire de Nazianze, Apollinaire de Laodicée, Théodore de Mopsueste, Jean Chrysostome, Théodoret de Cyr, Epiphane, Ambroise, Innocent, Pélage, Jérôme, l'auteur arien de l'Opus Imperfecum, Léon Grand, Augustin et son contradicteur manichéen, Faustus de Milève." Crouzel, *L'Église primitive face au divorce*, 360.

18. Ibid., 361: "abusant de l'argument du silence, s'accrochant à des détails et ne tenant pas compte du contexte, défigure l'intention profonde du passage."

the Fathers of that period would take us far afield.[19] Moreover, settling that question is not critical to understanding the mind of Council fathers at Trent (whether or not their opinions are justified by the historical record), so no more will be said on the matter in this chapter.

By the sixth century, civil divorce legislation in the East was well developed. Beginning with the first Christian emperor in the fourth century, the Byzantine rulers sought to chart a compromise between the permissive practices of pagan Rome and the demands of the teachings of Jesus. This effectively meant attempting to render divorce more difficult, but not legally prohibiting it.[20] The dissolution of unified political authority in the Western Empire from the fifth century provided the Latin bishops more opportunity to exercise authority over the sacrament of marriage. But the survival of unified political rule in the East guaranteed the greater influence of the state upon the business of the church. Beginning with Constantine, the Byzantine emperors exercised considerable authority over the Eastern church, presiding over ecumenical councils, controlling episcopal appointments, drawing jurisdictional boundaries, overseeing forms of worship, and wading into doctrinal disputes.

No emperor was more influential upon marriage matters in the East than the great reformer of Roman law, Justinian I (527–65). Although his solicitude for the welfare of the church was sincere, he coveted the traditional prerogative of the pagan emperors to rule supreme over both the political and religious realms. Mackin refers to Justinian as "the quintessential Byzantine caesaro-papist."[21] Justinian knew that the non-Christian population of the empire, still great in number, had no desire to give up its pagan practice of dissolving unwanted marriages. His extensive sixth-century legislative reform included widespread revisions in the civil marriage code. Though it curtailed the reasons under civil law permitting divorce and re-

---

19. The Crouzel/Joyce conclusion, however, seems far more probable. As the writings of Gregory of Nazianzus illustrate, the fourth-century Eastern church both knew about and rejected the divorce practices of the Empire: "divorce is utterly repugnant to our laws, though the laws of the Romans judge otherwise" (Letter 144, in Patrologiae Cursus Completus, Series Graeca, ed. J.-P. Migne [Paris, 1857–66], 37:248 [hereafter, PG]; quoted in Joyce, *Christian Marriage*, 326). Since we have no evidence that any Eastern Church Father ever defended remarriage after divorce, or said they believed marriage was dissolved by any circumstance, the Gallagher and Meyendorff argument from silence is unpersuasive.

20. Peter L'Huillier, "The Indissolubility of Marriage in Orthodox Law and Practice," in *Catholic Divorce: The Deception of Annulments*, eds. Pierre Hegy and Joseph Martos (New York: Continuum, 2000), 108–26, esp. 114–55; originally published in *St. Vladimir's Theological Quarterly* 3 (1988).

21. Mackin, *Divorce and Remarriage*, 107.

marriage, it by no means eliminated the ancient practice. In the short run, this neither had nor was intended to have canonical effects. In the long run, however, the effects were very significant.

Justinian's most extensive legislation on divorce can be found in his *Novellae* (Novels) 22 and 117, published in 536 and 542 respectively. He begins novel 22 with a panegyric to marriage. He says the institution is so honorable that it is through it that God gives immortality to the human race, perpetually renewing it through the procreation of children. Since marriage laws alone, over all others in force, concern the whole human race, and are not restricted to certain men or times, marriage is more worthy of solicitude than all other subjects.[22] Having said this, however, he declares that marriage is a human institution; and "in matters pertaining to humans, whatever is bound together can be dissolved."[23] Brundage states that novel 22 is especially significant "because it was based on the explicit premise that marriage was dissoluble."[24]

The Notion of a "Legitimating Cause" for Divorce

In the *Novellae*, Justinian appeals to the notion of a legitimating cause for divorce using several different terms: proper cause, just cause, reasonable cause, sufficient cause, and reasonable excuse.[25] In the codex the terms are

---

22. "Si enim matrimonium sic est honestum, ut humano generi videatur immortalitatem artificem introducere, et ex filiorum procreatione renovata genera manent iugiter, dei clementia, quantum est possibile, nostrae immortalitatem donante naturae, recte nobis studium de nuptiis est. Alia namque omnia, quae sancita sunt, non omnibus competunt nec hominibus nec rebus neque temporibus, studium vero nuptiarum totius est, ut ita dicatur, humanae sobolis, ex quo etiam renovatur solo, et ampliori quam alia sollicitudine dignum est." Novel 22, "Preface," in *Corpus Iuris Civilis* (Cambridge Library) (Cambridge: Cambridge University Press, 2014), 3:147 [hereafter, CIC].

23. Novel 22, chap. 3: "quoniam horum quae in hominibus subsequuntur, quidquid ligatur, solubile est" (CIC 3:149). It should be kept in mind that Justinian is speaking here about civil marriage; his statements should not necessarily be taken as representing his own views of the spiritual meaning of marriage.

24. James A. Brundage, *Law, Sex, and Christian Society in Medieval Europe* (Chicago: The University of Chicago Press, 1987), 116.

25. "The idea which motivated the emperor was the divorce must be the exclusive result of reasonable causes, expressly stated in law." L'Huillier, "Marriage in Orthodox Law and Practice," 114. Novel 22, chap. 5: "secundum occasionem itaque inculpabilem" (CIC 3:150). Fred H. Blume translates "inculpabilem occasionem" as "proper cause"; see http://www.uwyo.edu/lawlib/blume-justinian/ajc-edition-2/novels/. Novel 22, chap. 6: "necessariam occasionem et non irrationabiliem" (CIC 3:150). Blume translates this as "just cause." Novel 22, chap. 19: "rationabili ... causa" (CIC 3:159). Novel 117, chap. 14: "aliqua causarum, quas contra uxores ad matrimonii solutionem sufficere iussimus" (CIC 3:564). Novel 22, chap. 7: "bona gratia distrahere

not legally synonymous, but for our purposes, they amount to the same thing: a ground under law legitimating divorce and remarriage. Novel 117, a stricter revision of novel 22, specifies more than ten such grounds, with remarriage in each instance being permitted to at least one of the spouses.[26] They include a wife's adultery; either spouse conspiring against the emperor; plotting to kill one's spouse; a wife dining or bathing with other men against the consent of her husband, or staying at someone else's house, other than her parents, against her husband's consent, or attending a circus, theater, or arena without the knowledge or against the prohibition of her husband; a husband attempting to involve his wife in unchastity or adultery with others; a husband living with another woman in the same house in which he lives with his wife and disregarding the repeated censures of his wife; a spouse choosing to enter religious life; a husband's impotence for a period of three years after entering into the marriage; and either spouse being carried away into captivity and subjected to slavery.[27]

Justinian's *Novellae* greatly influenced the development of the first texts of canon law in the East, as well as on "the whole theory and practice concerning divorce in the Orthodox Church."[28] The earliest extant Greek canonical collection, attributed to John Scholastikos, patriarch of Constantinople in 565–77, includes as a supplement eighty-seven imperial constitutions dealing with ecclesiastical matters, all taken from Justinian's *Novellae*.[29] The compendium, referred to as the *Synagoge (or Collection) in Fifty Titles*, does not include excerpts from novels 22 and 117. This suggests

---

matrimonium" (CIC 3:151); "bona gratia" literally translates "by mutual consent" referring to the consent of the spouses. Blume translates "bona gratia" as "reasonable excuse."

26. See chaps. 8–15. See also novel 127 (548 A.D.), which enacted that equal penalties should be imposed on husband and wife for extralegal divorces; and novel 134 (556 A.D.), chaps. 10–11, which specified quite precise penalties for adultery. Justinian's 168 *novellae* are available at http://www.uwyo.edu/lawlib/blume-justinian/ajc-edition-2/novels/.

27. Each of these grounds except the final is specified in novel 117, chaps. 8, 9, 12; note that in chap. 10, the longstanding practice of "divorce by mutual consent" is prohibited. The ground of captivity is specified in novel 22, chap. 7, and is not abrogated by the provisions of novel 117, chap. 11. For English versions of the two novels, see http://www.uwyo.edu/lawlib/blume-justinian/ajc-edition-2/novels/; cf. Joyce, *Christian Marriage*, 364–65. Justinian refers to divorce by the final three causes as "bona gratia," i.e., a divorce where the party divorced was not particularly at fault. See novel 22, chap. 4, including Blume's note following chap. 4.

28. Gallagher, *Church Law*, 32.

29. Ibid., 21–22. John's collection is dated around 550, before he began his reign. Scholars identify an earlier canonical collection, *Collectio LX titulorum*, compiled around the time of the completion of Justinian's *Corpus Iuris* (534), but the text has not survived. It contained the 85 canons of the apostles, 193 canons of eight church councils, the canons of the Council of Ephesus (431) and the canons of the Council of Sardica (343). Ferdinand Feldbrugge, *Law in Medieval Russia* (Leiden: Brill, 2009), 76 and 76n60.

that still in the late sixth century, the permissiveness of the civil divorce legislation of the empire was not yet presumed within the Eastern church. Vasil' makes a point of noting that the Greek church in the sixth century resisted a simplistic conflation of civil and ecclesiastical laws in matters of marriage: "the Byzantine Church, quite radically and often at the cost of conflicts with the will of emperors, justified the distinction between the application of civil and ecclesiastical laws."[30] Nevertheless, the decision of John to combine into a single text for use as church law both ecclesiastical precepts and imperial legislation on church matters became normative for Greek canon law.

In the middle of the seventh century, a jurist of Constantinople altered the *Synagoge* by taking the excerpts of imperial law from the supplement and placing them side-by-side with ecclesiastical canons under appropriate titles in the main body of the text. The *Synagoge* was transformed into a *Nomokanon*: a compendium of ecclesiastical law where civil laws (*nomoi*) and ecclesiastical canons are placed together.[31] The significance of this transformation for the assimilation of imperial marriage legislation into the practices of the Eastern church can hardly be overestimated. The juxtaposition of the canonical set of laws with the imperial laws implied that the two sets of laws shared the same normative force. As Gallagher writes: "The imperial ecclesiastical laws were to be seen just as authoritative for the Church as the canons issued by church councils. This makes an important ecclesiological statement concerning the place of the emperor in the Church."[32] Consequently, over time, the marriage legislation of Justinian was received as authoritative throughout the Greek church. His novel 117, L'Huillier writes, "constitutes the basic element of the future Byzantine nomocanonic synthesis."[33]

Vasil' claims that early signs of the Greek church's official acceptance of divorce and remarriage can be seen in canon 87 of the Quinisext Council (also called the Council of Trullo, the name of the hall in which the council took place) held in 692 at Constantinople under Emperor Justinian II.[34] The Eastern churches consider Quinisext to be an Ecumenical Council. The Catholic church does not.

---

30. Vasil', "Separation, Divorce," 102.
31. Gallagher, *Church Law*, 40.
32. Ibid.
33. L'Huillier, "Marriage in Orthodox Law and Practice," 114.
34. Vasil', "Separation, Divorce," 102. For a rendering of c. 87 in Latin and English, see appendix A, 195.

The grounds for this claim of Vasil' are very weak. Canon 87 begins with a reference to the "holy and divine Basil"—whose views in the East were held with the kind of authority that Augustine's were in the West—who taught that a woman who remarries after leaving her husband is an adulteress. The canon then continues: "If therefore she appears to have departed from her husband without reason, he is deserving of pardon and she of punishment. And pardon shall be given to him that he may be in communion with the Church."[35] The formulation raises at least two questions. First, by decreeing that the husband can be pardoned, does the Council mean to teach that he is free to remarry while his first wife is still living? Second, should we understand the canon to imply that if the woman departed *with* "reason," she too could be deserving of pardon, even without repudiating her second spouse? Neither the words of the canon, nor anything said in the other 101 canons, gives us any strong reason for concluding that Trullo meant to sanction divorce and remarriage here. The quoted text seems more likely to mean that the aggrieved husband deserves no punishment for the separation. The canon continues:

> But he who leaves the wife lawfully given him, and shall take another is guilty of adultery by the sentence of the Lord. And it has been decreed by our Fathers that they who are such must be "weepers" for a year, "hearers" for two years, "prostrators" for three years, and in the seventh year to stand with the faithful and thus be counted worthy of the Oblation [if with tears they do penance].[36]

Since this does not explicitly state as a condition for being restored to ecclesial communion that the man must repudiate his second union, some believe the canon implies that after performing the prescribed penance, he may return to the eucharist even though he remains within the second union and his first spouse still lives. This would support the archbishop's claim.

Such an interpretation however is not only implausible, but preposterous. It would mean that Trullo knowingly prescribed a penance for an offense that the sinner had no intention of discontinuing and that the Council knew he had no intention of discontinuing. Since this would be unprecedented in the East before the Photian Schism (863–67), the burden of proof rests with those who argue that Trullo meant here to permit divorce and remarriage. Otherwise, the only reasonable interpretation is that the Council firmly understood, without stating, that the man

---

35. Canons of the Council in Trullo, 14:402.
36. Ibid. (bracketed phrase included in the text).

had repudiated his second "wife." In the absence of some other evidence demonstrating that the contrary reading is plausible, this text provides no witness whatsoever of an emerging tradition of permissiveness in the late seventh-century Byzantine church.

The first unambiguous evidence is found in the ninth-century Eastern compendium of canon law referred to as the *Nomokanon in XIV Titles*.[37] The collection, compiled in 883 and attributed to Patriarch Photius of Constantinople, formally incorporates the list of legitimating causes to dissolve a marriage set forth in Justinian's novel 117.[38] The Nomokanon, citing esteemed Eastern Church Fathers, at first affirms that marriage is indissoluble, but then goes on to itemize the reasons justifying divorce and remarriage.[39] Shortly thereafter the Byzantine Emperor, Leo VI, surnamed "the Wise" (886–912), added to Justinian's list the causes of madness and voluntary abortion.[40] The revised *Nomokanon* was approved as the official collection of laws for the Eastern church at the Synod of Constantinople in 920, establishing its list of legitimating causes "as a rule for the practice of the Church."[41]

Alexius I, patriarch of Constantinople 1025–43, seems to be the first patriarch explicitly to grant approval to divorce and remarriage in the form of synodical decrees, appealing to the familiar notion of a legitimating cause. Among his decrees, we find the following: "no censure is incurred by the priest who blesses the marriage of a divorced woman, where the husband's conduct gave cause for the divorce"; and "if women divorced from husbands whose conduct gave cause for the divorce, desire to form new marriages, no blame attaches either to them or to the officiating priest: and similarly as regards men."[42] In the twelfth century, when the three most

---

37. Gallagher, *Church Law*, 38.
38. Feldbrugge claims the attribution is spurious; see *Law in Medieval Russia*, 78.
39. Photii Constantinopolitani Patriarchae, *Opera Omnia*, "Nomokanon," 13 (PG 104:1210). This disparity between what is taught and what is practiced is still common today in the Orthodox churches.
40. Luigi Bressan, *Il divorzio nelle Chiese orientali: ricerca storica sull'atteggiamento cattolico* (Bologna: Edizione Dehoniane Bologna, 1976), 22–23.
41. Vasil', "Separation, Divorce," 103. Quotation from Joyce, *Christian Marriage*, 372.
42. Printed in Joyce, *Christian Marriage*, 374. Dacquino's suggestion that the patriarch's ruling might merely refer to fiancés "because the fourth decree punishes severely a priest who performs the nuptial blessing for those who divorce by mutual consent" is unpersuasive because *bona gratia* divorce (by mutual consent) had generally been viewed since the time of Justinian as worse than divorce for a *iusta causa*. See Pietro Dacquino, *Storia del matrimonio cristiano alla luce della Bibbia. 2. Inseparabilità e monogamia* (Leumann: Elle Di Ci, 1988), 298–99; referenced in Vasil', "Separation, Divorce," 104.

important commentators on Byzantine canon law—Zonaras, Aristenes, and Balsamon—address the issue of divorce, they do not debate the question of its legitimacy, but rather focus on the importance of fulfilling the "conditions established by the law."[43] By the middle of the fifteenth century Greek canon law admitted divorce and remarriage for at least eighteen "just causes," including adultery, a spouse conspiring against the emperor or plotting to kill the other spouse; a wife dining or bathing or residing at another's house against her husband's consent; her attending a circus, theater, or arena without his knowledge; madness; a wife's voluntary abortion or premarital unchastity; a husband's unnatural vice; irksome cohabitation; apostasy from the Christian religion, etc.[44]

A footnote in the history of the fifteenth century illustrates how common the notion of a *legitimating cause* for divorce and remarriage had become a hundred years before the beginning of the Council of Trent. At the end of the Council of Florence (1445), where a short-lived union was established between the Catholic and Byzantine churches, Pope Eugene IV summoned together the Greek bishops who remained in the city and asked them to correct their problematic practice of divorce. The bishops replied that although his demand seemed fair, they could not speak on behalf of all their church and in any case divorce was not permitted "sine iustis causis."[45]

Trent and the Greek *Ritus*

Orthodox writers today frequently argue for the indissolubility of Christian marriage while simultaneously defending ecclesiastical divorce and subsequent remarriage in various forms.[46] One form it takes is called *oiko-*

---

43. Vasil', "Separation, Divorce," 104–5.
44. Joyce, *Christian Marriage*, 374–75.
45. Quoted in Bressan, *Il Canone Tridentino*, 71; cf. Joyce, *Christian Marriage*, 387, and L'Huillier, "Marriage in Orthodox Law and Practice," 116.
46. In 1918, the Pan-Russian Council of the Russian Orthodox church adopted revised regulations on marriage and divorce. The Council began by affirming that a marriage blessed by the Orthodox church is indissoluble. It then went on to say that divorce "is admitted by the Church only in condescension to human weakness and out of care for the salvation of man" (sometimes called the principle of *economia*); the council itemized ten approved reasons for dissolving a marriage, listed in Vasil', "Separation, Divorce," 110n17 (see also 109). In 2000, the Anniversary Council of Hierarchs of the Russian Orthodox Church (ACHROC) reaffirmed the 1918 Council's reasons for dissolution, stating (again) that "the marriage of Orthodox spouses is a lifelong and indissoluble union" before affirming the approved reasons for divorce. The ACHROC's document states that when the marital relationship has irreparably broken down, a "Church divorce is allowed on the basis of pastoral considerations." Second marriages, after obtaining an ecclesiastical divorce, are "not encouraged although permitted for the inno-

nomia (or *economia*). Although it is difficult if not impossible to identify a universal Orthodox conception of *economia*, it seems to represent at minimum a pastoral solution permitting the restoration to full communion of divorced and remarried Orthodox Christians, after a time of penance, while consigning the second "marriage," albeit a true marriage, to a kind of second-class status in the ecclesial community. Orthodox authors do not consider the disparity between the professed belief in the doctrine of indissolubility and the practice of divorce and remarriage to be problematic. Rather than conceiving of indissolubility as a permanent property of the marriage itself, as in Roman Catholicism, indissolubility in Orthodox Christianity seems merely to constitute a moral reality that establishes permanence as an ideal towards which all Christian spouses should aim. Clearly, Orthodox churches, despite their profession of indissolubility, deny the Catholic belief that Christian marriage is absolutely indissoluble.

The Council fathers at Trent knew well that the Greek Orthodox believed that Jesus made a definite exception to indissolubility for cases of adultery.[47] They also knew that the Greeks justified divorce on grounds much wider than adultery, as if through the "adultery breach" in the doctrinal fence, as it were, streamed an abundance of other exceptions, principally ones defended by civil law. A century before the Council began, Greek canon law had already noted more than fifteen legitimating causes for divorce. Those Council fathers who were more familiar with the beliefs of the Greeks would have known that apostasy, enmity between spouses, and prolonged absence were among those "exceptions." When, in November 1563, the Council published canon 5, consistent with Lorraine's request, addressing the dissolution of marriage in cases of heresy, enmity between spouses, and the willful desertion of a spouse, the canon condemned *anyone,* not just Calvin or Protestants, who held the errors.[48] The *ritus* of the Greeks

---

cent spouse." The guilty spouse, however, who is responsible for the separation, can only be permitted to remarry under condition of performing canonical penances (ACHROC, Bases, X3). Vasil' states that "in the exceptional case of a third marriage, these penances are more severe" ("Separation, Divorce," 111). Most prominent contemporary Orthodox theologians—e.g., John Meyendorff, Kallistos Ware, Paul Evdokimov—affirm the same incongruous propositions: marriage is a lifelong indissoluble union; divorce and remarriage are possible and permissible.

47. John Meyendorff writes: "The Byzantine Church ... never understood indissolubility to be a *legal* absolute. It condoned the famous exception found in Matthew ... and recognized adultery as a legitimate cause of divorce." Meyendorff, "Christian Marriage in Byzantium: The Canonical and Liturgical Tradition," *Dumbarton Oaks Papers* 44 (1990): 102–3.

48. On the request, see Lotharingus (CT, IX, 642.25–28). "Si quis dixerit, propter haeresim aut molestam cohabitationem aut affectatam absentiam a coniuge dissolvi posse matrimonii vinculum: anathema sit." (If anyone shall say that the bond of matrimony can be dissolved

was clearly not spared under this formulation, and many of the Council fathers would have understood this very clearly.

Moreover, it was obvious to all that the extensive catalogue of Greek exceptions was not purely grounded in the Matthean exceptive clause. The accepted ground was rather the notion, made prominent by Roman law, and recurring throughout the civil (and later ecclesiastical) law codes of the Eastern Empire for a thousand years, of a legitimating cause (*iusta causa*) for divorce. The Council fathers certainly would have seen that exempting the Greek *ritus* would not simply have been a matter of excusing a highly restrictive instance of divorce and remarriage out of respect for an apparently ancient interpretation of the Gospel of Matthew. It would have amounted to what it had amounted to in the Greek church by the time of Trent—an effective denial of the doctrine of indissolubility. The Council fathers also would have recognized other points of similarity between Protestant and Greek views on marriage, including that both Greeks and Protestants permitted latitude to civil law to determine what constituted justifiable grounds for divorce; and that both Byzantine civil law and Protestant theology defended reasons for divorce using an analogy with death.[49] As Bressan notes, the real difference between the Protestants and the Greeks had little to do with the actual practice of divorce or the beliefs grounding the practice, but in the fact that the Protestants "accused the Church of tyranny and error," while the Greeks carried on with their practice "without referring to the Church of Rome."[50]

Moreover, in August 1563, immediately after the indirect formulation of canon 7 was first proposed to the Council fathers, Lorraine recommended adding to the formulation the words *iuxta Scripturas* (in accordance with scripture).[51] With that addition the formulation read:

If anyone says that the holy Roman catholic and apostolic church, which is the teacher of all the others, has erred or errs, when she has taught and teaches *in ac-*

---

on account of heresy, or irksome cohabitation, or the willful desertion of one of the spouses: let him be anathema.) DEC, 2:754; see also CT, IX, 682.17–18.

49. Meyendorff says that beyond adultery, the Byzantine church defended other grounds for dissolution "where the mystical union of husband and wife had, in reality, ceased to exist, that is, situations practically equivalent to the death of one of the partners (disappearance, insanity, violence)." Meyendorff, "Christian Marriage in Byzantium," 102–3; see also John H. Erickson, "Eastern Orthodox Perspectives on Divorce and Remarriage," in *Divorce and Remarriage: Religious and Psychological Perspectives,* ed. William P. Roberts (Kansas City, Mo.: Sheed and Ward, 1990), 15–26, esp. 22.

50. Bressan, *Il divorzio nelle Chiese orientali,* 77.

51. CT, IX, 687.7–9.

cordance with the Scriptures [iuxta Scripturas] that on account of the adultery of one of the spouses, the marriage cannot be dissolved, and that both of the spouses, or at least the innocent one who gave no cause for adultery, should not contract another marriage while the other spouse is living, and that he commits adultery who dismisses an adulteress and remarries, and she commits adultery who dismisses an adulterer and remarries: let him be anathema.[52]

We will see in chapter 4 that Trent ultimately consented to the Cardinal's recommendation by adding to the final formulation of canon 7 the even stronger phrase: *iuxta evangelicam et apostolicam doctrinam*. The Cardinal obviously wanted to guarantee that the proposition asserting the permanence of the marriage bond was understood to be in close agreement with the teaching of scripture. Was he concerned that the turn to an indirect formulation might be taken as an indication of the Council's lack of resolve to define indissolubility as a *de fide* doctrine? The conclusion is reasonable. The fact that thirty-eight Council fathers, including two members of the *deputatio*, followed Lorraine in his comments on the second reform, tells us that others likely shared his concern.[53] When the Council finally published its dogmatic canon affirming that the indissolubility of marriage is "in accordance with the evangelical and apostolic doctrine," it exposed the inconsistency of the Greek practice with the teaching of divine revelation.[54]

Given that some of the beliefs of the Greek church on divorce and remarriage were identical to the *errores* of the Protestants, and others were similar, when Trent stated in its *doctrina* that it intended to condemn not only the *haereticos* but also their *errores*, those errors wherever they were found—on the lips of the great Reformers or in the nomocanonical collections of the Greek church—were singled out as erroneous.[55] This gives us another reason for concluding that the Council did not intend to exempt

---

52. Emphasis added. "Si quis dixerit, sacrosanctam Romanam catholicam et apostolicam ecclesiam, quae est aliarum omnium magistra, errasse vel errare, quando propter adulterium alterius coniugum docuit et docet, matrimonium non posse dissolvi, et utrumque coniugum, vel saltem innocentem, qui causam adulterio non dederit, non debere, altero coniuge vivente, aliud matrimonium contrahere, et moechari eum, qui dimissa adultera aliam duxerit, et eam, quae dimisso adultero alii nupserit: anathema sit." CT, IX, 686.28–33.

53. See appendix table B-4, column 2.

54. The final formulation of canon 7 reads: "Si quis dixerit, ecclesiam errare, cum docuit et docet, iuxta evangelicam et apostolicam doctrinam, propter adulterium alterius coniugum matrimonii vinculum non posse dissolvi, et utrumque, vel etiam innocentem, qui causam adulterio non dedit, non posse, altero coniuge vivente, aliud matrimonium contrahere, moecharique eum, qui dimissa adultera aliam duxerit, et eam, quae dimisso adultero alii nupserit: anathema sit." CT, IX, 967.31–35.

55. CT, IX, 967.15. For the doctrinal preface in Latin and English, see appendix B.

the divorce practices of the Greeks from the scope of its teaching on indissolubility.

Finally, recall that in canon 5 Trent defined the impossibility of divorce and remarriage in cases of heresy, irksome cohabitation, and spousal abandonment, so condemning three grounds for divorce defended variously by Protestants and Greeks. Recall also that the rapid turn to an indirect formulation for canon 7 was preceded two weeks earlier by a vote of a large majority of the General Congregation in support of a direct condemnation of anyone who denies indissolubility in cases of adultery. Is it likely that these same fathers would suddenly, indeed almost instantaneously, vote to exempt adultery—the most common ground justifying divorce and remarriage in both the Greek and Protestant communities—from its definitive teaching on the permanence of marriage?

If the Council really meant to make an exception to the Catholic church's ancient teaching on the indissolubility of marriage in cases of adultery we would expect it to say that it was doing so, or otherwise to provide evidence that a majority of fathers believed it should be done. We find neither. The only apparent piece of evidence is the about-face in favor of an indirect formulation for canon 7. We will see in chapter 4 that no more than a tiny minority ever stated that it supported the carving out of an exception, whereas a large majority stated repeatedly that it supported a reaffirmation of the strict teaching. Thus we should not take the about-face as signifying the decision to approve a limited instance of divorce, but rather the intention of the Council to spare the Greeks—who though practicing their contrary *ritus*, did not obstinately argue for it against the church of Rome—direct condemnation under canon 7. The canon struck the Protestants with an anathema, while simultaneously teaching as a truth of faith the absolute indissolubility of marriage in cases of adultery, and thus implicitly rejecting the Greek practices as contrary to the truth of faith.

CHAPTER 3

INDISSOLUBILITY AND THE 1547 BOLOGNA SESSIONS

Luther's ninety-five theses were posted in 1517. The Council of Trent did not open until 1545. During the intervening years, civil and ecclesiastical authorities, universities and theologians, and preachers and men on the streets all tried in vain to douse the conflagration lit in central Europe by the new religious ideas. Finally it became clear that nothing short of a universal church council was adequate to reply. History demonstrates that that reply was too late to save the unity of European Christianity, but it was not too late to preserve the integrity of Christian doctrine within the Catholic church.

Pope Paul III first convoked an ecumenical council in June 1536 and ordered all patriarchs, archbishops, bishops, and abbots of the Catholic church to assemble at Mantua in Italy on May 23, 1537. Political obstructions caused by the duke of Mantua delayed the date until May 1538. The venue was set for Vicenza. The date arrived and the papal legates were dispatched, but almost no bishops showed up. After another lengthy delay, Paul again convoked the Council on May 22, 1542, to meet at Trent, a city in northern Italy near the Swiss and Austrian borders, on November 1 of the same year.[1] Because Trent was a free city of the Holy Roman Empire, the location was widely accepted by the states of the Empire, even originally by the Protestants, who in the end refused the pope's invitation.

---

1. Paul convoked the Council with his bull "Initio nostri huius pontificati" (known as the "Bull of the Convocation"). See Hubert Jedin, *Crisis and Closure of the Council of Trent* (New York: Sheed and Ward, 1967), 8.

The Council formally opened in Trent on December 13, 1545. In March 1547, the papal legates, who served as Council presidents—Cardinals Giovanni del Monte and Marcello Cervini—recommended the transfer of the Council on account of the threat of a typhus outbreak in the imperially controlled city.[2] Supporters of the emperor denied the existence of an epidemic. But the majority of the fathers, eager to escape the emperor's influence, voted to move the Council south to the city of Bologna. Since Bologna was in the Papal States, Emperor Charles V and his delegation of Spanish bishops opposed the transfer. The transfer occurred anyway in March, but the emperor's protests led the pope to agree that the Bologna sessions *would engage in analysis and debate only* and pass no resolutions.[3] The dozen or so bishops of the emperor's party remained behind in Trent.

Formal discussions on marriage began at Bologna in spring 1547. Although the Bologna sessions resulted in no resolutions, the discussions of the Conciliar theologians and voting prelates illustrate the points of doctrinal concern shared by the Council members when they discussed the sacrament of marriage. The Council's threefold method was first to identify the errors of the Protestants, especially Luther, by quoting their own texts, then to clarify the corresponding Catholic truths, and finally, to formulate condemnations against the heretics and the corresponding heresies.[4]

THE "BOLOGNA SESSIONS"

The Bologna discussions on marital indissolubility took place during three sessions beginning respectively in April, June, and September 1547. Recorded in the *Acta* are the names and opinions of the Conciliar theologians and the voting prelates of the General Congregation (cardinals, archbishops, bishops, abbots, and superiors of religious orders).

The promulgation of a universal council, especially the publication of a dogmatic canon, is an act of the church. But the means by which the promulgation is arrived at is not any act of the church, but rather a process of the church comprised of innumerable acts of large numbers of people. The opinions these people hold when they begin their discussions; the proce-

---

2. Reginald Pole was also a papal legate and Council president, but was absent from Trent at the time. The decree of translation is printed in CT, VI, 3–4. The original *Acta* of this collection are recorded by Angelo Massarelli, bishop of San Severino and secretary of the Council.

3. Hubert Jedin, *Ecumenical Councils of the Catholic Church: An Historical Outline* (London: Herder and Herder, 1960), 164.

4. Bressan, *Il Canone Tridentino*, 81.

dural dynamics to which they are subjected, the force of good arguments, the influence of the interventions of council presidents and papal legates, episcopal peers and prominent theologians; the momentum that builds for shared conclusions and the sway of dissenting opinions, the bearing of internal and external political pressures; the skirmishes, collisions, and conflicts arising from the clash of hundreds of contending personalities; even the impact on the mind of a digestion distressed by the influence of soured cabbage and boiled eggs: these all come together and bear fruit in the formulation of propositions that we call the "teachings of the Council." These human dynamics, assisted by the invisible *actionem Spiritus sancti*, are the workshop, the church believes, for advancing Christ's divine will for his Body.[5] But when his will is not evident from the promulgated writings, we must investigate inferentially the recorded statements of individual members, especially the voting members, in order to understand what they thought about the topics at hand and what they would have meant had they individually formulated the Council's statement.

In November 1563, the problematic canon 7 was published. As we noted in the introduction, the canon's meaning, the scope of its application, and its authoritative status are disputed. Many believe that in using an indirect formulation ("If anyone says the Church errs") the Council meant only to single out the Reformers' denial of church authority in matters pertaining to marriage, but to accommodate the practices of divorce and remarriage of "the Greeks". Moreover, they believe the propositions asserted by the canon are not truths of faith taught in divine revelation, but longstanding conclusions of Catholic practice grounded merely in a firm legal tradition; consequently they may be understood as *de fide* only in the very wide sense that they are embraced within the wider Catholic belief system.

To begin to construct an argument against these conclusions, this chapter examines what truths on marriage the members of the Council of Trent believed needed defending at the time of the Bologna sessions, what status the truths held in Catholic teaching, with what type of formulation the truths should be taught, and the degree of authority with which they should be taught.

---

5. Vatican Council II, *Lumen Gentium*, no. 25, in DEC, 2:870.

First Bologna Session

Earliest Recorded Statements on the Sacrament of Marriage (April 1547)

The first Bologna session began on April 21, 1547. Angelo Massarelli, the general secretary of the Council, recorded the proceedings. Before it began, he presented the Conciliar theologians with a list of heresies on marriage for discussion. They are included in a list of erroneous propositions drawn from the writings of Luther and Melanchthon on the sacraments of holy orders, extreme unction, and matrimony.[6] The propositions were not themselves discussed, but provided the basis for the first formulation of the *articuli haereticorum* (articles of the heretics). The fifteen propositions on matrimony address marriage's sacramentality, grounds of invalidity, grades of affinity (i.e., relations to another by marriage) and consanguinity (relations to another by blood), polygamy, clandestine and clerical marriage, and divorce. I mention them simply to illustrate what teachings of the Reformers were most at issue when the Council's discussion on marriage began.

Proposition 8 asserts that because Christ only allowed *divortium* (divorce) for the cause of *fornicationem* (adultery), the pope errs whenever he grants a divorce for any other cause.[7] "Divortium" here means any formalized separation between spouses from bed or from cohabitation. Going back to early Christianity, the Catholic church permitted separation for a variety of reasons. Luther argued that only sexual misconduct justified it. Proposition 10 asserts that it is licit to remarry after divorce.[8] The *Acta* keys both propositions to Luther's *Babylonian Captivity*, published in 1520. For

---

6. The articles are recorded at CT, VI, 90–95. They are excerpted from a polemical text published by Girolamo Seripando (Hieronymum Seripandum), superior general of the Augustinian order, whose influence at the Council was considerable. He later became cardinal and papal legate to the Council, and was the Council's president from 1562 until his death in March 1563.

7. "Errare papam, dum divortium facit extra causam fornicationis." The text is drawn from the following statement from Luther's *Babylonian Captivity* as recorded in the *Acta*: "Christus concedit divortium in causa fornicationis dumtaxat. Quare errare papam necesse est, quoties divortium in aliis causis facit" (CT, VI, 93.12–15).

8. "Licere post repudium iterum contrahere." This also is from *Babylonian Captivity*: "Sed hoc admiror magis, cur coelibem cogant esse hominem, qui divortio separatus est a coniuge sua, nec aliam ducere permittant" (*Luthers Werke*, 6:559.27–29). Also from Luther's *Epithalamio*: "In his casibus, ubi coniugum unus alterum ad vitam non christianam urget aut se ab eo separat, ibi alter non est captus nec obligatus ei adhaerere; potest cum alio contrahere, perinde ac si mortuus esset prior ille coniux" (CT, VI, 93.23–29 and n7).

proposition 10 it also references the 1523 biblical commentary, *On 1 Corinthians 7* (referred to in the proceedings as the "Epithalamium").⁹ Luther's attack on papal authority in *Babylonian Captivity* was well known and so the inclusion of proposition 8 is unsurprising.¹⁰ More interesting is that papal authority in cases of divorce, and church authority in marriage issues more widely, is never again mentioned at Bologna. This is in contrast to the sustained and collective interest with the substantive doctrinal issue of the legitimacy of divorce and remarriage, as referred to in proposition 10.

First Theological Discussion on Marriage (April 1547)

The first formal theological discussions of marriage were undertaken by the *congregatio theologorum*, experts not possessing the rank of bishop and so not entitled to vote at the Council, but invited to provide theological guidance for the bishops as they formulated the canons and decrees. On April 26, Massarelli presented to the *congregatio* six "articles of heresy" on marriage. Three of the six (nos. 3–5) address the legitimacy of remarriage after divorce, two referring specifically to cases of adultery. (The other three concern clandestine marriages, polygamy, and grades of consanguinity and affinity.)¹¹ The *Acta* cross-references all three to the precise text in Luther's *Babylonian Captivity* that was cross-referenced in the *Acta* for proposition 10 above.¹² They read:

A. 3: "A married woman who has committed adultery has therefore ceased to be a wife; it is therefore licit for both spouses, or at least for one of them [the one who gave no cause for divorce], to remarry [i.e., to take a new spouse]."¹³

---

9. The Greek term "epithalamion"—from epi (ἐπί) meaning "upon" and thalamos (θάλαμος) meaning marriage chamber—is a song or poem written in honor of a wedding. Luther's *Epithalamium* can be found in *Luthers Werke*, 12:95–142.

10. "Tamen in iis nihil definio (ut dixi), quamquam nihil magis optarem esse definitum, cum nihil magis me et multos mecum vexet hodie. Sola auctoritate Papae aut Episcoporum hic diffiniri nihil volo" (*Babylonian Captivity*, in *Luthers Werke*, 6:560).

11. CT, VI, 98–99.

12. Luther, *Babylonian Captivity*, in *Luthers Werke*, 6:559.24–35 (for mistaken reference, see p. 56, note 19).

13. CT, VI, 98.17–19: "Mulier, quae alteri viro sui fecit copiam, adeo uxor esse desiit, ut utrique aut alteri saltem coniugum, (qui causam non dedit divortio), liceat (novare coniugium, hoc est) aliam uxorem ducere vel alteri nubere." The Latin has two gender-specific constructions for "to marry." A more precise rendering, which would be awkward and add nothing to the meaning, would include after the second parenthesis: "if the innocent party is the husband,

A. 4: "He does not commit adultery who has married another after dismissing an adulterous wife."[14]

A. 5: "Divorce annuls marriage; wherefore after a divorce has been lawfully performed, it is licit for both spouses to remarry."[15]

All three articles concern the question of the indissolubility of marriage. The third and fourth imply that adultery dissolves marriage; the fifth asserts that divorce dissolves it. Fransen and Bressan both argue that the articles should be seen as concerning merely the inner or intrinsic indissolubility of marriage (Fransen's "innere Unauflöslichkeit").[16]

It is highly doubtful that Massarelli, his drafters, or the *congregatio* had any such distinctions in mind when preparing the three articles. Each of the three is intentionally drawn from Luther's writings. Since Luther denied the doctrine of indissolubility—intrinsic, extrinsic, or otherwise—he could have had no such concept in mind when drafting *Babylonian Captivity*. Moreover, the terms "intrinsic" and "extrinsic indissolubility" were never used at the Council, nor was the distinction between the concepts ever obviously alluded to.[17] Moreover, there is no indication from the theological discussion over article 3 that the formulation was taken by anyone as pertaining explicitly to a denial of intrinsic indissolubility. It is interesting to note that Theobald Freudenberger, editor and annotator of the sixth volume of *Concilium Tridentinum*, cross-references article 3 with Luther's famous text on divorce from *Babylonian Captivity* noted above.[18]

---

for him to take another wife, or if the innocent party is the wife, for her to have another husband."

14. CT, VI, 98.21: "Non moechatur, qui dimissa adultera aliam duxerit."

15. CT, VI, 99.1–2: "Divortium dirimit matrimonium, unde ab illo rite celebrato licet repudianti et repudiatae reiterare coniugium."

16. See Piet F. Fransen, "Ehescheidung Im Falle Von Ehebruch," 535, in *Hermeneutics of the Councils and Other Studies*, ed. Mertens, 135; Bressan, *Il Canone Tridentino*, 85.

17. Although Palmieri in the late nineteenth century (1880) refers to the two terms in his discussion of canon 7 (see *Tractatus De Matrimonio Christiano,* cap. III, § II, thesis XVI, 125–40), his use does not support Fransen's claim.

18. In CT, VI, see 98n10: "Concedit ergo Christus divortium, in causa fornicationis duntaxat. Quare errare Papam necesse est, quoties divortium facit aliis causis.... Sed hoc admiror magis, cur caelibem esse cogant hominem, qui divortio separatus est a coniuge sua, nec aliam ducere permittant. Si enim Christus divortium concedit in causa fornicationis et neminem cogit esse celibem, et Paulus magis velit nos nubere quam uri (1 Cor. 7:9), videtur omnino admittere, ut in locum repudiatae aliam ducat. Quae res utinam plane discussa et certa esset, ut posset consuli infinitis periculis eorum, qui sine culpa sua hodie celibes esse coguntur, hoc est, quorum uxores vel mariti aufugiunt et coniugem relinquunt, decennio vel nunquam reversuri" (Freudenberger mistakenly references *Luthers Werke* 7:559; it should be 6:559). For an English translation of this passage from *Babylonian Captivity*, see Luther, *Works*, 36:105.

But the third article, as Fransen notes, does not correspond to Luther, but rather to a text from Erasmus. (The unique phrase *sui fecit copiam* is clearly Erasmian.)[19] On December 16, 1527, the faculty of the University of Paris condemned Erasmus's proposition, along with three others.[20] This ensured that the heretical proposition was widely known by the time of the Council. Massarelli singled out the three articles, not because he, his drafters or the *congregatio* believed they implied or would imply a reference merely to the property of intrinsic indissolubility, but because he believed (wrongly in the case of article 3) that they belonged to Luther and he intended to present for discussion Luther's most prominent articles against the Catholic doctrine of the indissolubility of marriage.

Statements of the "Congregatio Theologorum"

The role of the *congregatio* was to assist the Council fathers in their examination of the "articles of heresy" by offering expert theological opinion on whether the propositions under consideration were erroneous and indeed constituted heresy; and they were to support their opinions by appeal to authorities such as scripture, councils, Church Fathers, history, and natural law. Thirty-six theologians commented on the three articles from Friday, April 29, to Saturday, May 7, 1547. Of the thirty-six, not a single doubt was expressed regarding the heretical nature of the propositions.[21] Some simply assert that the articles are heretical.[22] Others support their opinions by

---

19. "Uxor enim, quae sui corporis copiam fecit alteri, jam, etiamsi non repudietur, desiit esse uxor. Et maritus, qui sui corporis copiam fecit alienae, jam ante divortium maritus esse desiit." Erasmus, "Paraphrases in Novum Tetamentum, In Marcum 10," in *Opera Omnia* (Leiden: Lugduni Batavorum, 1706), t. VII, 233 F. See also Erasmus, "Annotationes in Matthaeum 19:9," *Opera* (1705), VI, 97–98: "Quae alteri viro sui fecit copiam iam uxor esse desiit et matrimonii ius ademit sibi, divisa carne quam Deus unam et indivisam esse voluit."

20. The Paris condemnation reads: "Hae quatuor propositiones, quatenus per eas praetendi videtur matrimonium per adulterium dissolvi quoad vincula, *haereticae sunt*: est enim vinculum matrimonii jure divino indissolubile ut ad Corinthios scribens Apostolus demonstrat." In Charles Du Plessis d'Argentré, *Collectio Judiciorum de novis erroribus qui ab initio saec. XII [to 1735] in Ecclesia proscripti* (Lutetiae Parisiorum [Paris], 1728), II, I, 53. For discussion of Erasmus's condemned propositions, see Piet Fransen, "Ehescheidung Im Falle Von Ehebruch: Der fundamentaltheologisch-dogmatische Ertrag der Bologneser Verhandlungen (1547)," *Scholastik* 27 (1952); reprinted in *Hermeneutics of the Councils and Other Studies*, ed. Mertens, 128n12, 128–29n15, 131n30, 134–35n45. Erasmus's denial of indissolubility was influential on the permissive views of the Reformers; see Gordon Wenham and William Heth, *Jesus and Divorce* (Eugene, Ore.: Wipf and Stock, 2010), 78–79.

21. See CT, VI, 99–121.

22. For example, Conventual Franciscan John Bernerius (de Coregio), doctor of metaphysics at the University of Bologna, where he was taught by Felice Peretti (later Pope Sixtus V),

quoting church authorities. For example, French Franciscan and Parisian scholar, Richard Cenoma, references scripture (Lk 16:18, Rom 7:3, 1 Cor 7:10–11), the writings of Church Fathers (Ambrose, Augustine, Jerome), the Councils of Mileve (416 A.D.) and Elvira (300 A.D.), the Canons of the Apostles (c. 47), and the writings of a pope (Innocent I, *Letter to Exsuperius*).[23] Similarly, Franciscan theologian Padua Barletano asserts that the third and fourth articles are heretical since they are contrary to Matthew 5:32 and 19:9.[24]

Parisian scholar, John Consilium, says that although Ambrose (really Ambrosiaster) in his commentary on 1 Corinthians 7 held that divorce was licit on account of adultery, "all other doctors judge to the contrary."[25] Consilium refers here to a biblical commentary wrongly believed at the time of Trent to be written by Ambrose. The pseudonymous text seems to defend a double standard: a wife who dismisses her husband for adultery is not permitted to remarry, but a husband who dismisses an adulterous wife is not prohibited.[26] The text posed a problem for the fathers at Trent because they believed the great Milanese bishop himself wrote it.[27] The actual position

---

says: "tertius et quartus articuli haeretici sunt" (CT, VI, 105.10); Philip Braschi (Faventinus), metaphysician at the University of Ferrara, states: "Tertius articulus eiusdem matrimonii etiam falsus est" (119.19–20); Paris scholar Nicolas Grandis states: "omnes alios articulos haereticos censet" (120.2–3); and Italian Franciscan theologian Christopher de Bagnacavallo states: "omnesque alios propositos articulos hereticos iudicat" (120.12).

23. CT, VI, 101.17–21, 102.1–2. The Canons of the Apostles, also referred to as "Ecclesiastical Canons of the Same Holy Apostles," is a fourth-century collection of ecclesiastical statutes treating issues of government and discipline in the early church. Their attribution to the twelve apostles is without historical basis.

24. Barletano's examination is at CT, VI, 104.8–9. He does not address the question of the exceptive clause in the two Matthean passages.

25. "Ambrosius in 7. cap. I ad Corinth. tenet propter fornicationem uxorem dimitti posse. Sed omnes alii doctores contrarium senserunt, scilicet quod non possit dissolvi matrimonium propter fornicationem" (CT, VI, 107.15–16).

26. *Commentary on 1 Cor. 7:* "It is not permitted for the wife to marry, if she dismisses her own husband because of adultery .... It is licit for a husband to remarry if he dismisses a sinful wife, because he is not thus bound by the law as is his wife, because a husband is head of his wife." (Non permittitur mulieri, ut nubat, si virum suum causa fornicationis dimiserit .... Viro licet ducere uxorem, si dimiserit uxorem peccantem, quia non ita lege constringitur vir, sicut mulier; caput enim mulieris vir est.) The text is quoted at CT, IX, 411n3.

27. The commentary was probably written during the papacy of Pope Damasus I (366–84). Its author, believed to be an aristocratic Roman cleric, wrote commentaries on the letters of Paul, which, because of their Ambrosian attribution, were disseminated widely. In the sixteenth century, Erasmus questioned their origin, and by the seventeenth century, the pseudonymous author was referred to as Ambrosiaster, or pseudo-Ambrose. Consilium's purpose for referencing the commentary is obscure since the text was usually referenced as an example of toleration for divorce and remarriage during the Patristic period. For background on Ambrosiaster,

of Ambrose is that a Christian marriage cannot be dissolved for any reason or under any circumstance.[28] Consilium also references Chrysostom, Origen, Hillary, Jerome, Augustine, and Pope Leo I.[29] He appeals to scripture (Lk 16:18 and Mk 10:11), as well as the Council of Mileve, which, he says, affirms what is taught "secundum apostolicam et evangelicam doctrinam."[30]

The Parisian scholar then raises the sensitive question of the exceptive clause in Matthew's Gospel (19:9; 5:32). He says that although Christ may seem to make an exception to the norm against divorce and remarriage for adultery, Augustine makes clear that the exception is only apparent. He refers to Augustine's famous reasoning from *On Adulterous Marriages*.[31] There the saint argues that if we begin from the premise asserted in Matthew 19:9—that anyone who divorces his wife, except for adultery, and marries another, commits adultery—it does *not* follow that someone who divorces his wife on account of her adultery and marries another, does not commit adultery. Augustine says this would be tantamount to arguing from the premise that anyone who knows the good but does evil sins, to the conclusion that anyone who does evil, not knowing the good, does not sin, which is obviously false. It is worse to divorce a wife who has not committed adultery and to marry another than to remarry after divorcing a wife for committing adultery. Both are adulterers. But the Lord in Matthew's Gospel desires to focus on the more serious sin. But being a less serious sin does not make it no sin at all. Augustine's interpretation exercised enormous influence over the fathers at Trent and is frequently appealed to as a reply to the pseudo-Ambrosian text. Consilium then condemns the arguments of Erasmus that marriage can be dissolved on account of irksome

---

see David G. Hunter, "Ambrosiaster," in *Dictionary of Major Biblical Interpreters*, ed. Donald K. McKim (Downers Grove, Ill.: InterVarsity Press, 2007), 123. Hunter shows elsewhere that among Ambrosiaster's unorthodox ideas are that women are not created in God's image and that they are inferior to men; David G. Hunter, "The Paradise of Patriarchy: Ambrosiaster on Women as (Not) God's Image," *Journal of Theological Studies* 43 (1992): 447–69. Cf. Rist, "Divorce and Remarriage," esp. 82n14.

28. See appendix B.

29. Chrysostom is referenced at CT, VI, 107.16–17. Freudenberger (107n11) refers to the texts *In Matt. Hom.* 17 and *De Virginitate* 40. Origen is referenced at CT, VI, 107.17. The CT text references homily 7 of Origen's *Comment. In Matthaeum*; the homily number is actually 19. See also CT, IX, 409n3. Hillary, *Comm. In Matt.* 4, 22; referenced at CT, VI, 107n13. Jerome, *Commentary on Matthew 19:9*; referenced at CT, VI, 107.17–18. Augustine, *De Adulterinis Conjugiis ad Pollentium* I, 9, 9; referenced at CT, VI, 107.18. Pope Leo I, *Epist.* (77) *ad Nicetam Episcopum Aquileiensem* 159; referenced at CT, VI, 107.18.

30. CT, VI, 107.19.

31. CT, VI, 107.20–23. *De Adulterinis Conjugiis ad Pollentium* I, cap. 9.

cohabitation, proof of murder, and witchcraft and incantations.³² He recommends that to the third article should be added: "neither from adultery nor any other cause does she cease to be a wife."³³

A very influential sixteenth-century theologian, Peter Canisius, SJ, just twenty-six years old at Bologna, in one of his two interventions on marriage at Trent, asserts unambiguously his agreement with the traditional doctrine: "Indeed, whatever marriages exist, provided that they are rightly contracted, they cannot be dissolved by anyone, not even by the Church herself, in accordance with the words of Christ, 'what God has joined, let no man separate'; for this reason, St. Paul said [in Rom 7:2–3], as long as a wife lives she is bound to her husband."³⁴ This defense of the absolute indissolubility of marriage as a *de fide* truth is either explicit or taken for granted in the writings of all the theologians who contributed to this discussion.

For example, Fr. Augustine Montealcino, priest of the Eremites of St. Augustine, rejects the third article as false on account of Paul's words in 2 Corinthians 11:2: "I espoused you to one husband to present you as a chaste virgin."³⁵ Neapolitan Franciscan, Peter Paul Caporella ("de Potentia"), states that the "bond [of marriage] is indissoluble and cannot be dissolved for any reason, even by the natural law."³⁶ Roman theologian, Vincent Placentia, OP, says "a contracted marriage, since it comes into existence by divine law, cannot be dissolved, not even by the Church."³⁷ We know he is referring to consummated marriages because he says that "article

---

32. CT, VI, 107.23–24. Erasmus, *In novum testamentum annotationes, in priorem ad Corinth. c. 7* (Basel, 1555), 499. CT, VI, 107n20, notes that Erasmus defends the following "causae divortio": "graviora discrimina, nimirum caedes, veneficia, incantamenta."

33. CT, VI, 107.24–25.

34. CT, VI, 118.29–31: "Quaecunque enim sint matrimonia, dum contracta sunt, dirimi non possunt a quoquam neque etiam ab ipsa ecclesia iuxta illud Christi: 'Quos Deus coniunxit homo non separet.' Propterea Paulus dicebat: Mulier quandiu vixerit, coniuncta erit viro suo." The young Jesuit accompanied Cardinal von Waldburg of Augsburg to the Council before travelling to Rome to be tutored by his order's saintly founder. Canisius was founder of the first German-speaking university and author of three enormously influential sixteenth-century catechisms written between the second and third periods of the Council: *Summa doctrinae christianae* (A Summary of Christian Teachings) (1555); *Catechismus minor* (A Smaller Catechism) (1556); *Parvus catechismus catholicorum* (A Little Catechism for Catholics) (1558). Canisius returned to the Council as a papal theologian during the third period of the Council of Trent, but was not present for the final discussions on marriage in 1563.

35. CT, VI, 108.12: "Spondi uni viro virginem castam."

36. CT, VI, 108.28: "Matrimonium sacramentum est a Christo institutum, cuius vinculum est indissolubile, et nulla ratione, etiam lege naturae, dissolvi potest." He repeats the same at 109.1: "matrimonium nulla ratione dissolvi potest."

37. CT, VI, 109.24–25: "Matrimonium, cum sit de iure divino, contractum dirimi non potest neque etiam ab ecclesia."

five is false after a couple has performed an act of sexual intercourse, but not before."[38] He says that adultery justifies a separation "of bed and no more," and references the Councils of Constance, Florence, and Lateran IV, as well as the authority of Augustine.[39] Augustinian theologian Gaspar de Valentia says that article 3 is false because it is contrary to the teaching of Paul in 1 Corinthians 7:11.[40] Francis Salazar, a Spanish Franciscan, says that "all six articles on marriage are heretical, because marriage is a sacrament instituted by God," and references both Old and New Testament passages.[41] Parisian scholar Gentianus Hervetus, associate of Cardinal Cervini, writes that "the third, fourth, and fifth articles are heretical, because nothing dissolves a marriage, as was declared by the Council of Mileve, not even adultery, which only separates the bed."[42] Conventual Franciscan, John Baptist Vastinius Moncalvius, says he "judges all the articles [on matrimony] heretical"; "since a marriage among Christians is a sacrament in Christ and the Church, when it has been legally contracted in any way whatsoever, it *cannot [non potest]* be dissolved."[43] Finally, Augustinian theologian Cherubim of Cassia states: "marriage cannot be dissolved as is evident from Matt. 16 [actually 19] and Mark 10. These passages show that marriage was instituted from the beginning."[44] Addressing the exceptive clause in Matthew, he repeats the familiar maxim, *bed, not bond*: "when Christ said, 'except on account of adultery,' he meant that a spouse can send away an adulterous spouse, but cannot remarry; so there is a separation of bed, not of the marriage; emphasizing that a spouse can send an adulterous spouse away for reasons of adultery and cannot marry again. Thus, nothing can dissolve a marriage."[45]

38. CT, VI, 109.5–6: "Quintus articulus etiam falsus est post carnalem copulam, ante autem non."

39. CT, VI, 110.3–4: "Per fornicationem vero dirimitur quoad torum tantum, ut ait concilium Constantiense, Florentinum et Lateranense, Augustinus." The text refers to "Augustinus, c. *Licet* 32, q. 2"; Freudenberger identifies this with *De Adulterinis Conjugiis* II, 4–5. See CT, VI, 110n4.

40. CT, VI, 112.38–39: "Tertius articulus falsus est, contra Paulum 1 Cor. 7." He adds: "Quartus et quintus articuli etiam falsi sunt."

41. CT, VI, 113.14–15: "Quoad matrimonium omnes sex articuli haeretici sunt, quia matrimonium sacramentum est a Deo institutum, Gen. 1 [27], Paulus ad Eph. [5:32] et [1] Cor [7:10]."

42. CT, VI, 115.28–30: "Tertius, quartus et quintus etiam haeretici sunt, quia nulla ex causa matrimonium dirimitur, ut Milevitanum concilium declarant, etiam propter fornicationem, que solum torum separat."

43. CT, VI, 117.24: "Omnes articulos propositos haereticos censet." CT, VI, 118.8–9; emphasis added: "apud Christianos, cum matrimonium sacramentum sit in Christo et ecclesia, dirimi, postquam est quoquo modo rite contractum, non potest."

44. CT, VI, 121.3–4.

45. CT, VI, 121.5–8.

These earliest formal considerations by the *congregatio theologorum* illustrate the challenges facing the Catholic teaching on marriage. The Reformers and others (e.g., Erasmus) argued that marriage is dissoluble under certain circumstances, especially in cases of adultery, and consequently that the spouses—at least the innocent ones who gave no cause for the divorce—are free to remarry. The theologians reply by unanimously rejecting any cause for the dissolution of marriage (although they do not reject the possibility of a spousal separation presuming the spouses do not remarry while both are still living). By their frequent appeals to scripture, the Church Fathers, the teachings of popes, the judgments of councils, and the writings of other eminent authorities, they demonstrate that they believe that the absolute indissolubility of marriage is not merely a legal discipline, but rather a truth of faith rooted in divine revelation and consequently an irreformable part of Catholic teaching. Moreover, no theologian limits his remarks on marital indissolubility to a defense of intrinsic indissolubility. Fransen argues that Peter Caporella meant to do so because the Franciscan, when commenting on the fourth article ("he is not an adulterer who dismisses an adulterous wife and marries another"), says: "Polygamy was permitted to the fathers in the old testament by a divine dispensation. But if today by some chance it should turn out that in some place there were a great number of women and very few men, then it [polygamy] could be granted by a law of nature, especially if God were thus to proclaim it to the Church."[46]

But the conclusion must be rejected. If Caporella was in doubt as to whether the church could dissolve a marriage, why did he say twice that no reason, not even the law of nature, can dissolve marriage?[47] He does not merely say the bond of a Christian marriage *should* not be dissolved, he says it cannot (*potest*) be dissolved. Moreover, he begins his comments on the fourth article saying that Paul (1 Cor 7:10) refutes the proposition that remarriage after adultery is licit.[48] We note that Paul's command to spouses to "not separate" or "to remain single" is not limited to any specific circumstances; and the apostle says the command is from "the Lord," suggesting

---

46. CT, VI, 109.3–5: "Polygamia in veteri testamento licita patribus fuit ex dispensatione divina; hodie vero si quo casu eveniret, ut aliquo in loco magna esset copia mulierum et paucissimi homines, tunc iure naturae possit concedi, praesertim ita Deo renuntiante Ecclesiae." See Fransen, "Ehescheidung Im Falle Von Ehebruch," 136 and 136n53.

47. CT, VI, 108.28–29: "Matrimonium sacramentum est a Christo institutum, cuius vinculum est indissoluble et nulla ratione, etiam lege naturae, dissolvi potest." CT, VI, 109.1–2: "Primus igitur articulus haereticus est et etiam Tertius eadem ratione, quia matrimonium nulla ratione dissolvi potest."

48. CT, VI, 109.2: "Item quartus, cum a Paulo repraehendatur."

that Caporella thinks the teaching on indissolubility is a part of divine revelation. He concludes his comments on article 4 by saying that the dispensation for polygamy in the Old Testament was given "because of the hardness of the hearts of the Jews [ad duritiem cordium Iudaeorum]," but that "*Christ* prohibited it in the gospel law."[49] It is clear that Caporella thinks indissolubility is a truth of divine revelation and that the property of indissolubility precludes the possibility of dissolution. So the *ius natura* that allows polygamy in extreme cases must refer to an exception to the negative norm—the publication of which he thinks deserves the support of a divine command to the church—prohibiting living in a marital-type relationship with more than one woman, and not to any law that dissolves marriage.[50]

Summarizing the responses of the theologians on May 7 to articles 3, 4, and 5, Massarelli recorded the following statement:

> Regarding articles three, four and five, concerning whether a wife can be dismissed because of [lit. "through"] adultery, all the theologians defended the negative position. And because some said that Erasmus in his commentary on 1 Cor. 7 refers to some of the causes for which a marriage can be dissolved, they [the theologians] desired to be added to their comments on the third article that neither by adultery, nor by any other cause, can marriage be dissolved.[51]

---

49. CT, VI, 109.10–11: "in lege evangelica Christus prohibuit" (emphasis added).

50. Fransen says that Aquinas's limited defense of polygamy in his *Commentary* on the *Sentences* of Peter Lombard supports his claim that Caporella means only to address his remarks to inner indissolubility. But Aquinas's remarks justify only the conclusion that in extreme situations exceptions can be made to the prohibitions arising from indissolubility in natural marriages (*In IV Sent*, d. 33, q. 2, a. 1, co.). This seems to be the reasoning that Caporella appeals to in his comments above. Aquinas states explicitly that there can be *no* exceptions to the indissolubility of a sacramental marriage, unless that exception is supernaturally ordained by a divine dispensation ("secundo modo dispensationis"): "Inseparabilitas quamvis sit de secunda intentione matrimonii prout est in officium naturae, tamen est de prima intentione ipsius prout est sacramentum ecclesiae; et ideo ex quo institutum est ut sit ecclesiae sacramentum, manente tali institutione non potest sub dispensatione cadere, nisi forte secundo modo dispensationis" (a. 2, ad 3). Most of the Conciliar theologians, though never explicitly rejecting the indissolubility of natural marriage, were explicitly defending the indissolubility of sacramental marriage. So Aquinas's limited defense of exceptions to the indissolubility of natural marriage has no relevance to the question of whether the Council theologians intended to limit their remarks to instrinsic indissolubility.

51. Entitled "Summa responsionis theologorum": "In tertio, quarto et quinto articulo, an per fornicationem uxor dimitti possit, omnes defenderunt partem negativam. Et quia dicebant aliqui Erasmum in cap. 7 primae ad Corinthios referre aliquas causas, ob quas matrimonium dirimi possit, cupiebant addi in ipso tertio articulo, quod nedum adulterio, sed nulla etiam alia causa dirimi posse matrimonium" (CT, VI, 121.31–35). The Erasmus passage can be found in his *In novum testamentum annotationes, in priorem ad Corinth. c. 7* (Basel, 1555), 499; referenced at CT, VI, 107.23–24n20.

The reproduction of these quotes from the *Acta*, though tedious, is necessary for establishing at the outset of our consideration of the Council's preliminary discussions on marriage the important point—crucial to our argument—that from the very first deliberations at Trent on marriage, there is no hesitation whatsoever to affirm the absolute indissolubility of marriage and to ground the truth of that doctrine firstly in divine revelation and secondly in councils, Church Fathers, and natural law.

First Recorded Canons

Sometime before March 24, 1547, while the Council was still at Trent and before the *congregatio theologorum* took up their considerations, six canons on the sacrament of matrimony are recorded in the *Acta*.[52] These are the first recorded canons on marriage at the Council. Their preparation is attributed to Ambrose Pelargi, Secretary to the archbishop of Trier. Pelargi remained behind in Trent when the Council transferred to Bologna. He gave his draft of the articles to Robert Wauchope, the archbishop of Armagh (Armacanus), who subsequently conveyed them to Cardinal Cervini, papal legate and Council president.[53] Using the traditional condemnation *anathema sit*, canons 4, 5, and 6 single out for condemnation the heretical propositions asserted in articles 3, 4, and 5 above. The canons read:

C. 4: "If anyone says that a married woman who has committed adultery has ceased to be a wife, so that it is licit for both spouses, or at least the innocent spouse, who evidently gave no cause for the divorce, to marry whom he or she wishes, let him be anathema."[54]

C. 5: "If anyone says that a man who after dismissing an adulterous wife has married another does not commit adultery, let him be anathema."[55]

C. 6: "If anyone says divorce annuls marriage, wherefore after a divorce has been lawfully performed, it is licit for either spouse to contract a marriage with another person, let him be anathema."[56]

---

52. The transfer from Trent to Bologna took place on March 11, 1547.
53. See CT, VI, 125n1.
54. CT, VI, 129.12–14: "Si quis d[ixerit] mulierem, quae alteri viro sui fecit copiam, adeo desinere esse uxorem, ut utrique coniugum aut saltem innocenti, qui scilicet causam non dedit divortio, liceat cui velit nubere, a. s. [anathema sit]."
55. CT, VI, 129.15: "Si quis d[ixerit] non mechari, qui dimissa adultera aliam duxerit a. s."
56. CT, VI, 129.16–17: "Si quis d[ixerit] divortium dirimere matrimonium, ideoque ab illo rite celebrato licere utrique cum alia persona contrahere, a. s."

Pelargi's canons, as we shall see below, will be used to formulate the "disputed articles" that Massarelli distributes on August 29 to the General Congregation for discussion.

Second Bologna Session

The second Bologna session began on June 6, 1547. Later that summer (around August 5), Cardinal Cervini charged Massarelli with drafting canons on marriage in preparation for the discussions of the General Congregation (the bishops and others holding the rank of bishop) scheduled to be held in the first week of September. Massarelli apparently found this a difficult job to complete. On August 7, he showed his draft to four prominent French theologians (Consilium, Cenomani, Grandis, and Salazar) who gave him critical feedback.[57] Grandis was obviously not satisfied because on August 16 he requested more changes.[58]

On August 28, Massarelli again had in hand a revised draft of the canons. The draft did not include canons for two particular articles that were causing difficulty. The first dealt with clandestine marriage. The second, which interests us, concerned adultery, divorce, and remarriage. President and papal legate, Cardinal del Monte, decided to delay distribution of all canons on matrimony until the fathers had a chance to express their opinions on the two articles.[59] On August 29, Massarelli distributed to the members of the General Congregation the two articles. The second is a positive rendering of the propositions condemned in Pelargi's canons 4 and 5. Numbered as article 2, it reads: "A married woman who has committed adultery has ceased to be a wife, so that it is licit for either spouse, or at least the innocent spouse, who evidently gave no cause for the divorce, to marry whom he or she wishes. And a man who after dismissing an adulterous wife has married another does not commit adultery."[60] The article is referred to

---

57. See CT, VI, 445–46n7.

58. CT, VI, 446n7: "Nic. Grandis die 16. Aug. dedit Massarello, qui eodem die vacavit 'aptandis canonibus matrimonii, ut in congregationibus generalibus proponi possint.'"

59. CT, VI, 402.11–14: "Ideo super eis prius (audire cupimus sententias patrum), quid (videlicet eis) videatur, an relinquendi sint, ut non necessariae quaestiones evitentur etiam inter catholicos, decisioni iuris communis (sunt enim ambo in iure decisi), an etiam determinandi cum aliis."

60. CT, VI, 402.19–21: "Mulier, quae alteri viro sui fecit copiam, adeo uxor esse desiit, ut utrique coniugum aut saltem innocenti, qui scilicet causam non dedit divortio, liceat cui velit nubere. Neque mechari eum, qui dimissa adultera aliam duxerit." See also 407.10–12. A simplified formulation is also stated at CT, VI, 409.37–38: "Quod per fornicationem non solvatur vinculum matrimonii" (That on account of adultery, the bond of marriage is not dissolved).

as "heretical" and is said to be "also disputed among Catholics."⁶¹ This is the first time the article on divorce and remarriage is referred to them as "disputed."

The text introducing the article tells us something of how the Council looked at its subject matter in August 1547. It says the article concerns "matrimonium ipsum" (marriage itself), meaning it pertains to the *nature* of marriage. This indicates that early in the Bologna proceedings, the fathers' interest with divorce and remarriage included not only questions of the church's authority over marriage, but a substantive concern with the nature of marriage itself. The text says the corresponding canon was delayed because article 2 "seem[ed] to contain some difficulty." "Difficulty" is obviously referring to its disputed nature (more on this below). Further, the "thoughts of the Fathers" are to be solicited "so that unnecessary questions, even among Catholics, may be avoided" and the Council will follow the judgments of the Church Fathers. The *Acta* says that as a practical matter, the issue under dispute was already settled in common law, and consequently there is a question as to whether the matter should be left to the decisions of common law or settled by the publication of canons. This seems to me the most important point. It tells us that at least Cardinal del Monte believed that if there was no need doctrinally to settle the matter raised by article 2, the Council may have prescinded from it altogether. Why might there be no need? The two most obvious reasons are that the matter was already settled with sufficient clarity, or that the will of Christ regarding the matter was not (at the time of Trent) sufficiently clear for the Council to render a definitive judgment. We will see that the Council did in fact choose to publish canons treating the question of divorce and remarriage, from which we gather both that the Council did not consider the matter in question to be (already) sufficiently clear, and that it believed that the will of Christ at the time of Trent *was* sufficiently clear to render a definitive judgment. Finally, the text says the article is to be formulated in the "precise words of the Lutherans."⁶² The attribution of article 2 to Luther also indicates that concern with Protestant heresies stretched beyond questions

---

61. CT, VI, 407.7.
62. "Restat quoad dogmata sacramenti matrimonii, super quo formati sunt canones, qui examinandi proponentur quoad materiam et quoad formam, ut hactenus factum est in examinatione aliorum sacramentorum. (Verum quoad ipsum matrimonium sunt) duo alii articuli, de quibus canones formati adhuc non sunt, cum habere videantur aliquam difficultatem. Ideo super eis prius (audire cupimus sententias patrum), quid (videlicet eis) videatur, an relinquendi sint, ut non necessariae quaestiones evitentur etiam inter catholicos, decisioni iuris communis (sunt enim ambo in iure decisi), an etiam determinandi cum aliis; (patrumque sententiis

of ecclesial jurisdiction to include the Protestant rejection of the Catholic doctrine on the nature of marriage.[63]

Demonstrating the disputed nature of the article, Massarelli distributed on August 30 a list of *auctoritates* who "seem" to support and oppose the simplified proposition.[64] In support of the proposition, Massarelli identifies twenty-two authorities: four texts from scripture (Mk 10, Lk 16, Rom 7, 1 Cor 7), the testimony of five popes (Innocent I, Leo I, Gregory I, Alexander III, Innocent III), four regional councils (Mileve, Elvira, Quinisext, Seventh Council of Carthage), and eleven additional writings of theological authorities (including from the Canons of the Apostles, two references to the Venerable Bede, two to Augustine, two to Jerome, Rupert, Origen, Tertullian, and Chrysostom).[65] These are followed by eleven writings of authorities that "seem to oppose [*contra videtur facere*]" the proposition: the two instances in the Gospel of Matthew where the exceptive clause is repeated (Mt 5:32, 19:9), the opinions of three regional councils (Arles, Venice, and three canons from Tribur), two popes (Zachary, Gregory II), and two theologians (Pseudo-Ambrose, Augustine).[66]

---

auditis eorum iudicium sequemur). Articuli (igitur ipsi) duo in verbis propriis Lutheranorum proponentur, qui ita se habent." CT, VI, 402.7–16.

63. The attribution of the first sentence of article 2 to Luther (line 15) is, as we have noted, an error since it comes from Erasmus.

64. CT, VI, 407.13: "Auctoritates, quae videntur favere et adversari ... articulis."

65. Innocent I, *Second Letter to Victricius*; referenced at CT, VI, 410.9–13. Pope Leo I, *Epist. (77) ad Nicetam Episcopum Aquileiensem* 159; referenced at 410.14–16. Pope Gregory (590–604), *Li vero*: q. 7, c. 22; referenced at 410.17–21 (see also CT, IX, 649.11 and 649n5). Alexander III (1159–81), *X De divortiis* [IV 19], cap. 2; referenced at 411.3–8. Innocent III (1198–1216), *X De divortiis* [IV 19], c. [7] *Quanto*; referenced at 411.9–16. Council of Mileve (Milevitanum), c. 17; referenced at 410.25–27. Council of Elvira (Eliberitanum), c. 9; referenced at 410.30. The Quinisext Council (Council of Trullo) (692), c. 87; Greek referenced at 410.22–24, Latin at CT, IX, 649n6. Seventh Council of Carthage; referenced at 410.28–29. Canons of the Apostles, c. 47; referenced at 410.7–8. Venerable Bede (673–735), *Commentary on Mark 10* and *Commentary on 1 Cor. 10*; referenced at 411.17–32. Augustine, *De Sermone Domini in Monte* I, cap. 16, and *De Adulterinis Conjugiis ad Pollentium* II, cap. 4–5; referenced at 411.33–40. Jerome, *Epist. 77 (ad Fabiolam)* and *Epist. 55 (ad Amandum)*; referenced at 411.41–412.3. Rupert of Deutz, *De trinitate et operibus eius*, in Gen. Lib. II, c. 35; referenced at 412.4–6. Origen, *Comment. In Matthaeum*, hom. 19, no. 23; referenced at 412.7–12. Tertullian, *Adversus Marcionem*, IV, 34; referenced at 412.13–17. John Chrysostom, *In Matthaeum homil. 17*; referenced at 412.18–19.

66. Council of Arles I, cap. 10; referenced at CT, VI, 412.24–26. Council of Venice (465), cap. 2 (c. 2); referenced at 412.27–30. Contrary to what is sometimes believed, the Council of Venice (*Venetum*) was held in Vannes, not in Venice (see 412n8). Council of Tribur, in Germany (895), cc. 19, 24, 41; referenced at 412.31–413.3. Pope Zachary, "Concubuisti," referenced at 413.4–7. Gregory II, *Letter to Boniface* (ca. 726), cap. 18; referenced at 413.8–12. Ambrosia-

General Congregation Discusses Article on Divorce and Adultery

From September 2 to 6, the General Congregation considered the two August 29 articles in accord with Cardinal del Monte's plan. Twenty-six Council fathers comment on article 2. Twenty-one explicitly defend the proposition that adultery does not dissolve the bond of marriage.[67] For

---

ster, *Commentary on 1 Cor. 7*; referenced at 413.13–17. Augustine, *De Fide et Operibus,* chap. 19; referenced at 413.18–23.

67. Materanus: "per separationem tori non separatur vinculum matrimonii" (CT, VI, 420.3). Naxiensis: "non solvitur vinculum, licet solvitur thorus" (420.19–20). Sibinicensis: "fornicatio non vinculum, sed thorum solvit" (421.15); contrary authorities should be understood according to the traditional interpretation. Chironensis: "de fornicatione tenet, quod non solvitur vinculum, sed thorus" (421.24–25); scripture should be interpreted according to the teaching of the church and the holy doctors "de solutione tantum thori, non vincula" (421.26). Maioricensis: "fornicatio non rumpit vinculum matrimonii" (421.31). Aquensis Vorstius: "fornicatio non solvit vinculum matrimonii, sed thorum" (421.42). Sebastensis: "fornicatio non solvit vinculum matrimonii, sed thorum, ut doctors omnes tenet" (424.9–10). Motulanus: "fornicatio non solvit vinculum, sed thorum matrimonii" (424.19–20). Parentinus: "fornicatio non rumpit vinculum matrimonii" (424.31–32); in response to contrary authorities, Mt 19 should be read according to the interpretation of the church; Council of Tribur, cap. 41, should be read in light of cap. 46; Ambrose should be read in accord with Gratian's remarks (recall Gratian: "the insert by Ambrose is spoken by deceptive men …". (*Decretum Gratiani,* tom. I, part II, causa 32, q. 7, cap. 18 [PL 187:1501]). Veronensis (Verona): "per fornicationem non solvitur vinculum matrimonii" (425.1–2); lengthy reply to contrary authorites. Mylonensis Ferrettus: "fornicatio non solvit vinculum matrimonii, sed thorum" (425.24–25). Caprulanus: "[fornicatio] non rumpit vinculum matrimonii" (425.31–32). Aquinatensis: "ob fornicationem mulier non desinit esse uxor" (426.14). Lavellinus: "respondet per eam [fornicationem] non solvi vinculum matrimonii" (426.22–23); he says that if a man dismisses his wife for adultery and remarries, "he has two living wives at the same time" ("ille duas haberet uxores vivas eodem tempore"; 426.26–27); contrary authorities should be interpreted according to the maxim "vinculum non solvitur ex fornicatione, sed thorus" (426.27–28). Mylonensis: "De fornicatione, tenet quod ecclesia sentit" (426.30). Feltrensis: "per heresim non solvitur vinculum matrimonii, multo minus per fornicationem, cum heresis sit maius delictum quam fornicatio" (the bond of matrimony is not dissolved through heresy, much less through adultery, since heresy is a greater wrongdoing than adultery) (427.17–18); to contrary authorities he replies: "argumentum a contrario sensu non procedit, quando sequitur pravus intellectus vel absurdum, ut omnes doctores tenent" (the argument from the contrary sense is not successful, since it follows a distorted or absurd understanding, as all doctors hold) (427.26–28). Bellicastrensis: "fornicatio non rumpit vinculum matrimonii, sed thorum tantum" (427.37). Cardinal Cervini (S. Crucis), president and papal legate: he follows Aquinas in interpreting the Matthean exceptive clause: "exceptio comprehendat dimissionem tantum, non licentiam aliam ducendi" (the exception includes dismissal only, not the license to remarry) (430.11–13). Robert Vauchop, archbishop of Armagh: "fornicatio non rumpit vinculum matrimonii" (431.16–17); he asks, why cannot an adulteress remarry?; "Quia adhuc est uxor prioris viri" (because she is still the prior man's wife) (431.34–35), and then states definitively: "Opinio semper in ecclesia servata est, ita ut illa habeatur ex traditione apostolorum, quae traditio eiusdem est auctoritatis, cuius scriptura

example, Giovanni Michele Saraceni, the archbishop of Matera (Materanus), states that the article on divorce and remarriage is not consistent with the teaching of the Council of Florence, which affirmed that in cases of adultery, spouses may separate only as far as bed, but "non separatur vinculum matrimonii."[68] This, he says, follows from the teachings of the Gospel (Mk 10) and Paul (1 Cor 7), as well as from the teachings of the doctors noted into the record on August 30.[69] In response to the exceptive clause in Matthew 19:9, Materanus states that the passage should be interpreted according to the exposition of Aquinas in *Commentary* on the *Sentences* of Peter Lombard.[70] Replying to the question, "whether a man may remarry after divorce," Aquinas says:

Nothing that happens after a marriage [has been brought into existence] can dissolve it; and therefore, adultery can do nothing to a marriage such that it does not remain a true marriage. For the marital bond remains, as Augustine says, between the two living spouses, and neither separation nor union with another can take the bond away; and therefore it is not licit for one spouse to remarry while the other spouse still lives.[71]

Materanus then responds to Arles and other apparently contrary authorities saying they actually do not stand in opposition to the proposition because they should be understood "eodem modo" (in the same way),

---

sacra, ut iam decisum est in concilio Tridentino" (this opinion has always been preserved in the church, thus as it is held from the tradition of the apostles, which tradition is of the same authority as sacred scripture, as now it has been decided in the Council of Trent) (431.35–37). Salutiarum: "fornicatio non rumpit vinculum matrimonii" (432.8). Olaus Magnus, Archbishop of Upsala (Upsalensis): "[fornicatio] non rumpit vinculum matrimonii" (433.5). President and papal legate, John Mary Cardinal Del Monte from Arezzo in Tuscany: "Tenet tamen ipse cum tota ecclesia, quod vinculum non solvitur ex fornicatione, sed tantum thorus" (Nevertheless, he [Del Monte] holds with the entire church, that the bond is not dissolved by adultery, but only the bed) (433.19–20).

68. Council of Florence (1439), bull *Exultate Deo*, Decree for the Armenians, no. 16: "Quamvis autem ex causa fornicationis liceat tori separationem facere, non tamen aliud matrimonium contrahere fas est, cum matrimonii vinculum legitime contracti perpetuum sit" (Although separation of bed is lawful on account of *fornicationem*, it is not lawful to contract another marriage, since the bond of a legitimately contracted marriage is perpetual). CT, VI, 420n1; in DEC, 1:550.

69. CT, VI, 420.4–5: "Est consequens 10 cap. Marc. et 1 ad Cor. 7 et doctoribus, de quibus supra die 30. Augusti."

70. *In IV Sent.*, d. 35, q. 1, a. 5, in Aquinas, *Opera Omnia* (Parma, 1858), t. 7, 2:992.

71. "Respondeo dicendum, quod nihil adveniens supra matrimonium potest ipsum dissolvere; et ideo adulterium non facit quin sit verum matrimonium: manet enim, ut dicit augustinus, inter viventes conjugale vinculum, quod nec separatio nec cum alio junctio potest auferre; et ideo non licet uni, altero vivente, ad aliam copulam transire" (ibid.). The question is: "utrum post divortium vir alteri nubere possit" (ibid.).

namely, "separatio tori, non vinculi" (separation of bed, not bond).[72] The archbishop of Naxos, Sebastiano Leccavella de Chio, OP (Naxiensis), repeats the maxim, "bed, not bond."[73] He agrees that Matthew 19:9 should be construed according to Aquinas's interpretation, and replies to the contrary statements of regional councils saying: "it is difficult to respond since they speak so clearly contrary [to the tradition]." But he ventures a response anyway, which, I think, is important for understanding the relative disinterest the fathers at Trent took in the contrary judgments of these regional councils. Referring to the Councils of Arles (cap. 10), Venice (cap. 2), and Tribur (cap. 41), "et alia," Naxiensis states: "since the councils were provincial, they were able to err, since they were in the act of judging, in which even popes sometimes err."[74]

The bishops of Sibinicensis, Chironensis, Aquensis Vorstius, Sebastensis, Motulanus, Parentinus, Verona, Mylensis, Caprulanus, Aquinas, Lavellinus, Feltrensis, and Bellicastrensis each affirm the familiar maxim *bed, not bond*. Peter van der Vorst, bishop of Acqui (Aquensis Vorstius) adds that the statements of authorities who seem to speak contrary to this should be interpreted according "to the understanding of the Church and the holy doctors," and says "Matt. 19:9 should be understood according to what St. Paul says in 1 Cor. 7, that is that the bed, and not the bond, is dissolved."[75] Egidius Falsetta, bishop of Caprulanus, adds that Matthew 19:9 admits of no exception (*neque exceptio*).[76] And Tommaso Stella, OP, bishop of Lavellum (Lavellinus) adds that Matthew 19 should be understood in relation to the creation narratives of Genesis:

God made them male and female; it did not say [male and] *females*. Again, *a man shall cleave to his wife*; it did not say *wives*. And the same again, *they are two in one flesh*; it does not say, *three, four,* or *more*. If therefore anyone after dismissing a wife on account of adultery marries another, he has two wives living at the same time, which has not been granted by any law. Therefore, the church and doctors have un-

---

72. CT, VI, 420.6–8.
73. CT, VI, 420.21–22.
74. CT, VI, 420.23–26: "Difficile est respondere, cum clare loquantur in contrarium; sed respondet, cum sint concilia provincialia, potuisse errare, cum fuerint in facto iudicandi, in quo et pontifices aliquando errant."
75. CT, VI, 421.43–45: "declarari debent secundum intelligentiam ecclesiae et doctorum sanctorum; et 19 Matth. intelligendum est secundum id, quod dicit Paulus 1 Cor. 7, ut solvitur thorus, non vinculum."
76. CT, VI, 425.34–37: "Neque exceptio, quae ponitur Matth. 19[9], est de regula, cum sequeretur pravus intellectus et correctio iuris, ut doctores tenent etc. Ad alias auctoritates contrarias respondet, quod intelligendae sunt secundum ecclesiam etc."

derstood from [these verses] that the bond [*vinculum*] is not dissolved from adultery, but [only] the bed.⁷⁷

Angelus Paschalis, bishop of Motula (Motulanus), adds that "Christ says in the same place [i.e., Mt 19] that *not all* are able to understand *this teaching, but [only those] to whom it was given* evidently from above through the holy spirit. Therefore, St. Paul, to whom it had been given from above to understand these words, says in Romans 7 and 1 Cor. 7 that one whose wife has been dismissed is not permitted to remarry." The church "instructed by the Holy Spirit teaches the same."⁷⁸ Giovanni Campeggio, bishop of Parenzo (Parentinus), replies to canon 41 of the Council of Tribur with canon 46 of the same council.⁷⁹ To the pseudo-Ambrosian text, Parentinus says "he responds just as Gratian and the other doctors (of the church), especially since so many authorities—e.g., Pope Alexander III—stand against [the contrary view]."⁸⁰ Replying to the same text, Luigi Lippomani, coadjutor

---

77. CT, VI, 426.23–28: "Respondit ad 19[9] Matth., quod ibi patet eodem tempore non licere habere plures uxores, cum dicat: *Fecit Deus masculum et foeminam*, non dixit *feminas* etc. *Adherebit vir uxori suae*, non dixit *uxoribus*. Item: *Et erunt duo in carne una*, non dicit *tres, quattuor vel plures*. Si igitur dimissa uxore ob fornicationem aliam quis duceret, ille duas haberet uxores vivas eodem tempore, quod nullo iure concessum est. Propterea ecclesia et doctores ita interpretati sunt, ut vinculum non solvatur ex fornicatione, sed thorus etc."

78. CT, VI, 424.20–24: "Christus eodem loco dicit: *Non omnes* intelligere possunt *hoc verbum, sed quibus datum est* desuper, scilicet per spiritum sanctum. Unde Paulus, cui desuper datum fuerat ea verba intelligere, inquit ad Rom. 7 [2 s.] et 1 Cor. 7 [10 s.], quod dimissa non potest alteri nubere etc., quod idem facit ecclesia a spiritu sancto edocta."

79. C. 41: "if anyone marries a legitimate wife and is hindered by a domestic infirmity from fulfilling his marital duty with her, and his brother ... secretly humiliates her and violates her, they shall be completely separated and henceforth she shall not be touched by anyone .... Because indeed human nature is fragile and inclined to fall, it shall be strengthened in some way to be able to rise. Therefore, the bishop, having considered their weakness of mind, after they carry out the penance he instituted, shall let them be consoled with a lawful marriage if they are unable to contain themselves, lest, while hoping to raise themselves higher, they fall into the mud" (CT, VI, 412.31–37). C. 46: "Si cuius uxor constuprata fuerit ... Maritus vero, quamdiu ipsa vivat, nullo modo alteram ducat" (If a man's wife is defiled ... the husband indeed under no circumstances may remarry as long as his wife lives) (CT, VI, 424n11).

80. Pope Alexander III, in X *De divortiis* [IV 19], cap. 2, teaches that if a husband persists in the evil of infidelity, his wife can separate from him, "but it will not be licit for her to marry another; because although they may be separated, they are nevertheless always spouses. This same judgment also applies to husbands" (CT, VI, 411.3–8). Gratian's harsh words against Ambrosiaster's *Commentary on 1 Cor. 7* were well known to the Council fathers. Gratian writes: "the insert by Ambrose is spoken by deceptive men .... But because no authority permits a husband with a living wife to remarry, that statement of Ambrose in the above passage is understood to mean ... not that a man is able to marry again if the spouse he dismissed is living, but rather that after the death of the adulterer ... he who was innocent of adultery, either the man or the woman, is permitted to remarry. However, if the adulterers survive, under no circumstances may they remarry" (*Decretum Gratiani*, tom. I, part II, causa. 32, q. 7, c. 17–18 [PL 187:1501]; see also

of the bishop of Verona (Veronensis), replies, "as Gratian says, it is not the testimony of Ambrose."[81] Cardinal Cervini adopts the analysis of Aquinas who "divides Christ's elocution in Matt. 19 into two parts, so that the exception includes dismissal only, not the license to remarry."[82] The archbishop of Armagh offers a forceful opinion: "adultery does not dissolve the bond of marriage as is clearly stated in Mark 10, Luke 16, Romans 7 and 1 Cor. 7." He says Matthew 19 does not oppose this when it teaches

if anyone divorces his wife, except on account of adultery, he makes her commit adultery, that is, he is the cause of his wife being an adulteress and committing adultery. But the man who divorces an adulteress does not make her commit adultery since she already had committed adultery and is an adulteress. Therefore, one who divorces an adulteress does not make her commit adultery, i.e., does not give to her the cause or occasion to commit adultery, since she will have already committed adultery.[83]

CT, VI, 424n13). Gratian's twelfth-century treatment exercised significant influence at Trent. When the Greek churches were conceding multiple exceptions to the indissolubility of marriage, Gratian's text illustrates the Western church's commitment to the absolute indissolubility of marriage in the high middle ages. Gratian begins asking whether a husband who dismisses his wife for adultery can take another wife while his first spouse still lives. He summarizes the responses of ten Catholic authorities: Cap. 1: the bond of marriage cannot be dissolved on account of adultery (Augustine, *De Bono Conjugali*, c. 7; PL 187:1494–95). Cap. 2: after a marriage has been entered into, there is no cause (*ratio*) that can dissolve it (Augustine, *De Adulterinis Conjugiis*, lib. II, cc. 4–5; PL 187:1495). Cap. 3: whether a husband is dismissed by his wife for adultery, or a wife by her husband, both are prohibited from remarrying (Bede, *1 Corinth. 7*, quoted by Augustine, *De Sermone Domini in Monte*, lib. I, cap. 26; PL 187:1495–96). Cap. 4: "It can happen that a man dismisses his wife for the cause of adultery .... She is not allowed to remarry during the lifetime of her husband from which she has departed, nor he to take another while the wife is living" (Augustine, *De Sermone Domini in Monte*, lib. I, cap. 25; PL 187:1496). Cap. 5: regarding either a husband or wife who has been dismissed, they should be brought back to repentance, and either choose to live as they are or be reconciled to one another (Council of Mileve, c. 17; PL 187:1496). Cap. 6: she commits adultery who remarries after having been dismissed by her husband (Augustine, *De sermone Domini in monte*, lib. I, cap. 25; PL 187:1496). Cap. 7: she proves herself an adulteress who marries another while her [first] husband still lives (Jerome, *Epist. ad Amandum*; PL 187:1497). Cap. 8: a faithful wife who dismisses and adulterous husband is not permitted to remarry (Council of Elvira, c. 9; PL 187:1497). Cap. 9: anyone who is joined to more than one spouse should be made to do penance (Council of Elvira, from a chapter by Saint Martin of Braga, cap. 80; PL 187:1498). Cap. 10: whoever dismisses his wife on account of adultery and marries another commits adultery (Augustine, *De Adulterinis Conjugiis*, lib. I, cap. 9; PL 187:1498).

81. CT, VI, 425.11–12: "non est testus Ambrosianus, ut ait Gratianus."
82. CT, VI, 430.11–13: "Igitur bona est responsio b. Thomae, qui dividit elocutionem Christi in duas partes, ut excepto comprehendar dimissionem tantum, non licentiam aliam ducendi."
83. CT, VI, 431.16–22: "Fornicatio non rumpit vinculum matrimonii, ut clare loquuntur Marc. 10 et Luce 16 et Paulus 7 ad Rom. et 1 Cor. 7. Neque obstat 19 Matth., qui intelligitur, quod, si quis dimittit uxorem nisi ex causa fornicationis, facit eam mechari, i.e., est causa, quod

This, he says, is consistent with the parallel passages in the other Gospels and in Paul. Moreover, when Christ repeated Genesis 2:24 to the Jews and added the words "what God has joined let no man separate ... he thus shows that marriage is indissoluble."[84] Vauchop then asks why it is that, as Christ said, one who marries a divorced woman commits adultery, and that the woman dismissed for adultery cannot marry another? He answers: "because she is still the first man's wife."[85] He concludes: "This opinion has always been preserved in the Church, just as it is held from the tradition of the apostles, which derives from the same authority as sacred scripture."[86] And he ends by forcefully asserting: "Now it is decided by the Council of Trent."[87] Finally, Italian prelate, Sebastiano Pighino, bishop of Alife (Alyphanus), says

> marriage is defined as the inseparable communion of souls, which is why Christ says *because of this, [a man] shall leave father, mother* etc. and *they shall be two in one flesh*. Accordingly this great communion is not only of the body, but of the souls, as Leo and Gregory explain; and St. Paul says: *This is a great mystery* .... This communion endures for ever. The communion of body signifies and represents the unity of flesh with divinity in Christ.[88]

Of the four prelates that do not explicitly defend indissolubility in cases of adultery, one prelate, Alexander Campegius, bishop of Bononi-

---

ipsa adulteretur et mechetur; qui autem dimittit adulteram, non facit eam mechari, cum iam ipsa mechata fuerit et sit adultera. Igitur qui sic adulteram dimiserit, non facit eam mechari, i.e., non dat ei causam vel occasionem moechandi, cum iam mecha sit."

84. CT, VI, 431.28–29: "indissolubile esse matrimonium ostendit."

85. CT, VI, 431.34–35: "quia adhuc est uxor prioris viri."

86. CT, VI, 431.35–37: "Quae opinio semper in ecclesia servata est, ita ut illa habeatur ex traditione apostolorum, quae traditio eiusdem est auctoritatis, cuius scriptura sacra."

87. CT, VI, 431.37: "iam decisum est in concilio Tridentino."

88. CT, VI, 427.45–428.1–2 and 4–5: "Propterea diffinitur matrimonium esse coniunctionem individuam animorum, unde Christus dicit: *Propter hoc relinquet patrem, matrem* etc., *et erunt duo, sed una caro*; propter magnam coniunctionem non solum corporis, sed animorum, ut Leo et Gregorius interpretantur etc. Et Paulus dicit: *Hoc est magnum sacramentum* etc.... Quae coniunctio perpetuo durat. Et coniunctio corporis denotat sacramentum repraesentatque unionem carnis cum divinitate in Christo." Alyphanus replies to Mt 19:9 saying that when Jesus tells the Jews that whoever divorces his wife, except for the cause of adultery, commits adultery and who marries a dismissed wife commits adultery, it "should be understood according to the Hebrews, for whom it was not only permitted to divorce wives for adultery, but to put the adulterous wife to death. Therefore, since the adulterous wife was now condemned to death by the judgment of God, her husband [under the Old Law] was also permitted to remarry before the actual death itself" (Hoc intelligi secundum Hebreos, quibus non solum erat licitum dimittere uxores ex fornicatione, sed erat uxori fornicanti poena mortis. Igitur, cum uxor fornicata esset iam iudicio Dei ad mortem damnata, etiam ante ipsam mortem realem vir poterat ducere aliam). CT, VI, 428.24–27.

ensis, says he "does not think that something should be decreed now, but that the tradition of the church should be upheld."[89] Another, Benedetto de Nobili, bishop of Accia (Aciensis), argues that Matthew 19:9 requires only that "we profess that Christ does not permit divorce and remarriage except on account of adultery." Nevertheless, he holds that "according to the conclusions reached by the Church it is not licit to enter into a second marriage."[90] We see here he appeals to a disciplinary tradition to ground the prohibition against remarriage, and not to a teaching of divine revelation.

Only two bishops argue that remarriage after divorce can be legitimate. The first was the influential Italian bishop-theologian, Ambrosius Catharinus Polito, bishop of Minori (Minoriensis). He was known at Bologna for his exceptionist reading of the divorce precept in the Gospel of Matthew, having published on it five years earlier his *Annotationes contra Cajetanum* (1542). There he agrees with the great Cardinal Cajetan, that Christ's words in Matthew permit remarriage after divorce in cases of adultery.[91] At the same time, he defended the church's strict prohibition of remarriage, not as a teaching of divine revelation but as an ecclesiastical law that is warranted to prevent an increase of adultery.[92] Replying to the opinion that no human being can dissolve marriage, Minoriensis replies, "Christ himself, not man, dissolves it when he himself says (Matt. 19:9), *except for the cause of adultery.*"[93] Why then do Mark 10, Luke 16, and Paul teach to the rule that nothing dissolves marriage? The bishop replies, "to this rule

---

89. Bononiensis: "non censet aliquid nunc statuendum, sed standum consuetudini ecclesiae" (CT, VI, 421.7–8).

90. CT, VI, 421.3–5: "Ergo cum Christus respondere dicatur ad propositum, oportet necessario confiteri, quod Christus noluerit, nisi ob causam fornicationis, dimittere et alias ducere. Tenet ipse tamen, quod ad secundas [nuptias] non licet transire ex determinatione ecclesiae."

91. See Joyce, *Christian Marriage*, 390. Cajetan's position is referenced by a Conciliar theologian in 1563 (see remarks of Ioannes Ramirez, CT, IX, 417.9–10); but otherwise, Cajetan and Catarino's opinions seem to have had little influence on the Council's discussions on marriage.

92. Ibid. The comments of the Council president and papal legate, Cardinal Del Monte, are ambiguous. At first he seems to follow Catarino and Cajetan: "the words of Matthew are sufficiently clear that it is permissible in cases of adultery to dismiss a wife and marry another" (Verba Matthei sunt satis clara, quod liceat propter fornicationem uxorem dimittere et aliam ducere) (CT, IX, 433.14–15). But then he says he holds "with the whole church that the bond of marriage is not dissolved on account of adultery, but only the bed, as all the holy doctors hold, especially St. Augustine." Had he said only that he holds the church's universal prohibition against remarriage after divorce, we would conclude he believes Christ made an exception for adultery, but that the church's strict rule against remarriage is justifiable. But he says that he "holds," that is, accepts as a true proposition, that "the bond of marriage" is indissoluble in cases of adultery. "Tenet tamen ipse cum tota ecclesia, quod vinculum non solvitur ex fornicationem, sed tantum thorus, ut sancti omnes doctores tenant, praesertim Augustinus" (CT, VI, 433.19–21).

93. Minoriensis: "Ad contraria, quod Matrimonium non potest dissolvi ab homine, et

there is an exception: the cause of adultery." He says "it is not unfitting that what one evangelist left out another supplied."⁹⁴ The second, Alvaro de la Guarde, bishop of Venusia (Venusinus), says, "it appears from the words of Christ, that on account of adultery it is permissible to divorce the adulterer and marry another."⁹⁵ To Christ's words that "one who marries a divorced woman commits adultery," he replies, "certainly the woman who gave cause for the divorce may not remarry."⁹⁶ Massarelli summarizes in the *Acta* the strong consensus of the General Congregation in defense of absolute indissolubility on September 6: "The responses of the fathers varied; but the *vast majority* affirmed that adultery *cannot* dissolve a marriage; that one who takes another wife while his first wife is living commits adultery; and that for no reason can they be separated except as far as the bed."⁹⁷

In his comments on this early discussion of the General Congregation, Fransen makes three unfounded claims. First, he states three times that the fathers' consensus position—encapsulated in the oft-repeated maxim *fornicatio non rumpit vinculum matrimonii, sed thorum*—pertains only to the quality of "intrinsic indissolubility."⁹⁸ Second, he states that it can be "proven" that the consensus is "principally" against the positions of the Reformers; and third, that "it is certain" that not all Council fathers believed that marital indissolubility was a truth of revelation; and although they identify

---

quod indissolubile est etc., respondet, quod Christusmet solvit, non homo, cum ipse dicat [Mt 19:9]: *excepta causa fornicationis*" (CT, VI, 429.9–11).

94. CT, VI, 429.12–14: "Ad Marc. 10 et Luc. 16 et Pa[u]lum respondet, quod illud est regulariter, cui regule est exceptio: causa fornicationis; quod non est inconveniens, quod unus evangelistarum reliquit, per alium suppleatur."

95. CT, VI, 426.6–9 (Venusinus): "Ex verbis Christi apparet, quod ob fornicationem licet aliam ducere dimissa adultera.... Igitur ob fornicationem licet viro dimittere uxorem et aliam ducere."

96. CT, VI, 426.9–10: "Respondet ad verba Christi: *Et qui dimissam duxerit, mechatur*, quod scilicet mulierem, quae causam dedit divortio, ducere non licet."

97. CT, VI, 434.28–30 (emphasis added): "Patres etiam varie responderunt; sed longe maior pars confirmavit matrimonium ob fornicationem dissolvi non posse, mecharique eum, qui vivente uxore aliam duxerit, nullamque separationem fieri posse nisi quoad thorum." An additional summary recorded in the *Acta* states that the two articles under consideration "are to be condemned." "Summa autem sententiarum partum super ipsis articulis haec fuit, ut ambo ipsi articuli damnentur in verbis haereticorum" (CT, VI, 431.42–43).

98. "Es sei noch auf einen anderen Punkt, in dem auch alle übereinstimmten, hingewiesen. Die allgemeine Formel, mit der die Besprechung dieses Punktes eingeleitet wurde, lautete: Respondet quod fornicatio non rumpit vinculum matrimonii, sed thorum. Hieraus geht wieder hervor, daß es sich um die "innere Unauflösbarkeit" der Ehe handelte" (Fransen "Ehescheidung Im Falle von Ehebruch," 143). "In seinem Diarium schreibt er [i.e., Massarelli]: 'Conclusumque ...', weider die 'innere Unauflösbarkeit'" (144–45).

indissolubility with Catholic *fides*, the term here means no more than an authoritative legal determination of the church.[99] These are strong claims, which if true would substantially weaken my argument that the Council during the Bologna sessions overwhelmingly supported the indissolubility thesis.

The first might lead one to believe that the fathers took no position on the question of absolute indissolubility, but only meant to speak to whether couples by their own acts can and may dissolve their marriage; and that the fathers meant to leave open the question of whether the church—as in the Greek practice of *oikonomia*—may intervene to permit dissolution and subsequent remarriage. The second claim might lead one to think that the fathers were not also interested in addressing the substantive question of the nature of marriage; that they were merely interested in condemning Reformation denials of papal authority. And the third might lead one to conclude that in the last analysis, the fathers did not believe that marital indissolubility was a doctrine of faith taught in divine revelation, but merely an eminent legal tradition passed on since the early church. In fact, this is the story that Piet Fransen tells over the course of his many painstaking and pedantic essays on Trent's teaching on divorce and remarriage.[100]

The image on Fransen's tapestry is woven out of the narrow thread of opinions set forward by three dissenting bishops, Aciensis, Venusinus, and Minoriensis. Not only does it not represent the opinions of the "vast majority" of Council fathers, but the Council itself at the end of the Bologna sessions can be said to be firmly and almost unanimously committed to the contrary of each of the three propositions.

Of the twenty-six fathers who offer comment on the heretical article, none of them explicitly mentions the concept of "intrinsic dissolubility" (under any title). It is nowhere alluded to, not part of the conversation, obviously on nobody's mind. Even to interpret the opinions of Aciensis,

---

99. "Verschiedene Punkte können wir also wiederum belegen: Es geht um die 'innere Unauflösbarkeit' und an erster Stelle gegen die 'positiones' oder sogar gegen die 'petitiones' der Reformatoren. Trotz der dieser Diskussion eigenen Mehrdeutigkeit ist es sicher, daß nicht alle eine geoffenbarte Wahrheit festlegen wollten, obschon alle die innere Unauflösbarkeit bestimmt zur 'fides' rechneten, jedoch im weiteren Sinne des Wortes." Fransen, "Ehescheidung Im Falle von Ehebruch," 145.

100. For a concise summary of his account, see Piet Fransen, "Divorce on the Ground of Adultery," 89–100. A more recent version of the same story is told by Pani, "Matrimonio." I reply at C. Brugger, "Damnatio Memoria? The Council of Trent and Catholic Teaching on Divorce," *La Chiesa*, October 17, 2014; available at http://chiesa.espresso.repubblica.it/articolo/1350897?eng=y; also published at *Public Discourse*, October 17, 2014; available at http://www.thepublicdiscourse.com/2014/10/13934/.

Venusinus, and Minoriensis through the lens of the doctrine is anachronistic (although their opinions could be argued to accommodate the concept). Moreover, Massarelli's summary is perfectly precise: "the vast majority agreed that adultery *cannot* dissolve a marriage; that one who takes another wife while his first wife is living commits adultery;..."[101] It does not tell us that the fathers agreed to condemn the Reformers, but tells us rather what the fathers believed about the nature of marriage, namely, that it is indissoluble in cases of adultery, that "separation" should not be understood as dissolution, and that one who remarries while his spouse is still living commits adultery. Furthermore, in his official diary for September 6—the same day he summarizes in the *Acta* the consensus of the General Congregation—Massarelli writes: "It was concluded that the petitions of the Lutherans should be condemned and clandestine marriages should be prohibited with severe punishments, and that the bond of marriage is not broken through adultery."[102] These three propositions, each separated by "et," are three separate conclusions of the Council fathers. The first, obviously concerning the teachings of the Reformers, is distinct from the third, which obviously concerns the nature of the marriage bond itself.

Finally, to say that not all Council fathers believed that absolute indissolubility was a truth of divine revelation is undoubtedly correct. A small number were in doubt. But inasmuch as Fransen's claim suggests that the revealed status of the doctrine was in any sense "in doubt" by the Council, it is wrong and misleading. As demonstrated, a large majority of Conciliar theologians and voting prelates affirmed its status as a truth of divine revelation. Moreover, when Massarelli summarizes the response of the General Congregation to the problem of dissenting authorities, he says the fathers agree that "separation should be understood to extend to the bed, but not to the bond," and he adds the words, "as the doctors of the Church declare (and St. Paul declared in 1 Cor. 7 and Romans 7, and as found in Mark 10 and Luke 16 and Matthew 5:32 itself), and that the scriptures are to be interpreted according to the declaration of the Church."[103]

---

101. CT, VI, 434.28–30 (emphasis added): "Patres etiam varie responderunt; sed longe maior pars confirmavit matrimonium ob fornicationem dissolvi non posse, mecharique eum, qui vivente uxore aliam duxerit, nullamque separationem fieri posse nisi quoad thorum."

102. From Massarelli Diarium IV, September 6: "Conclusumque fuit ut damnarentur petitiones Lutheranorum et clandestina matrimonia prohiberentur gravissimis poenis, et quod per fornicatioinem non rumpatur vinculum matrimonii" (CT, I, 690.7–9).

103. CT, VI, 435.2–6: "Cui auctoritati contrarium tenentes responderunt eam separationem intelligi debere quoad thorum, non quoad vinculum, ut doctores interpretantur (et Paulus declarat 1 Cor. 7 et ad Rom. 7 ac Marci 10 et Luce 16 et ipsemet Matth. 5:32), quodque

In summary, the proceedings for the first General Congregation on the sacrament of matrimony demonstrate that a large majority of fathers believe that the bond of a Christian marriage is absolutely indissoluble—not only that adultery "should not" dissolve it, but "cannot."[104] The fathers believe that this is not only an eminent canonical tradition, but also and more importantly the teaching of Jesus as found in scripture; and that contrary opinions and interpretations of scripture are untrue and that anyone who holds and teaches them, including the Reformers, holds and teaches error.

The Third Bologna Session

First Consideration of General Congregation on Canons on Marriage

The third Bologna session began on September 14, 1547. One week earlier, on September 8, Massarelli distributed six canons on the sacrament of marriage to the bishops for examination. This is the first time the General Congregation considered canons on marriage.[105] The third is familiar as it constitutes a condemnation of the propositions taught in the second "disputed" article distributed to the General Congregation by Massarelli on August 29 (c. 3):

If anyone says that a woman who falls into adultery thereby ceases to be a wife, so that it is licit for both spouses or at least the innocent one who gave no cause for adultery to take a new spouse, and that he does not commit adultery who dismisses an adulterous wife and marries another and she is not an adulteress who is dismissed for adultery and marries another, let him be anathema.[106]

---

scripturae intelligendae sint secundum declarationem ecclesiae." The other summary notes that because some disagreed over the interpretation of Mt 19, a canon would be formulated on the issue and presented to the fathers for examination (CT, VI, 431.47–50).

104. CT, VI, 434.28–30

105. In late August Massarelli entered two sets of canons into the record, which are not discussed but rather used as references for the developing of future canons. Freudenberger says that both sets were formulated in light of the criticisms (mentioned above) of Nicolas Grandis. The first set seems to include the canons that Massarelli "had in hand" on August 28, because it excludes any canon dedicated to the "disputed" article on divorce and remarriage, and includes in its place quotes from canons 17 and 9 of the Councils of Mileve and Elvira, respectively. Canon 5 of the second set was obviously referenced in formulating canon 3 distributed to the fathers on September 8. It reads: "Si quis dixerit mulierem in adulterio lapsam adeo desinere esse uxorem, ut utrique coniugum vel saltem innocenti, qui causam adulterio non dederit, liceat novare coniugium, neque mechari eum, qui dimissa adultera aliam duxerit, neque eam, quae dimisso adultero alii nupserit, a. s." (CT, VI, 448.3–5).

106. CT, VI, 446.5–8: "Si quis dixerit mulierem in adulterio lapsam adeo desinere esse

The prelates of the General Congregation comment on the canons on September 10–24.[107] Thirty-nine offer comment on canon 3.[108] Twenty-nine approve the canon in the words "tertius canon placet" or similar words with little or no qualification.[109] Four more approve the canon with qualifica-

---

uxorem, ut utrique coniugum vel saltem innocenti, qui causam adulterio non dederit, liceat novare coniugium, neque mechari eum, qui dimissa adultera aliam duxerit, neque eam, quae dimisso adultero alii nupserit, a. s."

107. The third session began in the middle of the General Congregation's discussion, but had to be prorogued because imperial troops on September 12 under the command of Don Ferrante Gonzaga, the governor of Milan, on behalf of Emperor Charles V himself, entered and occupied the city of Piacenza and expelled the remaining members of the Farnese family (CT, VI, 456.9–11). Pope Paul III was a Farnese. Pier Luigi Farnese, duke of Parma and Piacenza and illegitimate son of Paul III, had been murdered at the family castle in Piacenza on September 10 by imperialist insurgent aristocrats, which paved the way for the occupation (see 451.36–41). Since Bologna was in the Papal States, and nearby Piacenza was imperially controlled, Council members were forced to respond to the threat of war. The opinions of four fathers (Lavellanus, Pistoriensis, Maceratensis, and Aprutinus) are recorded on September 14 during the prorogued session (see 457–59). The prorogation ceased on September 16 (see 469) and discussions on matrimony resumed on September 19 (see 470).

108. See CT, VI, 448–80.

109. Materanus: "Primus, secundus et tertius placent quoad ... formam et materiam" (CT, VI, 448.25–17). Upsalensis: "Tertius canon: Cuperet renovari canonem concilii Milevitani; placet tamen canon, ut iacet" (449.15–16). Armacanus: "Tertius canon placet"; he recommends minor changes of wording (449.23–24). Feltrensis: "Tertius canon placet" (449.37). Chironensis: "Placet igitur canon tertius" (451.16). Aquensis Vorstius: "Tertius placet in omnibus" (451.29). Sibinicensis: "Tertius [canon placet], cum per fornicationem matrimonium non solvitur quoad vinculum .... Tertius posset adaptari secundum concilium Milevitanum" (450.35 and 451.1–3). Camerinensis: "Tertius placet, quia fornicatio non rumpit vinculum matrimonii, sed tantum thorum" (452.7–8). Veronensis coadiutor: "Tertius canon placet" (452.27); he disagrees with Parentinus that the clause "*neque mechari eum* etc." should be deleted (453.2–3). Salutiarum: "Tertius placet." He also says the clause "*neque mechari* etc." should *not* be deleted ("neque deleatur *neque mechari* etc"), since Jesus did not mention any exception in Mk 10 (453.14–15). Mirapicensis: "Reliqui placent" (453.34). Mylonensis Ferrettus: "Tertius etiam placet, ut stat; neque aliquid mutandum" (453.37–38). Vigorniensis: "placent canones" (455.15). Bituntinus: "Tertius canon: Materia placet ... neque enim matrimonium dissolvitur nisi per mortem" (455.27, 31). He says that Mt 19:9 should be interpreted as Augustine does in his letter to Polentius (455.33–36). Lavellanus offers an interesting reply. He says "the third canon should be noted lest the words of the canon come in conflict with the words of the gospel, that adultery is an exception, although it itself [i.e., the gospel] holds that the bond of marriage is dissolved for no reason, not even because of adultery" (In tertio canone est advertendum, ne verba canonis pugnent cum verbis evangelii, quod fornicationem excipit etc., licet ipse teneat, quod nulla ex causa, etiam fornicationis, vinculum matrimonii solvitur). He is clear that "according to the law of nature marriage is indissoluble," and says that this is "on account of its end, so that children may be procreated"; Christ confirms this when he says (in Mt 19:6): "What God has joined, man must not separate" (Matrimonium autem etiam iure naturae indissolubile est propter finem, ut proles procreetur; unde [ait] Christus: *Quod Deus coniunxit, homo non separet*). The indissolubility of marriage in fact has a twofold ground: because of the "union of souls" and from the fact that it is "divinely instituted." Having said this, Lavellanus argues, somewhat novelly, that although the man who dismisses his wife for

tion.[110] Finally, six suggest that the canon should either be reconsidered, reformulated, or suppressed.[111] A few examples of the three groups will illustrate the mind of the Council in September 1547.

---

adultery and marries another does not (according to Mt 19) commit adultery, he still does wrong if he remarries. But if he does, he does not commit adultery, he just sins. "Duo igitur ista vincula faci[un]t matrimonium indissolubile: coniunctio animorum et institutio divina.... Ergo potest aliam accipere? Non, quia Christus alibi prohibet [Lk 16]; sed si aliam ducit, non mechatur, sed peccat tantum" (458.7–9, 16–18, and 459.1–8). Pistoriensis: "Quoad tertium tenet cum ecclesia, quod fornicatio non rumpat vinculum matrimonii" (459.14, 16–17). Mylonensis Graecus: "Placent canones cum censuris Veronensis et Salutiarum," both of whom said that the clause "neque mechari etc." should be retained (459.22–23). Maceratensis: "Tertius placet, quia matrimonium obligat contrahentes per totam vitam; ergo per fornicationem non rumpitur" (459.26–27). Aprutinus: "Tertius canon placet, quia uxor propter fornicationem non desinet esse uxor, quia fornicatio non rumpit vinculum matrimonii, sed thorum." He says the Matthean exception was prescribed by Christ "secundum legem veterem" (according to the old law); this is not infrequent in the New Testament, e.g., the command to "go and show yourself to the priest, along with similar verses, and the circumcision of Timothy by Paul" (*Vade et ostende te sacerdoti* cum similibus, et Paulus Timotheum circumcidit). But all such commands were afterwards prohibited and annulled by the church for good reason (470.11–15). Alyphanus: "Tertii canonis materia placet, quia per adulterium seu fornicationem matrimonium non solvitur quoad vinculum, sed tantum quoad thorum" (471.29–30). Minoriensis: "Tertius canon quoad materiam placet, quia matrimonium non solvitur per fornicationem, neque uxor esse desinit, si fornicator." He says "non mechatur, qui dimissa uxore ob fornicationem aliam ducit, sed peccat, cum sint aperta verba Matth. 19" (one who dismisses his wife for adultery and marries another does not commit adultery, but he does sin, since the words of Christ are clear). He recommends the clause "*neque mechari eum* and what follows should be deleted from the canon" (472.13–14, 24–25). Aquensis: "Tertius canon: Placet material, quia adulterium non separat vinculum matrimonii, sed tantum thorum" (473.23–24). Sarsinensis: "Tertius canon: Materia placet, cum clarum sit per adulterium non rumpi vinculum." He says, however, he does "nollet poena anathematis feriri, qui contrarium dicit" (not wish [him] who speaks to the contrary to be punished with [the penalty of] anathema) (474.10–11). Britonoriensis: "Tertius canon: Materia placet, quia vinculum matrimonii nullo modo, etiam per fornicationem, solvi potest" (474.36–37). Albinghanensis: "Tertius canon placet, ut stat" (475.22–23). Calvensis: "laudat canones" (475.32). Alatrinus: "Tertius canon placet, quia fornicatio non rumpit vinculum matrimonii. Et dictio *nisi* Matth. 19 posset intelligi pro *neque* in Graeco, ut intelligit Theophilactus" (And the term *nisi* [except] could be understood in the place of *neque* [and not] in Greek, as Theophilactus understood) (475.40–42). Portuensis: "Tertius canon placet, quia nulla ex causa licet uxorem dimittere et aliam ducere, neque etiam ob fornicationem" (477.18–20). Girolamo Seripando, General of the Hermits of Saint Augustine: "Tertius et quintus canon: Forma et materia placent, quia cum matrimonio non potest stare divortium neque pollygamia neque solutio vinculi matrimonialis" (479.28–30).

110. Parentinus: delete the clause "*neque mechari* etc" (CT, VI, 452.15). Thermularum: delete the clause "*neque mechari* etc" (453.29–30). Maioricensis: delete the clause "*neque mechari eum, qui* etc., cum videatur dicere idem prima pars, praesertim cum nullum concilium id damnaverit eo modo; sed posset damnari, ut concilium Milevitanum et Florentinum fecit. Posset addi eius loco: *quasi per fornicationem solutum sit vinculum matrimonii, quod tamen nisi per mortem solvi [non] potest*" (451.22–26). Caprulanus: the formula should be briefer (455.9). Armacanus, who firmly approved the canon (see note 109), tentatively recommends at the end of his remarks that the clause "*neque mechari eum* etc" be deleted (449.24–26).

111. Naxiensis: "Tertius canon advertatur: Quia ecclesia Graeca observat contrarium ri-

Peter van der Vorst (Aquensis Vorstius) says he "approves of the third canon *in all respects*."[112] Giovanni Pietro Ferretti, bishop of Melos (Mylonensis Ferrettus), says something similar and adds, "and nothing should be altered."[113] Fourteen fathers say that adultery does not dissolve the bond of marriage.[114] Cornelio Musso, bishop of Bitonto (Bituntinus), argues that Matthew 19:9 should be interpreted as Augustine does in his letter to Polentius.[115] Tommaso Stella (Lavellanus) argues that remarriage after divorce for adultery is impermissible because the marriage bond is "indissoluble" and therefore Christ forbids it; but adds that according to the exceptive clause, the one who does remarry after dismissing an adulterer "does not commit adultery, but only sins [non mechatur, sed peccat tantum]."[116] Sebastiano Pighino (Alyphanus) argues that marriage is indissoluble because the "sacrament of marriage signifies the union now made between the divinity and humanity in Christ, and just as it is not able to be dissolved, thus also marriage cannot be dissolved; and therefore marriage cannot be dissolved, just as the union between Christ and the church—which is also imaged through marriage—cannot be dissolved."[117] Minoriensis agrees

---

tum et tot doctores et concilia contrarium dixerunt, non deberet damnari iste articulus sub anathemate" (CT, VI, 449.8–10). Aciensis: "Tertius canon est considerandus, ne damnentur sub anathemate et Graeci et doctores, qui contrarium dicunt" (450.22–23). Bononiensis: "Tertius canon posset reformari, cum videatur nimis longus" (450.30). Venusinus: "Placent canones, excepto tertio de fornicatione, cum sit contra Matth. 19" (456.1–2). Aquinatensis: "Quoad materiam tertii canonis: Non placent ultima verba *neque mechari eum* etc. cum aliter sonent verba Matth. 19, qui excepit fornicationem in dimissione uxoris et aliam ducenda" (Regarding the content of canon three: Aquinas does not agree with the final words 'and he commits adultery etc.,' since they sound different from the words of Matthew 19 who makes an exception for the dismissing of a wife for adultery and marrying another) (456.3–5). Generalis Praedicatorum: "Tertius canon non deberet poni inter hos canones, sed silentio praeteriri, quia utraque pars habet multos doctores et pios et doctos, praesertim cum contrarium teneat ecclesia Graeca et Armena" (The third canon should not be placed among these canons but passed over in silence because each side has many doctors, both pious and learned, [and] especially since the Greek and Armenian church[es] hold the contrary view) (478.23–26).

112. CT, VI, 451.29.
113. CT, VI, 453.37–38.
114. Sibinicensis (450), Camerinensis (452), Veronensis coadiutor (452), Lavellanus (458), Pistoriensis (459), Maceratensis (459), Aprutinus (470), Alyphanus (471), Minoriensis (472), Aquensis (473), Sarsinensis (474), Britonoriensis (474), Alatrinus (475), and Seripando (480).
115. CT, VI, 455.34–35. For Augustine's letter see appendix A (Augustine, *De Adulterinis Conjugiis ad Pollentium*).
116. CT, VI, 459.8.
117. "Nam hoc sacramentum significat coniunctionem iam factam inter divinitatem et humanitatem in Christo, quae quemadmodum dissolvi non potest, ita et matrimonium [dissolvi] non potest, prout neque coniunctio inter Christum et ecclesiam, quae coniunctio etiam per matrimonium figuratur" (CT, VI, 471.30–34).

with Lavellanus that the man who remarries after divorcing his wife for adultery sins, but does not commit adultery; consequently, he requests that the words "and that he does not commit adultery who dismisses an adulterer and marries another, nor does she who is dismissed for adultery and marry another" should be deleted from canon 3.[118] John James Barba, the Apostolic Sacristan and bishop of Aprutinus, says the Matthean exception was prescribed by Christ "according to the old law"; other instances in the New Testament where a prescription from the Old Law persists include the command to "go and show yourself to the priest" (Lk 5:14) and the "circumcision of Timothy by Paul" (Acts 16:3). The exception, however, was "later prohibited from its cause and abrogated by the Church."[119]

The bishop of Porto, Balthasar Lympus (Portuensis), says boldly that Matthew 19 should be interpreted as the "holy church" interprets it, namely,

to mean a separation only as far as bed, as the other Evangelists clearly have written; and St. Paul says that *a married woman is bound to her husband as long as he lives*, adding no exceptions. And the council of Mileve declared the same. And this also always has been observed in the Catholic Church and held by the holy doctors: Gregory, Augustine, Jerome, Tertullian, Origen and Chrysostom and others.[120]

Finally, the influential Girolamo Seripando, general of the Order of Saint Augustine, approves the "form and matter" of the third canon "because divorce cannot stand with marriage, nor can polygamy, nor the dissolution of the marriage bond." He says that when Christ was teaching in Matthew 5:32 and 19:19, he addressed himself "ad legem et ad Phariseos" (to the law and the Pharisees)—to the law when he spoke about divorce *for any reason* and to the Pharisees who held and taught this law. Since the law had not been totally abrogated, he taught "no divorce except for adultery." But in Mark 10 and Luke 16, Christ did not have the law in mind, but the Gospel, the church, and his disciples; he therefore does not mention adultery

Therefore, when Christ taught the Gospel to his disciples he asserted that for no reason may a man dismiss his wife and marry another. Moreover, when a passage of scripture seems doubtful, it should be decided by the interpretation of the Church, which has always held and taught the same thing, [namely,] that adultery does not

---

118. CT, VI, 472.24–25.
119. CT, VI, 470.11–15.
120. CT, VI, 477.20–25: "ut de separatione tori tantum intelligatur, ut clare scribunt alii evangelistae; et Paulus dicat, quod *vivente viro mulier ligata* est, nullam addens exceptionem. Et ita declaravit concilium Milevitanum. Et ita etiam observatum semper fuit in ecclesia catholica et tenuerunt sancti doctores: Gregorius, Augustinus, Hieronymus, Tertullianus, Origenes, Chrisostomus et alii."

destroy the bond. And St. Paul clearly says without any exception that *a wife is not to depart from her husband*, and *if she departs, she should remain single or be reconciled to her husband*. And Paul adds: and a husband similarly should not depart from his wife. The Council Mileve declared the same, and said the teaching was *according to the law of the Gospel and of the apostles*.[121]

Finally, he recommends that the canon be reformulated according to the words of the Council of Florence (1439).[122]

Criticisms ("censurae") of Canon 3[123]

Parentinus, together with Vincent de Durantibus, bishop of Thermularum, and Gianbattista Campeggio, bishop of Mallorca (Maioricensis), suggest that the clause "*and he does not commit adultery* etc. [*neque mechari* etc.]" should be deleted from the canon.[124] Alexander Campegius (Bononiensis) and Egidius Falsetta (Caprulanus) think the formula is too long.[125] Sebastiano Leccavella (Naxiensis) and Benedetto de Nobili (Aciensis) believe that because of the contrary observances of the Greeks and opinions of contrary authorities the article should not be condemned under an anathema.[126] The general of the Order of Preachers, Franciscus Romeus, agrees but says the canon should be "passed over in silence."[127] Alvaro de la Guarde (Venusinus) and Galeazzo Florimonte, bishop of Aquino (Aquinatensis), both express concern that the canon conflicts with Matthew 19.[128]

---

121. CT, VI, 479.28–37 and 480.1, 3–10: "Igitur Christus cum docuit evangelium discipulis, nulla ex causa dimittendam uxorem et aliam ducendam esse asserebat. Praeterea cum aliquis locus scripturae videtur dubius, standum est interpretationi ecclesiae, quae idem semper tenuit et docuit, ut fornicatio non rumpat vinculum. Et Paulus clare sine ulla exceptione dicit, quod *uxor a viro non discedat* et *si discedit, maneat innupta vel viro reconcilietur.* Et addit Paulus: Et vir similiter non discedat ab uxore sua. Idem declaravit concilium Milevitanum, quod dixit esse *secundum legem evangelicam et apostolicam.*"

122. CT, VI, 480.10–11. On Council of Florence, "Bull of Union with the Armenians," no. 16, see CT, VI, 420n1.

123. Summarized at CT, VI, 485–86.

124. CT, VI, 452.15 and 453.29–30 respectively.

125. CT, VI, 450.30 and 455.9 respectively.

126. CT, VI, 449.8–10 (Naxiensis): "Tertius canon advertatur: quia ecclesia Graeca observat contrarium ritum et tot doctores et concilia contrarium dixerunt, non deberet damnari iste articulus sub anathemate." CT, VI, 450.22–23 (Aciensis): "Tertius canon est considerandus, ne damnentur sub anathemate et Graeci et doctores, qui contrarium dicunt."

127. CT, VI, 478.23–26.

128. CT, VI, 456.1–2 and 3–5 respectively.

Prelate Theologians Consider the Criticisms of Canon 3

On October 10, twenty-one prelate members of the Council were elected to serve as a "Congregatio Praelatorum Theologorum" to examine more deeply the criticisms offered on the canons on the sacraments.[129] On Saturday, October 15, Cardinal Cervini presented to the *Congregatio* for examination the two most common criticisms of canon 3 made by the General Congregation. The first was the question of whether adultery dissolves the bond of marriage; the second whether the words "*neque mechari eum* etc." should be deleted from the canon's formulation.[130] Ten prelates offer comment. Nine affirm that adultery does not dissolve the bond of marriage.[131] Robert Senalis, bishop of Abrincensis, adds that the exception in Matthew 19 should be understood to mean "bed, not bond" in accord with the church's interpretation.[132] Dionisio de Zanettini, bishop of Chironissa (Chironensis) adds that this is clear from Mark 10, Luke 16, and 1 Corinthians 7, which tell us how Matthew 19:9 is to be interpreted (consistent with the church's exposition); he then says, the words "*neque mechari eum* etc." should be retained.[133] Minoriensis, Romeo, and Seripando (who affirmed that adultery does not dissolve marriage) disagree with Chironensis, arguing that the words "*neque mechari* etc." should be deleted from the canon because of the opinions of contrary authorities.[134]

Cervini ends the discussion by saying that the canon will be reformulated in accordance with the recommendations of the fathers and returned to them for examination to see if a second formulation is more acceptable. He instructed them to consider what responses should be made to authori-

---

129. CT, VI, 524.1–21.
130. CT, VI, 535.2–3: "an ea [fornicatio] rumpat vinculum matrimonii et an ex canone delenda sint illa verba *neque mechari eum* etc."
131. Abrincensis, Chironensis, Motulanus, Veronensis, Bituntinus, Minoriensis, Francis Romeo (Dominican general), Girolamo Seripando (Augustine general), and Simon Stampensis (general of the Order of Minims). Aciensis questions (but does not conclude) whether it is true that in all cases adultery does not break the bond of marriage (CT, VI, 535.4–22).
132. CT, VI, 535.7–8: "Respondit ad Matth. 19, quod intelligitur de thoro, non vinculo."
133. CT, VI, 535.15–18: "cum sit clarum Marci 10, Luce 16, ad Corinth. 7, qui loci declarant locum Matth. 19, qui intelligendus est secundum expositionem ecclesiae. Circa verbum *neque mechari eum* placet poni."
134. Minoriensis: "Propterea delea[n]tur ex canone verba illa *neque mechari* etc." (CT, VI, 535.24). Romeo: "Videretur tamen ei de hoc canone non esse faciendam mentionem propter diversas doctorum altercationes" (535.26–27). Serapand: "Verba autem illa canonis *neque mechari eum* etc. cuperet immutari per ea, quae dixit Minoriensis" (535.29–30).

ties that seem to say that the bond of marriage is dissolved by adultery.[135] On October 18, Cervini made good on his promise, returning three reformulated canons on matrimony to the prelate theologians for criticisms, including the following (c. 3): "If any one says that the bond of a legitimately contracted marriage is not by divine law indissoluble, and consequently that on account of adultery it is licit for both spouses or the spouse who gave no cause for the adultery, not only to have a separation of bed, but to contract another marriage, let him be anathema."[136]

A significant transition occurs here. In place of the more unwieldy Erasmian formulation referring to the adulterous woman who "ceases to be a wife," this new, shorter, and uncomplicated formulation directly condemns a denial of the indissolubility of a rightly contracted marriage. By suggesting the legitimacy of a separation of bed and using the phrase "legitimately contracted marriage," we see the influence of the teaching of the Council of Florence: "Although separation of bed is lawful on account of fornication, it is not lawful to contract another marriage, since the bond of a legitimately contracted marriage is perpetual."[137] Also, in teaching that indissolubility is grounded in "divine law," we see the influence of the Council of Mileve's reference to "the Gospel and apostolic discipline."[138]

Among the criticisms of the new formulation, which mostly amount to minor terminological suggestions, are recorded the more extensive remarks of the Dominican general, Francis Romeo.[139] Recall that in the discussion of the canon's prior formulation, although Romeo affirmed with emphasis

---

135. CT, VI, 535.36–38: "Monuit tamen eos, ut cogitarent, quid respondendum illis auctoritatibus, qui videa[n]tur dicere per fornicationem rumpi vinculum matrimonii."

136. CT, VI, 537.9–12: "Si quis dixerit matrimonii (legitime contracti) vinculum non esse iure divino indissolubile, ac proinde ex causa fornicationis licere utrique aut alteri coniugum, qui fornicationi causam non dederit, non solum thori separationem facere, sed aliud contrahere matrimonium, a.s."

137. Council of Florence, "Bull of Union with the Armenians," no. 16: "Quamvis autem ex causa fornicationis liceat tori separationem facere, non tamen aliud matrimonium contrahere fas est, cum matrimonii vinculum legitime contracti perpetuum sit" (CT, VI, 420n1); translation from DEC, 1:550.

138. Council of Mileve, c. 17: "Be it resolved that according to the Gospel and apostolic discipline, neither a husband dismissed by his wife nor a wife dismissed by her husband may be joined to another; but they should remain as they are or be reconciled to each other" (CT, VI, 447.24–26). Fransen argues that "iure divino" here should not necessarily be understood as pertaining to something *revealed* by God. He gives no argument for this, only his "belief" that at Trent, the term did not necessarily carry this meaning. But the continuous referencing of scripture by the fathers in order to ground the truth of indissolubility belies Fransen's insouciant dismissal of the more obvious meaning of "iure divino" (as well as Mileve's "evangelicam et apostolicam disciplinam").

139. The criticisms (labeled "Censurae censurarum") are summarized at CT, VI, 577.21–42.

(*firmiter*) that adultery does not dissolve the bond of marriage, he asked that the words "*neque mechari* etc." should be deleted.[140] Here he recommends a revised formulation of the canon: "If anyone says that the bond of a consummated marriage is not by divine law indissoluble, and consequently that in cases of adultery not only has it been permitted but also licit for living spouses to contract a marriage with others, let him be anathema."[141] In a commentary on his own formulation Romeo says he recommends that "consummati" replace "contracti" because the pope can dissolve the bond of a non-consummated marriage.[142] This demonstrates that he believes that a consummated marriage is absolutely indissoluble. He then recommends that the canon condemn those who assert that remarriage after adultery is both "permissible" *and* "licit." This, he says, will "save" (preserve, protect) those authorities, including councils and decrees (*concilia et decreta*), which hold that on account of adultery and other causes, a new marriage may be contracted. It will also "save the *ritus* of the Greeks and Armenians and judgements of some fathers" that for similar reasons say divorce and remarriage are permissible, but do not say it is licit.[143]

His distinction between sources that permit but do not (morally) approve divorce and remarriage is obscure. None of the classical "authorities" permitting divorce and remarriage make such a distinction. He may be drawing on reasoning similar to Lavellanus and Minoriensis, who argued that if a man remarries after divorcing his wife for adultery he is not guilty of adultery, but he still sins.[144] Fransen asserts that "licitum" here refers to the personal initiative of the married persons or at least the guiltless

---

See also "Francisci Romei generalis ord. Praedicatorum: censura super his canonibus de sacramento matrimonii; ante diem 7 Novembris 1547" (CT, VI, 537.12–13).

140. CT, VI, 535.25–27: "Generalis Praedicatorum tenet firmiter per fornicationem non rumpi vinculum matrimonii, ut semper tenuit ecclesia. Videretur tamen ei de hoc canone non esse faciendam mentionem propter diversas doctorum altercationes."

141. CT, VI, 537.18–20 (repeated at 577.37–39): "Si quis dixerit consum[m]ati matrimonii vinculum non esse iure divino indissolubile, ac proinde ex causa fornicationis non solum fuisse permissum, sed etiam licitum viventibus coniugibus cum aliis contrahere matrimonium, a.s."

142. CT, VI, 537.26–27: "In tertio canone apposui li *consum[m]ati*, quia matrimonii non consum[m]ati vinculum est dissolubile a papa."

143. Freudenberger references CT, VI, 412, where several authorities are itemized that "seem to oppose" the proposition "that on account of adultery, the bond [*vinculum*] of marriage is not dissolved." CT, VI, 537.27–23, and 538.1–3: "Addidi quoque *non solum fuisse permissum* ad salvanda concilia et decreta omnia, quae censent propter fornicationem et alias causas posse contrahi nova matrimonia. Salvantur quoque ritus Grecorum et Armenorum et sententie quorundam patrum, qui propter dictas causas etc. permissive enim intelliguntur ac per consequens non videntur anathemate feriendi, cum non dicant ea esse licita, sed permissa."

144. CT, VI, 459.7–8 and 472.13–14, 24–25.

spouse, and "permissum" implies the "right of the church to 'dispense' in this matter [i.e., from marriage] for particular reasons."[145] If this is true, and neither Romeo's remarks nor anything from the 1547 discussions sheds any light whatsoever on whether or not it is, then it is the first remark—implicit, unelaborated, and obscure—in the Council's proceedings on the distinction between "intrinsic" and "extrinsic" indissolubility, which Fransen argues dominates the discussion of adultery, divorce, and remarriage at Bologna.

Revealingly, Romeo's wording—intending to "save" the Eastern *ritus* and opinions of the Church Fathers—is not accepted. On November 7, 1547, the final formulation of canon 3 of the Bologna sessions is recorded in the *Acta*, reformulated on the basis of the criticisms of the prelate theologians. It is similar to the formulation of October 18 (canon 3): "If anyone says that the bond of marriage contracted between legitimate persons is not by divine law indissoluble, and consequently that on account of adultery it is licit for both spouses or the spouse who gave no cause of adultery, not only to have a separation of bed, but to contract another marriage, let him be anathema."[146]

Changing the phrase "the bond of a legitimately contracted marriage" to "the bond of marriage contracted between legitimate persons" seems to shift the sense of legitimacy away from the contracting to the status of the persons. I presume "legitimate persons" means legally defined persons, but the Council's rationale for the alteration is unclear. Still, the canon continues to teach that the bond of marriage is indissoluble, that the indissolubility arises by divine law, and that remarriage after adultery is wrongful.

CONCLUSION: FOUR QUESTIONS

Our purpose for reviewing the Conciliar discussions of 1547 has been to establish the "mind of the Council" on the doctrine of indissolubility throughout and concluding Trent's Bologna sessions. The lengthy debates, and especially the final formulation of canon 3, establish the doctrinal context for the discussions sixteen years later when the Council again takes up

---

145. "'Permissum' deutete dem Text gemäß das Recht der Kirche an, in dieser Angelegenheit aus besonderen Gründen zu 'dispensieren.'" Fransen, "Ehescheidung im Falle von Ehebruch," 154.

146. CT, VI, 578.7–10: "Si quis dixerit matrimonii inter legitimas personas contracti vinculum non esse iure divino indissolubile, ac proinde ex causa fornicationis licere utrique aut alteri coniugum, qui fornicationis causam non dedit, non solum thori separationem facere, sed aliud contrahere matrimonium, a.s."

its considerations of the doctrine. What can we conclude about the beliefs and intentions of the Council fathers at the end of the Bologna sessions? At the beginning of the chapter it was stated that the answers to four questions would become clear by looking at the consensus of the Council fathers on the doctrine of indissolubility. By "consensus" I mean the positions held and defended by the vast majority of voting prelates.

Question 1

What truths did the Council fathers believe needed to be defended and what errors condemned? From the first discussions in April 1547 through the final formulation of canon 3 in November of the same year the fathers agreed that:

> the bond of a validly contracted marriage is indissoluble
> no cause, not even adultery, dissolves it
> indissolubility is taught in divine revelation
> remarriage after divorce is always illicit

And the contrary propositions are to be condemned:

> not all validly contracted marriages are indissoluble
> adultery dissolves the marriage bond
> the doctrine of indissolubility is not divinely revealed
> remarriage in cases of adultery is not always prohibited

We see that the fathers are interested in answering the question of what is true about the nature of the bond of marriage. Besides the article drawn from the writings of Luther that "the pope errs whenever he grants a divorce for any cause other than adultery," published in the *Acta* prior to the first discussion of the council theologians in April 1547, the issue of papal authority to teach on marriage is not mentioned. It does not appear in any formal discussions of the Conciliar theologians, the General Congregation, or the prelate theologians. We are therefore justified in excluding the thesis that the Council, at least in November 1547, was only interested in correcting the Reformers' denial of papal and ecclesial authority over the marriages of Christians.

Question 2

What status did the Council fathers believe these truths held in Catholic teaching? They judged them to be truths of divine revelation, with frequent appeals to the teachings of Jesus in the Gospels (Mk 10, Lk 16) and of Paul (1 Cor 7, Rom 7) and even to the first chapters of Genesis. To the view that Matthew 5:32 and 19:9 teach something contrary, and establish a real "exception" to indissolubility and the norm against remarriage, they almost unanimously respond that these passages "are to be interpreted according to the clear explication of the Church," namely, that Jesus' reference to "separation" in cases of adultery should be understood to extend only as far as a separation of bed, but not to the dissolution of the bond.[147] The conclusion that the views of contrary authorities—the decrees of regional councils and the apparently permissive views of some Church Fathers—"forced a compromise" by which the Council grounded its anathema on purely canonical (i.e., legal) grounds is unfounded.[148] The vast majority of Council fathers grounding their arguments in the writings of Church Fathers, scripture, church councils, history, and even the prescriptions of the natural law, indicate they believed that indissolubility is a dogmatic truth, revealed by God, and in this sense *de fide*.

Question 3

With what type of formulation did the Council fathers believe the truths should be taught? They had available to them several authoritative forms. They could teach a truth in the form of a *doctrina* (general teaching), *canon de reformatione* (reform canon), *decretum de reformatione* (reform decree), or in the form of a *canon fidei* (canon of faith). We see that despite objections from a small number of fathers, the propositions denying indissolubility and justifying remarriage are condemned using the formulation *anathema sit*, which the fathers make clear should be understood as a *de fide* definition.

---

147. CT, VI, 435.2–6: "Cui auctoritati contrarium tenentes responderunt eam separationem intelligi debere quoad thorum, non quoad vinculum, ut doctores interpretantur (et Paulus declarat 1 Cor. 7 et ad Rom. 7 ac Marci 10 et Luce 16 et ipsemet Matth. 5:32), quodque scripturae intelligendae sint secundum declarationem ecclesiae."

148. "Durch die ältere Tradition, sowohl die dekretalische als auch die patristische, stellten sich aber Schwierigkeiten ein, die zu einem Kompromiß zwangen, d.h. man mußte die Lösung auf rein kirchlichem Gebiet suchen, um in jedem Fall das Anathem bebehalten zu können." Fransen, "Ehescheidung Im Falle Von Ehebruch," 155.

Question 4

With what degree of authority did they believe it should be taught? In formulating the truth of indissolubility as a canon of faith, the Council fathers believed that the teaching should express the full and solemn authority of the Catholic church and result in an irreformable doctrine of faith.

Finally, does the final formulation of canon 3 assert that the marriage bond is *absolutely* indissoluble? It does not seem so. Because the term *contracti* remains and was not replaced, as Romeo recommended, with *consummati*, the November 1547 formulation of the canon on adultery leaves open the question of the dissolution of non-consummated marriages. Moreover, remarriage is excluded in normative terms (*non licere*) and not substantive terms (*non posse*), leaving open the question of whether the dissolution of marriage is still possible, even if wrongful.

CHAPTER 4

DISCUSSIONS AT TRENT ON MARRIAGE (1563)

The third period of the Council at Trent, under Pope Pius IV (Giovanni Angelo Medici), ran from 1562 to 1563 and included sessions 17–25. The General Congregation formally debated canons on marriage on July 24–31, August 7–23, September 7–10, and October 26–27, 1563, all during session 23. The twelve canons on the sacrament of marriage were authoritatively published on November 11, 1563, during session 24.

Theological deliberations on the sacrament of matrimony began in February 1563 during session 22. On February 4, eight heretical articles were submitted for discussion to a small group of theological experts, referred to as *theologi minores* ("minor theologians," analogous to *periti* at Vatican II). The third reads: "It is licit after repudiating a wife on account of adultery to contract another marriage while the first wife still lives; and divorce for a cause other than adultery is an error."[1] The first sentence refers only to a wife's adultery and the legitimacy of a husband's entering into a second marriage, following the example of Matthew 5:32 and 19:9 which refer only to the dismissal of a wife.[2] The second sentence rejects causes for divorce

---

1. CT, IX, 380.7–8: "Licere post repudiatam uxorem causa fornicationis iterum contrahere, vivente priore uxore, erroremque esse, extra illam causam fornicationis divortium facere." Discussion of this article can be found in CT, IX, 409–20.

2. The one-sided formation was also likely influenced by the widely known text of Pseudo-Ambrose (Ambrosiaster), believed to be Ambrose of Milan, which stated: "It is not permitted for the wife to marry, if she dismisses her own husband because of adultery.... It is licit for a husband to remarry if he dismisses a sinful wife, because he is not thus bound by the

other than adultery. This is obviously derived from Luther's criticism of the Catholic church's practice of permitting spousal separation (but not remarriage) for a variety of reasons.³ Notwithstanding these particularities, the theologians reply to the more fundamental question of whether adultery annuls marriage.

Six theologians offer replies. The first is by the prominent Spanish Dominican Peter de Sotto, who begins by asserting that the article is heretical.⁴ He says that although this was doubted by some, the question is now "in ecclesia explicata est" (settled in the church). "It is therefore never permissible to marry another when one's spouse is still living."⁵ Lest one understand him to mean the question has been settled merely by a "firm legal tradition" leaving open the dogmatic question, he adds: "this has been proved/sanctioned by the decrees of Sacred Scripture."⁶ He references Mark 10:11, Luke 16:18, 1 Corinthians 7:39, and Romans 7:2. He says the exceptive clause in Matthew 19:9 should be understood in relation to the parallel passages in Mark and Luke.⁷ "Moreover," he says, "since marriage is a sacrament and the bond [as sacramental] is supernatural and not from nature—not depending on free choice, but indissoluble—it *cannot be dissolved by any cause*; for those whom God has joined, let no man separate."⁸ Sotto's assertion is not merely normative—marriage *should* not be separated. It is a statement of fact about the unbreakable nature of the marriage bond—it *cannot* be (*non potest*) divided. Sotto ends by condemning Car-

---

law as is his wife, because a husband is head of his wife" (*Commentary on 1 Cor. 7*; see appendix A for the Latin text).

3. Recall that before the first Bologna session in April 1547, Massarelli distributed to the Conciliar theologians a list of ten erroneous propositions on marriage drawn from the writings of Luther and Melanchthon (they are referenced at CT, VI, 92–96). The eighth proposition is: "the pope errs whenever he grants a divorce for a cause other than adultery [divortium facit extra causam fornicationis]" (CT, VI, 93.12).

4. CT, IX, 409.2: "respondit, haereticum esse."

5. CT, IX, 409.10–11: "Non igitur umquam licet vivente altero coniugum alii nubere."

6. CT, IX, 409.5–7: "Nunc autem haec quaestio in ecclesia explicata est, ut nullo modo liceat adulteris uxorem ducere, (quod auctoritatibus sacrae Scripturae comprobatum est)." Authors at Trent generally used the male-specific construction, rendered here as "uxorum ducere" (to take a wife), following the Vulgate rendering of Mt 19:9, "aliam duxerit," in which Jesus is referring to the Mosaic exception for husbands (cf. Mk 10:11, Lk 16:18). On the legal tradition, see Fransen, "Divorce on the Ground of Adultery," 90n4.

7. CT, IX, 409.14–16: "Neque intelligendam exceptionem *nisi causa fornicationis*, cum Matthaeus 19, 9 iuxta Marcum et Lucam intelligendus sit."

8. CT, IX, 409.27–29 (emphasis added): "Praeterea cum matrimonium sit sacramentum et vinculum supernaturale, non ex natura, neque ex libero arbitrio pendens, sed indissolubile, nulla ex causa dissolvi potest; quos enim Deus coniunxit, homo non separet."

dinal Cajetan for defending a theological position contrary to the truth in opposition to the definitions of popes and consensus of the whole church.[9]

Parisian theologian Antonius Demochares is the second to comment. The article is heretical, he says. He dismisses pseudo-Ambrose's contrary opinion as false.[10] He resolves interpretive questions in the writings of Pope Gregory III and Origen in favor of indissolubility. To ground the church's ancient understanding, he appeals to scripture (1 Cor 7), popes (Innocent I, Gregory I, Alexander III, and Innocent III), councils (Elvira, Mileve, and Florence), Church Fathers (Clement, Tertullian, Origen, Ambrose, and Augustine) and sacred writings (Canons of the Apostles). And he repeats twice the common formula that although it is licit to dismiss a spouse ("separation of bed") on account of adultery, since the bond is indissoluble, remarriage is never permissible.[11]

The third reply comes from the French Franciscan Jacob Hugo. Replying to the difficulty raised by the exceptive clause, he argues for indissolubility from both the Old and New Testaments. In addition, he mounts an argument from sacramental theology that presumes marriage is indissoluble in virtue of the sacrament.[12]

The fourth, by Spanish Franciscan John Ramirez, appeals to the writings of Paul and the Gospels to argue that remarriage after divorce, even for an innocent spouse, is impossible if the first spouse is still living.[13] He offers an exegetical solution to the problem of the Matthean exceptive clause. He notes that in Matthew 5:32, the apparent exception comes after the first clause "everyone who dismisses his wife," but is not repeated after the second clause "and whoever marries a divorced woman commits adultery." It follows that a divorced woman cannot remarry for any reason. Moreover, the first clause says "*makes* her commit adultery" and not "he commits adultery," since it is speaking only about the husband who dismisses his wife and not about remarriage; so that it refers only to separation from the bed,

---

9. CT, IX, 410.6–9: "Responditque ad id, quod Caietanus contra hanc veritatem dicit .... Nam Romanorum Pontificum diffinitiones reiici non possunt, cum praesertim accedit universalis ecclesiae consensus."

10. CT, IX, 411.8: "Ambrosii dictum falsum esse."

11. CT, IX, 411.28.29: "liceat fornicationis causa separationem facere, scilicet thori, non licet tamen aliam ducere, cum Matrimonium indissolubile sit." See also CT, IX, 412.3–4: "Licite dimittitur uxor ob causam fornicationis; sed remanet vinculum, quare non licet aliam ducere." Again the male-specific construction "aliam ducere" is used. See p. 91, note 6.

12. CT, IX, 414.21–23: "Si licuisset aliam ducere, vinculum matrimonii non fuisset indissolubile, ergo nec rationem sacramenti habuisset. Nam de ratione sacrameti est indissolubilitas."

13. CT, IX, 416.8–9: "Si uxor innocens discesserit a viro, non potest eo superstite alium ducere, et oppositum est haereticum."

because when a husband dismisses his wife for something other than adultery, he makes her commit adultery, that is, he is the cause of her committing adultery. But if he dismisses her for committing adultery, then he does not make her commit adultery, since from her own adultery she already is an adulteress.[14] Ramirez goes on to say that when the Lord is confronted by the question of the Pharisees, who are trying to trap him, he replies by proposing principles from which clear conclusions may be drawn. From the principle "they will be two in one flesh" it is clear that they cannot contract a second marriage; and from the principle "what God has joined no one shall separate" he demonstrates that marriage is indissoluble.[15]

The fifth, Calabrian theologian and secular cleric Matthew Guerra, begins by saying that although it is licit to dismiss one's wife for adultery, it is not licit to remarry while she lives.[16] "This is proved by Matt. 5 and 19."[17] Jesus taught that anyone who dismisses his wife except in cases of adultery makes her an adulteress and the man who marries a wife who has been dismissed for adultery is an adulterer. Therefore it is not licit to dismiss one's wife for just any cause, but "only on account of bodily or spiritual adultery" (he does not specify what he believes "spiritual" adultery entails),[18] adding that the wife "cannot" remarry and neither can the husband, since husband and wife are judged equally.[19] Although the law of Moses permitted husbands to give a bill of divorce to their wives "in order to avoid greater evils," the law of the Gospel "perfects the law of Moses and returns the law of nature to the state of innocence at which time [man and woman] were

14. CT, IX, 416.16–25: *"Omnis, qui dimiserit uxorem suam, excepta fornicationis causa, facit eam moechari, et qui dimissam duxerit, adulterat,* ubi notandum, quod posteriori parti nulla apparet exceptio, quam tamen priori adiunxerat, ostendens ex hoc, nulla ob causam dimissam ab alio duci posse; ergo non fuit solutum matrimonium, quamvis adulterium commissum sit. Notandum etiam, quod in priori parte dicitur *facit eam moechari,* non *adulterat,* quia loquebatur de eo, qui dimisit solum, non duxit aliam, ut significetur separatio a thoro solum; quando ergo iste dimittit propter alias causas quam propter fornicationem, is facit uxorem moechari, id est in causa est, cur uxor moechetur. At si fuerit propter fornicationem, non facit eam moechari, quia ipsa iam ex se moecha erat."

15. CT, IX, 416.39–42: "[Christus] ponit principium, ex quo ipsi possunt elicere conclusionem. Principium est: *Erunt duo in carne una;* quodsi una caro, ergo non licet secundo contrahere. Secundo ostendit indissolubilitatem Dominus: *Quod Deus coniunxit, homo non separet;* subobscure ergo Pharisaeis respondit."

16. CT, IX, 418.2–3: "Licet repudiare uxorem ob causam fornicationis; sed non licet, ea vivente, cum alia contrahere."

17. CT, IX, 418.3: "Probatur Matth. 5 et 19."

18. CT, IX, 418.5–6. "non licere dimittere uxorem ex quacumque causa, sed tantum ob fornicationem corporalem vel spiritualem."

19. CT, IX, 418.6–7: "Uxor non potest alium virum accipere, neque vir uxorem, cum non ad imparia iudicentur."

[first] joined to one another in matrimony."²⁰ Husband and wife are bound together; they become one flesh: "they may separate only as far as the bed, but the bond of matrimony remains indissoluble."²¹ He quotes Augustine who says, "the indissolubility of the bond of marriage is an image of Christ and the church," and references scripture (Mt 5 and 19, Mk 10, Lk 16, Rom 7, 1 Cor 7, Eph 5), church councils (Mileve, Lateran III, Florence), and Church Fathers (Augustine, Chrysostom, Jerome) in defense of this position.²²

Finally, Spanish priest of the Holy Trinity, Diego de Sarra, argues that from the words in Matthew 19:9 it is not entirely clear what the Lord himself wills. When the Lord is questioned about divorce he says it is not permissible "excepta causa fornicationis." Therefore, in cases of adultery, it seems licit to divorce one's spouse and marry another. But the words leave room for doubt. And in cases of doubts, we must return to the conclusions reached by the church. Before those conclusions were proposed, doubt was permitted regarding the meaning of the proposition. Nevertheless, acting against the doubt was prohibited by the church. And after the conclusion of the church, not the slightest bit of doubt is permitted. For there is a great difference between speculative and practical doubt. The latter involves a doubt of conscience, before which it is not permissible to act. He says, "if it should be asked whether the church is able [posit] to permit divorce and remarriage, it seems that it could, because at times this was done for reasons less grave than fornication, for instance, because of infirmity."²³ We see that

20. CT, IX, 418.8: "ad evitanda maiora mala." CT, IX, 418.9–10: "Lex autem Evangelica perfecit legem Mosaicam et legem naturae reduxitque ad statum innocentiae, quo tempore altera alteri matrimonio iungebatur."
21. CT, IX, 418.12–13: "Separantur tantum quoad thorum; sed vinculum matrimonii manet indissolubile." Several lines later he says (418.24–26): "Quamvis autem ex causa fornicationis liceat thori separationem facere, non aliud matrimonium contrahare fas est, cum matrimonii vinculum legitime contracti perpetuum sit" (Although it may be licit because of adultery to make a separation of bed, it is not permissible to contract another marriage, since the bond of a legitimately contracted marriage is perpetual).
22. CT, IX, 418.37: "Indissolubilitas vinculi coniugalis instar Christi et ecclesiae," from Augustine, *De nuptiis et concupiscentia*, lib. 1, c. 10, no. 11 ad Matt. 5:32 (PL 44:420).
23. CT, IX, 420.26–40: "Nam Dominus interrogabatur de dimissione, quae, ut dictum est, includebat, quod posset aliam ducere. Interrogabatur itaque, an omnem ob causam liceret; respondit, non omnem ob causam licere. Ob quam igitur? Ob nullam, inquit, excepta causa fornicationis. Ergo propter fornicationem licet ita dimittere et aliam ducere. Nam regula est, quod exceptio firmat regulam in contrarium. Quare quantum sit ex his verbis, hac de re licet dubitare. Et Augustinus dubitavit, atque Ambrosius. His subnectam secundam conclusionem: In dubiis recurrendum est ad determinationem ecclesiae.... Aliquando licuit dubitare de hac propositione; non licuit tamen facere contra illam, et post determinationem ecclesiae ne tantillum quidem dubitare licet.... Nam magna est differentia inter dubium speculativum et practi-

de Sarra's opinion situates the doctrine of indissolubility in the realm of the disciplinary and not the dogmatic tradition of the church.

SESSION 23

First Formulation on the Canons on Matrimony (July 20, 1563)

Session 23 opened on July 15, 1563, under the papacy of Pius IV.[24] Three weeks earlier, on June 21, a deputation (*deputatio*) of fourteen prelates was appointed by the General Congregation to prepare a preliminary draft of the decree on marriage.[25] This included the important task of drafting canons on marriage. On July 20, the work was complete and eleven canons on the sacrament of marriage, each ending "anathema sit," were presented to the fathers. Canon 6 reads: "If anyone says, that on account of the adultery of one of the spouses a marriage can be dissolved, and that it is licit for both spouses, or at least the innocent spouse who gave no cause for adultery, to remarry, and that he does not commit adultery who dismisses an adulteress and marries another, nor she commit adultery who dismisses an adulterer and marries another, let him be anathema."[26]

Dissecting the canon, we see that three related propositions are condemned and their contraries asserted:

Condemned:

The adultery of a spouse dissolves the marriage;
One who dismisses one's spouse for adultery may remarry;

---

cum. De primo licet dubitare. At de secundo ex ante dubia conscientia nihil licet facere. Si quaeratur, utrum ecclesia posit permittere, videtur, quod quandoque factum sit ex leviori causa, quam ob fornicationem, puta propter infirmitatem."

24. See CT, IX, 617.

25. Georg Draskovics (Quinqueecclesiensis), Marcantonio Bobba (Augustensis), Pedro Guerrero (Granatensis), Pietro Emilio Verallo (Rossanensis), Bartolomé de Los Mártyres (Bracarensis), Marcantonio Colonna (Tarentinus), Pierre du Val (Sagiensis), Urban de Ruere (Senogalliensis), Francois de Beaucaire (Metensis), Jacob Lomelli (Mazariensis), Andrés Cuesta (Legionensis), Hugo Buoncompagni (Vestanus), Nicolas Sfondratus (Cremonensis), and Augustine Moligni (Trivicanensis). CT, IX, 590 and 591.1–16; see also CT, III, 77.5, and CT, II, 683.27.

26. CT, IX, 640: "Si quis dixerit, propter adulterium alterius coniugum posse matrimonium dissolvi, et utrique coniugum vel saltem innocenti, qui causam adulterio non (dederit, licere) novare coniugium, neque moechari eum, qui dimissa adultera aliam duxerit, neque eam, quae dimisso adultero alii nupserit, anathema sit." The General Congregation's first formal examination on the canons ran from July 24 to 31. The prelates' comments are recorded at CT, IX, 642–79.

One who remarries after dismissing an adulterous spouse does not commit adultery.

Taught:
Marriage *cannot* be dissolved by adultery.
It is not licit to remarry after adultery.
One who remarries after dismissing an adulterous spouse commits adultery.

If we compare canon 6 with heretical article 3 of February 4, we note significantly that the one-sided reference to a wife's adultery has been universalized to include both spouses; the legitimacy of remarriage, even situated in the best possible context (namely, for the innocent spouse free of fault), is rejected; and remarriage is judged to be adultery.[27]

We also see the continuity between the propositions affirmed here and the propositions affirmed by the fathers at the end of the Bologna sessions. The final formulation of the canon on indissolubility at Bologna taught that the marriage bond is indissoluble; that no cause, not even adultery, ruptures the bond; and that remarriage after divorce is always illicit.[28] These propositions are repeated in the theological remarks of Sotto, Demochares, Hugo, Ramirez, and Guerra.[29] The *deputatio* plainly developed canon 6 on the basis of these prior deliberations.

But the *deputatio* made one alteration that is extremely important to the way the Council henceforward would understand the doctrine of indissolubility. In the final formulation of Bologna, remarriage is excluded in normative terms (*non licere*) leaving open the question of whether the dissolution of marriage is still possible, even if wrongful. Canon 6 excludes dissolution in cases of adultery using the term *posse* ("non posse dissolvi"). The sense of the term as used here is that the dissolution of marriage in cases of adultery is not simply wrongful but impossible. The result is a stronger

---

27. CT, IX, 380.7–8: "Licere post repudiatam uxorem causa fornicationis iterum contrahere, vivente priore uxore, erroremque esse, extra illam causam fornicationis divortium facere" (It is licit after repudiating a wife on account of adultery to contract another marriage while the first wife still lives; and divorce for a cause other than adultery is an error).

28. CT, VI, 578.7–10: "Si quis dixerit matrimonii inter legitimas personas contracti vinculum non esse iure divino indissolubile, ac proinde ex causa fornicationis licere utrique aut alteri coniugum, qui fornicationis causam non dedit, non solum thori separationem facere, sed aliud contrahere matrimonium, a.s." (If anyone says that the bond of marriage contracted between legitimate persons is not by divine law indissoluble, and consequently that on account of adultery it is licit for both spouses or the spouse who gave no cause of adultery, not only to have a separation of bed, but to contract another marriage, let him be anathema).

29. Remarks are recorded at CT, IX, 409–19.

affirmation of the doctrine than at Bologna. The canon affirms the indissolubility of marriage in cases of adultery not merely on grounds of the moral law or legal precedent, but on the substantive nature of marriage itself.

The General Congregation began its analysis of the eleven canons on Wednesday, July 24, and ended a week later on July 31. Two hundred Council fathers registered comments that bear on canon 6. Of these fathers, by far the greatest number approved canon 6 with no mitigating comments. Forty-seven explicitly note their approval, with more than twenty adding strengthening clauses either rejecting opposing interpretations, stating that the canon's content is contained in divine revelation, or adding statements such as "publish as is," "with anathema," and "do not alter."[30] Another fifty-five approve the canon's content with general statements such as "placent omnes canones."[31] Among this group is the influential Charles de Guise, cardinal of Lorraine (Lotharingus), who in Jedin's words was "a youthful, energetic and highly-gifted cardinal."[32] One of his contributions to this discussion proved very significant.

Two years earlier, in September 1561, de Guise led the Catholic delegation to the Colloquy of Poissy, a conference attended by Calvinist and Catholic theologians aimed at religious reconciliation.[33] Calvin's chief theologian at the meeting was Théodore de Bèze, who presented on the Reformed doctrine of sacraments. Lorraine delivered the Catholic reply. He was therefore especially familiar with Calvin's sacramental theology. On Wednesday, July 24, Lorraine proposes that an additional canon should be formulated condemning three propositions held by John Calvin contrary to the doctrine of absolute indissolubility: marriage may be dissolved on account of disparity of cult, disharmony between the spouses, and prolonged absence.[34] Forty-eight fathers follow him on this recom-

---

30. On rejecting opposing interpretations, see the comments of the bishop of Justinopolis (or Caesarea, modern Turkey) at CT, IX, 654, and of the French bishops of Verdun (Virdunensis) at 657 and Paris (Parisiensis) at 658. For content as contained in divine revelation: Clugiensis, 655; Interamnensis, 655. For "as is": Larinensis, 662; Vaurensis, 664; Quinqueecclesiensis, 665; Hyprensis, 669; etc. For "with anathema": Ilerdenisis, 666; Dertusensis, 671; Columbriensis, 673; Achadensis, 676; Usellensis, 677; etc. For "do not alter": Civitatensis, 668.

31. See appendix table B-2, column 6.

32. Jedin, *Ecumenical Council of the Catholic Church*, 176.

33. G. Goyau, "Versailles," in *The Catholic Encyclopedia*; available at http://www.newadvent.org/cathen/15366a.htm.

34. Lotharingus: "cuperetque novum addi canonem, in quo damnentur tres propositiones Calvini, videl. quod dirimatur matrimonium propter disparitatem cultus, propter non convenientiam in conversatione et propter longam absentiam" (CT, IX, 642.25–28).

mendation.³⁵ The next day (July 25), Nicolaus de Pelleve, the archbishop of Senonensis proposes a minor but important addition to the content of the Lorraine formulation. The Council should teach: "if anyone says that the willful absence [affectatam absentiam] of either spouse, or etc."³⁶ We shall see that the Council of Trent ultimately follows Lorraine's recommendation (with Senonensis's addition), publishing not one, but two canons on indissolubility: first, the successor to canon 6 (promulgated as canon 7), and second, the Lorraine canon, ultimately numbered as canon 5.³⁷

Another thirty-four fathers, although not explicitly approving canon 6, register no opposition.³⁸ The total number of Council fathers who approve canon 6 as is, with minor non-substantive emendations, or who express no opposition, is 136 out of 200, or 68 percent of the voting prelates.³⁹ If we add to this number the eighteen who approve the canon while recommending the addition of a condemnation of those who say the church cannot prohibit remarriage after divorce, the number comes to 154, or 77 percent of the voting prelates.

Bressan argues that "the majority of the Fathers rejected the Deputatio's proposal," arguing that "just over 40 were willing to approve the proposed canon."⁴⁰ He derives this number from Piet Fransen's "careful examination" of the opinions of the General Congregation.⁴¹ The number indeed comes from Fransen. But the number is untrustworthy and misleading. Fransen considers only those fathers who register an unqualified approval without any recommendations as having "accepted" the canon. Fransen's number (forty-one) roughly corresponds to the number I found who explicitly note their approval with no suggested emendations (forty-seven). But if we really want to know whether or not the fathers of Trent agreed with the general propositions being taught in canon 6 we need also to look at fathers who approve the canon while offering only minor non-substantive

---

35. For the names, see appendix table B-1.
36. Senonensis: "apponatur alius canon iuxta id, quod dixit Lotharingus: *Si quis dixerit, affectatam utriusque coniugis absentiam, aut* etc." (CT, IX, 652.29–30).
37. "Si quis dixerit, propter haeresim aut molestam cohabitationem aut affectatam absentiam a coniuge dissolvi posse matrimonii vinculum: anathema sit" (If anyone shall say that the bond of matrimony can be dissolved on account of heresy, or irksome cohabitation, or desertion by a spouse: let him be anathema). DEC, 2:754; see also CT, IX, 682.17–18.
38. See appendix table B-2, column 9.
39. See appendix table B-2, columns 1, 2, 6, and 9.
40. Bressan, *Il Canone Tridentino*, 136, no. 61.
41. He references Fransen, "Ehescheidung Bei Ehebruch," 547; reprinted in *Hermeneutics of the Councils and Other Studies*, ed. Mertens, 167.

recommendations, and who register no opposition, which rightly is taken as approval. When we do this, as I said, we get a minimum number of 136, which tells a very different story about the fathers' opinions from the story Fransen and Bressan tell.[42]

Only fifteen of two hundred prelates register a "non placet" (i.e., disagreement with the canon's content), eleven of whom specify that it is because of the opinions of the Greeks and pseudo-Ambrose.[43] An additional twenty-one, although approving canon 6, say it should be published without an anathema.[44] This indicates they are doubtful about elevating the canon's content to a solemn condemnation, effectively carrying a sentence of excommunication on those who reject it. Another ten fathers approve the canon, but say more generally that the Council should avoid offending contrary authorities. This includes the Italian archbishop of Rossano (Rossanensis), Giovanni Battista Castagna, the future Pope Urban VII.[45] It also includes the Spanish bishop of Segovia, Martin Pérez de Ayala (Segobiensis), who on the morning of July 26, announces that he approves the canon's content (*materiam*), but not its formulation (*dispositionem*). He claims the text of the Gospel was understood by pseudo-Ambrose, Basil, Origen, Hilary, and Gregory the Great to concern not simply the separation of bed, but also of bond.[46] (As my commentary in appendix B suggests, this stretches the truth out of all proportion.) He ends by proposing an indirect formulation to replace the direct formulation: "If anyone says the Church has erred in saying that the bond of marriage is not dissolved through adultery, let him be anathema."[47]

Fransen claims that the "only true interpretation" for this can be that Segovia means merely to affirm "intrinsic indissolubility" and that he means to ground the canon's authority "on a generally existing canon law."[48] Sego-

---

42. Fransen states: "*the canon in its immediate and strict form was rejected by the first general congregation of the council, which was all too obvious, in fact, mainly because of the uncertain tradition of the catholic church itself*" ("Ehescheidung Bei Ehebruch," 168–69). Fransen's characterization of the first General Congregation as opposed to the strict formulation of indissolubility in canon 6 badly misrepresents the results.

43. See appendix table B-2, columns 7–8.

44. See appendix table B-2, column 4.

45. His papacy lasted thirteen days, from September 15 to 27, 1590, the shortest in history.

46. CT, IX, 656.42–43, 657.1: "Nam textus Evangelii ab Ambrosio, a Basilio Magno, Origene, Hilario et Gregorio Magno intellectus fuit de separatione quoad vinculum."

47. CT, IX, 657.4–6: "Si quis dixerit, ecclesiam errasse dicentem, non dissolvi matrimonium quoad vinculum per fornicationem: anathema sit."

48. Fransen, "Ehescheidung Bei Ehebruch," 170: "It is very obvious from the context that this is only a matter of inner indissolubility and based on a generally existing canon law. 'Si quis

via's intervention does not justify this conclusion. Because the bishop says he agrees with ("placet") the content of canon 6, we know he intends to assert nothing substantially different from the direct formulation. Moreover, in asserting that the church does not err in teaching proposition X, his formulation indirectly asserts that X is true. So why propose an indirect formulation? Because he wants the force of the anathema to fall on the Reformers who deny both the indissolubility of marriage and the church's authority in matters pertaining to the sacrament of marriage and not on authorities in Catholic tradition who doubt the doctrine. Given Segovia's (tendentious) opinion on the views of the five Patristic authors, the indirect formulation permits the truth in canon 6 to be asserted, while directing the anathema with the specificity he desires. This seems to be how the fathers at Trent understood Segovia's proposal, since six fathers who explicitly register a "placet" on Canon 6 also affirm Segovia's suggestion.[49] Two additional fathers specifically oppose Segovia's recommendation, arguing that the canon's direct formulation should be strengthened.[50]

Also on July 26, the bishop of Modena, Egidio Foscarari (Mutinensis), commented on the canons. As a leader of the Italian humanistic reform, and having participated in consultations of the Council of Trent both as theologian and bishop, his interventions were influential.[51] He generally approves the canon, but specifically says only: "Canon 6 should condemn those who say the church cannot prohibit remarriage after adultery."[52] He offers no explanation, but the implicit reference to Luther's challenge of church authority seems likely. Since he does not formulate his statement as an alternative to the direct formulation, we conclude that he means the canon, in addition to condemning those who deny indissolubility in cases of adultery, should *also* condemn those who say the church cannot prohibit remarriage.[53]

---

dixerit ecclesiam erasse' refers without doubt to the Lutheran 'contumacia' and their denial to concede to the church a certain jurisdiction in the matter of the indissolubility of marriage. Out of the broader context ... this is really the only true interpretation."

49. Calamonensis (CT, IX, 659); Laguedonensis (659); Montismarani (660); Casertanus (661); Uxentinus (667); Lucensis (674). In addition, one prelate who registers a "non placet" also follows Segovia (Aliphanus, 675), and one other who does not mention canon 6 follows Segovia in his general approval of the canons (Vulturariensis, 660).

50. Virdunensis (CT, IX, 657); Parisiensis (658).

51. Fransen, "Ehescheidung Bei Ehebruch," 170–71 and 170n67.

52. CT, IX, 658.47–48: "Damnari eos, qui dicunt, ecclesiam non posse id prohibere, videl. ob (fornicationem non ducendam) aliam uxorem."

53. Four fathers (2 percent of the total) follow him in this recommendation: Aurelianensis (CT, IX, 660); Brixiensis (668); Aemoniensis (675); General of the Franciscans (679). Thir-

On July 31, a summary of the prelates' criticisms on the eleven canons is registered in the *Acta*, entitled "judgments/opinions [censurae] made by the fathers in the aforementioned assembly regarding the canons on the sacrament of marriage."[54] The two concerning indissolubility include: (1) the canon should be formulated without an anathema because of the teaching of (pseudo) Ambrose and others who hold a contrary position, especially the Greeks; (2) the canon should condemn those who say the church is not able to prohibit remarriage after adultery.[55] This summary is important because it demonstrates that as of July 31, 1563, the Council had set before itself the two most prominent reasons against a direct formulation of the canon on indissolubility. And, as we shall see, when one week later a revised schema is published, the *deputatio* plainly rejects those arguments by re-proposing a direct formulation.

One other very important initiative from this discussion must be mentioned. Until now, the canons on the sacrament of marriage were set down with no preface or introduction. On July 26, the French bishop of Verdun, Nicolas Psaulme (Virdunensis), proposes the addition of a "doctrina" preceding the canons in which questions concerning the essential nature and ecclesiastical rites of the sacrament of marriage can be clarified.[56] This request for some type of introduction—referred to variously as a "doctrina," "praefatio," "praefatiuncula," or "titulus"—is repeated by more than twenty-five bishops over the course of the discussions. (We shall see that the Council adopts this proposal.) In addition to the reasoning of Virdunensis, two main reasons are adduced. First, a *doctrina* would allow truths pertaining to the sacrament of marriage to be set down firstly in positive form and then what is contrary to them to be singled out and condemned

---

teen additional fathers, who do not explicitly mention canon 6, say in general terms that they approve the canons "following Mutinensis" (or the remaining canons, if they have already commented on one or two). Since the remarks of Mutinensis on the eleven canons number eighteen lines—a large body of material—it is not clear that we should take their statement that they "follow Mutinensis" as specifically endorsing the proposition about condemning those who say the church cannot prohibit remarriage. But if we do, then a total of seventeen fathers follow Mutinensis in his recommendation for this additional condemnation; with Mutinensis a total of eighteen (9 percent).

54. The title reads: "Censurae factae a patribus in suprascriptis congregationibus super canonibus de sacramento matrimonii" (CT, IX, 680).

55. CT, IX, 680.18–22: "In 6. non ponatur anathema, ne feriatur Ambrosius et alii, qui contrarium tenent, praesertim Graeci, qui non sunt omnino reiiciendi ab ecclesiastica unione.... Item damnentur ii, qui dicunt, ecclesiam non posse id prohibere."

56. CT, IX, 657.19–20: "Proponatur doctrina, in qua tractetur de institutione et gratia et ritibus ecclesiasticis, quae circa hoc sacramentum servanda sunt."

by the canons that follow.⁵⁷ Second, and similar to Virdunesis, it would allow questions to be answered, such as what elements of the teaching on marriage are matters of divine law and what are of human law, and what are the matter, form, and minister of the sacrament.⁵⁸ In Trent's final promulgated text on the sacrament of marriage, this *doctrina* plays an extremely important role as an interpretive instrument for uncertainties surrounding the meaning and scope of canon 7.

Second Formulation on the Canons on Matrimony (August 7, 1563)

The second examination of canons on marriage took place on August 7–23. On August 7, the *deputatio* proposed to the General Congregation a revised schema with a set of reformulated canons, now numbering twelve. The first thing to note is that an introductory statement precedes the canons.⁵⁹ It is more of a *titulus* or formula stating the intention to condemn the principal heresies on the sacrament of marriage, than it is a *praefatio* or doctrinal introduction to Catholic truths concerning the sacrament of marriage. Nevertheless the rapid formulation and inclusion of the introduction illustrate the seriousness with which the *deputatio* took the recommendation.

Of the eleven canons published on July 20, the contents of ten, with minor emendations, are reasserted in the twelve reformulated canons.⁶⁰ Most remarkable is the fact that the full content of canon 6, now num-

---

57. E.g., Aurelianensis: "Fiat doctrina, in qua comprehendantur omnia, quae dicuntur in canonibus, et tandem unico canone anathematizentur, qui contraria sentiunt" (CT, IX, 660.3–4); Madrutius: "desiderat canones uberiores et pleniores, aut fieri compendiosam doctrinam, in qua haeretici feriuntur" (643.20–21); General of the Augustinians: "Praeponatur praefatiuncula canonibus, et magis placet, ut praeponeretur doctrina ampla" (679.25–26).

58. See Aliphanus (CT, IX, 674.44–675.1); Dertusensis (671.1–3); Augustinus (678.10–11). Other bishops who propose some sort of introduction include: Virdunensis, "doctrina" (657); Niciensis, "doctrina" (658); Mutinensis, "titulus" (658); Calamonensis, "doctrina aut prooemium aut titulus" (659); Cauriensis, "doctrina" (659); Vulturariensis, "doctrina" (660); Larinensis, "doctrina" (662); Gerundensis, "praefatio" (663); Auriensis, "doctrina" (663); Brixiensis, "praefatio brevis" (668); Hyprensis, "doctrina" (669); Namurcensis, "doctrina" (669); Niochensis, "doctrina" (671); Troianus, "praefatiuncula" (671); Guadiscensis, "doctrina" (672); Aemoniensis, "doctrina" (675); Faventinus, "doctrina" (676); Marsicanus, "praefatio" (677); Sagonensis, "praefatiuncula" (677); Usellensis, "doctrina" (677).

59. See appendix B.

60. Canon 3, which affirmed that clandestine marriages freely contracted were true and ratified marriages, was dropped from the reformulated list of twelve (compare CT, IX, 639–40, with 682); the content of the canon excluding the anathema is contained in the lengthened Decree on Clandestine Marriages following the canons (683).

bered canon 7, is restated against the recommendations of the "non placet" and "without an anathema" minorities:

> If anyone says, that on account of the adultery of one of the spouses a marriage can be dissolved, and that it is licit for both spouses, or at least the innocent spouse who gave no cause for adultery, to remarry while the other spouse is living, and that neither does he commit adultery who dismisses an adulteress and marries another, nor she commit adultery who dismisses an adulterer and marries another, let him be anathema.[61]

In formulating canon 7, the *deputatio* obviously noted the strong support for the first direct formulation. When coming to a judgment about the intentions of the fathers for ultimately using an indirect formulation for canon 7, this fact cannot be overemphasized. The alternative narrative, defended by Bressan and Fransen, is that the fathers of the General Congregation substantially rejected the first formulation. But if this were true, the *deputatio* would have revised the canon's second formulation accordingly. The role of the *deputatio* was principally administrative. It did not possess authority to ignore the voice of what Bressan alleges is a "strong majority" of voting prelates.[62] From the fact that the *deputatio* essentially repeated the content of the first formulation in its second formulation of the canon on adultery, we must conclude that no such majority ever existed.

The canon immediately following this, canon 8, asserts: "If anyone says the Church errs when on account of causes other than adultery she separates the spouses as far as their bed or cohabitation for a time or perpetually, let him be anathema."[63] This addresses the objection of the Reformers that adultery alone justifies separation and the church cannot decree otherwise. It also supports the Augustinian interpretation of the "exceptive clause" that what the Lord permits is only a separation "quoad thorum." The emendation proposed by Mutinensis to condemn those who say the church cannot prohibit remarriage after adultery is nowhere mentioned.[64]

61. CT, IX, 682.21–24: "Si quis dixerit, propter adulterium alterius coniugum posse matrimonium dissolvi, et utrique coniugum vel saltem innocenti, qui causam adulterio non dederit, licere, altero coniuge vivente, aliud matrimonium contrahere, neque moechari eum, qui dimissa adultera aliam duxerit, neque eam, quae dimisso adultero alii nupserit: anathema sit." "Novare coniugium" from the July 20 formulation is replaced with "aliud matrimonium contrahere," both translating "remarry." Also, after "remarry" the words "altero coniuge vivente" are added, which I have translated "while the other spouse is living."
62. "A strong majority, though divided into various group for a diversity of reasons, rejected the proposed canon" (Bressan, *Il Canone Tridentino*, 146; see also Fransen, "Ehescheidung Bei Ehebruch," 168–69).
63. CT, IX, 682.25–27.
64. For the proposal of Mutinensis, see CT, IX, 658.45.

In addition, a new canon, canon 5, is added in response to the July 24 recommendation of the cardinal of Lorraine (Lotharingus) to condemn three heretical propositions of John Calvin: "If anyone says the bond of marriage can be dissolved on account of heresy, or irksome cohabitation, or the willful desertion by one of the spouses: let him be anathema."[65] Read together with canon 7, the Council singles out the most common causes of separation and denies that any of them dissolves marriage. The intention is to support a strict interpretation of the doctrine of indissolubility.

Intervention of the Venetian Delegation

The General Congregation began formal discussions on the reformulated canons on August 11.[66] The Congregation began with the granting of a petition to the Conciliar delegation of the Republic of Venice to speak on the most recent iteration of canon 7.[67] In the sixteenth century, Venice's political rule extended to territories as far as Greece and the Mediterranean. As noted above, the Greek majority in some of these places, especially on the islands in the Mediterranean, lived in singular but fragile unity with the Roman church. The Venetian government permitted the Greek archpriests to exercise limited rule over Greek clergy and liturgy, while the Greek inhabitants agreed to submit to the loosely defined jurisdiction of the islands' Rome-appointed bishops and periodically to profess acknowledgement of the authority of Rome.[68]

The legates from the Republic of Venice announced that on islands such as Crete, Cyprus, Corfu, Zakynthos, and the Ionian island of Cephalonia, Greek Christians live subject and obedient to Roman authority, yet they maintain a "most ancient custom [*ritus*] of their fathers" which permits them to dismiss an adulterous wife and marry another.[69] They say the tradition was long known to the Roman church and yet never condemned by an ecumenical council or struck with an anathema, and argue that publishing

---

65. CT, IX, 682: "Si quis dixerit, propter haeresim aut molestam cohabitationem aut affectatam absentiam a coniuge dissolvi posse matrimonii vinculum: anathema sit." See Lotharingus (642.26–28).

66. See appendix B, part A, for the full text of the Venetian intervention in Latin and English.

67. CT, IX, 686.3–37.

68. For example, at Crete the Greek Christians agreed to sing solemnly the "Laudes" to the pope and archbishop of Crete three times per year; see G. Hofmann, "Wie stand es mit der Frage der Kircheneinheit auf Kreta im XV. Jahrhundert?," *Orientalia Christiana Periodica* 10 (1944): 91–115, esp. 92.

69. CT, IX, 686.19–20: "antiquissimum ritum suorum patrum."

an anathema now would burden the Greeks, confuse them, and incite their rebellion against Rome. Consequently, the delegation entreats the Council to moderate the language of the canon in such a way as to fulfill the intentions of the Council and satisfy the words of our Lord, yet while relieving the Greeks of the burden of falling under an anathema. At the end of the oration, the Venetians propose a reformulated canon, replacing the first clause of the August 7 formulation with wording similar to what was proposed by Sevovia and Modena in the debate over the first reformulation:

If anyone says that the most holy Roman catholic and apostolic church, which is the teacher of all the others, has erred or errs, when she taught and teaches that on account of the adultery of one of the spouses, the marriage cannot be dissolved, and that both of the spouses, or at least the innocent one who gave no cause for adultery, should not contract another marriage while the other spouse is living, and that he commits adultery who dismisses an adulteress and remarries, and she commits adultery who dismisses an adulterer and remarries: let him be anathema.[70]

Rather than condemning directly anyone who denies the indissolubility of marriage in cases of adultery, the formulation condemns anyone who says the church erroneously teaches that marriage is indissoluble in cases of adultery. From a direct assertion of the doctrine of indissolubility and its implications for divorce and remarriage, the Venetian delegation proposes an indirect formulation of the same.

The cardinal of Lorraine (Lotharingus) was the first to speak on the reformulation.[71] He endorses Venice's proposal for an indirect formulation, but immediately recommends adding to the canon the words "iuxta Scripturas" (in accordance with the scriptures) after the clause "when she has taught and teaches." Clearly he meant to ensure that the canon asserted the close agreement between the church's teaching—that is, the proposition asserting the indissolubility of marriage in cases of adultery—and the teaching of divine revelation.

Mackin writes that the "great majority of the bishops favored the Venetians' proposal."[72] If by "proposal" he means approved the recommendation for an indirect formulation of canon 7, then his statement is undoubtedly

---

70. CT, IX, 686.28–33: "Si quis dixerit, sacrosanctam Romanam catholicam et apostolicam ecclesiam, quae est aliarum omnium magistra, errasse vel errare, quando propter adulterium alterius coniugum docuit et docet, matrimonium non posse dissolvi, et utrumque coniugum, vel saltem innocentem, qui causam adulterio non dederit, non debere, altero coniuge vivente, aliud matrimonium contrahere, et moechari eum, qui dimissa adultera aliam duxerit, et eam, quae dimisso adultero alii nupserit: anathema sit."

71. CT, IX, 687.7–9.

72. Mackin, *Divorce and Remarriage*, 388.

true. A total of 192 Council fathers offer comment on the second revision of the canons on matrimony.[73] Eighty-eight explicitly approve the Venetian formulation.[74] Another thirty-eight, while not explicitly mentioning Venice's formulation, say that they follow Lorraine, either specifically in his comments of canon 7 or in his general comments on the second formulation.[75] Of these, only three state that they disagree with Lorraine's proposal to add the words "iuxta Scripturas."[76] We presume that the other thirty-five agree. Another nine indirectly indicate their agreement with the Venetian proposal by endorsing the comments of fathers who support Venice.[77] Together the number of fathers indicating directly or indirectly their agreement with Venice's proposal for canon 7 totals 135, or 71 percent of the fathers, a significant majority indeed.[78]

Despite the powerful momentum in the direction of an indirect formulation, twenty-seven fathers still held firm for the direct formulation as published on August 7.[79] Giovanni Battista Sighicelli, bishop of Faenza (Faventinus), added that the formulation should illustrate that the church teaches that the doctrine is from the scriptures ("ex Scripturis"), recommending the addition of the Milevian phrase "according to the evangelical and apostolic teaching."[80] Bernardo del Bene, bishop of Nimes (Nemausensis), recommends adding the words "by the tradition of the ancient fathers."[81] Finally, Thomas Lili, bishop of Soranus, says to retain the direct formulation "lest we seem to approve the errors of the Greeks."[82] Another fifteen register no opposition, but say nothing explicit about the canon. In total, forty-two fathers do not follow the Venetian proposal, but indicate they favor the direct formulation.[83]

Some may conclude that a vote in favor of the Venetian formulation

---

73. See CT, IX, 687–741.
74. See appendix table B-4, column 1.
75. See appendix table B-4, column 2.
76. Aquilegiensis (CT, IX, 688.15), Granatensis (689.16), and Bracarensis (697.15–16). Bishop Marco Laureo (Campaniensis), in his summary of judgments of the fathers (743.2), adds Hydruntinus, Genuensis, and Messanensis. The mention of Hydruntinus appears to be a mistake since he makes no mention of the phrase. Genuensis and Messanensis say they follow Granatensis in canon 7 ("in 7. Granatensi," 697.40; "in 7. Granatensem," 698.34). Since Granatensis's comments on canon 7 constitute twenty-two lines of text in CT, IX, it is not clear that the two bishops mean to follow him in everything he says.
77. See appendix table B-4, column 3.
78. Marco Laureo numbers this total as 137. See CT, IX, 747.14–15.
79. See appendix table B-4, column 5. Laureo numbers these as twenty-six; CT, IX, 747.17.
80. CT, IX, 735.21–22: "secundum evangelicam et apostolicam doctrinam."
81. CT, IX, 725.44–45: "patrum antiquorum traditione."
82. CT, IX, 735.12: "ne Graecorum errors approbare videamur."
83. Another ten say ambiguously that they follow the "majority of the fathers" (see ap-

meant agreement with the whole argument put forward by the delegation. The delegation asked the council "to moderate" the words of canon 7 "so that it may not be prejudicial [praeiudicium] to the Greeks especially by placing them under pain of anathema."[84] Both the classical sense of *praeiudicium*, meaning pre-judgement, and its post-classical sense of damage or disadvantage suggest that Venice wished to exempt the Greek divorce practices (their *ritus*) from the scope of the canon's condemnation.[85] But as we shall see, this cannot plausibly be held as the judgment of the majority who approved the indirect formulation.

As shown, just one week earlier, 136 fathers explicitly supported or expressed no opposition to a direct condemnation of the denial of indissolubility in cases of adultery. In other words, they were willing solemnly to define as a truth of faith marriage's indissolubility on grounds of adultery. The Venetian orators then rise and say that Greek Christians practice divorce in territories under their jurisdiction, the Catholic hierarchy tolerates it, the toleration supports a measure of religious and political stability, and that condemning the practice would disrupt that stability; and they ask that the Council not teach what the vast majority had resolved to teach, but to teach a qualified doctrine of indissolubility that exempts the Greek practice. We know from our considerations in chapter 2 that the substantive truth about the nature of marriage was first and foremost on the minds of the Council fathers and theologians from the beginning of the Council's consideration on matrimony. In every consideration of articles of heresy and canons condemning those heresies a large majority of bishops defended the proposition that marriage is not and cannot be dissolved in cases of adultery, and that consequently a separation of bed can be permissible, but remarriage is neither permissible nor possible while one's first spouse still lives. Just days earlier the bishops of Virdunensis, Parisiensis, and Iustinopolitanus had dismissed the popular pseudo-Ambrosian opinion that the Gospel of Matthew permits dissolution of the bond; Vaurensis, Hyprensis, Civitatensis, and Lunaevillae had stated that the direct formulation of the

---

pendix table B-4, column 7); and five others say the canon should be published without an anathema (see table B-4, column 4).

84. CT, IX, 686.23–24: "verba illius canonis ita moderentur, ut Graecis (sub anathemate praesertim) non fiat praeiudicium."

85. Fransen concludes similarly: "a clear determination could be seen with the Venetian party to avoid any way of condemnation with anathema, which could endanger the religious and political peace on the Greek islands taken by Venice and Genoa. *They intended to accept the Greeks handling of divorce in cases of adultery as a 'ritus'* (in the very blurred sense of the word in these times) which the Greeks had adopted from the Eastern Church before the Schism" ("Ehescheidung Bei Ehebruch," 181–82; emphasis added).

canon should be published "as is"; and Sulmonensis and Vicensis (Italus) had explicitly asserted that it should be published "with anathema."[86] After the August 11 intervention, each of these prelates suddenly supports an indirect formulation. Rather than concluding that these and many others who supported a direct formulation suddenly see the logic of the Catholic church permitting divorce and remarriage, it is much more plausible to conclude that they believed they were saying the same thing, although in a formulation less offensive to the Greeks.

Two influential errors of Piet Fransen, which Luigi Bressan perpetuates, need dispelling. First, he claims that a majority of Council fathers before the Venetian intervention opposed the direct formulation of the canon: "Already at Bologna, even more so at Trent in July 1563, a majority of the fathers of the council declared openly against the strict phrasing of the canon about divorce in case of adultery, i.e., against the direct and absolute condemnation of this form of divorce under anathema."[87] This flatly contradicts the historical record, which demonstrates that both at Bologna and at Trent's session 23 only a small minority, insignificant in relation to the size of the assembly, declared their opposition to the direct phrasing of the canon on indissolubility in cases of adultery.

Second, he says they opposed the direct formulation because they believed it would cause Ambrose (really Ambrosiaster) and others holding contrary views to fall under excommunication: "The main reason for it was the opposing view of Holy Ambrose and others [Ambrosius et alii], who would have fallen under the excommunication in the absolute and direct phrasing of such a canon."[88] This too misrepresents the record. Neither at Bologna nor at Trent do more than a few fathers mention the problem of Ambrose et al. For example, of the two hundred fathers who remark on the first formulation on canon 6 (later canon 7) from July 24 to 31, 1563, only seven mention the problem of the opinions of Ambrose et al.[89] These make comments such as: "do not proceed by way of anathema ... lest Ambrose be attacked"; "the text of the Gospel [of Matthew] was understood

---

86. Iustinopolitanus (CT, IX, 654.16–17); Virdunensis (657.26–29); Parisiensis (658.18–19). For "as is": 664.15, 669.24, 668.30, and 678.22, respectively. For "with anathema": 656.11–12 and 666.24–25, respectively.

87. Fransen, "Ehescheidung Bei Ehebruch," 182.

88. Ibid. Bressan writes: "The fundamental reason why the [direct formulation of the] canon was rejected was always the same: the text would have condemned Ambrose and others, including the Greeks" (*Il Canone Tridentino*, 137).

89. Cretensis (CT, IX, 644), Verallus (644), Rossanensis (645–46), Segobiensis (656), Pactensis (658), Guadiscensis (672), and Aliphanus (675).

by Ambrose to permit a separation of bond"; "formulate Canon 6 so as not to oppose the custom of the Greeks and the authority of Ambrose."[90] The vast majority, however, express no such concern. In fact, four fathers explicitly reject the Ambrosian interpretation.[91] For example, Thomas Stella, bishop of Iustinopolitanus, says, "even if Ambrose is struck [by anathema], it matters little, for any doctor is capable of error."[92] Quinqueecclesiensis, who defends the direct formulation of canon 6 ("prout iacet"), replies to the problem of pseudo-Ambrose with the maxim of Vincent of Lerins: "we should follow the common judgment of the fathers, but not any particular person, however holy."[93] Virdunensis and Cassinensis both defend their "*placet*" by referencing Ambrose as a *positive* witness to indissolubility![94] Moreover, of the 192 fathers whose remarks are recorded on the second formulation on August 7–23, only *one* mentions Ambrose, whereas twice as many—Legionensis and Ilerdensis—argue that the texts from Ambrose are either falsely attributed or too ambiguous to draw any conclusions from.[95]

This is not to say that the text of pseudo-Ambrose was unknown to the Council fathers.[96] All knew of its existence and the opinion it adopted. This is beyond dispute. The salient point for our consideration is that the

---

90. Verallus: "[non] procedendum per viam anathematis ... ne feriatur Ambrosius" (CT, IX, 644.35–36). Segobiensis: "textus Evangelii ab Ambrosio ... intellectus fuit de separatione quoad vinculum" (656.42–657.1). Pactensis: "6. conficiatur non obstante ritu Graecorum et auctoritate Ambrosii" (658.8).

91. Iustinopolitanus (CT, IX, 654), Virdunensis (657), Quinqueecclesiensis (665), and Cassinensis (678).

92. CT, IX, 654.16–17: "etiamsi feriatur Ambrosius, parum refert, quia quilibet particularis doctor potens errare."

93. CT, IX, 665.9–11: "nec his obstat auctoritas Ambrosii, quia iuxta sententiam Vincentii Lerinensis debemus sequi communem sensum patrum, non autem alicuius particularis quantumvis sancti."

94. CT, IX, 657.26–29 and 678.17–18, respectively.

95. Granatensis (CT, IX, 689). The bishops Ostunensis (723), Segobiensis (709), and Aliphanus (734) each reference contrary authorities but do not mention Ambrose. See also Legionensis (721.5–6) and Ilerdensis (722.27–32).

96. For example, on July 19, 1563, the Milanese bishop, Charles Vicecom (Ventimiliensis), wrote to Cardinal Borromeo about the canons on marriage as they were being conceived but before they had been proposed, noting that the words of the sixth canon were contrary to "the opinion of Ambrose" and that the Council fathers will have to decide whether to publish the teaching as a "decree without anathema." "Perché le parole del sesto son contrarie all'opinione di Ambrose, i padri deputati per non dannar l' opinione di quel santo dottore, sì come avverrà, formando i canoni per Anathema: hanno fatto sopra di ciò un altro decreto senza Anathema, qual sarà notato in margine; i quali canoni si proporranno alla sinodo, che in ciò eleggerà quel che li parrà più espediente." CT, IX, 640n1.

vast majority of fathers simply did not regard this contrary opinion as an obstacle to a solemn definition of the indissolubility of marriage in cases of adultery.

Fransen says something worth underlining: "The attempt not to condemn the Greeks together with the Protestants was only a secondary reason, because it would have been defended in each case merely by a particular group of fathers of the council especially the Venetians."[97] This is true. The other fathers were far removed from the pastoral concerns of the Venetian prelates, and certainly would not have been willing to compromise the doctrinal content of the canon in order to accommodate what to them would have been a very narrow concern.

Proposed Reformulation of Canon 7 by Lotharingus

Recall that Lorraine was the first to speak after the Venetian delegation sat down. He recommended adding the words "iuxta Scripturas" after the phrase "when she taught and teaches."[98] In this way, he meant to ensure that the proposition "that on account of adultery marriage cannot be dissolved" was understood to be in accord with scripture. At the end of the discussion of the second formulation, on or around August 23, Lorraine proposes a reformulated version of canon 7:

> If anyone says the catholic church has erred or errs when she taught and teaches by the Sacred Scriptures, that on account of the adultery of a spouse the bond of marriage cannot be dissolved, and that both of the spouses, or at least the innocent one who gave no cause for adultery, cannot contract another marriage while the other spouse is living, and that he commits adultery who dismisses an adulteress and remarries, and she commits adultery who dismisses an adulterer and remarries: let him be anathema.[99]

We see that Lorraine adopts an indirect approach consistent with the Venetian proposal. But he amends the proposal in certain important ways. First, he changes the normative phrase "non debere ... contrahere" ("should

---

97. Fransen, "Ehescheidung Bei Ehebruch," 182.
98. CT, IX, 687.
99. CT, IX, 724.44–49: "Si quis dixerit, ecclesiam catholicam errasse vel errare, quando, propter adulterium alterius coniugum, docuit et docet, idque per Scripturas sacras, matrimonii vinculum non posse dissolvi, et utrumque coniugum, vel saltem innocentem, qui causam adulterio non dederit, non posse, altero coniuge vivente, aliud matrimonium contrahere, et moechari eum, qui dimissa adultera aliam duxerit, et eam, quae dimisso adultero alii nupserit: anathema sit."

not...contract") to "non posse...contrahere" ("cannot...contract"). This suggests that indissolubility is a property of the marriage bond; that not only is it wrong to attempt remarriage after divorce, but impossible. Second, consistent with Lorraine's earlier recommendation, he introduces the phrase "per Scripturas sacras" (by sacred scripture) to ensure that the doctrine of indissolubility is understood to have its origin in the teaching of divine revelation; that not only is it a matter of church law, but also of divine law.[100] In addition, Lorraine tightens Venice's formulation by replacing the term *matrimonium* (marriage) with the more precise term *matrimonii vinculum* (bond of marriage).

Third Formulation on the Canons on Matrimony (September 5, 1563)

Before we consider the final phase of the process of development of Trent's teaching on marital indissolubility, let us take stock of the Council's deliberations on indissolubility up to this point. Stemming from its earliest recorded statements at Bologna in April 1547 on the nature of marriage and the question of divorce and remarriage, through each stage of deliberation between the Congregation of Theologians, the Prelate Theologians and especially the General Congregation, up to the second formulation of the canons on matrimony at Trent in August 1563, the great majority of fathers affirmed that the bond of a validly contracted marriage is indissoluble; that no cause, not even adultery, can rupture that bond; that marital indissolubility is taught in divine revelation; and that remarriage after divorce is always illicit. We see their willingness to define solemnly marriage's indissolubility as a truth of faith in cases of adultery and directly condemn those who denied the teaching.

After the Venetian intervention, the opinion of the majority turns in favor of an indirect condemnation of the denial of indissolubility. They now resolve to make the blunt weight of the anathema fall on the Protestant Reformers, who denied both the indissolubility of marriage and the church's power of jurisdiction over the sacrament, and not on Greek Christians living on Mediterranean islands under Venetian (i.e., Roman Catholic) control. At the same time, they want to teach definitively the truth of marital indissolubility and rule out the possibility of remarriage after divorce. This

---

100. Spanish bishop, Anthony Gueron (Almeriensis), expressed this concern earlier: "ne innuatur, hoc esse iuris ecclesiastici tantum, non autem divini" (lest it give the impression that this is only a matter of church law, but not divine law) (CT, IX, 721.30–31).

gives rise to a clear but delicate *modus operandi* that maintained features from prior Council discussions, but also expressed a distinct concern: how to formulate a dogmatic canon that would condemn the Protestants, teach absolute indissolubility, and cause the least disturbance possible for mixed communities of Greek and Latin Christians.

On September 5, 1563, the *deputatio* presented to the General Congregation a third schema with twelve reformulated canons on marriage. The third formulation of canon 7 reads:

If anyone says the church errs because she taught that in accordance with the evangelical and apostolic doctrine, marriage cannot be dissolved on account of the adultery of a spouse, and that neither spouse, even the innocent one, who gave no cause for adultery, can contract another marriage while the other spouse is living, and that he commits adultery who dismisses an adulterous wife and marries another, and she commits adultery who dismisses an adulterous husband and marries another; let him be anathema.[101]

We see first that the *deputatio* adopts an indirect formulation consistent with the Venetian proposal. But it departs from Venice's formulation in two important ways. In adapting Lorraine's suggestion, the Council adds the phrase "iuxta evangelicam et apostolicam doctrinam" (in accordance with the evangelical and apostolic doctrine). This formula is derived from canon 17 of the Second Council of Mileve (416): "secundum evangelicam et apostolicam disciplinam."[102] The term's inclusion has a double significance. At Trent the Council of Mileve was held to have the authority of an ecumenical council. Not only was Augustine believed to have attended it, but Pope Innocent was thought to have solemnly confirmed its teachings. The Spanish bishop Didacus of Leon (Columbriensis) says as much in his approval of the first formulation of canon 6.[103] Because the Council of Mi-

---

101. CT, IX, 760.21–25: "Si quis dixerit, ecclesiam errare, quod iuxta evangelicam et apostolicam doctrinam propter adulterium alterius coniugum matrimonium non posse dissolvi docuit, et utrumque vel etiam innocentem, qui causam adulterio non dedit, non posse, altero coniuge vivente, aliud matrimonium contrahere, moecharique eum, qui dimissa adultera aliam duxerit, et eam, quae dimisso adultero alii nupserit: anathema sit."

102. See appendix A, p. 194, for discussion of the authenticity of the canon's origins at Mileve.

103. CT, IX, 673.12–14: "Canon 6 should remain as it is, with an anathema, because this was decreed by the Council of Mileve, which has the authority of a General Council." The Spanish Dominican archbishop of Bracarensis (Braga, now in Portugal), Bartolomé de Los Mártyres, says this even more strongly. Bracarensis led the Spanish delegation to Trent; he was considered a respected theologian and historian, authoring a history of church councils while in attendance at the Council. In that work, Bracarensis states: "Here are placed the letters of the Councils of Carthage and Mileve sent to the aforementioned Innocent in which the errors

leve's authority had been referenced many times during the discussions on marriage by the theologians and fathers, we can be certain that by September 1563, most everyone would have been familiar with canon 17. Adopting the Milevian formula in its affirmation of indissolubility suggests that the Council wanted to strengthen the *de facto* authority of the new and indirect formulation by its identification with the fifth-century Council. Second, in affirming that the doctrine of indissolubility is "iuxta evangelicam et apostolicam doctrinam," the Council closely identifies it with sources of revelation. But notice that Trent changes the word *disciplinam* to *doctrinam*. This reinforces this identification by reducing the likelihood that the proposition affirming indissolubility would be misunderstood as simply a custom or changeable rule of conduct.[104]

The reformulation also departs from Venice's formulation by changing—in accord with the recommendation of Lorraine—the normative phrase "non debere aliud matrimonium contrahere" (should not contract another marriage) to the substantive phrase "non posse ... contrahere" (cannot ... contract another marriage). As stated above, this suggests that marital permanence is not merely a disciplinary norm, but rather a substantive quality of marriage denoting the impossibility of remarriage after divorce.[105]

A further addition is made on the same day. For the first time, the *deputatio* proposes a formulation of a developed doctrinal *praefatio* (preface) to the canons on matrimony.[106] In order to obviate a time-consuming discussion by the General Congregation, the two prefaces (i.e., the August 7 *titulus* and this doctrinal *praefatio*) are juxtaposed and the Council fathers are asked to choose between them.[107] The preface will undergo consider-

---

of the Pelagians are condemned, and he himself responds to them with a letter, and confirms the condemnation of the named errors, and confirms the things determined at the Council of Mileve" (Hic ponuntur epistolae Concilii Carthaginensis, & Concilii Milevitani ad dictum Innocentium, in quibus damnantur errores Pelagianorum, & ipse respondet illis per epistolam, & confirmat damnationem dictorum errorum, & confirmat definita in Concilio Milevitano). Venerabilis Servi Dei, D. Bartholomaei a Martyribus, "Summa Conciliorum Omnium: tam generalium, quam provincialium," in *Opera Omnia*, tom 1 (Rome: Jerome Mainardi at Monte Citatorio Square, 1734), 363.

104. This point is also made in Ryan and Grisez, "Indissoluble Marriage," 401n145.

105. Two further points are worth noting. First, the term "marriage" remains as in Venice's proposal rather than Lorraines's "matrimonii vinculum" (bond of marriage). Second, the phrases "errasse vel errare" (has erred or errs) and "docuit et docet" (taught and teaches) are rendered simply "errare" (errs) and "docuit" (in having taught).

106. See appendix B.

107. The title reads: "Nova praefatio canonibus sacramenti matrimonii praeponenda, si patribus absque disceptatione placuerit loco illius, quae incipit *Sacrosancta* etc." (CT, IX, 761.5).

able expansion before finally being promulgated, but this first formulation teaches the following: the bond of marriage is "perpetual and indissoluble"; this is taught under the inspiration of the Holy Spirit in the book of Genesis (2:23–24), and again more clearly (*diserte*) by Jesus in the Gospels (e.g., Mt 19:5–6); Jesus further confirmed the permanent nature of the indissolubility of marriage when he said: "What God has joined, let no man separate"; the law of the Gospel, perfecting natural love, infuses marriage with grace thus making the spousal union holy; and finally, in order to root out these errors and heresies against the doctrine of the indissolubility and sacramentality of marriage, the Council "hos in ipsos haeresiarchas eorumque sectatores decrevit" (decree[s] against these very heresiarchs and their followers) twelve anathemas.

The preface serves as a theological introduction establishing a doctrinal framework within which to read and understand the twelve canons. This is critically important to our considerations. On the same day that the Council proposes for the first time an indirect formulation for canon 7, it concurrently proposes a hermeneutical framework for understanding and interpreting that canon (and the others).[108] More will be said on this in chapter 5. Finally, it is worth noting that no changes were made in the third schema to canon 5 condemning anyone who says that marriage can be dissolved on account of heresy, irksome cohabitation, or willful desertion.[109]

Examination of the Third Formulation of Canons

The discussion of the third schema by the General Congregation ran from September 7 to 10, 1563. The opinions of 202 fathers are recorded.[110] Lorraine again leads off the discussion. The cardinal reiterates his earlier recommendations that the more precise term *matrimonii vinculum* (bond of marriage) replace *matrimonium* (marriage) and the more capacious term *docuit and docet* (taught and teaches) replace the simpler *docuit* (having taught).[111] Significantly, fifty-six Council fathers follow Lorraine, including the archbishop of Rossano (Rossanensis), the future Pope Urban VII.[112] Two more,

---

108. Among those who offer opinions on the introductory statements, fifty-six bishops preferred the new preface, seven of whom suggested it should be expanded; nineteen preferred the old one; ten said that they approved both; and three said that both should be combined into a single preface. See appendix table B-5, for the opinions of the bishops.

109. CT, IX, 760.17–18.

110. CT, IX, 779–94.

111. CT, IX, 779.23–24.

112. See appendix table B-6, column 2. Most of these say generally that they follow Lorraine in his annotations of the canons, not mentioning canon 7 explicitly.

Reginus and Ilerdensis, affirm the addition of "vinculum matrimonii."[113] Interestingly, five fathers request that the prior direct formulation be restored.[114] Among these is the bishop of León (Legionensis), member of the *deputatio*. He says the canon should be formulated as it had been when it was first drafted; or if an indirect approach is used, then the canon should assert plainly: "If anyone says, the church erred when she taught and teaches the evangelical doctrine."[115] In directly calling the doctrine of indissolubility an "evangelicam doctrinam" and not merely "iuxta evangelicam doctrinam" all ambiguity is removed that what the church has taught and teaches is "identical with what is taught by the gospel and Paul."[116] The bishop of Nicosia in Cyprus (Nicosiensis) is even more to the point: canon 7 should assert that "marriage is—by divine law—indissoluble."[117] The largest number, ninety-six—46 percent of the fathers—offer no comment on canon 7, indicating that they are content with the formulation.[118]

Significant to our considerations is the fact that fifteen bishops either directly or indirectly disapprove of the new canon because it conflicts with the practices of the Greeks and/or condemns the "holy fathers."[119] This includes the influential bishops of Segovia (Segobiensis) and Granada (Granatensis), both leaders of Council factions arguing that scripture does not prohibit remarriage after adultery.[120] Several argue that the canon should be published without the anathema.[121] This raises an obvious problem for those who argue that the turn to an indirect formulation signaled the intention of the Council fathers to overcome the problem of conflict-

---

113. Reginus (CT, IX, 783.37–38); Ilerdensis (789.34–35).

114. Augustensis (CT, IX, 789), Legionensis (789), Almeriensis (789), Columbriensis (792), Jesuits (794)

115. CT, IX, 789.26–28: "[Canon] 7. ponatur qui erat in principio, vel: *Si quis dixerit, ecclesiam errasse, cum evangelicam doctrinam docuit et docet.*"

116. Fransen, "Divorce on the Ground of Adultery," 95.

117. CT, IX, 782.31: "In 7 dicatur, matrimonium divino iure esse indissolubile."

118. See appendix table B-6, column 7.

119. Granatensis (CT, IX, 780), Segobiensis (785), Naulensis (786), Mutinensis (786), Calamonensis (786), Alessanensis (788), Aquensis (789), Ostunensis (790), Uxentinus (790), Massaelubrensis (791), Lucensis (792), Praemisliensis (793), and Cauriensis (794).

120. During the General Congregation's discussion of the first formulation of the canon on indissolubility, Segobiensis says that prominent Church Fathers understood the gospels to permit a separation of bond; he is the first to propose an indirect formulation for the canon (CT, IX, 656.42–657.1, 4–6). During the General Congregation's discussion of the second formulation, Granatensis approves the Venetian formula recommending that the words "secundum Scripturas" be removed (689.16). Each has a cohort of bishops who follow his recommendations.

121. Praemisliensis (CT, IX, 793); Mutinensis (786); three bishops follow Mutinensis: Alessanensis (788), Aquensis (789), and Massaelubrensis (791).

ing authorities and the divorce practices of Greek Christians. By focusing exclusively on the denial of the Catholic church's jurisdiction over marriage, and not the substantive issue of indissolubility, the canon should be understood to exempt the divorce practices of the Greeks. But because some of the strongest defenders of a limited doctrine of indissolubility still see the canon as representing a strict conception of the doctrine, we may conclude that in the mind of these fathers at least, and probably in the mind of the majority, the turn to an indirect formulation was not taken as overcoming the doctrinal obstacle to the Greek divorce practices.

Fourth Formulation on the Canons on Matrimony (October 13, 1563)

The *deputatio* proposed the fourth schema on October 13 offering minor revisions on canons 1, 3, 4, 7, and 9. Canon 7 reads:

If anyone says the Church erroneously taught and teaches, in accordance with the evangelical and apostolic doctrine, that the bond of marriage cannot be dissolved on account of the adultery of a spouse, and that neither spouse, even the innocent one, who gave no cause for adultery, can contract another marriage while the other spouse is living, and that he commits adultery who dismisses an adulterous wife and marries another, and she commits adultery who dismisses an adulterous husband and marries another; let him be anathema.[122]

Two noticeable changes have been made consistent with the recommendations of the influential cardinal of Lorraine. In the first, the term "marriage" is changed to the more precise "bond of marriage." In the second alteration, the *deputatio* replaces *docuit* (taught) with *docuit et docet* (taught and teaches). We will discuss both alterations in more depth in chapter 5.

The *deputatio* also distributed a new formulation of the *praefatio*.[123] Like the first formulation, the new version asserts that the bond of marriage is perpetual and indissoluble; and that this is a teaching of divine revelation, found in both the Old and New Testaments. When it refers to the sacramentality of Christian marriage, it adds that Christ's grace "indissolu-

---

122. CT, IX, 889.14–18: "Si quis dixerit, ecclesiam errare, quod iuxta evangelicam et apostolicam doctrinam propter adulterium alterius coniugum matrimonii vinculum non posse dissolvi docuit et docet, et utrumque, vel etiam innocentem, qui causam adulterio non dedit, non posse, altero coniuge vivente, aliud matrimonium contrahere, moecharique eum, qui dimissa adultera aliam duxerit, et eam, quae dimisso adultero alii nupserit: anathema sit."

123. CT, IX, 888–89.22; the reformulation is reproduced in Latin and English in appendix B.

bilem unitatem confirmaret" (strengthen[s] the indissoluble unity) of the spouses. Finally, whereas in the first formulation, anathemas are said to be decreed against the heresiarchs and their followers, in the second, they are against "ipsos errores et haeresiarchas" (these very errors and heresiarchs).

Examination of the Fourth Formulation of Canons

The General Congregation's examination of the canons ran from October 26 to 27, 1563. A total of 162 fathers comment with the briefest statements of the four examinations.[124] Eighty-one fathers either explicitly or indirectly approve of canon 7, and another twenty-four offer no comment, suggesting they have no problem with the fourth formulation.[125] Several argue for minor emendations. For example, two bishops argue that the canon should be made more precise and clear and an additional eight recommend that *docuit et docet* (taught and teaches) be replaced by *docuisse* (has taught).[126] Seven fathers, led by Archbishop Pedro Guerrero (Granatensis), still believe the formulation is incompatible with the opinions of *multorum sanctorum* (many saints) or at least should be published without the anathema; most are familiar critics, especially Guerro himself, but also Spanish bishop Melchior a Vosmediano, who had argued against both the canon's first and second formulations because they were published with an anathema.[127] One member of this cohort, however, is new to the opposition. The English bishop Thomas Godvellus (Assaphaensis), who had approved the first

---

124. See appendix tables B-7 and B-8.
125. See appendix table B-8, columns 1, 2, and 7.
126. The recommendation is made by the Cardinal Deacon Madruzio of Trent (Madrutius) (CT, IX, 898) and followed by seven other bishops: Rheginus (899), Pragensis (899), Senonensis (900), Pactensis (901), Atrebatensis (903), Caprulanus (904), and Rossensis (905). Panormitanus: "6. et 7. lucidiores fiant" (900.7–8); Civitatis Castelli: "clarius concipiatur" (904.33).
127. Granatensis (CT, IX, 899), Callarensis (899), Montismarani (902), Assaphaensis (903), Guadiscensis (905), Oppidensis (905), and Bobiensis (905). Interestingly, Archbishop Guerrero defended the *direct* formulation during the General Congregation's discussion of the first formulation of canon 6 in July 1563 (644.14). But he seems to have been persuaded by the Venetian intervention because he begins to defend an indirect formulation in his comments on the second formulation (688.15–16); he begins to worry that a direct formulation will "sancti doctores damnentur" (condemn the holy doctors) who hold contrary opinions (689.15). In the third formulation his position hardens; he even rejects the first indirect formulation of canon 7 (third formulation) believing it too condems "plures sancti patres" (many holy fathers) (780.51–52). Spanish bishop Melchior a Vosmediano (Guadiscensis) disapproves of the first and second formulations of the canon saying in both cases it should be published without the anathema (see 672.12 and 732.3).

indirect formulation of canon 7, now argues it should be published without an anathema.[128] The reason for his change is not disclosed.

Most revealing, however, is that the largest cohort of disapprovals is made up of bishops who are dissatisfied with the indirect formulation. Sixteen fathers reject it outright, arguing for a return to a stricter formulation.[129] The two leaders of this cohort are the Hungarian bishop, George Draskovic of Quinqueecclesiensis, and the Spanish bishop, Andres Cuesta (Legionensis). Draskovic says frankly he "rejects the formulation because it says: *if anyone says the church errs,*" and again later, that he rejects it "because of the added clause *ecclesiam errare*," adding that "the canon remains most reasonable and catholic even without [the clause]."[130] Seven bishops follow him in his remarks.[131] Moreover, Cuesta says "the canon should be restored to the first (direct) formulation."[132] Recall that on the first formulation, Cuesta had argued "pluribus rationibus" (for many reasons) for a direct formulation of the canon on indissolubility.[133] He continued to defend it when the fathers were turning towards the Venetian formulation in August, specifically noting the need for the anathema.[134] And in September, when the *deputatio* formally proposed the indirect formulation, he argued

---

128. He followed Lorraine's recommendations (see CT, IX, 788.25–26). Two other bishops who disapprove of the canon both offered no comment on the prior formulation (third formulation): Bobiensis (792) and Oppidensis (793).

129. Gerundensis (CT, IX, 903), Quinqueecclesiensis (903), Legionensis (903), Almeriensis (903), Clusinus (904), Neocastrensis (904), Hyprensis (904), Namurcensis (905), Columbriensis (905), Pennensis (905), Pampilonensis (905), Monopolitanus (905), Achadensis (905), Usellensis (906), Stephanus (906), and Eutitius (906).

130. For the first quotation, see Quinqueecclesiensis (CT, IX, 903.39–40). We might wonder why he reacts so strongly in October when his two immediately previous opinions (on the second and third formulations) were more detached. In August on the direct formulation of canon 7 he says simply that he agrees with a majority of fathers (recall the majority at the time was turning towards the Venetian recommendation; see 721) and in September that he generally approves the canons following Lotharingus, who recommended that "bond of marriage" replace "marriage" and "taught and teaches" replace "taught" (see 790; for Lotharingus's remarks see 779). We gain clarity, however, when we go back to his remarks on the first formulation of the canon (c. 6) in July; there he argues the canon should be published "as is" and replies to the problem of conflicting authorities with the maxim of Vincent of Lerins, that we should hold to the "common judgment of the fathers," and not to the opinions "of some particular saint" (665.9–13). For the second quotation, see CT, IX, 975.26–27: "7. canon non placet propter adiectam clausulam *ecclesiam errare*, quia etiam absque eo canon verissimus est et catholicus"; this was from his final *votum* during the solemn session.

131. Clusinus (CT, IX, 904), Neocastrensis (904), Pennensis (905), Monopolitanus (905), Achadensis (905), Stephanus (906), and Eutitius (906).

132. CT, IX, 903.42: "Legionensi 7. non placet, sed maneat (primus canon prius positus)."
133. See CT, IX, 665.34.
134. See CT, IX, 721.8–9.

for a return to the direct formulation, but added that if this could not be done, then the Council should explicitly refer to indissolubility in cases of adultery as an "evangelicam doctrinam" (doctrine of the Gospel).[135] Spanish bishops Peter Fragi (Usellensis) and Arias Gagliego (Gerundensis), and Flemish bishop Martin Rithovius (Hyprensis), follow Cuesta in his call for a return to a stricter formulation.[136] This strengthened opposition is in contrast to the only five bishops who during the discussion of the third formulation argued for a return to a direct formulation.[137]

Fransen asks why so many bishops opposed canon 7 in October 1563 when just a month earlier there were "almost no objections."[138] He says it is because of the phrasing of the preface. The first preface of September 5 announces the intention of the Council to condemn "in ipsos haeresiarchas eorumque sectatores" (these very heresiarchs and their followers). This, Fransen believes, was "an unambiguous way" of ensuring that the Protestants were solely affected by the canons that followed, leaving untouched the Greeks with their divorce practices. In October, the formulation was changed to "these errors and heresiarchs." This, he says, changes the "Tragweite" (scope) of the canons that followed. By condemning now not only the heretics, but also the "errores," the formulation apparently raised the concern that "the Greeks and even the older fathers of the church could be affected by this anathema," and so we see an upsurge in disapprovals.[139]

When subjected to scrutiny, this interpretation shows itself to be without foundation. First, Fransen says that "45 bishops oppose Canon 7," but only thirty-one can be reliably categorized as opponents of the fourth formulation.[140] Second, we have already demonstrated that the most frequent reason given for opposing the October formulation was disapproval of the indirect formulation. Far from fearing that the teaching on marriage was too strict, these fathers opted to make it stricter. Third, among the fathers arguing that the fourth formulation condemns the opinions of many saints, only the motives of Thomas Godvellus (Assaphaensis)—who first approved of indirect formulation, then later argues it should be published without an anathema—are left unclear. Fourth, if the implications of the new preface were a concern, we would expect at least a few fathers to men-

135. See CT, IX, 789.26–27.
136. Usellensis (CT, IX, 906), Hyprensis (also called Yprensis) (904), and Gerundensis (903).
137. See appendix table B-6, column 6.
138. Fransen, "Ehescheidung Bei Ehebruch," 195.
139. Ibid., 195–96.
140. See the introductory remarks to appendix table B-7.

tion this. But of the 162 opinions, not one mentions or even hints at a problem with the words "ipsos errores et haeresiarchas."[141]

SESSION 24

Final and Definitive Formulations of the Canons (November 11, 1553)

On November 11, at the start of session 24, Trent published its final teaching on the sacrament of marriage in the form of twelve canons (*canones*) each setting forth erroneous propositions and ending in "anathema sit," preceded by a doctrinal preface (*doctrina*), and followed by ten paragraphs or chapters (*capita*) on reform.[142] Other than the simple rearrangement of a few words, canon 7 is identical to the fourth formulation.[143]

If anyone says the church errs, when she has taught and teaches, in accordance with the evangelical and apostolic doctrine, that the bond of marriage cannot be dissolved on account of the adultery of a spouse, and that neither spouse, even one who is innocent and gave no cause for adultery, can contract another marriage while the other spouse is living, and that he commits adultery who dismisses an adulterous wife and marries another, and she commits adultery who dismisses an adulterous husband and marries another; let him be anathema.[144]

---

141. There are however multiple suggestions for strengthening the *doctrina*. Madrutius: replace the words "two only are to be coupled by this bond" with words of Paul saying "Christ loved the church," and refer to the authority of the apostle John (CT, IX, 898.37–40). S. Severinae: note two effects of the sacrament, i.e., "God is pleased with the couple, and they have children" (899.22–23). Corcyrensis: change "indicates" to "testifies" (899.33). Verdunensis: change "perpetual" to "stable" (901.14–16). Both Lucensis and Aliphanus: *doctrina* should be "uberior" (expanded) (905.28, 32–33). Usellensis: "condemn not only the heresiarchs, but also their followers" (906.1–3). Servites: replace "idem Christus" with "ipse Christus" (906.18–19).

142. These too are referred to in the record as canons; but they are expository with no anathemas.

143. The four words "cum docuit et docet" are moved from the second line to the third clause in the first line and the word "quod" is dropped. The canon's translation is not effected.

144. CT, IX, 967.31–35: "Si quis dixerit, ecclesiam errare, cum docuit et docet, iuxta evangelicam et apostolicam doctrinam, propter adulterium alterius coniugum matrimonii vinculum non posse dissolvi, et utrumque, vel etiam innocentem, qui causam adulterio non dedit, non posse, altero coniuge vivente, aliud matrimonium contrahere, moecharique eum, qui dimissa adultera aliam duxerit, et eam, quae dimisso adultero alii nupserit: anathema sit."

The Doctrinal Preface[145]

The third and final version of the doctrinal preface is also nearly identical to the previous formulation.

Inspired by the Holy Spirit, the forefather of the human race pronounced marriage to be a perpetual and indissoluble bond when he said: *This at last is bone of my bones and flesh of my flesh. Therefore a man shall leave his father and mother and cleave to his wife, and the two shall become one flesh.*

Christ our Lord taught more clearly that the two are to be coupled and joined only by this bond when, referring to the words just quoted as spoken by God, he said: *So they are no longer two, but one flesh*, and went on at once to confirm the lasting nature of the same bond, declared by Adam so much earlier, with these words, *What therefore God has joined, let no man separate.*

And the grace that would perfect that natural love, strengthen the indissoluble unity, and sanctify the spouses, Christ himself—the instituter and perfecter of the venerable sacraments—merited for us by his passion. The Apostle Paul implied this, saying: *Husbands love your wives, just as Christ loved the church and gave himself up for her*, adding shortly after: *This is a great mystery*; but I mean, in Christ and the church.

Since therefore marriage in the law of the Gospel exceeds the old marriages by means of grace through Christ, our holy fathers, and councils, and the universal tradition of the church have always taught that marriage is rightly to be numbered among the sacraments of the new law. Against this tradition, impious and senseless men of this age have not only thought falsely about this venerable sacrament, but introducing the license of the flesh as is their habit under pretext of the Gospel, they have said and written many things that are inconsistent with the understanding of the catholic church and with custom approved from apostolic times, causing great damage to the Christian faithful. Desiring to confront their temerity, the holy and universal council has decided that the more glaring heresies and errors of the aforementioned schismatics must be rooted out, lest more people be drawn to their deadly contagion, decreeing against these heretics themselves and their errors the following anathemas:

All the modifications are matters of minor punctuation, non-substantial grammatical alterations, or change of functional location of words.[146] Even

---

145. CT, IX, 966.28–967.15. For all three versions of the doctrinal preface in Latin and English, see appendix B.

146. In the first paragraph "ex carne" is changed to "de carne," and "suam" is deleted from "matrem suam." In the third paragraph, "ipsos" is deleted from "ipsosque coniuges" and the conjunction is changed to "coniugesque," and "idem Christus" is changed to "ipse Christus" in accord with the recommendation of the General of the Servites (see 906.18–19). In the final paragraph the term "connumerandum" is changed to "annumerandum," "praefatorum" is

the change in the final sentence from "hos in ipsos errores et haeresiarchas" (against these very errors and heresiarchs) to "hos in ipsos haereticos eorumque errores" (against these heretics and their errors) leaves unchanged both the meaning of the preface and the scope of the canons that follow, since, as chapter 5 will demonstrate, the "errors of the heretics" (meaning especially Luther and Calvin) include a denial of the doctrine of indissolubility not only in cases of adultery, but in other cases as well.

The *Vota* of the Council Fathers on the *Doctrina* and Canon 7

The Council secretary, Angelo Massarelli, assisted by two Council notaries, questioned each father singly as to whether he approved of the finalized formulation of the *doctrina* and twelve canons.[147] Each father responded with a solemn *votum*—his final and definitive judgment on the texts. The comments of 200 fathers are recorded; 194 say they approve the *doctrina* and canon 7.[148] Three register disapproval with canon 7. Quinqueecclesiensis says it is because of the indirect formulation beginning with the words "the Church errs"; he says "the canon remains most reasonable and catholic even without [this clause]."[149] Praemisliensis disapproves because the canon is published with the anathema.[150] Pampilonensis registers a *non placet* with no explanation. But we infer from his comments on the fourth formulation that he disapproves of the indirect formulation.[151] Three others offer no direct or indirect judgment on canon 7 or the doctrina.[152]

The primate of the Mediterranean island of Cyprus, Filippo Mocenicos, archbishop of Nicosia (Nicosiensis), still fears that suspicion may be aroused in Greek Christians living on the Mediterranean islands by the addition of canon 7. So supported by his suffragans, Girolam Ragazzonus,

---

changed to "praedictorum," and the words "errores et haereses" are reversed to read "haereses et errores."

147. See CT, IX, 971.15–20.

148. See appendix table B-9.

149. CT, IX, 975.26–27: "7. canon non placet propter adiectam clausulam *ecclesiam errare*, quia etiam absque eo canon verissimus est et catholicus."

150. CT, IX, 976.50–51: "6. et 7. can., quod illis canonibus sit appositum anathema, non placet."

151. CT, IX, 977.9; for comments on fourth formulation, see 905.26, where he says he follows Almariensis's *non placet*.

152. Two papal legates, Moronus (CT, IX, 971) and Varmiensis (see 1007–8n343), and Bishop Iprensis (976). Since none opposed canon 7 or the *doctrina*, silence was taken as an approval.

auxiliary bishop of Famagusta (Famagustanus) and Francesco Contarini, bishop of Paphos (Paphensis)—all three, incidentally, were members of the Venetian delegation—Nicosiensis asks that an excerpt be printed under his name in the Council proceedings.[153] The excerpt is taken from a letter published in the proceedings of a provincial council held at Cyprus in 1340.[154] By way of introduction, the excerpt sets forth a lengthy avowal of the fidelity of Greek, Maronite, and Armenian bishops and Christians (presumably under Roman jurisdiction) to the articles of faith and teachings on the sacraments of the Roman church, of the free and open confession by these same Christians of everything said to be true by that fourteenth-century council, and of their promise to respect and be obedient to the Roman pontiff.[155] It culminates in the request: "We humbly ask, that they be permitted to remain in their customs, which are not contrary to the faith, and we entreat the said lord Archbishop to deign to make known to the Supreme Lord Pontiff their devotion."[156] The phrase "in suis ritibus" recalls the phrase "antiquissimum ritum suorum patrum" (the most ancient custom of their fathers) used by the Venetian delegates, referring, of course, to the Greek divorce practices.[157]

153. Famagustanus: "sed petit, quod petiit D. Nicosiensis quoad Graecos" (CT, IX, 977.3-4). Paphensis: "approbat ea, quae dixit Nicosiensis quoad Graecos" (CT, IX, 977.32).

154. CT, IX, 972.43-46, 973.2-3: "Peto tamen, ne de recta et orthodoxa Graecorum, qui in regno Cypri sunt, fide aliqua suspicio in hac sancta synodo, occasione eorum, quae circa septimum canonem adducta fuerunt, oriri possit.... Verba excerpta ex concilio provinciali regni Cypri, celebrato sub R. P. D. Helia archiep. Nicosiensi etc. a. 1340, quae in fine dicti concilii sunt."

155. CT, IX, 973.3-18: "Memorati Graecorum, Maronitarum et Armenorum episcopi, et praemissarum aliarum nationum maiores pro se et subditis suis, intellectis omnibus et singulis supradictis, et super singulis articulis fidei, et ecclesiae sacramentis, ac aliis in dicta serie comprehensis, singuli singulariter, universaliter universi iuxta religionem infrascriptorum interpretum clare, aperte, distincte et singulariter et explicite recognoverunt humiliter et devote et spontanea voluntate, omni timore semoto, et quacumque [co]actione cessante, humili professione confessi sunt, et devote confessione professi, illa omnia et singula, <in dicti scripti serie> comprehensa, vera esse, et quod illa omnia et singula firmiter credebant, prout superius explicite declarantur, adiicientes rationes, quod ita erat ab omnibus Catholicis absque dubietate credendum, et quod sacrosancta Romana ecclesia erat mater omnium fidelium et magistra, super omnes ecclesias plenum principatum obtinens et primatum, et quod S^{mus} in Christo pater D. Benedictus, divina providentia Papa XII, successor B. Petri et in terris vicarius Iesu Christi, erat cunctorum fidelium pater, pastor et dominus, cui singuli praelati ecclesiarum omnium debent reverentiam humilem, ipsique reverentiam eidem et obedientiam promittebant."

156. CT, IX, 973.18-20: "Petentes humiliter, quod eis liceret, in suis ritibus, fidei non contrariis, permanere, ac deprecantes dictum D. archiepiscopum, ut devotionem eorum intimare D. Summo Pontifici dignaretur."

157. CT, IX, 686.18-19: "consuevisse Graecos, fornicariam uxorem dimittere et aliam ducere."

Fransen argues that the inclusion of this excerpt into the record implies that "the council approves and declares that the Greeks are not affected by the 7th canon."[158] Fransen's claim is plainly false. The included excerpt stands simply as the recorded statement of the Mediterranean primate and his suffragans and should not be taken as expressing the will of the Council. We know this because at the end of the voting, after Cardinal Moroni announced that "the *doctrina* and canons on the sacrament of marriage were approved by all," he adds, "in some instances, however, some fathers desired some things [quaedam] to be added or subtracted."[159] These *things* included requests both that the words "ecclesiam errare" be deleted from canon 7, as well as that the canon be published without the anathema. Obviously neither of these suggestions is carried out. We know therefore that the simple inclusion of a statement in the *Acta* during the *vota* should not be taken as an affirmation by the entire Council of the proposition asserted in it. Indeed, *pace* Fransen, Nicosiensis's demand for the excerpt's inclusion illustrates his anxiety that the final formulation does not in fact leave Greek Christians free to practice their "most ancient custom."

158. "Damit wird zum letzten Male und in offizieller Weise—da diese Erklärung ausdrücklich in die Akten der Session aufgenommen wurde—vom Konzil gutgeheißen und bestätigt, daß die Griechen vom 7. Kanon nicht betroffen werden." Fransen, "Ehescheidung Bei Ehebruch," 196–97.

159. CT, IX, 977.47–49: "Doctrina et canones de sacramento matrimonii approvata fuere ab omnibus; aliqui tamen in nonnullis desiderarent quaedam adiici et detrahi."

CHAPTER 5

TRENT'S TEACHING ON INDISSOLUBILITY

The Council of Trent published its final and definitive teaching on the sacrament of marriage on November 11, 1563 (session 24). Relating specifically to the doctrine of indissolubility, the Council promulgated two dogmatic canons, canons 5 and 7, and a doctrinal preface. Chapter 4 reviewed the minor distinctions between the fourth reform/revision and the Council's final formulations, and summarized the *vota* of the General Congregation on the final teaching. This chapter considers the meaning of the three promulgated texts.

DOCTRINAL INTRODUCTION

Recall that on the same day that the *deputatio* first proposed an indirect formulation for canon 7, it also proposed the first formulation of a preface introducing the canons on marriage. This was consistent with the petitions of Virdunensis and twenty-four bishops, who in July had requested that an introduction precede the canons. Its purpose would be to set forth truths on the sacrament of marriage first in positive form, followed by the canons which would single out certain of those truths that were being denied by heretics.[1] Between July and November, the preface underwent two signifi-

---

1. It also serves as an introduction to the ten "Canones super reformatione circa matrimonium" (Canons on the reform of marriage) that follow the twelve dogmatic canons on marriage (CT, IX, 968–71).

cant reformulations. On November 11, it was published with the title "*doctrina*" and read as follows.[2]

Inspired by the Holy Spirit, the forefather of the human race pronounced marriage to be a perpetual and indissoluble bond when he said: *This at last is bone of my bones and flesh of my flesh. Therefore a man shall leave his father and mother and cleave to his wife, and the two shall become one flesh.*

Christ our Lord taught more clearly that the two are to be coupled and joined only by this bond when, referring to the words just quoted as spoken by God, he said: *So they are no longer two, but one flesh,* and went on at once to confirm the lasting nature of the same bond, declared by Adam so much earlier, with these words, *What therefore God has joined, let no man separate.*

And the grace that would perfect that natural love, strengthen the indissoluble unity, and sanctify the spouses, Christ himself—the instituter and perfecter of the venerable sacraments—merited for us by his passion. The Apostle Paul implied this, saying: *Husbands love your wives, just as Christ loved the church and gave himself up for her,* adding shortly after: *This is a great mystery; but I mean, in Christ and the church.*

Since therefore marriage in the law of the Gospel exceeds the old marriages by means of grace through Christ, our holy fathers, and councils, and the universal tradition of the church have always taught that marriage is rightly to be numbered among the sacraments of the new law. Against this tradition, impious and senseless men of this age have not only thought falsely about this venerable sacrament, but introducing the license of the flesh as is their habit under pretext of the Gospel, they have said and written many things that are inconsistent with the understanding of the catholic church and with custom approved from apostolic times, causing great damage to the Christian faithful. Desiring to confront their temerity, the holy and universal council has decided that the more glaring heresies and errors of the aforementioned schismatics must be rooted out, lest more people be drawn to their deadly contagion, decreeing against these heretics themselves and their errors the following anathemas.

Paragraphs 1–2: Indissolubility of Natural Marriage

Four points are made in the first two paragraphs. First, the opening sentence makes clear that the "bond" of marriage is the oneness that marriage itself is. Marriage *is* the bond. So when the term "bond of marriage" is used in canons 5 and 7, it does not refer to something separable from mar-

---

2. CT, IX, 966.28–967.15, translation supplied. For all three versions of the doctrinal preface in Latin and English, see appendix B. The complete heading in CT is "Teaching and canons together with other matters concerning the sacrament of marriage" (doctrina et canones cum aliis concernentibus sacramentum matrimonii) (CT, IX, 966.28).

riage, a property *of* marriage, but to marriage itself. Second, marriage is a natural institution. It begins with Adam. Third, that natural institution is "perpetual and indissoluble." Marriage is not indissoluble simply in virtue of its sacramentality, but in virtue of the fact that it "joins" (coniungere) and "couples" (copulare) spouses: recall Aquinas's term *coniunctio*, "joining together."[3] Fourth, the indissolubility of marriage is a teaching of divine revelation—proclaimed under the inspiration of the Holy Spirit by our forefathers, and taught by Christ more clearly in the Gospels, ratifying that earlier proclamation as one "spoken by God."

A fifth point should be noted. When the Council uses the term "marriage" in the *doctrina*, it is referring to consummated marriages. We know this because when Jesus says, "what God has joined," he is clearly talking about the one-flesh relationship of a husband and wife and so a consummated marriage, since a couple are not one flesh until the marital union is consummated. So although the term "consummated marriage" is not found in the preface, the text is clearly referring to it.

Paragraph 3: Indissolubility of Sacramental Marriage

In the third paragraph, the Council turns its attention to sacramental marriages. The text states that "grace" is given by Christ to *confirmare* (strengthen) the indissoluble unity of the spouses. Why say that grace *strengthens* indissolubility? The first paragraphs teach that consummated natural marriages are indissoluble. Some fathers at Trent thought that marriage was *absolutely* indissoluble as a natural realty, others that sacramentality makes it so. *Confirmare* could be taken to mean that grace strengthens what already is the case, or that it strengthens the bond which makes it to be that way. Trent leaves the question open. The drafting committee provided a formula that can be understood in either way. But the *doctrina* is certainly saying that consummated sacramental marriages are absolutely indissoluble.

Paragraph 4: Defense of the Indissolubility of Sacramental Marriage

The fourth paragraph makes clear that the principal concern hereafter, including in the canons, is to defend sacramental marriage. It singles out those who hold, say, or write things *aliena* (inconsistent) with the church's

---

3. See preface, **ix**.

belief and practice, and refers to the latter as "custom approved from apostolic times." The *doctrina* ends by stating the intention of the Council to condemn those who deny what the church believes and practices about sacramental marriage, as well as their errors. The proximate reference of *haeretic[i] eorumque errores* is, of course, the Reformers, especially Luther and Calvin, and their teachings. But inasmuch as the Council condemns the errors of the heretics, those errors are condemned not merely in the writings or mouths of the Reformers, but wherever they are found.

Do the Statements in the *Doctrina* Constitute Solemn Definitions?

The Council formulates its teaching in the *doctrina* as affirmations of positive truths, not as condemnations of errors ending with the traditional formula *anathema sit*. It employs hyperbole ("senseless men") and metaphor ("deadly contagion"), neither of which is given to the precision necessary for solemn definitions.[4] And recall that in its development during the conciliar deliberations, the Council did not permit discussion of the *doctrina*'s parts, restricting comments to an approval or disapproval of the whole text. Its statements therefore do not constitute solemn definitions.

Summary

The Council of Trent in the *doctrina* authoritatively teaches without defining that the absolute indissolubility of a consummated, sacramental marriage is a divinely revealed truth. We conclude for two reasons that *absolute* indissolubility is its meaning: first, as stated above, from the Council's affirmation that in sacramental marriage "grace" *strengthens* the indissoluble unity of the spouses; second, from the fact that the *doctrina*'s account pertains to Christian marriage in general, with no mention of individual cases, whereas canons 5 and 7 specify common individual cases for the application of the general teaching. The twelve canons that follow the *doctrina*, which single out for emphasis truths taught in the *doctrina*, presume this teaching and so can only be understood rightly in the light of it.

---

4. For contemporary renderings of the way infallibility is exercised by an ecumenical council, see Vatican II, *Lumen Gentium*, no. 25; Congregation for the Doctrine of the Faith, "*Instruction Donum Veritatis*" (On the Ecclesial Vocation of the Theologian) (1990), no. 15.

CANON 5

The two canons (5 and 7) bearing directly on the indissolubility of marriage each address reasons for divorce and remarriage considered acceptable by Protestants and Greek Orthodox in the sixteenth century. Recall that in his remarks on the first draft of the canons on marriage in July 1563, the cardinal of Lorraine (Lotharingus), tutored by his experience at the Colloquy of Poissy in 1561, recommended the addition of a new canon condemning three errors of John Calvin, namely, that marriage "dirimatur" (may be) dissolved on account of disparity of cult, disharmony between the spouses, and "propter longam absentiam" (prolonged absence).[5] Nearly fifty bishops supported the recommendation. Until then, the only canon specifying any circumstance for the application of the doctrine of indissolubility was canon 6 (later canon 7) on adultery. Lorraine's plea was made more than two weeks before the Venetian delegation's appeal for an indirect formulation. At the time, canon 6 still retained its direct form condemning anyone who denied the indissolubility of marriage in cases of adultery. Recall that between 68 and 77 percent of the voting prelates (depending how they are numbered), including Lorraine, were content with that form. Because of the Matthean exceptive clause, adultery was the only circumstance that raised any doubt at the Council about the exceptionless nature of the doctrine. We saw in chapter 1 that the Reformers defended divorce and remarriage not only on the ground of adultery, but on several other grounds as well, as did the Greeks as shown in chapter two. Lorraine's proposal singled out three reasons defended by Calvin. Again, the formulation mentions disparity of cult, disharmony between the spouses, and prolonged absence. The final formulation of canon 5 replaces "disparity of cult" with "heresy" and "prolonged absence" with "willful desertion." It reads: "If anyone says that the bond of marriage can be dissolved on account of heresy, or irksome cohabitation, or the willful desertion of one of the spouses: let him be anathema."[6]

The canon defines the proposition that marriage is indissoluble in these three cases, and it means cannot be dissolved, not should not be dissolved (*posse*, not *debere*). My translation follows the current English edition of

---

5. Lotharingus: "cuperetque novum addi canonem, in quo damnentur tres propositiones Calvini, videl. quod dirimatur matrimonium propter disparitatem cultus, propter non convenientiam in conversatione et propter longam absentiam" (CT, IX, 642.25–28).

6. CT, IX, 967.27–28: "Si quis dixerit, propter haeresim, aut molestam cohabitationem, aut affectatam absentiam a coniuge dissolvi posse matrimonii vinculum: anathema sit."

Denzinger in rendering "affectatam" as "willful" and connecting "a coniuge" to "affectatam absentiam."[7] This is consistent with the older translation found in *The Church Teaches*, which translates "affectatam absentiam a coniuge" as "willful desertion by one of the parties."[8] The influential Tanner translation (*Decrees of the Ecumenical Councils*), however, renders "affectatam absentiam" as "continued absence" and "a coniuge dissolvi posse" as "can be dissolved by a spouse." The translation reads: "If anyone says that the bond of marriage can be dissolved by a spouse on the grounds of heresy, or irksome cohabitation, or continued absence." The difference is very significant. Tanner's translation has Trent teaching only that one spouse cannot dissolve the marriage, as if it wished to leave open the possibility that both spouses acting together could do so, or that one or both could have it dissolved by ecclesiastical authority. The thought that the Council had, or could have had, such an intention is without foundation, indeed absurd. Though Latin grammar in the abstract does not exclude the Tanner translation, the historians of the Council unhesitatingly take the meaning of canon 5 to be, as Jedin puts it, that the Council condemned "the teaching that heresy, difficulty in living together, and absence, deliberately brought about, of one of the spouses could be a valid ground of dissolution."[9]

Lorraine had called for the canon as a condemnation of errors of Calvin. He knew that in Calvin's revised *Marriage Ordinances* of 1561, the Reformer approved divorce and remarriage in cases of prolonged abandonment.[10] He also knew that the reformer considered questions of dissolution to be open and public affairs (e.g., in Calvin's revised Marriage Ordinance of 1546 great care was taken to guard *against* the practice of dissolution

---

7. "If anyone says that the marriage bond can be dissolved because of heresy or difficulties in cohabitation or because of the willful absence of one of the spouses let him be anathema." Heinrich Denzinger, *Enchiridion Symbolorum*, 43rd ed., ed. and trans. Peter Hünermann (San Francisco: Ignatius Press, 2012), no. 1805 (426) [hereafter, Denz.].

8. Jesuit Fathers of St. Mary's College, *The Church Teaches: Documents of the Church in English Translation* (Freiberg: Herder, 1955), no. 861 (975).

9. Hubert Jedin, *Geschichte des Konzil von Trent IV/2* (Freiburg: Herder, 1975), 108; "bewusst herbeigeführte Abwerweheit eines Gatten als Scheidungsgründe gelten könnten." The editors of CT, IX, say (642n2) that canon 5 had its beginning (after Lorraine's call) in the *votum* of Senonensis: "Si quis dixerit, *affectatam utriusque coniugis absentiam*, aut ..." (emphasis added). Like Jedin's paraphrase, this absolutely excludes the Tanner translation. The drafters tweaked Senonensis's *utriusque*, which suggested of *both* spouses, into *a coniuge,* the deliberate absence of one of them, to make the canon's insistence on indissolubility even more airtight.

10. John Calvin, "Les Ordonnances Ecclesiastiques De 1561," in *Opera Quae Supersunt Omnia*, eds. Guilielmus Baum, Eduardus Cumtz, Eduardüs Reüss (Brunsvigae: C. A. Sohwetsohke and Son, 1871), 10.1:110–12.

by spouses).[11] Lorraine plainly did not mean that marriage's dissolubility (merely) *by spouses* should be denied, because Calvin *never said it should be permitted*. Calvin's concern was to assert what the canonists called extrinsic—absolute—dissolubility. The clear sense of the condemned proposition is that disparity of cult, hostile communication, and prolonged absence each result in the dissolution of the marriage bond. Lorraine wants the new canon to condemn anyone who says that these things ground dissolution of marriage because Calvin said precisely that. Moreover, the Tanner translation is excluded by the history of canon 5's formulation. Lorraine proposed "longam absentiam" (prolonged absence). The Council replaced "longam" with "affectatam." The alternative term came from a proposal made by the archbishop of Senonensis one day after Lorraine offered his proposal. Senonesis says the Council should say: "si quis dixerit, affectatam utriusque coniugis absentiam" (if anyone says that the *affectatam absentiam* of either spouse).[12] There is no doubt that Senonensis means to address the problem of the absence of a spouse. What kind of absence? Absence that is deliberately aimed at or intended (from *adfectare*). The English word "continued" is not a fitting translation for *affectatam*.[13] The eccentric Tanner translation is doubly indefensible.[14]

In conclusion, canon 5 solemnly defines the proposition that marriage cannot be dissolved on account of heresy, irksome cohabitation, or spousal abandonment. The canon clearly means *cannot*, and not should not or even must not; and it means *by anyone*, not just by the spouses themselves.

CANON 7

The final formulation of canon 7 reads:

If anyone says the church errs, when she has taught and teaches, in accordance with the evangelical and apostolic doctrine, that the bond of marriage cannot be dissolved on account of the adultery of a spouse, and that neither spouse, even one who is innocent and gave no cause for adultery, can contract another marriage while the other spouse is living, and that he commits adultery who dismisses an

---

11. "Calvin was as eager to safeguard against the prior canon law practices of private dissolutions as against the traditional canon law toleration of secret marriages." Witte, Jr., and Kingdon, *Sex, Marriage, and Family*, 1:45–46.

12. CT, IX, 652.30.

13. Ryan and Grisez also make this point; see "Indissoluble Marriage," 402n149.

14. Standard English (e.g., Schroeder 1941, Waterworth 1848) and other modern language translations (e.g., Schmets 1868) translate with "absence of one of the parties/spouses."

adulterous wife and marries another, and she commits adultery who dismisses an adulterous husband and marries another; let him be anathema.[15]

After tracking the history of canon 7 from its 1547 antecedents at Bologna through the four formulations of summer and fall 1563, we may now ask what it asserts, condemns, and concedes. For what it asserts is an irreformable dogma of Catholic faith, taught by the Council with full and supreme authority. Its dogmatic character is evident from its form. Its status as *de fide* (i.e., a doctrine of Christian faith) will become clear in what follows.

What Canon 7 Asserts

For the sake of simplicity the following three theses are labeled X, Y, and Z.

X: Even in cases of adultery: [a] the bond of marriage cannot be dissolved, [b] spouses cannot contract a second marriage while their first spouse lives, and [c] a spouse who attempts remarriage commits adultery.

Y: The church is certainly correct when it teaches proposition X.

Z: Proposition X is "iuxta evangelicam et apostolicam doctrinam."

Canon 7 as self-referential

Canon 7 is self-referential in two ways. The first and more obvious way is by teaching that the church is inerrant when it teaches, and then by specifying the proposition it teaches inerrantly.

"The church errs." By using the indirect formula—if anyone says the church errs, when she taught and teaches X, let him be anathema—rather than the direct formula—if anyone says not-X, let him be anathema—the Council chose not to define proposition X directly. It does however indirectly define it by directly defining propositions Y and Z. Proposition Y asserts that the church is certainly correct when it teaches proposition X. Therefore proposition X is free from error. If it is free from error, then the church teaches the truth in teaching X.[16] Proposition Z asserts that propo-

---

15. "Si quis dixerit, ecclesiam errare, cum docuit et docet, iuxta evangelicam et apostolicam doctrinam, propter adulterium alterius coniugum matrimonii vinculum non posse dissolvi, et utrumque, vel etiam innocentem, qui causam adulterio non dedit, non posse, altero coniuge vivente, aliud matrimonium contrahere, moecharique eum, qui dimissa adultera aliam duxerit, et eam, quae dimisso adultero alii nupserit: anathema sit." CT, IX, 967.31–35.

16. Palmieri recognized this in 1880: "for the Church cannot 'not err' in teaching that 'marriage cannot be dissolved,' unless that [proposition] be true" (Nam nequit Ecclesia non errare cum docet matrimonium non posse dissolvi, nisi id sit verum). *Tractatus de Matrimonio Christiano*, 142. Perrone drew the obvious conclusion in 1861: "for just as the evangelical and

sition X is "iuxta evangelicam et apostolicam doctrinam." The term is the Council's elaboration of Lorraine's "iuxta scripturas."[17] Its plain meaning here is that proposition X is in close agreement, even possessing equality of status with the teaching of the New Testament (of the Gospels and the apostles). The phrase is not as direct as the influential bishop of León would have wished; it does not assert straightforwardly that proposition X *is* an "evangelicam doctrinam."[18] But given the finalized teaching of the *doctrina*, Legionensis could not have been disappointed. The *doctrina* asserts twice that the perpetual and indissoluble character of the marriage bond is taught in divine revelation. So when the church teaches that the bond of marriage cannot be dissolved on account of adultery, it teaches what was pronounced under the inspiration of the Holy Spirit, by the forefather of the human race, and what was repeated (with clearer indication of its authoritativeness) by Christ. This excludes the view that the teaching is simply a question of church discipline, much less the possibility that it could conflict in some way with the teaching of Jesus.

"Taught and teaches." The second way that canon 7 is self-referential is less obvious and has been missed by most commentators on Trent's teaching on indissolubility.[19] Why did the Council introduce the present tense ("docet") into the formulation when in context the former simpler term *docuit* (in having taught) implied it? Because it wanted to draw special attention to instances where the church *presently* (i.e., at the time of Trent) taught the doctrine of indissolubility. This was meant to draw attention in particular to the church's teaching of indissolubility in the *doctrina*. There the church reaffirms the general proposition that marriage is absolutely indissoluble, not simply, as in canon 7, indissoluble in cases of adultery. *There-*

---

apostolic doctrine cannot not be true, so the opposite doctrine cannot not be false and erroneous, and whoever acts in accordance with this cannot be free of serious fault. Therefore, the Greeks sin gravely whenever they dissolve marriages unless they are in the grip of invincible ignorance; and any new marriage they contract is null and void on account of the impediment of the bond." (Nam sicut doctrina evangelica et apostolica non potest non esse vera, ita doctrina opposita non potest non esse falsa et erronea, et qui iuxta hanc operantur, nequeunt se a gravi culpa subducere. Graviter igitur peccant Graeci, quoties dissolvunt coniugia, nisi ignorantia invincibili detineantur, et novum, quod contrahunt, matrimonium ob impedimentum ligaminis nullum ac irritum est.) *De Matrimonio*, 3.385; see also Pallavicino, *History of the Council of Trent*, lib. XXII, cap. IV, nos. 47–50.

17. Recall that after approving the Venetian delegation's proposal for an indirect formulation for canon 7, Lorraine recommends adding the words "iuxta Scripturas" after the clause "when she has taught and teaches." See CT, IX, 687.9.

18. CT, IX, 789.27–28: "[Canon] 7 ponatur qui erat in principio, vel: *Si quis dixerit, ecclesiam errasse, cum evangelicam doctrinam docuit et docet.*"

19. It was not missed by Ryan and Grisez; see "Indissoluble Marriage," 400.

fore, in canon 7 Trent solemnly defines that the church teaches truth when it teaches what the church itself teaches in the doctrina. And anyone who says the church errs in teaching *that* falls under the anathema. In the very canon in which indirection is introduced, the Council reaffirms the truth of the proposition that condemns the Greek teaching.

Bond of Marriage

Canon 7 retains "bond of marriage" as originally recommended by Lorraine, and as introduced into the fourth formulation.[20] The use of *vinculum* (bond) has at least two purposes. First, it tells us the Council is referring to ratified consummated marriages. How so? Because in canon 6, when the Council teaches in principle that non-consummated marriages are dissoluble, there is no reference to *vinculum*: "If anyone says that a ratified marriage which is not consummated, is not dissolved by the solemn religious profession of one of the spouses, let him be anathema."[21] By using *bond* in canons 5 and 7, the Council refers to consummated—one flesh—marriage, as spoken about in the *doctrina*.

Second, without including "bond," the canon might have accommodated an interpretation that Trent wanted to exclude. The Catholic church permitted spouses to separate, but not remarry; *in this sense*, the church recognized that marriages can break down. Referring to the bond makes clearer that *even if marriage as a lived community* can dissolve, the *bond* does not, and cannot be dissolved either *de facto* or *de jure*. If we look at this in light of the debate over the apparent exceptive clause in Matthew, we see the Council adopting language consistent with Augustine's enormously influential interpretation of Matthew, rejected by both Protestants and Greeks, language that very clearly hearkens back to the maxim "bed, not bond," repeated continually at the Council of Trent.

Does Canon 7 Address the Nature of Marriage or
Merely Church Power?

The question bears upon two of the objections to the indissolubility thesis that were set forth in the introduction to this book. The first argued that Trent in canon 7 was mainly concerned with Luther's denial of pa-

---

20. For Lorriane's original proposal, see CT, IX, 742.44–49.
21. CT, IX, 967.30–31: "Si quis dixerit, matrimonium ratum, non consummatum, per solemnem religionis professionem alterius coniugum non dirimi: anathema sit."

pal prerogative and not with the nature of marriage; and the second that, because the Council fathers were doubtful as to whether the "exceptive clause" in Matthew establishes a real exception, Trent grounded canon 7 on the church's legal tradition prohibiting divorce and remarriage, not on the teaching of divine revelation. The consequence of both objections is essentially the same: canon 7 is concerned with the authority of the church to prohibit remarriage even in cases of adultery, not with the substantive nature of the marriage bond.

That canon 7 was interested in Luther, there is no doubt. But it also targeted the denial of the substantive doctrine of indissolubility in cases of adultery, which, as we have shown, represented the beliefs of both the Protestants *and* the Greeks. We know this because the direct formulation was clearly recognized to be targeting the Greeks, otherwise the Venetians would have had no reason to ask the Greeks to be dealt with in a certain way. Since it was already demonstrated that the same proposition affirming the indissolubility of marriage in cases of adultery is taught in the indirect formulation, we conclude that the final formulation of canon 7 also targeted the Greeks. For those who doubt the latter demonstration, we may recall that some of the Council's strongest defenders of the Greek divorce practices, even after an indirect formulation for canon 7 was proposed by the *deputatio*, still did not believe it overcame the doctrinal opposition to Greek divorce.[22] In other words, they still believed or at least strongly suspected that the indirect formulation affirmed the indissolubility of marriage in cases of adultery; this belief was again expressed when Nicosiensis insisted at the time of the final *vota* that an excerpt pleading for permission for the Greeks to "remain in their customs" be included into the conciliar register.[23]

"Ecclesiam errare." Both Fransen and Bressan argue that the Council's use of this phrase indicates that it was interested only in addressing the exercise of the authority of the church and not interested in defining dogma. They note that canon 8 too uses the term: "*If anyone says the church errs*" to begin that canon's formulation, which continues "when she decides for a variety of reasons a separation between spouses from bed or from cohabitation may take place for a certain or an indefinite time, let him be anathema" (emphasis added).[24] Since canon 8, they continue, clearly does not

---

22. See chapter 4, note 119.
23. See chapter 4, note 156.
24. CT, IX, 967.36–38: "Si quis dixerit, ecclesiam errare, cum ob multas causas separationem inter coniuges quoad thorum, seu quoad cohabitation, ad certum incertumve tempus, fieri posse decernit: anathema sit."

mean to define "separability" as a dogma of faith, but concerns rather the right of the church to exercise disciplinary power in establishing grounds for legitimate separation; therefore canon 7 is not defining any irreformable dogma of faith, but rather addressing a disciplinary teaching of the church, one that is "not easily to be dismissed," but that is open to "differing applications."[25] This argument is problematic.

Consider the two following statements: (1) "John is a bad father because he disciplines his children when they misbehave" and (2) "John is a bad father because he teaches his children that the Catholic faith is true." It is obviously fallacious to argue that because both begin with the same phrase "John is a bad father," and because the first is dealing with disciplinary issues, therefore so too is the second. It is true that when canon 8 refers to the church's act of deciding (*decernit*), it is referring to the church's exercise of disciplinary authority. But canon 7 refers to the church's act of teaching (*docuit, docet*). It is not referring to the church deciding anything, but to the church's act of defending true propositions.

"Error" is cognitively going wrong. Luther teaches that the church has erred in many ways, not only in teaching. Canon 8 denies the church is mistaken in its decision to permit spousal separation for a variety of reasons. Positively it asserts the church's correctness (absence of error) in making the judgment that spouses may separate for good reasons. Trent published canon 8 because Luther had said the church does not have power to decide that such separations can be licit.

Canon 7, on the other hand, denies that the church is mistaken in asserting propositional truths, in particular, that in cases of adultery, the bond of marriage cannot be dissolved, spouses cannot contract a second marriage while their first spouse lives, and a spouse who attempts remarriage commits adultery. The general form is that the church does not err in teaching these propositions. The Reformers were happy to say that the church errs in all sorts of ways, including in its teaching. But Luther does not explicitly assert that the church errs when it teaches proposition X.[26] Rather, Luther denies X. So while canon 8 deals with the church's exercise of disciplinary authority, canon 7 deals with the truth of propositions.

Moreover, when Trent in canons 3 and 4 address challenges to Catholic doctrine about the church's disciplinary authority, the language makes that clear:

---

25. Bressan, *Il Canone Tridentino*, 205–8, 221.
26. At the same time, if Luther denies X, he formally, albeit by entailment, teaches that the church (or anyone else) errs when it (or anyone else) teaches X.

C. 3: "If anyone says that only the grades of consanguinity and affinity expressed in Leviticus pose an impediment to contracting marriage and make one contracted invalid; and that the church can neither dispense from any of them nor enact others that prevent marriage or make it null: let him be anathema."[27]

C. 4: "If anyone says that the church did not have the power to establish diriment impediments to marriage, or erred in doing so: let him be anathema."[28]

Both address the extent of the church's authority, and the Council condemns anyone who denies the church's rightful exercise of that authority.

Again, canons 9 and 11 deal with the church's disciplinary authority, inasmuch as each entails an exercise of that authority:

C. 9: "If anyone says that clerics in holy orders, or regulars who have made solemn profession of chastity, may contract marriage, and that such a contract is valid, in spite of church law and the vow ... let him be anathema."[29]

C. 11: "If anyone says that the prohibition against the solemn celebration of marriage at certain seasons of the year is a tyrannical superstition, arising from pagan superstition; or condemns the blessings and other ceremonies used in the church at such celebration: let him be anathema."[30]

Canons 3, 4, 9, and 11 each in different ways concerns itself with the Catholic church's authority over the sacrament of marriage. And they all are clearly dealing with Luther. But none of them asserts anything about the substantive nature of the marriage bond.

Moreover, when the direct formulation was under consideration, *none* of the Council fathers thought the formulation referred merely to the dis-

---

27. CT, IX, 967.21–24: "Si quis dixerit, eos tantum consanguinitatis et affinitatis gradus, qui *Levitico* exprimuntur, posse impedire matrimonium contrahendum, et dirimere contractum; nec posse ecclesiam in nonnullis illorum dispensare aut constituere, ut plures impediant et diriment: anathema sit." Translation from DEC, 2:754.

28. CT, IX, 967.25–26: "Si quis dixerit, ecclesiam non potuisse constituere impedimenta matrimonium dirimentia, vel in iis constituendis errasse: anathema sit." Translation from DEC, 2:754.

29. CT, IX, 968.1–5: "Si quis dixerit, clericos in sacris ordinibus constitutos, vel regulares, castitatem solemniter professos, posse matrimonium contrahere, contractumque validum esse, non obstante lege ecclesiastica vel voto ..., anathema sit." Translation from DEC, 2:755.

30. CT, IX, 968.10–12: "Si quis dixerit, prohibitionem solemnitatis nuptiarum certis anni temporibus superstitionem esse tyrannicam, ab ethnicorum superstitione profectam; aut benedictiones et alias caeremonias, quibus ecclesia in illis utitur, damnaverit, anathema sit." Translation from DEC, 2:755.

ciplinary activity of the church, even the few who believed that the prohibition of divorce and remarriage in cases of adultery was no more than a canonical rule and not a norm derived from divine revelation. Nor did the Council fathers think that in not anathematizing the Greeks by publishing an indirect formulation they were dealing merely with disciplinary matters. Both the proposition asserted in X (that marriage is indissoluble in cases of adultery) and the erroneous belief of Greek Christians tolerated by the indirect formulation (that Matthew teaches a real exception) are matters of doctrine, not discipline.[31]

Finally, the decree *Tametsi* ("Canons on the reform of marriage"), which immediately follows the twelve dogmatic canons, shows us even more clearly how the Council dealt with matters of discipline. Teaching on the problem of clandestine marriages, chapter 1 sets forth the *doctrinal* principle "that secret marriages, entered by free consent of the parties, are true and valid marriages" (in the contemporary words of canon law, the consent of the parties makes marriage).[32] *Tametsi* then condemns those who deny this together with those who "falsely assert that marriages contracted by sons and daughters [filiis] still at home without the consent of the parents are null, and that the parents can make them either valid or invalid."[33] It then states that the Catholic church has always "prohibited such marriages for the best of reasons," but acknowledges that the prohibitions "have been ineffective owning to human disobedience," and states that the church must use "a more effective remedy."[34] Following these statements, the Council decrees that *in posterum* (from this day forward) certain conditions must be met for a true and valid marriage to be contracted. The text reads: "The holy synod *now renders* incapable of marriage any who may attempt to contract marriage otherwise than in the presence of the parish priest or another priest, with the permission of the parish priest or the ordinary, and two or three witnesses; and *it decrees* that such contracts are null and invalid, *and renders them so by this decree*" (emphasis added).[35] When the Council meant to teach doctrine—for example, "secret marriages, entered by free consent of the parties, are true and valid marriages"—its statements indicate this. When it performed disciplinary actions, the lan-

---

31. The formal object of toleration is the Greek Christians themselves who erroneously held that Matthew teaches a real exception.
32. DEC, 2:755.26–27. See Code of Canon Law, c. 1057, §1.
33. DEC, 2:755.28–31.
34. DEC, 2:755.32–34, 39.
35. DEC, 2:756.17–20.

guage it adopts signals this fact, for example, "from this day forward," "now renders," "it decrees," "renders them so by this decree." The Council knew exactly what it was doing both in teaching doctrinal principles and in performing disciplinary actions.

The Proposition Defined in Canon 7

What then does canon 7 define? It defines precisely what it asserts. It asserts that the church teaches the truth when it teaches that a Christian marriage is indissoluble in cases of adultery; it also asserts—given the canon's self-referential nature—that the church teaches truth when it teaches what it itself teaches in the *doctrina*, which is that consummated, sacramental marriages are absolutely indissoluble; and it asserts that this is in accord with the teaching of divine revelation. Because the canon does not directly assert proposition X, and does not directly assert what is taught in the *doctrina*, it does not directly define proposition X or the truth asserted in the *doctrina*. But it does indirectly define both inasmuch as it directly defines that the church teaches the truth when it teaches both. So the outcome is the same: *a dogmatic definition of the absolute indissolubility of marriage as a truth of divine revelation.*

Canon 7 Rejects the Greek Position without
Condemning the Greeks

We saw that canon 5 condemns some of the divorce practices of the Greeks. This did not seem to bother anyone and no one objected to it. Why not? Because the Greeks rationalized their wider practice on the basis of the Matthean exceptive clause. From the Greek point of view, if divorce and remarriage for the cause of adultery is licit, then other causes can be licit, since Matthew teaches a real exception, and if a real exception exists, then marriage is not indissoluble. To directly condemn anyone who holds or teaches that Matthew provides a real exception would have grabbed the Greeks by the throat and made it clear they were being anathematized. The Council did not want to do this. The intervention of the Venetian delegation had drawn attention to the imperfect communion that still existed between Greeks and the Catholic church. Trent valued this communion and did not want unnecessarily to destroy it.

This does not mean that canon 7 does not teach the falsity of the Matthean rationalization. The formal object of canon 7 is indeed the teaching that Matthew carves out a real exception. But the canon rejects this object by teaching the truth of proposition X, which entails that the denial of X is false. The canon defined the truth of proposition X without directly condemning persons who reject it. In so doing, it taught that the Greek premise that Matthew establishes a real exception to the indissolubility of marriage is false; but it did so without cutting off—anathematizing—the Greeks to the extent that they were still united with the Catholic church.

The Elusive Genius of Trent's Teaching

The skill of the Council of Trent in adopting a form that accomplished its longstanding purpose—clarified over many hours of discussion between April 1547 and November 1563—of solemnly defining the indissolubility of marriage as a truth of faith, while bringing the anathema down on the heads of Reformers, has been lost on many commentators. The common but sadly simplistic reading of Trent's teaching was summed up by the German moral theologian Ignaz Fahrner in 1903: "If the Council Fathers had intended to define the principle of indissolubility itself as a dogma, they would have kept the original wording of the canon."[36] We have demonstrated that their purposes were more subtle, a subtlety lost not only on Fahrner but on the 1978 International Theological Commission (ITC), which concluded: "It cannot be said then that the council [of Trent] had the intention of solemnly defining marriage's indissolubility as a truth of faith."[37] Fahrner's and the ITC's conclusion, as we have shown, must be rejected.[38]

The Council's threefold strategy should now be plain. It simultaneously intended: (1) to secure a clear condemnation against Luther's denial of ecclesiastical authority over the marriages of Christians; (2) to define the truth of the absolute indissolubility of consummated and sacramental marriages; and (3) to cause as little disruption as possible to the fragile relations between Greek and Latin Christians living in Venetian territories. The Council did indeed, as Mackin remarks, take a "circuitous route." But not to the destination he and others believe. Mackin writes: "the excommu-

---

36. Ignaz Fahrner, *Geschichte des Unauflöslichkeitsprinzips und der vollkommenen Scheidung der Ehe im kanonischen Recht*, in the series Geschichte der Ehescheidung im kanonischen Recht (Freiburg im Breisgau: Herder, 1903), 256.

37. International Theological Commission, "Propositions on the Doctrine of Christian Marriage," 238.

38. So too must be rejected the argument of Himes and Corriden that "there [is no] reason to believe that Trent saw the teaching as definitive doctrine" ("The Indissolubility of Marriage: Reasons to Reconsider," 463).

nication for heresy did not affect the Greek Catholics in their practice of permitting divorce and remarriage after proved adultery."[39] He overstates this point, but he is not entirely incorrect. Inasmuch as Greek Christians were not known to profess pertinaciously the proposition "the Church errs when it teaches indissolubility," the condemnation did not fall directly upon them. But Mackin is wrong when he says: "And it [i.e., Trent's teaching on indissolubility] seems to have left also untouched their practice of dissolving marriages." Inasmuch as the Council defined proposition X, it excludes as contrary to Catholic faith and discipline the Greek custom of dissolving marriages.

What Canon 7 Concedes

We have shown what Trent taught and what it condemned. But in moving to an indirect formulation for canon 7, it also conceded something. What did it concede? To answer this we must look closely at what the Venetian delegation's intervention implied. It implied the following:

1. When the Venetians, who were Catholic, took control of their island possessions, people there were Greek Orthodox and they practiced divorce and remarriage;

2. Bishops named by the pope were installed to govern those churches;

3. The priests and people accepted the bishops and acknowledged papal primacy;

4. Some of the priests and people did not give up practicing divorce and remarriage;

5. The bishops were tolerating that practice.

Had the Council kept the direct formulation, the anathema would have ended that toleration. The petitioners claimed doing so would result in ending those churches' acceptance of papal authority. Thus, by agreeing to the indirect formulation, the Council accepted divorce and remarriage within those particular churches of the Catholic church.

Does this show that the Catholic church admits that divorce and remarriage are possible and that marriage is dissoluble? Emphatically, *no*. The way the Council defined the truth of the Catholic church's teaching, which it also took great care to set out lucidly in the *doctrina*, makes very clear that the Council did not accept the truth of the necessary presupposition

---

39. Mackin, *Divorce and Remarriage*, 392.

of the Greek Orthodox practice, and thus did not admit that the practice was sound.

Still, what Trent did would seem to show that the Catholic church can tolerate the practice of divorce and remarriage by some who are in communion with the church but who do not believe that marriage is indissoluble.[40] Does this show that the Catholic church, as Walter Kasper argues, can adopt for *itself* a limited practice of divorce and remarriage, like the Orthodox pastoral principle of *economia*, where in the "economy" of salvation the church permits the spouses in consummated sacramental marriages to divorce and remarry as a way "to accompany people when they make their incremental approach to life's goal," and do so without denying the indissolubility of marriage?[41] No, it does not.

Real but Imperfect Communion

What it shows is that some particular churches can be in partial but not complete communion with the Catholic church, and that the Catholic church can welcome their communion such as it is while tolerating their residual schism despite its presupposition of a proposition that contradicts a truth that the Catholic church holds to be divinely revealed.[42] If the bishops

---

40. Joseph Ratzinger in 1972 set forth a similar account: "it is today completely clear what the Council of Trent condemned [in c. 7] and did not condemn. It did not condemn the eastern practice, but rather accepted [gelten lassen] it as part of a 'ritus' within the wider context of an effort aimed at continuing ecclesiastical unity [Kirchenunion]." He attributes this (very limited, not to say ambiguous) "clarity" to the scholarship of Piet Fransen; see Ratzinger, "Zur Frage nach der Unauflöslichkeit der Ehe: Bemerkungen zum dogmengeschichtlichen Befund und zu seiner gegenwärtigen Bedeutung," in *Ehe und Ehescheidung*, ed. Henrich, 49. It is true that Fransen says something similar: "There is not the slightest doubt that Trent accepted the proposal of the Venetians who definitively wanted to avoid an excommunication of the Easterns and a possible threat to the fragile and rather superficial ecclesiastical unity which existed in their territories in the East" ("Divorce on the Ground of Adultery," 98). The Council undoubtedly wanted to avoid condemning the Greek practice in canon 7. But *pace* Fransen, this does not mean it approved the practice, or either explicitly or implicitly taught that the practice was not contrary to the faith and life of the Catholic church.

41. Kasper, *Gospel of the Family*, 51. Kasper adds: "this practice [of *oikonomia*] does not violate the principle of indissolubility as such. What it does in fact is to provide the Christian who is ready to do penance, on the basis of God's mercy, with a new possibility of a human and Christian life within the Church in certain difficult situations." Kasper, *Theology of Christian Marriage*, 56–57.

42. The Council of Florence (1445), where a short-lived reunion with the Greeks was established, seems to set a precedent for what Trent did in canon 7. The fathers at Florence knew that the Greeks practiced divorce and remarriage, but the Council did not require as a condition for reunion that they profess what the Catholic church teaches about marriage.

of the Greek Orthodox churches declared their faith in the primacy of the pope, but continued allowing divorce and remarriage, the Catholic church could welcome the improved relationship with those particular churches even though communion with them remained imperfect. The church could tolerate for a time what it believes to be erroneous in those churches for the sake of actualizing a fuller and more perfect—but not yet full—communion in the hope that that partial communion and the toleration that helped facilitate it might one day give way to full communion.

But the proposal that the Catholic church adopt for itself a pastoral practice similar to *economia* means that the church itself adopts the practice of blessing divorced and remarried unions and readmitting the members in those irregular unions to the eucharist, which would presuppose the falsity of its belief that the absolute indissolubility of marriage is divinely revealed. This the Catholic church cannot do.

Two analogies might clarify this. If one's hand were partly but not completely severed, and if that injury led to an infection in the hand, one might have the hand amputated to get rid of the infection, or one might have the infected hand more closely attached despite the infection. Still, one would not deliberately bring about an infection in one's fully attached hand. Likewise, if a teenage son was not compliant with his parents' values on the immorality of illicit drug use, his parents might require him to live elsewhere, or they might tolerate some misconduct on his part for the sake of preventing the kind of rupture that would occur in the family by kicking him out, and do so in the hope that one day he will accept fully the family's values. Still, the parents would not deliberately introduce illicit drug use into the family's recreational practices.

Vatican II adopted a similar approach when it addressed ecumenism. It did not focus upon elements of disunity between Catholics and Orthodox, but elements of residual communion. It referred to the Eastern Orthodox as real churches, with real sacraments and holy orders. It avoided statements on the defects in the Eastern positions that make communion imperfect. By not condemning those defects, Vatican II does not mean the Catholic church believes those positions are not false and contrary to the faith, and that the practices founded upon them are not contrary to the moral order. It means the beliefs and practices are not incompatible with *some* degree of real communion. It means the Catholic church and Orthodox churches are not completely out of communion. Pope Paul VI's act of raising the anathema against the Orthodox church of Constantinople during the Council in November 1965 has a meaning similar to Trent's decision not to impose the anathema in canon 7. In neither case did the actions imply that all obstacles to full communion had been overcome. Yet both showed that real but imperfect communion exists.

SUMMARY OF THE COUNCIL'S TEACHING ON THE INDISSOLUBILITY OF MARRIAGE

Trent has two canons bearing directly on the doctrine of indissolubility. Canon 5 solemnly defines that marriage cannot be dissolved for various reasons. The canon clearly means *cannot*, not *should not or even must not*, and clearly means cannot by anyone, not just by the spouses themselves.

Canon 7 solemnly defines that the church did not and does not err in teaching that marriage cannot be dissolved on account of adultery—that is, in denying that the Matthean phrase singles out a real exception. It too clearly means *cannot* be dissolved (not *should not* or *must not*) and means dissolved by anyone, not just by the spouses themselves. The canon defines that the teaching is justified by scripture and the apostles' handing on of it *and* that the church got and gets it right when it reaffirms it. Since Trent was putting down people who were disagreeing with church teachings about consummated sacramental marriages, canon 7 is concerned with the church's teaching about them. So the definition is clearly doctrinal, not disciplinary. Trent also teaches in the *doctrina* that the bond of marriage is the oneness that marriage itself is, but canon 7 replaced "marriage" with "bond of marriage" to make it clear that the marriage as a lived relationship can be ended by permanent separation.

Trent did make a real concession in adopting an indirect formula for canon 7. It might seem the Council was not really conceding anything, because if one asserts proposition X, one is not asserting anything less about the content of X than if one asserts, *I was right when I asserted X*. What one is adding by the latter formulation is something about the one who asserted it. So although canon 7 does bear directly on the church's act of teaching (and not on the teaching itself), still if the church does not err in the act of teaching, it necessarily follows that what it teaches is true, and what is contrary is false. This allows the anathema in canon 7 not to bear directly on the Greeks' teaching or practice, and so permit both to go on within the jurisdiction of the Catholic church without approving of either. That was a very real concession.

What Trent did was somewhat similar to what Vatican II and Paul VI did in recognizing that the Orthodox are real churches existing in imperfect but real communion with the Catholic church and lifting the mutual anathemas. But what Trent and Vatican II did does not mean that the church can cooperate in initiating heresy and schism within herself.

Trent really does teach, though not define, in the *doctrina*, that it is a divinely revealed truth that consummated sacramental marriage is absolutely indissoluble. Because of the logical relationship between the canons and the doctrinal introduction, the definitive teaching that the church is not in error in its teaching on adultery logically entails that the church is not in error in teaching that consummated sacramental marriages are absolutely indissoluble.

The canons are dealing with some bad errors against the teaching, which implies that the teaching as a whole that is being defended includes the specific teachings of canons 5 and 7. The *doctrina* therefore includes within itself the teachings in canons 5 and 7, because it (the *doctrina*) teaches that consummated sacramental marriages are absolutely indissoluble and the canons are applications of that teaching. So when canon 7 definitively teaches that there is no error in the church's doctrinal, indeed dogmatic, denial that the Matthean exceptive clause is a real exception, that teaching applies to the teaching in the *doctrina* that consummated sacramental marriages are absolutely indissoluble. The church believes the Matthean clause is not a real exception because it believes Jesus' affirmation of indissolubility is absolute. So, the general proposition must be at least as certain as the church's certitude that the exception is unreal.

The Teaching versus the "Spirit" of the Council

Although the term is never used, the common misconstrual of Trent's teaching seems to rely on the idea of the "spirit of the council," an idea frequently appealed to in the last half-century by interpreters of the teachings of Vatican II. The idea suggests that there is some meaning to the Council's teaching beyond the teaching itself; that you figure it out not by reading the published texts at face value, or in the context of what was said and done by those who drew up and approved them, but by discovering in other ways what the Council fathers "really meant," and that to consider what is taught as being what is asserted is naïve.

The problem with this view is that a Council only has public acts. There is no "spirit of a council" over and above those acts. It is true that a body can be duplicitous in stating its intentions. Say, for example, the Supreme Soviet of a bygone era publishes a statement that it intends to treat all dissidents with toleration and fairness; the assembly may very well mean something other than it asserts. But when we are dealing with a group like an assembly of bishops of the Catholic church, who are meeting and deliberating publicly and publicly setting forth their ideas and conclusions, there is simply no basis for entertaining a doubt that what it publicly asserts is what it means to assert.

CONCLUSION

To properly assess what Trent publicly asserted has involved looking at a combination of factors—most significantly, the recorded proceedings of the preliminary discussions of the Council participants. We saw that a large majority of Council fathers from spring 1547 through autumn 1563 affirmed the absolute indissolubility of sacramental marriage; they believed it was a truth of divine revelation; and they taught it directly in the *doctrina* and self-referentially in canon 7.

The turn to an indirect formulation in mid-August 1563 expressed no alteration of their beliefs at all, and no fundamental alteration of their intentions. Being presented with good reasons for teaching the indissolubility of marriage with the least possible fallout for the delicate balance of relations between Eastern Christians and Roman Catholics, the majority willingly assented to a proposal for an indirect formulation. The final teaching of the Council confirms all this. Canon 5 directly asserts the indissolubility of the marriage bond in three cases. Canon 7 indirectly asserts it in a fourth case. As if anticipating that the turn to an indirect formulation might generate in the minds of some people a doubt that the Council intended to assert indissolubility in the fourth case—and consequently to doubt the truth of the doctrine of absolute indissolubility, Trent adds a *doctrina* which unambiguously and without restriction or qualification asserts the proposition that the bond of a Christian marriage is indissoluble, that this is a truth of divine revelation, and that the Council intends the scope of its teaching to stretch as far as the doubts against the teaching may extend.

Let Dead Dogs Lie

The nagging suggestion going back to Paulo Sarpi that the Council of Trent does not teach definitively the doctrine of absolute indissolubility should finally be put to rest. The direct proposition affirmed by canon 7 is the accuracy of the church in teaching the doctrine of indissolubility in cases of adultery. So it only directly condemns those who deny that. In this way the anathema fell on the Reformers. But the *doctrina* states that the canons will condemn not only the heretics, but their errors. Canon 7's condemnation of those who deny that the church teaches truth when it teaches the doctrine of indissolubility in cases of adultery entails that in teaching that doctrine the church teaches the truth. And the self-referential nature of canon 7 reiterates that the church teaches *absolute* indissolubility. Canon 7 thus teaches that the doctrine of absolute indissolubility cannot not be true.

The Magisterium of the Catholic church since Trent has presented the doctrine of the absolute indissolubility of a ratified and consummated Christian marriage as what must be held to be faithful to divine revelation. The teaching of the church since Trent justifies the conclusion that absolute indissolubility has been taught by the infallibility of the Ordinary Magisterium. So on the one hand we have the teaching of scripture, and on the other, we have the infallibility of the Ordinary Magisterium. In the middle we have the teachings of the Council of Trent.

APPENDIX A

AUTHORITIES REFERENCED AT TRENT

Referencing authorities to support a position—both formal ecclesiastical writings and the writings of prominent theologians or texts—was an important part of the debates at the Council of Trent. It was especially important for the debates on indissolubility because of questions raised by the meaning of the Matthean exceptive clause and the permissive divorce practices of the Greek churches. This appendix reproduces in Latin and English all of the authoritative texts cited by the conciliar theologians and council fathers on the topics of divorce, remarriage, and indissolubility during the debates from the 1547 and 1563 sessions.

For purposes of economy, the *Acta* usually quotes only fragments of texts, or simply cites the titles of works. In many of the excerpts reproduced below, I have judged that the cited text's understanding as well as the context in which it is being cited would be enhanced by additional material from the paragraphs or chapters from which the fragments are taken. In most cases I have taken the Latin from standard reference works (e.g., Migne, Mansi, etc.). In cases where such works are not available, I have quoted the *Acta's* Latin. Although there are at times minor differences between the Latin of the standard reference works and of the *Acta's*, the meanings of the texts are essentially the same. Standard English translations are used where available, and where they are not, translations are supplied. Following the Latin quotes are parenthetical references to the page and line numbers in *Concilium Tridentinum* where the particular quotation is cited.

In a few instances, where authorities under consideration have been especially influential on Christian ideas on indissolubility, I have quoted additional texts by the same author, texts not referenced in CT that are nonetheless helpful for understanding the author's wider thoughts on the indissolubility of marriage; for example, among influential Western Church Fathers, I have quoted additional passages from Augustine and Ambrose, and among Eastern Church Fathers, additional texts from Basil and Chrysostom. In cases where the meaning or application of a particular text is debated or in need of some explanation, appendix A provides commentary.

SCRIPTURE

The version of scripture read by the Council fathers was principally the Latin vulgate. I have reproduced here the biblical Latin from a contemporary scholarly version of the Vulgate: *Biblia Sacra Iuxta Vulgatam Versionem* (Stuttgart: Deutsche Bibelgesellschaft, 1969), hereafter, VUL." The English translations below are taken from the RSV.

Old Testament

Genesis 1:27–28 (referenced at CT, VI, 426.24):

So God created man in his own image, in the image of God he created him; male and female he created them. And God blessed them, and God said to them, "Be fruitful and multiply, and fill the earth and subdue it; and have dominion over the fish of the sea and over the birds of the air and over every living thing that moves upon the earth."

Et creavit Deus hominem ad imaginem suam ad imaginem Dei creavit illum; masculum et feminam creavit eos; benedixitque illis Deus et ait crescite et multiplicamini et replete terram et subicite eam et dominamini piscibus maris et volatilibus caeli et universis animantibus quae moventur super terram.

Genesis 2:24 (referenced at CT, VI, 426.25):

Therefore a man leaves his father and his mother and cleaves to his wife, and they become one flesh.

Quam ob rem relinquet homo patrem suum et matrem et adherebit uxori suae et erunt duo in carne una.

Gospels

Matthew 5:32 (referenced at CT, VI, 412.20, 425.3, 427.19, 434.32, 435.5; IX, 416.16–17, 417.8, 418.3):

But I say to you that every one who divorces his wife, except on the ground of unchastity, makes her an adulteress; and whoever marries a divorced woman commits adultery.

Ego autem dico vobis quia omnis qui dimiserit uxorem suam, excepta fornicationis causa, facit eam moechari et qui dimissam duxerit adulterat.

Matthew 19:3–9 (referenced at CT, VI, 121.4, 420.5, 420.21, 421.44, 425.5, 426.23, 427.19, 427.37–39, 428.31–32, 429.11.19–20, 431.18–20, 434.32; IX, 409.14–15, 416.45, 418.3):

And Pharisees came up to him and tested him by asking, "Is it lawful to divorce one's wife for any cause?" He answered, "Have you not read that he who made them from the beginning made them male and female, and said, 'For this reason a man shall leave his father and mother and be joined to his wife, and the two shall become one flesh'? So they are no longer two but one flesh. What therefore God has joined together, let not man put asunder." They said to him, "Why then did Moses command one to give a certificate of divorce, and to put her away?" He said to them, "For your hardness of heart Moses allowed you to divorce your wives, but from the beginning it was not so. And I say to you: whoever divorces his wife, except for unchastity, and marries another, commits adultery [and he who marries a divorced woman commits adultery]."

Et accesserunt ad eum Pharisaei temptantes eum et dicentes si licet homini dimittere uxorem suam quacumque ex causa qui respondens ait eis non legistis quia qui fecit ab initio masculum et feminam fecit eos et dixit propter hoc dimittet homo patrem et matrem et adherebit uxori suae et erunt duo in carne una itaque iam non sunt duo sed una caro quod ergo Deus coniunxit homo non separet dicunt illi quid ergo Moses mandavit dari libellum repudii et dimittere ait illis quoniam Moses ad duritiam cordis vestri permisit vobis dimittere uxores vestras ab initio autem non sic fuit dico autem vobis quia quicumque dimiserit uxorem suam nisi ob fornicationem et aliam duxerit moechatur et qui dimissam duxerit moechatur.

Mark 10:11–12 (referenced at CT, VI, 107.19, 121.4, 409.37–38, 420.4, 421.32, 425.2, 428.34, 429.12, 431.17, 435.5; IX, 409.12–13, 416.37, 418.12):

And he said to them, "Whoever divorces his wife and marries another, commits adultery against her; and if she divorces her husband and marries another, she commits adultery."

Et dicit illis quicumque dimiserit uxorem suam et aliam duxerit adulterium committit super eam et si uxor dimiserit virum suum et alii nupserit moechatur.

> Luke 16:18 (referenced at CT, VI, 101.20, 107.19, 409.39–40, 421.32, 425.2, 427.16, 428.34, 429.12, 431.17, 435.5; IX, 409.13–14, 416.14–15, 418.12):

Every one who divorces his wife and marries another commits adultery, and he who marries a woman divorced from her husband commits adultery.

Omnis qui dimittit uxorem suam et alteram ducit moechatur et qui dimissam a viro ducit moechatur.

Paul's Letters

> Romans 7:2–3 (referenced at CT, VI, 101.18, 410.1–3, 424.23, 427.16, 427.40, 431.17–18, 435.4; IX, 409.7–9, 418.13–15):

Thus a married woman is bound by law to her husband as long as he lives; but if her husband dies she is discharged from the law concerning the husband. Accordingly, she will be called an adulteress if she lives with another man while her husband is alive. But if her husband dies she is free from that law, and if she marries another man she is not an adulteress.

Nam quae sub viro est mulier, vivente viro alligata est legi. Si autem mortuus fuerit vir soluta est a lege viri. Igitur vivente viro vocabitur adultera, si fuerit cum alio viro; si autem mortuus fuerit vir eius, libertata est a lege, ut non sit adultera, si fuerit cum alio viro.

> 1 Corinthians 7:10–11 (referenced at CT, VI, 101.20, 109.2, 112.38, 410.4–6, 420.4, 421.31, 421.45, 424.23, 425.2, 426.15, 427.40, 429.12–13, 431.17–18, 435.4; IX, 409.16–18, 411.21–22, 416.9–10):

To the married I give charge, not I but the Lord, that the wife should not separate from her husband (but if she does, let her remain single or else be reconciled to her husband)—and that the husband should not divorce his wife.

His autem qui matrimonio iuncti sunt praecipio non ego sed Dominus uxorem a viro non discedere quod si discesserit manere innuptam aut viro suo reconciliari et vir uxorem ne dimittat.

> 1 Corinthians 7:39 (referenced at CT, IX, 409.9–10):

A wife is bound to her husband as long as he lives. If the husband dies, she is free to be married to whom she wishes, only in the Lord.

Mulier alligata est quanto tempore vir eius vivit quod si dormierit vir eius liberata est cui vult nubat tantum in Domino.

2 Corinthians 11:2 (referenced at CT, VI, 108.12):

I feel a divine jealousy for you, for I betrothed you to Christ to present you as a pure bride to her husband.

Aemulor enim vos Dei aemulatione despondi enim vos uni viro virginem castam exhibere Christo.

FATHERS, DOCTORS, THEOLOGIANS, AND OTHER WRITERS OF PROMINENCE

Ambrose (339–97)

De patriarcha Abraham, lib. 1, cap. 7, no. 79 (PL 14:442, referenced at CT, IX, 411n4):

It is not licit for you if your wife still lives to take another wife. For indeed to seek another when you have your own is the crime of adultery; this is most serious, because you think in your sin that you should seek freedom in the law [to divorce].

Non licet tibi, uxore vivente uxorem ducere. Nam et aliam quaerere, cum habeas tuam, crimen est adulterii, hoc gravius, quod putas peccato tuo auctoritatem lege quaerendam.

Expositio Evangelii secundum Lucam (In Luc):

Book 8, no. 2, commenting on Paul's advice to Christian spouses in 1 Cor 7:15 (PL 15:1765):

I must first, I think, speak of the law of marriage so as to treat afterward the prohibition of divorce. For some believe that every marriage is from God, especially since it has been written, "What God has joined together, let no man put asunder." Therefore, if every marriage is from God, no marriage may be dissolved. And yet how could the Apostle have said: "But if the unbeliever departs, let him depart"? In this he marvelously shows his unwillingness that there should be grounds for divorce among Christians, and at the same time shows that not every marriage is from God. For it is not by God's authority that Christians marry pagans, since the law forbids this.

Prius dicendum arbitror de lege conjugii, ut postea de prohibendo divortio disputemus. Quidam enim putant omne conjugium a Deo esse, maxime quia scriptum est: *Quae Deus conjunxit, homo non separet (Matt. xix, 6)*. Ergo si omne conjugium a Deo est, omne conjugium non licet solvi. Et quomodo Apostolus dixit: *Quod si infidelis discedit, discedat (I Cor. vii, 15)?* In quo et mirabiliter noluit apud Christianos causam residere divortii, et ostendit non a Deo omne conjugium; neque enim Christianae gentilibus Dei judicio copulantur; cum Lex prohibeat.

Trying to reconcile Paul's teaching with the words of Jesus in the Gospels, Ambrose introduces here the distinction between marriages "from God," meaning marriages between Christians, and marriages that are not from God. Ambrose argues that if a marriage is from God, it is absolutely indissoluble. But he suggests that if the marriage is not from God, it can be dissolved. This raises a problem for Catholic theological tradition, which teaches that marriage from the beginning is indissoluble ("but from the beginning it was not so," Mt 19:8).

Addressing the problem, Ryan and Grisez (hereafter, R/G) introduce the concept of "covenantal marriage," which permits the conclusion that some non-sacramental marriages are indeed not marriages at all (not "from God"), without yielding to the further conclusion that all non-Christian marriages are not from God. Addressing the concept of "covenant," they begin by saying that covenants between people have God as "witness" and "guarantor" (in the covenant on Sinai, God was an actual party to the covenant). Because they are "sacred, not secular," covenants "can be violated, but not broken"; they "are forever, not just for a time," not merely contracts.[1] Extending the notion of covenant to marriage, R/G argue that truly covenantal marriage has God as witness and guarantor. In covenantal marriage, the couple are united not "by their actions alone," but also by the action of God. The covenant entails an "indissoluble personal communion"; the two are united into "a single new reality"—"no longer two but one flesh" (Mt 19:6)—"without losing anything of their true selves."[2] R/G continue: "that oneness, as something really new, can be brought about only by the Creator, and once it has been brought about, it is not subject to human decision."[3] So the "bond" of marriage "is nothing but that covenantal union .... The bond *is* the couple, considered as no longer two but one."[4]

However, as God is its witness and guarantor, *what* it is that he witnesses and guarantees is not just any human coupling, but only unions that are according to his plan. If however a union "significantly deviated from God's plan," the marriage is not "*from God,*" indeed, not a covenantal marriage at all. Ambrose thought Jesus' words "what therefore God has joined together" referred only to marriages between Christians. But Jesus makes clear that marriage *from the beginning* was indissoluble. So, R/G conclude, only true covenantal marriages—which existed from the beginning—are what God joins; they alone are absolutely indissoluble. Quoting a contemporary biblical scholar: "The heart of this teaching has to do with those God joins together, not just any sort of hu-

---

1. Ryan and Grisez, "Indissoluble Marriage," 379.
2. Ibid., 380.
3. Ibid., 382.
4. Ibid., 383.

man coupling or official or legal marriage act." R/G continue: "The practice in most societies has been to marry by means of a secular contract or a covenant guaranteed by false gods, with the result that, though valid according to societal norms, those marriages have not been covenantal unions guaranteed by God. Thus, when fallen human beings married, they were hardly likely to undertake covenantal marriage."[5] R/G conclude: "People clearly do not do so when, for example, a woman is given in marriage against her will, a man marries one woman while planning to have a sexual relationship with another, or someone undertakes marriage with the intention of terminating it if ever he or she judges that it has completely broken down."[6]

Book 8, nos. 4–5 (PL 15:1766–67):

So do not dismiss your wife, lest you deny that God is the author of your marriage.... You dismiss your spouse as if rightly, without guilt; and you think this is permitted to you because human law does not prohibit it. But divine law forbids it. You who submit to men, have reverence for God. Hear the law of the Lord, to whom even those who propose the laws yield: *What God has joined, let no man separate.*

Noli ergo uxorem dimittere, ne Deum tuae copulae diffitearis auctorem .... Dimittis ergo uxorem quasi jure, sine crimine; et putas id tibi licere, quia lex humana non prohibet; sed divina prohibet. Qui hominibus obsequeris, Deum verere. Audi legem Domini, cui obsequuntur etiam qui leges ferunt: *Quae Deus conjunxit, homo non separet* (*Matth.* xix, 6).

Book 8, no. 9 (PL 15:1767–68):

After Jesus had said that not even the least part of the law falls away, he added, "Anyone who dismisses his wife and marries another commits adultery." So the Apostle rightly advises, saying that this is a great *sacramentum* [mystery] regarding Christ and the Church. Therefore you find a marriage that nobody doubts is joined by God, when Jesus himself said, "No one comes to me unless the Father who has sent me draws him." For the Father alone could join this marriage. And therefore Solomon said in a spiritual sense, "A wife is prepared by God for a man." Christ is the husband; the Church is the wife—by her love a wife and by her purity a virgin.

Cum dixisset de Lege unum apicem non posse cadere, subjecit: *Omnis qui dimittit uxorem suam, et ducit alteram, moechatur.* Recte admonet Apostolus dicens sacramentum hoc magnum esse de Christo et Ecclesia (*Ephes.* v, 32). Invenis igitur conjugium quod nemo dubitet a Deo con-

5. Ibid., 389.
6. Ibid., 389n99.

junctum, cum ipse dicat: *Nemo venit ad me, nisi Pater meus qui misit me, attraxerit eum* (Joan. vi, 44); ille enim solus potuit has nuptias copulare. Et ideo mystice Salomon dixit: *A Deo praeparabitur viro uxor* (Prov. xix, 14). Vir Christus, uxor Ecclesia est; charitate uxor, integritate virgo.

De Virginitate, lib. I, cap. VI, no. 31
(PL 16:273):

For although in the former passage he [Jesus] said that marriage should not be dissolved [non solvendum], except for the cause of adultery [fornicationem], he connected these words in the latter passage to the grace and gift of purity; in this way he could teach that marriage should not be condemned, but approved, nevertheless that a dedication to purity is to be preferred to marriage itself.

Nam cum in superioribus conjugium memoraverit non esse solvendum, nisi ex causa fornicationis, in posterioribus integritatis gratiam donumque contexuit. Ut doceret non damnandas esse nuptias, sed probandas; nuptiis tamen ipsis integritatis studia praeferenda.

Mackin argues that when Ambrose uses the verb *solvere* he most likely means that the adultery dissolves the marriage "even before the innocent spouse dismisses the adulterous."[7] In other words, the quote demonstrates that Ambrose does not think marriage is indissoluble. Mackin's interpretation has Ambrose flatly contradicting what he asserts in *In Luc 8*. Let us look at the text from *De Virginitate*, book 1, chap. 6, more closely.

The "former passage" refers to Christ's words in Matthew 19:9: "whoever dismisses his wife, except for *fornicationem*, and marries another, commits adultery," the relevant clause in the Vulgate Latin (which Ambrose does not reference) reading: "dimiserit uxorem suam nisi ob fornicationem." The "latter passage" refers to Matthew 19:10–12, where following Jesus' hard words, the disciples opine that it is better not to marry, and Jesus replies with his instruction on celibacy "for the sake of the kingdom of heaven" and commends anyone "who is able to receive this ... [to] receive it." The point of the passage—indeed of the entirety of *caput VI* and the whole book—is clear: celibacy is to be commended. Is it plausible that in a treatise on celibacy Ambrose would publish *in passing* a highly controversial judgment on the meaning of the so-called exceptive clause in Matthew 19? For if, as Mackin suggests, the use of *solvere* means that adultery dissolves the bond of marriage, implying that remarriage while one's first spouse still lives would not constitute adultery, then Ambrose would be saying what no known writer in the first five centuries ever said.

We would do well to follow Gilles Pelland's principle for interpreting the writings of the Church Fathers on marital indissolubility—that "one should not

---

7. Mackin, *Divorce and Remarriage*, 157.

facilely conclude that an author is contradicting what he maintains elsewhere."[8]
The following is a more plausible interpretation of Ambrose's words.

We see that Ambrose's *conjugium* replaces Matthew's *uxorem*, and *solvere* replaces *dimittere*. Otherwise, Ambrose's *nisi ex causa fornicationis* parallels the Vulgate's rendering of the Matthean passage. Rather than teaching the dissolubility of marriage, the phrase "marriage is not to be dissolved" means that spouses are not to separate except in cases of unchastity. This interpretation is supported by Palmer, who, considering a similar use of *solvere* by the Latin Father Lactantius, writes: "the conclusion [that marriage is dissolved by adultery, thus freeing the innocent party for a new marriage] is not drawn by Lactantius or by any known writer of the first five centuries." It would therefore "seem an anachronism" to interpret Lactantius—and also Ambrose—as referring to more than "the termination of the marriage," in the sense of the dissolution of the spousal commitment and community.[9]

Ambrosiaster (pseudo-Ambrose) (ca. fourth century)[10]

Commentary on 1 Cor. 7 (PL 17:218B, referenced at CT, VI, 101.19, 107.14–15, 413.13–17, 424.34, 425.11–12; IX, 411.7–10n3, 656.42, 675.20):

It is not permitted for the wife to marry, if she dismisses her own husband because of adultery.... It is licit for a husband to remarry if he dismisses a sinful wife, because he is not thus bound by the law as is his wife, because a husband is head of his wife.

Non enim permittitur mulieri, ut nubat, si virum suum causa fornicationis dimiserit.... Viro licet ducere uxorem, si dimiserit uxorem peccantem: quia non ita lege constringitur vir, sicut mulier; caput enim mulieris vir est.

---

8. *L'Osservatore Romano* 5 (February 2, 2000): 9.

9. See Paul F. Palmer, "Christian Marriage: Contract or Covenant?," *Theological Studies* 33 (1972): 617–65, at 626n19.

10. The Council fathers at Trent believed that Ambrosiaster was Ambrose and so that this text was written by the great bishop of Milan. See the discussion of Ambrosiaster in the introduction to this book, 3.

Thomas Aquinas (1225–74)

Summa Theologiae (Supp., q. 62, a. 5, ad 4) (Aquinas, *Opera Omnia*, referenced at CT, IX, 410.1–3, 658.3; translation from Fathers of the English Dominican Province, Christian Classics edition [London: Benziger, 1948], 5:2785):

The exception expressed in our Lord's words [Mt 19:9: "except for adultery"] refers to the putting away of the wife only and not to remarriage. Hence the objection is based on a false interpretation.

Quod exceptio illa, quae est in verbis Domini, refertur ad dimissionem uxoris. Et ideo obiectio de falso intellectu prodedit.

In IV Sent., dist. 35, q. 1, a. 5 (Aquinas, *Opera Omnia*, referenced at CT, VI, 425.5):

Nothing that happens to a marriage can dissolve it; and therefore adultery does not prevent a marriage from being a true marriage, for, as Augustine says, the bond of marriage among living spouses remains, and neither the separation of the spouses nor the joining together of one of the spouses with another removes the bond; and for this reason it is not licit for one spouse to join to another in spousal union while the other spouse is living.

Nihil adveniens supra matrimonium potest ipsum dissolvere; et ideo adulterium non facit quin sit verum matrimonium: manet enim, ut dicit augustinus, inter viventes conjugale vinculum, quod nec separatio nec cum alio junctio potest auferre; et ideo non licet uni, altero vivente, ad aliam copulam transire.

Augustine (354–430)

De Sermone Domini in Monte (394 A.D.):

Book I, cap. 14 (PL 34:1248–49):

Therefore, the Lord, to confirm the idea that it should not be easy to dismiss a wife, made an exception only for adultery; all the other annoyances [in marriage], however, if any by chance exist, he commands for the good of marital fidelity and for the sake of chastity to be borne with fortitude. And he also says that a man is an adulterer who has married a woman who has been dismissed by her husband. Of this matter, the Apostle Paul shows the limit, and he says it ought to be observed for as long as her husband lives; but with the death of her husband, he gives her permission to marry. For he himself also held by this rule, and in it he shows not his own advice, as in some of his admonitions, but a commandment of the Lord, when he says: "and to those who are married I command, yet not I but the Lord, a woman must not separate from her husband; but if she depart, let her remain unmarried, or be reconciled to her husband; and a man should not divorce his wife"; I believe in a similar manner that if he does divorce [his wife] he should not marry another woman, or he should be reconciled to his wife. Indeed, it can happen that a man dismisses his wife for the cause of adultery, which the Lord willed to be an exception. But now if she is not allowed to remarry during the lifetime of her husband from which she has departed, nor he to take another while the wife is living, whom he sent away, much less is it permitted to commit unlawful acts of fornication with anyone whomsoever.

Dominus ergo ad illud confirmandum, ut non facile uxor dimittatur, solam causam fornicationis excepit: caeteras vero universas molestias, si quae forte exstiterint, iubet pro fide coniugali et pro castitate fortiter sustineri. Et moechum dicit etiam virum qui eam duxerit quae soluta est a viro. Cuius rei apostolus Paulus terminum ostendit, qui tam diu observandum dicit, quamdiu vir eius vivit: illo autem mortuo dat nubendi licentiam (*Rom.* vii, 2, 3). Hanc enim etiam ipse regulam tenuit, et in ea non suum consilium sicut in nonnullis monitis, sed praeceptum Domini iubentis ostendit, cum ait: *Eis autem qui sunt in coniugio praecipio, non ego, sed Dominus, mulierem a viro non discedere; quod si discesserit, manere innuptam aut viro suo reconciliari; et vir uxorem ne dimittat* (*1 Cor. vii, 10, 11*). Credo, simili forma, ut si dimiserit non ducat aliam, aut reconcilietur uxori. Fieri enim potest ut dimittat uxorem causa fornicationis, quam Dominus exceptam esse voluit. Iam vero si nec illi nubere conceditur vivo viro a quo recessit, neque huic alteram ducere viva uxore quam dimisit; multo minus fas est illicita cum quibuslibet stupra committere.

Book I, cap. 16 (PL 34:1251, referenced at CT, VI, 411.33–37):

But let us consult the Apostle lest we say anything rashly: "To those who are married," he says, "I give charge, not I but the Lord, that a wife should not separate from her husband; but if she does, let her remain unmarried or be reconciled to her husband." For it is possible that she departs for that cause by which the Lord permitted [departure]. Or if it is licit for a woman to dismiss her husband for other reasons besides adultery and not licit for a husband, what shall we respond regarding that which he said later: "and the husband should not divorce his wife?" Why did he not add: "except for the cause of adultery," which the Lord permits, unless because he wishes a similar pattern to be understood that if he should dismiss his wife—which is permitted for the cause of adultery— she should remain unmarried, or [he should] be reconciled to his wife?

… And because he who says: it is not licit to dismiss one's wife except for the cause of adultery, obliges him to keep his wife, if the cause of adultery is not present; but if it is [present], he does not require him to dismiss her, but permits it; as it is said: let it not be permitted for a woman to marry another except upon the death of her husband; if she should marry before the death of her husband, she is guilty; if she does not marry after her husband's death, she is not guilty; for she has not been commanded to marry, but permitted.[11]

Sed consulamus Apostolum, ne aliquid temere dicamus: *His qui sunt in coniugio*, inquit, *praecipio, non ego, sed Dominus, uxorem a viro non discedere; quod si discesserit, manere innuptam, aut viro suo reconciliari*. Potest enim fieri ut discedat ea causa qua Dominus permittit. Aut si feminae licet virum dimittere etiam praeter causam fornicationis, et non licet viro; quid respondebimus de hoc quod dixit posterius, *Et vir uxorem ne dimittat*? Quare non addidit, *excepta causa fornicationis*, quod Dominus permittit; nisi quia similem formam vult intellegi, ut si dimiserit—quod causa fornicationis permittitur—maneat sine uxore, aut reconcilietur uxori? … Quia et qui dicit, Non licet dimittere uxorem, nisi causa fornicationis; cogit retinere uxorem, si causa fornicationis non fuerit; si autem fuerit, non cogit dimittere, sed permittit: sicut dicitur, Non liceat mulieri nubere alteri, nisi mortuo viro; si ante viri mortem nupserit, rea est; si post viri mortem non nupserit, non est rea; non enim iussa est nubere, sed permissa.)

De Bono Conjugali (401 A.D.):
Chap. 7 (PL 40:378–79; English translation from FOTC 27):[12]

To such a degree is that marriage compact entered upon a matter of a certain sacrament, that it is not made void even by separation itself, since, so long as her husband lives, even by whom she has been left, she commits adultery, in case she be married to another; and he who left her is the cause of this evil …. Even by divorce the marital covenant is not dissolved; so that they continue to be spouses to one another even after separation; and they commit adultery with those, with whom they shall be joined after their divorce, either the woman with a man, or the man with a woman. And yet not except in the City of our God, in his Holy Mountain, is such the case with a wife.

11. After reviewing Augustine's ideas in *De Sermone Domini in Monte*, Mackin makes the astonishing assertion: "there is one thing of which Augustine remains certain. There is no more than one cause justifying the dissolution of a marriage. This is *fornicatio*, understood as the religious infidelity he has defined in this chapter." Mackin, *Divorce and Remarriage*, 198.

12. FOTC is an abbreviation for the Fathers of the Church series by the Catholic University of America Press.

Usque adeo foedus illud initum nuptiale cujusdam sacramenti res est, ut nec ipsa separatione irritum fiat, quandoquidem vivente viro et a quo relicta est moechatur si alteri nupserit, et ille huius mali causa est qui reliquit.... Interveniente divortio non aboletur illa confoederatio nuptialis: ita ut sibi coniuges sint, etiam separati; cum illis autem adulterium committant, quibus fuerint etiam post suum repudium copulate, vel illa viro, vel ille mulieri. Nec tamen nisi in civitate Dei nostri, in monte sancto eius (*Psal.* xlvii, 2), talis est causa cum uxore.

Chap. 15 (PL 40:385; English translation from FOTC 27):

But once a marriage has been entered into in the City of God [i.e., if it is a Christian marriage], where even from the first joining of two human beings a certain sacrament of marriage was born, it can in no way be dissolved except by the death of one of the spouses. For the bond of marriage remains even if offspring because of obvious sterility should not be forthcoming. Thus even though the spouses know they will have no children, nevertheless it would not be licit to separate and remarry even for the sake of bearing children. Because if they did this, they would commit adultery with those whom they had intercourse, remaining still married to one another.

Semel autem initum connubium in civitate Dei nostri, ubi etiam ex prima duorum hominum copula quoddam sacramentum nuptiae gerunt, nullo modo potest nisi alicuius eorum morte dissolvi. Manet enim vinculum nuptiarum, etiamsi proles, cuius causa initum est, manifesta sterilitate non subsequatur: ita ut iam scientibus coniugibus non se filios habituros, separare se tamen vel ipsa causa filiorum atque aliis copulare non liceat. Quod si fecerint, cum eis quibus se copulaverint, adulterium committunt, ipsi autem coniuges manent.

Section 24 (32 in some editions) (PL 40:394, referenced at CT, VI, 102.1; English translation from FOTC 27):

Therefore the good of marriage through all nations and all men and women lies in the cause of procreation and the faith of chastity. But so far as the people of God are concerned, it lies also in the sanctity of the sacrament by reason of which it is forbidden for a woman, even one dismissed in divorce by her husband to marry another so long as her husband lives, and not even for the sake of bearing children. Although this alone is why they marry [viz., procreation], even if this for which the marriage took place does not come about, the nuptial bond is not dissolved except by the death of a spouse. Just as if the ordination of a cleric takes place in order to gather the people, even if the gathering of people does not follow, nevertheless there remains in those ordained the *sacramentum* of orders. And if, because of any fault, someone is removed from [clerical] office, he will not lose the sacramentum of the Lord once it has been imposed, although continuing to his condemnation.

Bonum igitur nuptiarum per omnes gentes atque omnes homines in causa generandi est, et in fide castitatis: quod autem ad populum Dei pertinet, etiam in sanctitate Sacramenti, per quam nefas est etiam repudio discedentem alteri nubere, dum vir eius vivit, nec saltem ipsa causa pariendi; quae cum sola sit qua nuptiae fiunt, nec ea re non subsequente propter quam fiunt, solvitur vinculum nuptiale nisi coniugis morte. Quemadmodum si fiat ordinatio cleri ad plebem congregandam, etiamsi plebis congregatio non subsequatur, manet tamen in illis ordinatis Sacramentum ordinationis; et si aliqua culpa quisquam ab officio removeatur, Sacramento Domini semel imposito non carebit, quamvis ad iudicium permanente.

De Fide et Operibus (413 A.D.):

Chap. 1 (PL 40:198):
They seem, however, to be prompted to this dispute, because it troubled them that those husbands who dismiss their wives and remarry, or women who dismiss their husbands and who remarry were not admitted to Baptism; because these are not marriages, but adulteries, Christ is without any doubt the witness. For since they cannot deny to be adultery what Truth without ambiguity affirms is adultery, they want to support those to receive Baptism whom they saw so caught by a snare of this kind, that if they were not admitted to Baptism, they would prefer to live or even die without any sacrament, rather than to be freed by breaking the bond of adultery.

Ad hanc autem disputationem videntur impulsi, quod eos moverit non admitti ad Baptismum qui dimissis uxoribus alias duxerint, vel feminas quae dimissis viris aliis nupserint; quia haec non coniugia, sed adulteria esse Dominus Christus sine ulla dubitatione testator (*Matth.* xix, 9). Cum enim negare non possent esse adulterium, quod Veritas adulterium esse sine ambage confirmat, eisque suffragari vellent ad accipiendum Baptismum, quos huiusmodi laqueo ita captos viderent, ut si non admitterentur ad Baptismum, sine ullo sacramento mallent vivere vel etiam mori, quam disrupto adulterii vinculo liberari.

Chap. 19 (PL 40:221, referenced at CT, VI, 413.18–23, 425.12; IX, 409.3–4, 675.21):
Also, whoever shall dismiss a wife caught in adultery and marry another, it does not seem he should be on the same level as those who dismiss wives for causes other than adultery and remarry: and in the divine

decrees it is so obscure whether even he to whom indeed it is without doubt allowed to dismiss an adulteress wife is nevertheless considered to be an adulterer if he remarries; so that, in my estimation, each one in this situation is guilty of venial sin.

Quisquis etiam uxorem in adulterio deprehensam dimiserit, et aliam duxerit, non videtur aequandus eis qui excepta causa adulterii dimittunt et ducunt: et in ipsis divinis sententiis ita obscurum est utrum et iste, cui quidem sine dubio adulteram licet dimittere, adulter tamen habeatur si alteram duxerit, ut, quantum existimo, venialiter ibi quisque fallatur.

De Genesi Ad Litteram Libri Duodecim (414 A.D.):

Book 9, chap. 7 (PL 34:397; English translation from FOTC 84):

This then is the threefold good of marriage: faith, offspring, sacrament. By faith spouses take care lest outside the bond of marriage they have intercourse with another man or woman. By offspring spouses take care to receive children lovingly, nourish them kindly, and educate them religiously. But by *sacramentum*, spouses take care not to separate the marriage; and if dismissed, not to be joined again in marriage even for the sake of offspring.

Hoc autem tripartitum est; fides, proles, sacramentum. In fide attenditur ne praeter vinculum coniugale, cum altera vel altero concumbatur: in prole, ut amanter suscipiatur, benigne nutriatur, religiose educetur: in sacramento autem, ut coniugium non separetur, et dimissus aut dimissa nec causa prolis alteri coniungatur.

De Nuptiis et Concupiscentia (418 A.D.):

Book I, chap. 11 (PL 44:420; English translation [with minor corrections] from NPNF-I, vol. 5)[13]

It is certainly not fecundity only, the fruit of which consists in offspring, nor chastity only, whose bond is fidelity, but also a certain sacramental bond in marriage which is recommended to believers in wedlock. Accordingly it is enjoined by the apostle: "Husbands, love your wives, even as Christ also loved the Church." Of this bond the substance [*res*] undoubtedly is this, that the man and the woman who are joined together in matrimony remain inseparable as long as they live; and that it should be unlawful for one consort to be parted from the other, except for the cause of fornication. For this is preserved in the case of Christ and the

---

13. NPNF is an abbreviation for Nicene and Post-Nicene Fathers of the Church, ed. Philip Schaff (Peabody, Mass.: Hendrickson, 1994), in two series.

Church; that a living one with a living one should be separated by no divorce for ever. And so complete is the observance of this bond in the city of our God, in His holy mountain—that is to say, in the Church of Christ—and among all married believers, who are undoubtedly members of Christ, that, although women marry, and men take wives, for the purpose of procreating children, it is never permitted one to put away even an unfruitful wife so that another fertile wife may be married. But if anyone whosoever does this is held to be guilty of adultery by the law of the gospel; though not by this world's law, which allows a divorce between the parties, without even the allegation of guilt, and the contraction of other nuptial engagements—a concession which, the Lord testifies, even the holy Moses extended to the people of Israel, because of the hardness of their hearts. The same condemnation applies to the woman, if she is married to another man. So enduring, indeed, are the rights of marriage once entered into between living persons, as long as they both live, that they [who are] spouses between themselves are more spouses than those who have separated from one another, rather than they between whom a new connection has been formed. Clearly they would not be adulterers with [these] others, unless they were remaining spouses to each other. Therefore, if the husband die, with whom a true marriage was made, a true marriage is now possible with whom before there was adultery. Thus between the conjugal pair, as long as they live, the nuptial bond remains, which neither separation nor union with another can take away. But it remains, in such cases, only for injury from the sin, not for a bond of the covenant. In like manner the soul of an apostate, withdrawing, as it were, from its marriage union with Christ, does not, even though it has cast its faith away, lose the sacrament of its faith, which it received by means of the laver of regeneration. It would undoubtedly be given back to him if he were to return, even if he had lost it on his departure from Christ. However, he who withdrew retains this apostasy, to the increase of his punishment, not for meriting the reward.

Non tantum fecunditas, cuius fructus in prole est, nec tantum pudicitia, cuius vinculum est fides, verum etiam quoddam sacramentum nuptiarum commendatur fidelibus coniugatis, unde dicit Apostolus: *Viri, diligite uxores vestras, sicut et Christus dilexit Ecclesiam* (*Ephes. v, 25*): huius procul dubio sacramenti res est, ut mas et femina connubio copulati quamdiu vivunt inseparabiliter perseverant, nec liceat, excepta causa fornicationis, a coniuge coniugem dirimi (Matth. v, 32). Hoc enim custoditur in Christo et Ecclesia, ut vivens cum vivente in aeternum nullo divortio separetur. Cuius sacramenti tanta observatio est in civitate Dei nostri, in monte sancto eius (*Psal. xlvii, 2*), hoc est, in Ecclesia Christi, quibusque fidelibus coniugatis, qui sine dubio membra sunt Christi, ut, cum filiorum procreandorum causa vel nubant feminae, vel ducantur uxores, nec sterilem coniugem fas sit relinquere, ut alia fecunda ducatur. Quod si quisquam fecerit, non lege huius saeculi, ubi interveniente repudio sine crimine conceditur cum aliis alia copulare connubia; quod etiam sanctum Moysen Dominus, propter duritiam cordis illorum Israelitis permisisse testator: sed lege Evangelii reus est adulterii; sicut etiam illa, si alteri nupserit (*Matth*. xix, 8, 9). Usque adeo manent inter viventes semel inita iura nuptiarum, ut potius sint inter se coniuges qui ab alterutro separati sunt, quam cum his quibus aliis adhaeserunt. Cum aliis quippe adulteri non essent, nisi ad alterutrum coniuges permanerent. Denique mortuo viro cum quo verum connubium fuit, fieri verum connubium potest cum quo prius adulterium fuit. Ita manet inter viventes quiddam coniugale, quod nec separatio, nec cum altero copulatio possit auferre. Manet autem ad noxam criminis, non ad vinculum foederis: sicut apostatae anima velut de coniugio Christi recedens, etiam fide perdita Sacramentum fidei non amittit, quod lavacro regenerationis accepit. Redderetur enim procul dubio redeunti, si amisisset abscedens. Habet autem hoc qui recesserit ad cumulum supplicii, non ad meritum praemii.

De Adulterinis Conjugiis ad Pollentium (419 A.D.):

Book I, chap. 9 (PL 40:456–57, referenced at CT, VI, 107.18, 455.35n10; IX, 414.28. English translation (with minor corrections) from "On Adulterous Marriages," in *Marriage and Virginity*, 147–48)

"Why, then," you say, "did the Lord introduce the cause of adultery, and not say more generally, 'Whosoever dismisses his wife and marry another, commits adultery,' if he is also an adulterer, who dismisses his wife for adultery and marries another?" I believe it is because the Lord wished to draw attention to that which is more serious. For who would deny that if someone takes another wife after divorcing a wife who has not committed adultery, this adultery is worse than remarrying after divorcing a wife who commits adultery? It is not because in the latter case there is no adultery, but it is less serious than where one remarries after dismissing a wife who commits adultery. For in a similar use of words, the Apostle James says: *If someone knows the right thing to do but does not do it, that person commits a sin* [Jas 4:17]. Does it follow from this that someone who does not know the right thing to do, and therefore does not do it, does not also commit a sin? This person does, certainly, commit a sin, but the sin is worse if the person should know and still does not do it. Being a less serious sin does not make it no sin at all. We can say similar things in both cases. Just as anyone who divorces his wife, except for adultery, and marries someone else, commits adultery, so anyone who knows the right thing to do, and does not do it, commits a sin. In the latter case, however, it is not correct to say, "Therefore, anyone who does not know does not commit a sin." There are also sins committed in ignorance, although they are less serious than sins committed knowingly. Similarly in the other case, it is not correct to say, "Someone who divorces his wife for committing adultery, and then remarries, does not commit adultery"; as there is also the adultery of those who remarry after leaving their first wives because of adultery, although this is certainly not as bad as the adultery of those who divorce their wives for reasons other than adultery and then remarry. In the same way as it was said, *If someone knows the right thing to do but does not do it, that person commits a sin* [Jas 4:17], it can also be said, "If someone divorces his wife, but not for adultery, and marries someone else, that person commits adultery." So then, if we say, "Anyone who marries a woman who has been divorced by her husband, though not for committing adultery, commits adultery," undoubtedly what we say is true; but we do not thereby absolve from similar guilt the one who marries a woman who has been divorced for committing adultery. We have no doubt at all that both are guilty of adultery. In a similar way, we declare that the man who divorces his wife, though not for committing adultery, and marries someone else, is an adulterer; and we do not thereby defend as untainted by this sin the one who divorces his wife and then marries someone else, when it is because she has committed adultery. Although one is worse than the other, we know that both are adulterers. No one would be so absurd as to say that someone who marries the woman cast aside by her husband because of adultery is not an adulterer, while someone who marries the one cast aside when it is not for adultery is an adulterer. So both are adulterers. Hence, when we say that anyone who marries a woman divorced by her husband for reasons other than adultery commits adultery, we are speaking of one of them, but we are not thereby denying that the other (the one who marries a woman rejected by her husband for committing adultery) also commits adultery. Accordingly, both commit adultery, both the one who divorces his wife when she has not committed adultery and then marries someone else, and the one who marries someone else after divorcing his wife because of her adultery. Therefore, when we read something about one of these, we certainly must not infer that if one is explicitly said to be guilty of adultery, the other is thereby said not to be.

Cur ergo, inquis, interposuit Dominus causam fornicationis, et non potius generaliter ait, Quicumque dimiserit uxorem suam et aliam duxerit, moechatur; si et ille moechus est, qui dimissa fornicante muliere alteram ducit? Credo, quia illud quod maius est, hoc Dominus commemorare voluit. Maius enim adulterium esse quis negat, uxore non fornicante dimissa alteram ducere, quam si fornicantem quisque dimiserit, et tunc alteram duxerit? Non quia et hoc adulterium non est; sed quia minus est, ubi fornicante dimissa altera ducitur. Nam simili locutione usus etiam Apostolus Iacobus ait: *Scienti igitur bonum facere, et non facienti, peccatum est illi (Jacobi* iv, 17). Numquid ideo non peccatum est illi etiam, qui nescit bonum facere, et ideo non facit? Utique peccatum est; sed hoc gravius, si etiam sciat et non faciat: nec illud ideo nullum, quia minus. Ut ergo eodem modo utrumque dicamus: sicut quicumque dimiserit uxorem, excepta causa fornicationis, et aliam duxerit, moechatur; ita quicumque scit bonum facere et non facit, peccat. Sed quemadmodum hic recte dici non potest, Ergo si nescit, non peccat; sunt enim etiam peccata ignorantium, quamvis minora quam scientium: ita nec illic recte dici potest, Ergo si causa fornicationis dimiserit, et aliam duxerit, non moechatur; est enim moechatio eorum etiam, qui alias ducunt, relictis propter fornicationem prioribus; sed utique minor quam eorum qui non propter fornicationem dimittunt, et alteras ducunt. Potest quippe, sicut dictum est, *Scienti bonum facere, et non facienti, peccatum est illi*; eodem modo et illud dici, Dimittenti uxorem sine causa fornicationis, et aliam ducenti, moechatio est illi. Quemadmodum igitur si dixerimus, Quicumque mulierem a marito praeter causam fornicationis dimissam duxerit, moechatur, procul dubio verum dicimus; nec tamen ideo illum qui propter causam fornicationis dimissam duxerit, ab hoc crimine absolvimus, sed utrosque moechos esse minime dubitamus: ita eum qui praeter causam fornicationis uxorem dimiserit et aliam duxerit, moechum pronuntiamus; nec ideo tamen eum qui propter causam fornicationis dimiserit, et alteram duxerit, ab huius peccati labe defendimus. Ambos enim, licet alterum altero gravius, moechos tamen esse cognoscimus. Neque enim quisquam ita est absurdus, ut moechum neget esse qui duxerit eam quam maritus propter causam fornicationis abiecit, cum moechum dicat eum, qui duxerit eam quae praeter causam fornicationis abiecta est: sic ergo isti ambo sunt moechi. Unde, cum dicimus, Quicumque mulierem praeter causam fornicationis a viro dimissam duxerit, moechatur; de uno quidem ipsorum dicimus, nec tamen ideo moechari negamus eum qui eam duxerit, quam propter causam fornicationis maritus dimiserit: ita, cum ambo sint moechi, et ille scilicet qui dimiserit uxorem suam praeter causam fornicationis et aliam duxerit, et ille qui propter causam fornicationis uxore dimissa se alteri copulaverit; profecto quando de uno eorum legimus, non ita intellegere debemus, quasi ex hoc alter moechus negatus sit, quod alter expressus sit.

Book II, chaps. 4–5 (PL 40:473, referenced at CT, VI, 110.4, 411.38–40, 425.6.13; English translation from Rotelle, 168):

It is not wrong, therefore, for a wife to be divorced for adultery; but her obligation of chastity remains, and this makes anyone who marries a divorced woman guity of adultery, even in this case of divorce because of adultery. When someone guilty of some crime is excommunicated, the sacrament of rebirth remains present in that person, and that person does not lose that sacrament even if he or she is never reconciled with God. In the same way, when a wife is divorced for committing adultery, the bond of marriage union remains in her, and she does not lose that bond even if she is never reconciled with her husband. She will lose it, however if her husband dies.

Licite itaque dimittitur conjunx ob causam fornicationis; sed manet vinculum prioris, propter quod fit reus adulterii, qui dimissam duxerit etiam ob causam fornicationis.... Sicut enim manente in se Sacramento regenerationis, excommunicatur cujusquam reus criminis, nec illo Sacramento caret, etiamsi nunquam reconcilietur Deo: ita manente in se vinculo foederis conjugalis, uxor dimittitur ob causam fornicationis, nec carebit illo vinculo, etiamis nunquam reconcilietur viro; carebit autem, si mortuus fuerit vir ejus.

Basil the Great

Moralia, rule 73, chap. 2 (PG 31:851; English translation from FOTC 9):

It is not lawful for a man to dismiss his wife and marry another. Nor is it permitted that a man should marry a wife who has been divorced by her husband.

Non licet viro, uxore dimissa, aliam ducere: neque fas est repudiatam a marito, ab alio duci uxorem.

Canonical Epistle 188, to Amphilochius (c. 9) (PG 32:678–79; English translation [with minor corrections] from Joyce, *Christian Marriage*, 322–23):

Our Lord's declaration that it is unlawful for one married person to depart from the other save because of fornication should logically hold good equally in regard of women and of men. Custom, however, has it otherwise. In the case of wives, we find great strictness: for as the Apostle says: "He that is joined to a harlot is one body with her" (1 Cor. 6:16): and Jeremiah, "If a wife shall have been with another man, she shall not return to her husband, but shall remain in her pollution" (Jer. 3:1): and again, "He who has joined to an adulteress is foolish and impious" (Prov. 18:22). Yet custom prescribes that even adulterous husbands who are living in fornication should be retained by their wives. Wherefore I do not know whether she who cohabits with a husband dismissed by his wife can be called an adulteress. In these cases the blame attaches to the woman who has dismissed her husband, and in proportion to the nature of the cause which led her to depart. If, having been beaten, she should not bear the blows, then in that case it was better for her to bear them than to be separated from her husband. If it was that she would not endure the wasting of her money, not even this is a just cause. But if it was that he lives in fornication, [even here] our ecclesiastical custom does not admit it. No, on the contrary, a woman is not bidden to be separated even from an unbelieving husband, but to wait because none can say what may be the result: "Indeed, how knowest thou, O wife, if thou shalt save thy husband?" Wherefore she who leaves her husband is an adulteress if she goes to another man. But the man who is left by his wife is to be worthy of pardon, and she who cohabits with him does not merit condemnation. But if the husband leaves his wife and goes to another woman he is himself an adulterer, "because he causes her to commit adultery" (Mt. 5:32): and she who cohabits with him is an adulteress, because she led over to herself another woman's husband.

Aeque viris et mulieribus convenit secundum sententiae consecutionem quod a Domino pronuntiatum est, non licere a matrimonio discedere, nisi ob fornicationem. Consuetudo autem non ita se habet, sed mulieribus quidem multa accurate observari deprehendimus, cum Apostolus quidem dicat, *Quod qui adhaeret meretrici, fit unum corpus*; Jeremias vero, *Quod si fuerit mulier cum alio viro, non revertetur ad virum suum, sed polluta polluetur;* et iterum, *Qui habet adulteram, stultus est et impius.* Consuetudo autem etiam adulteros viros et in fornicationibus versantes jubet a mulieribus retineri. Quare quae una cum viro dimisso habitat, nescio an possit adultera appellari. Crimen enim hic attingit mulierem, quae virum dimisit, quanam de causa a conjugio discesserit. Sive enim percussa plagas non ferat, ferre satius erat quam a conjuge separari: sive damnum in pecuniis non ferat, ne haec quidem justa excusatio: sin autem, quoniam ipse vivit in fornicatione, non habemus hanc in ecclesiastica consuetudine observationem, imo vero ab infideli viro non jussa est mulier separari, sed propter eventum incertum remanere. *Quid enim scis, mulier, an virum salvum sis factura*? Quare, quae reliquit, est adultera, si ad alium virum accessit. Qui autem relictus est, dignus est venia, et quae una cum eo habitat, non condemnatur. Sed si vir, qui ab uxore discessit, accessit ad aliam, est et ipse adulter, quia facit ut ipsa adulterium committat; et quae una cum ipso habitat, est adultera, quia alienum virum ad se traduxit.

Canonical Epistle 199, to Amphilochius (c. 48) (PG 32:731B, referenced at CT, IX, 656.42–43, 675.18):

If a wife has been abandoned by her husband, she should, in my opinion, remain as she is.

Quae a marito relicta est, mea quidem sententia, manere debet.

Although not quoted at Trent, Letter 188 is perhaps the most frequently quoted early Patristic text apparently witnessing to a tradition of toleration for divorce and remarriage in the Byzantine Church during the first five centuries of Christianity. So we must ask, are Basil's statements ("I do not know whether she who cohabits with a husband dismissed by his wife can be called an adulteress"; "the man who is left by his wife is to be worthy of pardon, and she who cohabits with him does not merit condemnation") sure indications that Basil rejects the doctrine of absolute indissolubility?

Gilles Pelland notes that the question that Amphilochius, bishop of Iconium, puts to Basil pertains to the exercise of the bishop's office of discipline; the text therefore must be read within this proper "penitential context."[14] Amphilochius is not asking Basil to render a moral judgment on particular practices or customs. He is asking what penances he should impose: should the woman be "called an adulteress" (i.e., should the canonical penalty for adultery be imposed upon her)? Is the husband "to be pardoned" or should he be punished as an adulterer? After explaining (with some diffidence) the "consuetudo" (custom) of the ecclesial community in Cappadocia, Basil replies to the question of whether the actions do or do not merit the full penalty for adultery.

The custom permits husbands to dismiss their wives for adultery, but not wives their husbands. What happens then when a wife does in fact wrongfully dismiss her husband, and the husband goes on to cohabit with another woman; should the paramour, if she wishes to return to ecclesial communion, have the full canonical discipline for adultery imposed upon her? Based upon the customary prescription, Basil expresses his opinion ("I do not know whether she ... can be called an adulteress"). Does this represent Basil's own view of the matter? It is unclear. Nor is it clear that he approves of the one-sided implications of the "ecclesiastical custom": viz., that wives should endure their husband's blows, recklessness with their (the wives') money, even their husband's adulteries without dismissing them. Because he passed on the custom and its implications to Amphilochius, we can be reasonably sure he does not strongly oppose them

---

14. Giles Pelland, SJ, "Did the Church Treat the Divorced and Remarried More Leniently in Antiquity than Today?," *L'Osservatore Romano* (English edition) 5 (February 2, 2000): 9.

(after all, he does say "*I* do not know ..."). Nevertheless, his reference to "great strictness" suggests that the opinion he renders does not—or at least does not fully—represent his own views.

But whether or not it does, the text tells us nothing whatever about Basil's views of remarriage after the "divorce," since the woman in question is the man's paramour, not his wife. Basil says that the man who is deserted by his wife "is to be pardoned." This must mean he should be pardoned when seeking to be reconciled to the church. Pardoned for what? It is not clear. Pardoned for the separation? But for this the man is not to blame; blame attaches rather to his wife. Pardoned for his fornication? Only if he repents of it. There is absolutely no basis for concluding that Basil (or any ancient Christian writer) thinks the man should pardoned—that is, restored to ecclesial communion—without first repenting for his illicit relationship. So it must mean pardoned after extricating himself from it. Could "pardoned" also mean that the man should not have the canonical penalty for adultery imposed upon him when seeking to be restored to full communion? If so, Basil chose an obscure way of expressing this.

But, again, none of this is relevant to the question of what Basil thought about divorce and remarriage for Christians, as the Greeks at the time of Trent (and some Orthodox scholars still today) assumed to be the case.[15] For, as Crouzel notes, the man is not remarried, but merely cohabiting.[16]

Basil also addresses the question of whether the bishop should impose the penance for adultery upon the paramour of the man wrongfully dismissed. Basil says the woman "does not merit condemnation" (i.e., condemnation under the canons for adultery). Commenting on this passage, Kampowski and Pérez-Soba write: "In speaking about a form of tolerance [the passage] clarifies neither the terms nor the limits within which it unfolds. The context is a set of widely varied 'canons' that deal with specific cases and are difficult to evaluate. It is something quite different from an established norm aimed at considering a divorced-and-remarried person as having a status that is accepted within the Church."[17]

Mackin claims that between 365, when the *Moralia* (at latest) was written, and 374/75 when *Canonical Epistle* 188 is dated, we see "an apparent change in [Basil's] judgement about the permissibility of remarriage after dismissal"; Basil clearly disapproves of remarriage after divorce in the *Moralia* (rule 73, chap. 2, quoted above); but over time, Mackin argues, he "appears" to come to "accept" some second marriages. Yet Mackin concedes that this is an argument from "si-

---

15. See John Meyendorff, *Marriage: An Orthodox Perspective* (Crestwood: N.Y.: St. Vladimir's Seminary Press, 1978), 49.

16. Crouzel, *L'Église primitive face au divorce*, 155–56.

17. Stephan Kampowski and Juan José Pérez-Soba, *The Gospel of the Family: Going Beyond Cardinal Kasper's Proposal in the Debate on Marriage, Civil Re-Marriage and Communion in the Church* (San Francisco: Ignatius, 2014), 118.

lence," since Basil actually never says this.[18] Fulbert Cayré, in his in-depth work on the canons of Basil, disagrees. He denies that Basil authorizes any second marriages in ep. 188; the most we can say is he does not think that all illicit sexual unions that include at least one married person should be punished *as* adultery: "One fact is assured and certain: one cannot affirm that Saint Basil, in the canonical letters, permits the divorced husband to contract a second marriage, licit and legitimate in the Church, during the lifetime of his wife."[19] Joyce writes: "it is evident that [ep. 188] affords no ground whatever for thinking that St. Basil tolerated divorce and remarriage. When he actually does speak of the subject, he declares it to be absolutely unlawful [reference to *Moralia*, rule 73]."[20]

Rist argues that Basil seems at least willing "to tolerate a second marriage after divorce in limited circumstances."[21] But what in ep. 188 leads Rist to this conclusion? The aggrieved husband is only cohabiting, he is not "remarried," that is clear. There is no evidence that he or his paramour have asked Amphilochius to restore them to communion as they are—that is, while continuing in their state of fornication. Moreover, no Patristic writer—except for the enigmatic Ambrosiaster—ever suggested that such could be licit. And no canonical process existed in the Byzantine church before the ninth century for returning couples in second unions to ecclesial communion without first rejecting the latter unions. It is anachronicistic to read Basil's text as implicitly sanctioning second marriages of any sort.

We do well here to attend to the words of Gilles Pelland: "One should be very wary of appeals to the argument 'ex silentio' (for example: 'the author does not say this or that, but there are reasons to believe he thought so'). This could be a way of making the texts say what one wants them to say."[22]

Bede (the Venerable) (673–735)

Commentary on Mark 10 (PL 92:230; referenced at CT, VI, 411.17–21):

He said to them, whoever dismisses ... In Matthew [19:9] it is written more fully: *whoever dismisses his wife, except on account of adultery, and marries another commits adultery*. Therefore, there is only one carnal reason, adultery, and one spiritual reason, the fear of God, for a wife to be

---

18. Mackin, *Divorce and Remarriage*, 146, 149.

19. "Ainsi, un fait reste acquis et certain: on ne peut affirmer que saint Basile, dans ses Lettres canoniques, permette au mari divorcé de contracter un second marriage, licite et légitime devant l'Église, du vivant de sa femme." F. Cayré, "Le divorce au IV siècle dans la loi civile et les canons de saint Basile," in *Échos d'Orient* 19 (1920): 295–321, at 319. Crouzel, Ryan/Grisez, and Joyce agree: Crouzel, *L'église primitive face au divorce*, 147; Ryan and Grisez, *Indissoluble Marriage*, 372–73n27.

20. Joyce, *Christian Marriage*, 324.

21. Rist, "Divorce and Remarriage," 90–91.

22. Pelland, "Divorced and Remarried," 9.

dismissed, just as many, we read, are to have done for the sake of religion. However, no reason has been written in the law of God that permits another woman to be wed while she who was abandoned is living.

Et dixit illis: Quicunque dimiserit ... In Matthaeo [19:9] scriptum plenius est: *Quicunque dimiserit uxorem suam, nisi ob fornicationem, et aliam duxerit, moechatur* (Matth v). Una ergo solummodo causa est carnalis, fornicatio: una spiritalis, timor Dei, ut uxor dimittatur, sicut multi religionis causa fecisse leguntur. Nulla autem causa est Dei lege perscripta, ut vivente ea, quae relicta est, alia ducatur.

Pseudo-Bede

Commentary on 1 Cor. 10 (from *Venerabilis Bedae Operum*, tom. VI, "In Omnes Divi Pauli Epistolas" [Coloniae Agrippinae, 1688], col. 322; referenced at CT, VI, 411.22–32):

Therefore the Lord, to confirm that a wife may not easily be dismissed, made the cause of adultery the sole exception. He commands that all other troubles are to be bravely endured and calls the man also an adulterer, who married a woman who has been divorced from her husband. The apostle Paul shows the limit of this state of affairs, because he says that it is to be observed as long as her husband lives. However, if he dies, she is free to marry. For he also held this rule, and in it he shows the precept of the Lord's command when he says, "But to those who are married, I do not command" ... I believe by a similar pattern that if the husband dismisses the wife, he should not marry another, or else be reconciled to his wife; for it is possible to send his wife away on account of adultery, which the Lord wanted to be an exception. Now indeed if she is not permitted to remarry while the spouse from whom she separated is living, and he is not permitted to marry another while the wife whom he dismissed is living, much less is it lawful for her to commit unlawful fornications with anybody whatsoever.

Dominus ergo ad illud confirmandum, ut non facile uxor dimittatur, solam causam fornicationis excepit; caeteras vero universas molestias ... iubet ... fortiter sustineri et moechum dicit etiam virum, qui eam duxerit, quae soluta est a viro. Cuius rei Paulus apostolus terminum ostendit, quia tamdiu observandum dicit, quamdiu vir eius vivit. Illo autem mortuo dat nubendi licentiam. Hanc enim etiam regulam ipse tenuit et in ea ... praeceptum Domini iubentis ostendit, cum ait: *Eis autem, quae nuptae sunt, praecipio non ego* ... Credo simili forma, ut, si dimiserit, non ducat aliam aut reconcilietur uxori; fieri enim potest, ut dimittat uxorem causa fornicationis, quam Dominus exceptam esse voluit. Iam vero si nec illi nubere conceditur vivo viro, a quo recessit, neque huic alteram ducere viva uxore, quam dimisit, multo minus fas est illicita eum cum quibuslibet stupra committere.

Cardinal Cajetan (d. 1534)

Commentary on Matthew 19:9 (quoted and referenced at CT, IX, 417.9 and 417n1):

Because whoever dismisses [his wife does so] completely. Indeed, the discussion [between the Pharisees and Christ] was about a dismissal of this kind; for to dismiss a wife without adding a condition means not to dismiss her according to something—for example, as far as the bed—but simply and absolutely, that is, to dismiss her completely; and it is certain that the question concerning absolute dismissal was put forward by the Pharisees and that Moses talks about it.

Quod quicumque dimiserit totaliter. De tali enim dimissione erat sermo; nam uxorem dimittere absque additione aliqua, significat non dimittere secundum quid, puta quoad thorum, sed simpliciter et absolute, quod est dimittere totaliter, constatque, de dimissione absoluta motam esse quaestionem a pharisaeis et loqui Moysen.

Commentary on Matthew 5:32 (quoted and referenced at CT, IX, 417n1):

The context invites those present to the understanding [that Jesus is referring to] a complete dismissal [of the wife], since from that law, for I will speak, saying, that the law is clear: "He that puts away his wife, let him give her a writing of divorce."

Contextus invitat ad intelligendum de dimissione totali, quoniam de illa constat legem loqui dicentem: "Qui dimiserit uxorem, det illi libellum repudii."

Canons of the Apostles

Canon 47 (Constitutiones Apostolorum, ed. F. X. Funk [Paderborn, 1905], 1:579.14–15; referenced at CT, VI, 101.21, 410.4–6; IX, 411.24–25, 649n2, 665.11–12):

If any layman drives away his wife and marries another, or marries a woman who has been dismissed by another, let him be excommunicated.

Si quis laicus uxorem suam expellens aliam duxerit aut ab alio dimissam, excommunicetur.

Erasmus (1466–1536)[23]

Annotationes in Matthaeum 19:9 (from *Opera Omnia* [Leiden: Lugduni Batavorum, 1705], t. VI, 97–98, 103 D–E):

A woman who has committed adultery has ceased forthwith to be a wife and has deprived herself of the right to marriage; she has divided the flesh that God willed to be one and indivisible.

Quae alteri viro sui fecit copiam iam uxor esse desiit et matrimonii ius ademit sibi, divisa carne quam Deus unam et indivisam esse voluit.

Paraphrases in Novum Tetamentum, In Marcum 10 (from *Opera Omnia* [Leiden: Lugduni Batavorum, 1706], t. VII, 233 F):

Among the Evangelists [i.e., the authors of the Gospels] only one reason dissolves a marriage, that is, the violation of marital faith [i.e., adultery].

Inter Evangelicos una dumtaxat causa dirimit conjugium, hoc est, violata conjugii fides.

For a wife who has committed adultery has ceased forthwith to be a wife, even if she has not been repudiated [by her husband]. And a husband who has committed adultery has ceased to be a husband even before the divorce.

Uxor enim, quae sui corporis copiam fecit alteri, iam, etiamsi non repudietur, desiit esse uxor. Et maritus, qui sui corporis copiam fecit alienae, iam ante divortium maritus esse desiit.

Commentarium in 1 Cor. 7 (from *Opera Omnia*, t. VI, 692 F; referenced at CT, VI, 107n20 and 107.23–24):

And so they may be divorced, so that each of the two is free to be joined to whom he pleases, or at least the one who gave no cause for the divorce.[24]

Et ita dirimantur, ut liberum sit utrique cui velit iungi, aut alteri certe, qui divortio non dedit causam.

Erasmus also defends the following "causes of divorce": "Dangers of a more serious nature, certainly including, murder, witchcraft, incantations." (Causae divortio: graviora discrimina, nimirum caedes, veneficia, incantamenta.)

---

23. The following propositions of Erasmus and the Paris condemnation are also available in d'Argentré, *Collectio Judiciorum*, II-I, 53–57.

24. The text is also available in Erasmus, *In novum testamentum annotationes, in priorem ad Corinth. c. 7* (Basel, 1555), 499.

Paris condemnation of Erasmus (December 16, 1527):

These four propositions, in so far as it seems that through them is proposed that the bond of marriage is dissolved on account of adultery, are heretical: for the bond of marriage is by divine law indissoluble as Paul's writings to the Corinthians demonstrates, ...; and the same judgment applies to the man as to the woman, because of the judgment of the same St. Paul: just as the wife hath not power over her own body, but the husband, so the man hath not power over his own body, but the wife.[25]

Hae quatuor propositiones, quatenus per eas praetendi videtur matrimonium per adulterium dissolvi quoad vincula, *haereticae sunt*: est enim vinculum matrimonii jure divino indissolubile ut ad Corinthios scribens Apostolus demonstrat, ...; et eadem omnino est ratio de viro sicut de muliere, quia eiusdem B. Pauli sententia, sicut mulier sui corporis potestatem non habet, sed vir, ita et vir sui corporis potestatem non habet sed mulier.

John Chrysostom (347–407)

In Matt. Homil. 17, 4 (PG 57:259; referenced at CT, VI, 107.17, 412.18–19; IX, 649n17 and n27):

For the wife who was cast off still remains wife to the one who cast her off.

Nam ejecta adhuc manet ejicientis uxor.

Μὴ γάρ μοι τοῦτο εἴπῃς, ὅτι ἐξέβαλεν ἐκεῖνος καὶ γὰρ ἐκβληθεῖσα μένει τοῦ ἐκβάλλοντος οὖσα γυνή.

In Matt. Homil. 62 (PG 58:597):

Then after quoting the ancient law ... [the Lord himself], with authority, both interprets and renders it sacred, saying: "Wherefore they are no

---

25. Erasmus's reply to the Paris condemnation of his propositions on marriage—in the form of revocations and denials—can be found in *Opera* (1706), t. IX, 814. A seventeenth-century author summarizes one of Erasmus's denials as follows: "[Erasmus] replies, that they [i.e., the censors] did well to add in the censure, that these propositions were condemned, *because he seemed to alledge*: for he had never entertained such a thought; that when he said, that an adulterous woman ceased to be a wife, it was by the same form of speaking as when one says that a son is no more a son; that is, she has lost the rights and advantages of a wife, such as are to continue in society with her husband, to dwell with him, to lie in the same bed, to govern his family together with him, and to share in his estate, etc." Lewis Ellies du Pin, *A New Ecclesiastical History* (London: H. Clark, 1699), 13:338.

longer two but one flesh." Therefore, just as it is execrable to cut off one's own flesh, so too it is unjust to cut off one's wife.

Deinde prisca recitata lege ... cum potestate illam interpretatur, et legem sancit dicens: Quapropter jam non sunt duo, sed una caro. Sicut ergo carnem secare scelestum est, ita et uxorem dirimere iniquum.

In epistolam primam (I) ad Corinthios: Hom. 19.3 (PG 61:154–55):

So why in this case [i.e., a spouse's idolatry] is impurity overcome, and therefore intercourse allowed; but in the case of the adulterous wife, it is not considered a fault, when he throws her out? Because in this case, there is hope that that part which was ruined would be made whole by means of marriage; but in the other case, the marriage was already dissolved: and in that case indeed both are corrupted; but here the fault only belongs to one of the two. To give an example: she who has committed adultery is assuredly accursed. If therefore he who clings to a prostitute is one body with her, he also becomes unclean who has intercourse with a prostitute; therefore in that case surely all purity flies away. But in the case of idolatry it is not so. But how? The idolater is unclean, but the woman is not unclean. For if she were a partner to him in that matter according to which he is unclean, I mean, in his impiety, she also would be unclean: but now the idolater is unclean in a different way; and in a different manner is his wife joined to him, in which manner he is not unclean. For marriage is also a mixing of bodies; in this mixing lies the union. And moreover there is hope that he will be called back by his wife, to whom he clings. But that other case will not be so easily be taken care of. How is that wife, who earlier dishonored him, and surrendered herself to another, and destroyed the rights of marriage, how will she be able to call him back who was treated unjustly; especially when he remains as if he were an alien to her? But moreover, after adultery, the husband is no longer a husband: but in this case, the husband's right is not lost, even though the wife worships idols.

Cur ergo hic victa est immunditia, ideoque concubitus permittitur; in muliere autem adultera non crimini datur viro, cum illam ejicit? Quia hic spes est fore ut per matrimonium pars illa quae peribat salutem consequatur; illic vero matrimonium jam solutum est: et illic quidem ambo corrumpuntur, hic vero alterius crimen est. Exempli causa: quae fornicata fuit, exsecranda certe est. Si ergo qui adhaeret meretrici, unum corpus est, et impurus ille fit qui cum meretrice miscetur; ideo certe tota munditia avolat. Hic autem non sic; sed quomodo? Immundus est idololatra, sed mulier non est immunda. Nam si consors ipsi esset in illa re secundum quam immundus est, in impietate, inquam, ipsa quoque immunda foret: nunc autem alio modo immundus est idololatra; in alia autem re ipsi jungitur uxor, in qua ille immundus non est. Connubium enim est et corporum mixtio, in qua est societas. Ad haec vero spes est illum ab uxore revocatum iri, cui adhaeret. Ille autem alius non ita facile (curabitur). Quomodo illa uxor, quae ipsum prius dedecore affecit, et alteri se dedidit juraque matrimonii abolevit, injuria affectum revocare poterit; cum maxime ille quasi peregrinus maneat? Praeterea autem post fornicationem maritus non est ultra maritus: hic autem mulier, licet idola colat, viri jus non amittit.

De Libello Repudii, II (PG 51:218–19):

The woman, he says, is bound to the law. It is necessary, therefore, that by no means should she be separated, while her husband lives, nor draw another husband to herself, nor enter upon a second marriage. And see with how much care he used the proper meaning of the words. For he [Paul] did not say, let her dwell together with her husband as long as he lives; but, *the wife is bound to the law for as long as her husband lives*: and indeed, even if he should give her a letter of divorce, even if she should leave the house, even if she should go to another man, even as an adulteress, she is closely bound to the law. *It is not lawful to marry a divorced woman. External laws yield to the divine law*. When therefore the man wishes to cast his wife out, or the wife to leave her husband, let them be mindful of this saying, and let them think that Paul is present and follows them exclaiming and saying: *The wife is tightly bound to the law*. For just as runaway slaves, even if they should leave their master's house, drag with themselves a chain: so also wives, even if they should leave their husbands, retain the law as if it were in the place of a chain, the law pursuing them and accusing them of adultery, and also accusing him who married her, and the law saying: the husband yet lives, and this crime is adultery. *For the wife is bound tightly to the law, as long as her husband lives. And anyone who marries a divorced wife, commits adultery.*

Mulier, inquit, *alligata est legi*. Oportet igitur ut minime separetur, vivente viro, neque alium superinducat maritum, neque secundas nuptias adeat. Et vide quanta cum diligentia verborum usus sit proprietate. Non enim dixit, Cohabitet viro quoad vixerit; sed, *Mulier alligata est legi quanto tempore vixerit vir illius*: atque adeo etiamsi libellum repudii det, etiamsi domum relinquat, etiamsi ad alium abeat, legi adstricta adulteraque est. *Non licet repudiatam ducere. Leges externae divinae legi cedunt.* Quando igitur vir ejicere vult uxorem, et uxor relinquere virum, hujus memor sit dicti, et Paulum putet esse praesentem, et persequi se clamando et dicendo: *Mulier adsctricta est legi*. Nam quemadmodum servi fugitivi, etiamsi domum herilem relinquant, catenam secum trahunt: ita et mulieres etiamsi viros relinquant, legem habent pro catena, se persequentem et adulterii accusantem, accusantem etiam eum, qui duxerit, ac dicentem: Adhuc superest maritus, et facinus hoc adulterium est. *Mulier enim adstricta est legi, quoad vixerit maritus illius. Et omnis qui dimissam duxerit, moechatur* (*Matth. 5:32*).

De Virginitate, 28 (PG 48:552):
But the husband, even though he marries the most difficult wife of all, must endure his servitude; and he is not able to enter on a path whereby he could free himself from this tyranny.

At vir, quamvis omnium difficillimam uxorem nactus sit, servitutem ferre cogitur, nec qua eo dominatu se absolvat, inire viam potest.)

Himes and Coriden say that Chrysostom "clearly endorsed the idea of divorce, seeing adultery as a cause for dissolution of a marriage"; as to whether he permitted remarriage, they are "less certain."[26] Their use of the terms "divorce" and "dissolution" is careless, since it implies that any restriction Chrysostom put on remarriage could only have been based on a legalistic custom. But Chrysostom's commitment to indissolubility, as expressed in *Homily 62*, seems to preclude a merely legalistic denial of remarriage. He does say in *Homily 19* that in the case of a wife's adultery, "the marriage was already dissolved" (illic vero matrimonium jam solutum est; ὁ γάμος ἤδη διαλελύσεται), and that "after the adultery, a husband is no longer a husband" (Praeterea autem post fornicationem maritus non est ultra maritus; μετά τὴν πορνείαν ὁ ἀνὴρ οὐκ ἔστιν ἀνήρ).[27] It is possible that this signifies Chrysostom's toleration for remarriage. But his position in *De Libello Repudii II*, as seen above, is that (quoting Tixeront) "as regards the woman, marriage is absolutely indissoluble. For whatever motive she is dismissed, she cannot remarry; once she has been joined to her husband, she remains his wife, as long as she lives."[28]

Yet Tixeront, Pospishil, and Mackin each wonder why Chrysostom nowhere plainly forbids an injured husband from remarrying.[29] Pospishil says it is because the early church "permitted a husband to remarry if he had divorced his wife because of adultery" and that Chrysostom did not want to speak against the law.[30] Tixeront and Mackin suggest Chrysostom approves of remarriage for husbands injured by their wives' infidelity: "we are left to interpret his silence."[31] But this ar-

26. Himes and Coriden, *Indissolubility of Marriage*, 471.
27. *In epist. I ad Corinth. Hom. 19.3*.
28. J. Tixeront, *History of Dogmas* (St. Louis, Mo.: Herder, 1914), 2:190.
29. Ibid. and Pospishil, *Divorce and Remarriage*, 157; Mackin, *Divorce and Remarriage*, 153–54.
30. Pospishil, *Divorce and Remarriage*, 157.
31. Mackin, *Divorce and Remarriage*, 155.

gument from silence is inconsistent with what Chrysostom plainly says in *Homily 62*, in which he "is emphatic that both the primal law of marriage and our Lord's renewal of that law make all severance of the tie impossible."³² As Palmer notes, "the concern of the early Church was not with reasons for remarriage but for separation." The conclusion from silence should be an affirmation of the traditional condemnation of remarriage after divorce, not the opposite.³³ Henri Crouzel agrees: Chrysostom "nowhere explicitly says that he who justifiably sends his wife away is able to marry, and all the texts commenting on the passages about dismissal constantly affirm the contrary."³⁴ Therefore, the phrase "already dissolved" should be taken to mean the breakdown of the moral commitment, and perhaps also dissolution of bed and board, not the dissolution of the *vinculum*.

Hilary of Poitiers

Commentary on Matthew 5:31 (PL 9:939–40; referenced at CT, VI, 107.17; IX, 656.43, 657n1, 675.20; English translation [with minor corrections] from FOTC 22, 69):

Establishing equity for all people, the Lord instructed the wife to remain above all in marital harmony. By adding many things to the Law, he subtracts nothing. Nor can one reasonably find fault with the progress made [by the Gospel]. Whereas the Law had granted the freedom to give a certificate of separation with authority, now the evangelical faith not only proclaimed its desire for concord with the husband, but also imposed guilt for forcing his wife into adultery, if, out of necessity of separation, she must be married to another, prescribing no other cause for leaving a marriage than that which defiles the husband through union with a prostituted wife.

Aequitatem in omnes concilians, manere eam maxime in conjugiorum pace praecepit: legi addens plura, nihil demens. Nec sane profectus argui potest. Nam cum lex libertatem dandi repudii ex libelii auctoritate tribuisset, nunc marito fides evangelica non solum voluntatem pacis indixit, verum etiam reatum coactae in adulterium uxoris imposuit, si alii ex discessionis necessitate nubenda sit: nullam aliam causam desinendi a coniugio praescribens, quam quae virum prostitutae uxoris societate pollueret.

---

32. Joyce, *Christian Marriage*, 326–27.
33. Palmer, "Christian Marriage," 626–27n19.
34. Crouzel, *L'église primitive face au divorce*, 203.

Jerome (ca. 341–420)

Epist. 55 (ad Amandum), no. 3 (PL 22:562–63; referenced at CT, VI, 101.18–19, 411.45–412.3; IX, 658.9; English translation from NPNF-II, vol. 6):

The apostle has thus cut away every plea and has clearly declared that, if a woman marries again while her husband is living, she is an adulteress. You must not speak to me of the violence of a ravisher, a mother's pleading, a father's bidding, the influence of relatives, the insolence and the intrigues of servants, household losses. A husband may be an adulterer or a sodomite, he may be stained with every crime and may have been left by his wife because of his sins; yet he is still her husband and, so long as he lives, she may not marry another.

Omnes igitur causationes Apostolus amputans, apertissime definivit, vivente viro adulteram esse mulierem, si alteri nupserit. Nolo mihi proferas raptoris et violentiam, matris persuasionem, patris auctoritatem, propinquorum catervam, servorum insidias atque contemptum, damna rei familiaris. Quamdiu vivit vir, licet adulter sit, licet sodomita, licet flagitiis omnibus coopertus, et ab uxore propter haec scelera derelictus, maritus eius reputatur, cui alterum virum accipere non licet.

Adversus Jovinianum, lib. 1, no. 14 (PL 23:233C; referenced at CT, IX, 418.31–34):

One rib was made into a wife from the beginning. "And they shall be," he says, "two in one flesh" (Gen. 2:24): not three, nor four, otherwise, they are no longer two if they are more. Lamech was first bloodthirsty and a murderer; he divided one flesh among two wives.

Una costa a principio in unam uxorem versa est. *Et erunt*, inquit, *duo in carne una* (Genes. ii, 24): non tres, neque quatuor, alioquin jam non duo, si plures. Primus Lamech sanguinarius et homicida, unam carnem in duas divisit uxores.

Epist. 77, no. 3 (PL 22:691; referenced at CT, VI, 411.41–44; English translation from NPNF-II, vol. 6):

The Lord has given the commandment that a wife must not be put away "except it be for fornication, and that, if put away, she must remain unmarried." Now a commandment which is given to men logically applies to women also. For it cannot be that, while an adulterous wife is to be put away, an incontinent husband is to be retained.

Praecepit Dominus uxorem non debere dimitti, excepta causa fornicationis: et si dimissa fuerit, manere innuptam (*Matth.* 5 *et* 19). Quidquid viris iubetur, hoc consequenter redundat in (ad) feminas. Neque enim adultera uxor dimittenda est, et vir moechus tenendus.

Commentary on Matthew 19:9 (PL 26:135A; referenced at CT, VI, 107.17–18; English translation [with minor corrections] from FOTC 117, 216–17):

It is adultery alone that conquers the affection for one's wife. Indeed, since she has distributed one flesh among another, and through adultery has separated herself from her husband, she ought not to be kept, lest she cause her husband to be under a curse, too, since the Scripture says: "He who retains an adulteress is foolish and impious." Therefore, whenever there is adultery and suspicion of adultery, a wife is freely divorced. And since it was possible that someone brought a false charge against an innocent person, and on account of the second marriage-union hurled a charge at the first wife, it is commanded to divorce the first wife in such as way that he has no second wife while the first one is living. For he says the following: If you divorce your wife not on account of lust, but on account of an injury, why after the experience of the first unhappy marriage do you admit yourself into the danger of a new one? And besides, it could have come to pass that according to the same law, the wife too could have given a bill of divorce to the husband. And so by the same precaution, she is instructed not to receive a second husband. And since a prostitute and she who had once been an adulteress were not afraid of reproach, the second husband is advised that if he marries such a woman, he will be under the charge of adultery.

Sola fornicatio est quae uxoris vincat affectum: immo cum illa unam carnem in aliam diviserit, et se fornicatione separaverit a marito, non debet teneri: ne virum quoque sub maledicto faciat, dicente Scriptura: *Qui adulteram tenet, stultus et impius est*. Ubicumque est igitur fornicatio, et fornicationis suspicio, libere uxor dimittitur. Et quia poterat accidere, ut aliquis calumniam faceret innocenti, et ob secundam copulam nuptiarum, veteri crimen impingeret, sic priorem dimittere jubetur uxorem, ut secundam, prima vivente, non habeat. Quod enim dicit, tale est: Si non propter libidinem, sed propter injuriam dimittis uxorem: quare expertus infelices priores nuptias, novarum te immittis periculo? Nec non quia poterat evenire, ut juxta eamdem legem uxor quoque marito daret repudium, eadem cautela praecipitur, ne secundum accipiat virum. Et quia meretrix, et quae semel fuerat adultera, opprobrium non timebat, secundo praecipitur viro, quod si talem duxerit, sub adulterii sit crimine.

Lactantius (d. ca. 325)

Divine Institutes, lib. 6, cap. 23, no. 33 (PL 6:720; referenced at CT, IX, 675.20 and 675n8):

He is an adulterer, who marries a woman dismissed by her husband; and [so is] he, who, except for the sin of adultery, dismisses his wife in order to marry another.

Adulterum esse, qui a marito dimissam duxerit, et eum, qui praeter crimen adulterii uxorem dimiserit, ut alteram ducat.

Origen (d. 254)

Comment. In Matthaeum 19:

[Book 8, chap. 23 (PG 13:1246A; a different version of the Latin with essentially the same meaning is referenced at CT, VI, 412.7–12; IX, 409.4–5, 411.12–15, 656.43, 675.18)]:

Moreover, certain leaders of the Church, contrary to the law of Scriptures, have permitted a woman to remarry while her husband is still alive. Acting contrary to that which is written, in which it is put thus: *A wife is bound to her husband as long as he lives*, and again, *She therefore will be called an adulteress if she lives with another man while her husband is still alive*. However they do not permit this without any reason at all. For although it is contrary to the law which was related and written down from the beginning, they permitted this accommodation complying with a judgment not their own; it was probably permitted to avoid worse things.

Jam vero contra Scripturae legem, mulieri vivente viro nubere quidam Ecclesiae rectores permiserunt, agentes contra id quod scriptum est, in quo sic habetur: "Mulier alligata est quanto tempore vir ejus vivit," et contra illud: "Igitur vivente viro mulier vocabitur adultera, si fuerit cum alio viro"; non omnino tamen sine ratione, haec enim contra legem initio latam et scriptam, ad vitanda pejora, alieno arbitrio morem gerentes eos permisisse verisimile est.

Book 14, chap. 24 (PG 13:1250A; referenced at CT, VI, 107.17)

For the ingenuousness of husbands oftentimes leads their wives into sins of this kind: but whether such husbands have grounds for excusing their own behavior, this you will explain, once you have carefully investigated it, regarding the questions proposed by us here. He also who keeps away (abstains) from a wife often brings it about that she commits adultery, since he does not satisfy her desire, even if he should do this led by the appearance of greater holiness or purity: and he perhaps is worthy of greater blame, who, however much it is in his own power, causes his wife to commit adultery, by not satisfying her desire, than he who without the reason of unchastity, but on account of sorcery, or murder, or some other rather serious wickedness, divorced her.

Nam virorum simplicitas uxores saepe numero in hujuscemodi peccata inducit: at utrum talibus viris in ejusmodi casibus sit necne sui excusandi locus, id super quaestionibus a nobis hoc loco propositis diligenter a te investigatum declarabis. Is quoque qui uxore abstinet, efficit saepe ut adulterium committat, cum ejus libidinem non explet, etiamsi majoris sanctimoniae, vel castitatis specie ductus id faciat: et is fortasse majori reprehensione dignus est, qui, quantum penes se est, efficit ut moechetur libidinem ejus non explens, quam qui sine causa stupri sed propter veneficium, vel eaedem [sic], aut gravius aliquod facinus, eam repudiavit.

Cardinal Walter Kasper, during an address to an Extraordinary Consistory of Catholic Cardinals at Rome in February 2014, referred to this text as a witness to an apparently widespread "customary law" of the early church—found "in many local Churches"—whereby "after a time of repentance, the practice of pastoral tolerance, of clemency and indulgence" towards divorced and remarried persons was practiced.[35] Kasper says: "this customary law is expressly discussed by Origen, who maintains that it is not unreasonable."

Since Origen refers only to a single instance where bishops apparently granted permission to remarry while a first spouse still lives, the text gives us little ground for concluding that the practice is widespread among Christians in the third century. Moreover, Kasper's statement that Origen "maintains that [the practice] is not unreasonable" suggests that Origen himself believes the accommodation can be acceptable or tolerable. But Origen's phrase in Latin, "Non omnino tamen sine ratione" means simply that the church leaders do not act without a rationale. John Rist suggests he means the bishops' actions "make pagan but not Christian sense."[36]

Origen leaves us with no doubts, however, as to what *he* thinks about the accommodation. Twice he states that the decision is contrary to scripture, and once that it is contrary to the natural law. The *rationem* and practice, therefore, are unacceptable to Christians. Although the passage testifies to the existence of periodic abuses in the pastoral care of married couples in early Christianity, it does not demonstrate what Kasper calls a "tradition of the early Church."

---

35. Kasper's address is published in *Gospel of the Family,* 37.
36. Rist, "Divorce and Remarriage," 84.

Rupert of Deutz (Abbot of the Benedictine Abby in Deutz, today Cologne) (ca. 1075–80 to ca. 1129)

De trinitate et operibus eius, in Gen. Lib. II, c. 24/35 (PL 167:283C; referenced at CT, VI, 412.4–6):

Therefore, only on account of adultery are divorces of rightly joined spouses excused; nevertheless, those who separate from one another on account of this cause must either remain as they are or be reconciled.

Igitur sola fornicationis causa recte coniugatorum excusantur divortia, ita tamen, ut aut permaneant sic, aut reconcilientur qui ab invicem discessere pro huiusmodi causa (1 Cor. vii).

Tertullian (d. 247)

Adversus Marcionem, IV, 34 (PL 2:442B; referenced at CT, VI, 412.13–17; IX, 675.20, 675n7):

Regarding the one who puts away his wife, so as to marry another, the Lord says: *he who shall dismiss his wife and marry another commits adultery, and he who marries a woman dismissed by her husband also commits adultery*, dismissed, at any rate, for the same reason whereby it is not permissible to be dismissed, namely so that the husband may marry another. For he who marries a woman unlawfully dismissed is an adulterer, just as one who marries a woman who is still married. For that marriage endures which was not rightly dissolved.

Si ideo quis dimittat uxorem, ut aliam ducat: *Qui dimiserit*, inquit, *uxorem, et aliam duxerit, adulterium commisit, et qui a marito dimissam duxerit, aeque adulter est*; ex eadem utique causa (dimissam), qua non licet dimitti, ut alia ducatur; illicite enim dimissam pro indimissa ducens, adulter est. Manet enim matrimonium quod non rite diremptum est.

POPES

Alexander III (1159–81)

De divortiis (*Decretals of Gregory IX*, lib. IV, tit. 19: "De divortiis," cap. 2, in CIC 2:720; referenced at CT, VI, 411.3–8, 424.35):

We, therefore, give this answer, that on account of her husband's deceit or any other crime, a woman should not be separated from her husband, or be joined for any reason to another, unless her husband attempts to draw her to his own evildoing, or wishes to corrupt the observance of her faith. But if he shall draw his wife to the crime of infidelity, a woman can withdraw from her husband and be separated, but it will not be licit for her to marry another; because although they may be separated, they nevertheless always will be spouses. This same judgment also applies to husbands.

Nos itaque taliter respondemus, quod mulier pro furto vel alio crimine viri sui, nisi *ipse eam ad maleficia sua trahere nitatur,* et fidei suae religionem corrumpere velit, ab eo separari non debet, *nec alii aliqua ratione copulari.* Verum si coniugem suam ad infidelitatis maleficium traxerit, *mulier* a viro *recedere* poterit *et* separari, ita, quod ei nubere alii non licebit, quia, licet separentur, semper tamen coniuges erunt. In viris quoque praesentis sententiae forma servetur.

Gregory the Great (590–604)

Li vero, q. 7, c. 22 (quoted from and referenced at CT, VI, 410.17–21; the quotation comes from a letter spuriously attributed to Gregory the Great: Pseudo-Gregory, cap. 32, q. 7, c. 22):

But husbands who catch their wives in adultery, it will not be licit for either the husband or the wife to remarry, as long as both live. If however the adulteress dies, her husband, if he wishes, may remarry, but only in the Lord. The adulteress however may never remarry, even if her husband dies; but for the remaining days of her life let her pay out lamentations of the most bitter repentance.

Hii vero, qui uxores suas in adulterio deprehedunt, non licebit nec eum nec illam aliam uxorem accipere vel alium virum, quamdiu ambo vivunt. Si autem adultera mortua fuerit, vir eius, si vult, nubat, tantum in Domino; adultera vero numquam, etiamsi mortuus fuerit vir eius. Omnibus tamen diebus vitae suae acerrimae penitenciae lamenta persolvat.

Innocent I (401–17)

Second Epistle to Victricius (bishop of Rouen)
(404 A.D.), chap. 13 (PL 20:479A; referenced at CT, VI,
410.9–13; IX, 411.31–32):

For if this rule is observed concerning every woman who marries another man while her husband still lives, that she should be held to be an adulteress, and must not be granted freedom to do penance unless one of the men dies, how much more should she be held to be an adulteress, who before had joined herself to an Immortal Spouse and afterwards migrated to a human marriage.

Si enim de omnibus haec ratio custoditur, ut quaecumque vivente viro alteri nupserit, habeatur adultera, nec ei agendae paenitentiae licentia concedatur, nisi unus ex eis defunctus fuerit: quanto magis de illa tenenda est, quae ante immortali se sponso coniunxerat, et postea ad humanas nuptias transmigravit.

Epistle to Exsuperius, chap. 6, no. 12 (405 A.D.)
(PL 20:500B; referenced at CT, VI, 102.1–2) [Exsuperius, bishop of Toulouse, has asked Pope Innocent several questions on marriage, and the pope replies]:

Your love has also asked concerning those who because a divorce has occurred have contracted another marriage. It is manifest that they are adulterers on both sides .... And therefore all of these should be held back from the communion of the faithful.

De his etiam requisivit dilectio tua, qui interveniente repudio, alii se matrimonio copularunt. Quos in utraque parte adulteros esse manifestum est .... Et ideo omnes a communione fidelium abstinendos.

Epistle to Probus, no. 36 (410 A.D.) (PL 20:602B–603A):

The confusion of a barbarous tumult brought an unfortunate event before the power of the laws. For the onset of captivity made a blemish on the well-established marriage between Fortunius and Ursa, unless they were being vigilant of the holy laws of religion. For while Ursa was being held in captivity, Fortunius is known to have entered into another marriage with Restituta. But when Ursa returned by the good-will of the Lord, she approached us, and without anyone denying it, thoroughly proved that she was the wife of Fortunius. Wherefore, lord and justly noble son, we decided, with the support of our Catholic faith, that the true marriage was that which was originally established by divine grace; and that the covenant with the second woman can by no means be legitimate, since the first wife survives, and was not dismissed by a divorce.

Conturbatio procellae barbaricae facultati legum intulit casum. Nam bene constituto matrimonio inter Fortunium et Ursam captivitatis incursus fecerat naevum, nisi sancta religionis statuta providerent. Cum enim in captivitate praedicta Ursa mulier teneretur; aliud conjugium cum Restituta Fortunius memoratus inisse cognoscitur. Sed favore Domini reversa Ursa nos adiit, et nullo diffitente, uxorem se memorati perdocuit. Quare, domine fili merito illustris, statuimus, fide Catholica suffragante, illud esse conjugium, quod erat primitus gratia divina fundatum; conventumque secundae mulieris, priore superstite, nec divortio ejecta, nullo pacto posse esse legitimum.

The letter to Probus is commonly appealed to as demonstrating the tolerance for divorce and remarriage in the early church. It has frequently been argued that the last clause implies that the second marriage *would* have been valid if the first wife had been dismissed by divorce.[37] The pope was replying to a pastoral situation not uncommon in the fifth century. During the Gothic invasion of Rome under Alaric in 410, a woman named Ursa, wife of a certain Fortunius, had been captured and carried away. Under such circumstances Roman law permitted the other spouse, after a set time, to contract another marriage. Under this liberty, Fortunius took another wife, Restituta. Ursa, however, regained her freedom and returned. But Fortunius failed to take her back. She brought her case to Rome and placed it before Pope Innocent. The pope sent his reply to a local *civil* magistrate named Probus. In order to properly interpret Innocent's words, it is important to understand that he was acting in his capacity as official arbitrator over matters of civil law, a power Constantine conferred upon bishops.[38] Innocent makes a point of saying that the case was submitted to him in virtue of his judicial competence to render legal decisions (*facultati legum*). His pronouncement renders the twofold verdict that the second marriage is invalid according to both divine law *and* civil law. If we had no other record of Pope Innocent's judgments on divorce and remarriage but this one, we might conclude that he admits here that the second marriage would have been valid if a civil divorce had preceded. But his letters to Exsuperius and Victricius preclude this as a reasonable possibility. Pope Innocent states emphatically that even in cases where a civil divorce has been issued (*interveniente repudio*) before contracting a second marriage, both the man and the woman in the second union are still judged to be adulterers.

Gregory II (715–31)
Letter to the Legates of Bavaria (*In Bavariam Ablegatis*)
(716 A.D.), cap. 6 (PL 89:533B; English translation from Bevilacqua, "History," 285):

The Apostle spoke of this: "You are bound to a wife. Seek not to be loosed." In other words, as long as your wife lives, do not seek to pass over to carnal relations with another woman. For the same Doctor of

---

37. See Pospishil, *Divorce and Remarriage*, 175; Mackin, *Divorce and Remarriage*, 163.

38. Both Joyce and Bevilacqua insist that when reading the passage we must keep in mind that the pope was acting in his capacity as legal arbitrator. Joyce, *Christian Marriage*, 317; Anthony Bevilacqua, "The History of the Indissolubility of Marriage," *Proceedings of the Catholic Theological Society of America* 22 (1967): 253–308, at 282.

the Gentiles instructs us: "He who commits fornication, sins against his own body," that is, against his own wife with whom he forms one body. By deceiving his wife through immoral embraces, he subjects himself to the guilt of sin.

Dicente de hoc ipso Apostolo: "Alligatus es uxori, noli quaerere solutionem" (1 Cor. 7); id est, superstite conjuge, ad alterius feminae concubitum non velle transire, quia eodem doctore gentium astruente: "Qui fornicatur, in corpus suum peccat" (1 Cor. 6), hoc est, in uxorem propria, cum qua unum corpus est, cui fraudando per amplexus illicitos semetipsum sub peccati reatu obstringit.

Letter to Boniface (ca. 726), cap. 18, c. XXIII, q. 7
(quoted from and referenced at CT, VI, 413.8–12;
IX, 411.10–11, 675.21; the *Acta* wrongly refers to the
author as Gregory III):

Because you asked, concerning a woman with a degenerative infirmity who is not able to pay the marriage debt to her husband, what should her husband do? It would be good if he were to remain in such a way that he devotes himself to abstinence. But because this is of great magnitude [i.e., requires virtue], he who will not contain himself may marry again. But let him not cease supporting her since she is kept from married life by her infirmity and not by a detestable fault.

Quod posuisti, si mulier infirmitate correpta non valuerit viro debitum reddere, quid eius faciat iugalis: bonum est, si sic permaneret, ut abstinentiae vacaret. Sed quia hoc magnorum est, ille, qui se non poterit continere, nubat magis. Non tamen subsidii opem subtrahat ab illa, cui ... non detestabilis culpa excludit.

Gregory's letter to Boniface has led some to conclude that the pope here expressly permits remarriage. But in treating the problem of impotence in this letter, the pope does not say whether the infirmity predates the marriage (and so could constitute an impediment to the marriage's validity), whether it occurred after marriage but before consummation (and so would be grounds for a legitimate dissolution of the marriage), or whether it arose after the marriage was consummated. Bevilacqua argues the second is plausible in light of the fact that German custom at the time tolerated the marriages of youth, and so it was not unusual for long periods to elapse before the spouses were old enough to consummate their marriage. Gratian understood the pope in the third sense, but strongly rejected the pope's judgment: "This [decision] of Gregory is found to be utterly contrary to the sacred canons, and even to the teaching of the Gospel and the apostles" (Illud Gregorii sacris canonibus, imo evangelicae et apostolicae doctrinae penitus invenitur adversum).[39] But if we read Gregory's reply in light of what he said ten years earlier in his letter addressed to the legates dispatched to Germany, we have very little reason for concluding that the pope accepts remarriage after divorce.

Zachary (741–52)

Concubuisti (Decretorum Liber Decimus Nonus (Book 19), of Burchardi, bishop of Worms, PL 140:965D; referenced at CT, VI, 413.4–7, 425.8–9):

> Have you had intercourse with your wife's sister? If so, you may have neither; and if she who was your wife was not aware of the evil and does not wish to remain with you, she may marry in the Lord whom she wishes. But you and the adulteress must remain without hope of a marriage spouse, and as long as you live, repent according to the instructions of the priest!

> Concubuisti cum sorore uxoris tuae? Si fecisti, neutram habeas. Et si illa quae uxor tua fuit, conscia sceleris non fuit, si se continere non vult, nubat in Domino cui velit. Tu autem et adultera sine spe coniugii permaneatis, et, quamdiu vixeritis, juxta praecepta sacerdotis, poenitentiam agite.

Some consider the declaration spurious; others suggest it refers to one who has relations with his future sister-in-law before marriage.[40] Whether spurious or otherwise, Pope Zachary's statement "she may marry in the Lord" offers doubtful proof of a tradition of tolerating remarriage in the Western church in the eighth century. The text's contents are inconsistent with a letter by Pope Zachary to Pepin dated January 5, 747. Replying to a question on divorce and remarriage, Zachary quotes two authoritative texts: the Canons of the Apostles, c. 47 (48), and c. 17 of the Council of Mileve (c. 8 of the Eleventh Council of Carthage):[41]

> Concerning a layman ejecting his wife, taken from the canon of the holy apostles, chapter 48: If any layman ejecting his own wife marries another woman or one dismissed by another husband, he is to be deprived of communion.

> Concerning those who dismiss their wives or husbands, that they remain single, taken from the above-mentioned African Council, in chapter 69: We decree that, according to the evangelical and apostolic discipline, neither the husband dismissed by his wife, nor the wife dismissed by her

---

39. *Decretum Gratiani*, tom. I, part II, causa 32, q. 7, cap. 18 (PL 187:1501).
40. See Pospishil, *Divorce and Remarriage*, 177–78.
41. Both quotations are taken from Bevilacqua, "History," 287.

husband may marry another; but they are to remain single or be reconciled to each other. If they disobey this law, they are to do penance.

Innocent III (1198–1216)

Quanto (*Decretals of Gregory IX*, lib. IV, tit. 19: "De divortiis," cap. 7, in CIC 2:723; referenced at CT, VI, 411.9–16):

If however one Christian spouse should fall into heresy or go over to the error of heathenism, we do not believe that in this case the spouse who is set aside is permitted to fly to a second marriage while the other spouse is still living; although in this case the insult to the creator appears to be greater.... But among the faithful, marriage is indeed true and exists as valid because of the sacrament of faith, which once it is received is never lost.... But through this response the malice of some is prevented, some who, because of hatred between the spouses, or even when each displeased the other, if they were able to dismiss their spouses in such a case, they might pretend heresy, in order to retreat from the spouses to whom they are married.

Si vero alter fidelium coniugum vel labatur in haeresim, vel transeat ad gentilitatis errorem, non credimus, quod in hoc casu is, qui relinquitur, vivente altero possit ad secundas nuptias convolare, licet in hoc casu maior appareat contumelia creatoris .... Inter fideles autem verum *quidem* et ratum exsistit [matrimonium], quia sacramentum fidei, quod semel est admissum, nunquam amittitur.... Per hanc *autem* responsionem quorundam malitiae obviatur, qui in odium coniugum, vel quando sibi invicem displicerent, si eas possent in tali casu dimittere, simularent haeresim, ut ab ipsa nubentibus coniugibus resilirent.

Leo the Great (440–61)

Epist. 159 ad Nicetam Episcopum Aquileiensem, cap. 1, 3–4 (PL 54:1136B–1137A; referenced at CT, VI, 107.18, 410.14–16):

Because we know what is written, that *a wife is joined to her husband by God* (Prov. 9: 14), and again, we recognize the precept that *what God has joined, let no man put asunder* (Matt. 19:6), it is necessary that we believe that the bonds of legitimate marriage must be reestablished, and, after the evils which hostility brought on have been removed, let that which each lawfully has be restored to him .... Therefore, if the men who have returned after long captivity should so persevere in their love for their wives that they desire to return into their partnership, what necessity brought on must be disregarded and judged blameless, and what faith demands must be restored. But if some women have been so captivated by love of their second husbands, that they prefer to be united with them rather than return to their legitimate partnership, they are rightly to be censured; in like manner they should be deprived of ecclesiastical communion [i.e., be excommunicated].

Quia novimus scriptum, quod *a Deo jungitur mulier viro* (*Prov. xix,* 14), et iterum praeceptum agnovimus ut *quod Deus junxit homo non separet* (*Matth. xix,* 6), necesse est ut legitimarum foedera nuptiarum redintegranda credamus, et remotis malis quae hostilitas intulit, unicuique hoc quod legitime habuit reformetur.... Et ideo, si viri post longam captivitatem reversi ita in dilectione suarum conjugum perseverent, ut eas cupiant in suum redire consortium, omittendum est et inculpabile judicandum quod necessitas intulit, et restituendum quod fides poscit. Si autem aliquae mulieres ita posteriorum virorum amore sunt captae, ut malint his cohaerere quam ad legitimum redire consortium, merito sunt notandae; ita ut etiam ecclesiastica communione priventur.

The bishop of Aquileia, Nicetas, was faced with a great pastoral problem after Attila the Hun invaded northern Italy in 452 and abducted many men. Believing their husbands to be dead, many women remarried. Then their husbands returned. What should the wives do in this instance, the pope was asked?

COUNCILS

Seventh Council of Carthage (258)

Canon 69 (Mansi, 3:956E; referenced at CT, VI, 410.28–29):

The bishop will be subject to a similar judgment [i.e., be deprived of the power to ordain], if he knowingly ordains a priest who married a widow or a divorced wife.[42]

Simili sententiae subiacebit episcopus, si sciens ordinaverit clericum eum, qui viduam aut repudiatam uxorem habuit, aut secundam.

---

42. Mansi = Giovanni Domenico Mansi, *Sacrorum Conciliorum Nova et Amplissima Collectio* (Florence and Venice, 1759–98; reprinted in Paris: H. Welter, 1901–27).

Council of Elvira (300)

Canon 8 (Mansi, 2:7B; referenced at CT, VI, 101.21, 410.30 [referred to as c. 7]; IX, 411.26):

Likewise women who have left their husbands with no preceding cause and have married others, shall not receive communion even at the end.

Item feminae, quae, nulla praecedente causa, reliquerint viros suos, et se copulaverint alteris, nec in fine accipiant communionem.

Canon 9 (Mansi, 2:7B; referenced at CT, IX, 411.27):

Likewise let a believing woman who has left a believing adulterous husband and is attempting to marry another, be prevented from marrying; if she does marry, let her not receive communion until the spouse whom she has left has died, unless perhaps illness compels that it be given to her.

Item foemina fidelis, quae adulterum maritum reliquerit fidelem et alterum ducit, prohibeatur ne ducat; si duxerit, non prius accipiat communionem, nisi quem reliquerit, prius de saeculo exierit; nisi forte necessitas infirmitatis dare compulerit.

Canon 10, part II (Mansi, 2:7C):

But if she is a believer—she who is being married by him who left behind a blameless wife; and if she found out that he had a wife whom he abandoned without cause, it is decided that communion is not to be given to her even at the end of her life.

Quod si fuerit fidelis, quae ducitur, ab eo qui uxorem inculpatam reliquit, et cum scierit illum habere uxorem, quam sine causa reliquit; placuit, nec in finem dandam esse communionem.

Council of Arles I (314)

Cap. 10 (Mansi, 2:472C; referenced at CT, VI, 412.24–26, 420.7.22–23, 425.6–7):

Concerning these husbands who catch their wives in adultery, husbands who are young believers and are forbidden from remarrying, we prescribe that in so far as it is possible, they be advised not to take a second wife as long as their first wife—even though an adulteress—is still alive.

De his qui coniuges suas in adulterio deprehendunt, et iidem sunt adolescentes fideles, et prohibentur nubere, placuit ut inquantum possit consilium eis detur, ne viventibus uxoribus suis, licet adulteris, alias accipiant.

Second Council of Mileve (Milevitanum) (416)

Canon 17 (Mansi, 3:806D; referenced at CT, VI, 101.20, 107.18–19, 410.25–27, 447.24–26; IX, 410.3–4, 411.27, 418.20–22, 658.9; the text can also can be found at *Decretum Gratiani*, tom. I, part II, causa 32, q. 7, cap. V [PL 187:1496]):

Be it resolved that according to the evangelical and apostolic teaching, neither a husband dismissed by his wife nor a wife dismissed by her husband may be joined to another; but they should remain as they are or be reconciled to each other. But if they disregard [this law], they should be compelled to repent.

Placuit, ut secundum evangelicam et apostolicam disciplinam, neque dimissus ab uxore, neque dimissa a marito, alteri coniungantur; sed ita maneant, aut sibimet reconcilientur. Quod si contempserint, ad poenitentiam redigantur.

The Council of Mileve is believed to have been held in 416 at Numidia in northern Africa under the presidency of Aurelius, bishop of Carthage. There is doubt as to whether this canon should be attributed to Mileve or to the Eleventh Council of Carthage (numbered canon 8) held on June 13, 407, also under the presidency of Aurelius. Hefele includes it under the canons of Carthage.[43] Gratian believes it was canon 17 of Mileve, as do Mansi and Migne.[44] Fransen seems to follow the opinion of Vacant and Mangenot from the *Dictionnaire De Théologie Catholique* (Tom X, 1928, 1753); he writes: "The *Concilium Milevitanum* was actually a fiction from Isidorus Mercator, who in his Hispana collected the resolutions of various African councils, et al. of the major African councils of 418 opposed to the Pelagians. In the 16th century it was thought that St. Augustine had attended this council and that Innocent I had solemnly approved it."[45] Whatever the case may be, the fathers at Trent believed it was canon 17 of Mileve. The canon was very influential at Trent, almost revered, because of the putative authority of Augustine and Pope Innocent. Gratian's inclusion of the canon in 1152 into his discussion of marriage in his *Concordia Discordantium Canonum* ensured its influence at Trent. Notice that the final wording of Trent's authoritative canon 7 includes the phrase "iuxta evangelicam et apostolicam doctrinam" most likely drawn from canon 17's "secundum evangelicam et apostolicam disciplinam."

---

43. See *Histoire Des Conciles D'Après Les Documents Originaux* (Paris: Letouzey et Ané, 1908), 2.1:156–58; see n3, "C. XXXIII" should read "C. XXXII".
44. Mansi, 3:806; PL 67:215–16.
45. Fransen, "Ehescheidung Bei Ehebruch," 158–59n7.

Council of Venice (465)

Cap. 2 (c. 2) (Mansi, 7:953C; referenced at CT, VI, 412.27–30, 420.23):

We have decided that those also, who, with their wives having been forsaken, just as it is said in the Gospel, "except for the cause of adultery," have married other women without the proof of adultery, should be similarly prevented from communion, lest sins overlooked through our indulgence incite others to the boldness of error.

Eos quoque, qui relictis uxoribus suis, sicut in evangelio dicitur: *excepta causa fornicationis*, sine adulterii probatione alias duxerint, statuimus a communione similiter arcendos: ne per indulgentiam nostram praetermissa peccata alios ad licentiam erroris invitent.

The Quinisext Council (Concilium Quinisextum), also known as the Council of Trullo (Concilium Trullanum) (692)

Canon 87 (Latin text from Mansi, 11:979D-E; referenced at CT, IX, 649n6 and 649.12; Greek text from Mansi, 11:980D-E; referenced at CT, VI, 410.22–24):

A woman who leaves her husband and marries another is an adulteress. A man who leaves the wife who was legitimately given to him is according to the words of the Lord, punishable by the judgment of adultery.

Quae maritum reliquit, est adultera, si venerit ad alium.... Qui legitime sibi datam uxorem relinquit, et aliam ducit, e domini sententia est adulterii iudicio obnoxius.

Ἡ τὸν ἄνδρα καταλιποῦσα μοιχαλίς ἐστιν, εἰ ἐπ᾽ ἄλλον ἦλθε .... Ὁ μέντοι καταλιμπάνων τὴν νομίμως αὐτῷ συναφθεῖσαν γυναῖκα καὶ ἑτέραν ἀγόμενος κατὰ τὴν τοῦ κυρίου ἀπόφασιν τῷ τῆς μοιχείας ὑπόκειται κρίματι.

The late seventh-century Concilium Quinisextum/Trullanum, held in Constantinople, was convened by Emperor Justinian II. Its purpose was to complete the work of the Fifth and Sixth Ecumenical Councils of Constantinople (hence the name *quini sext*), both of which failed to pass disciplinary canons. Quinisext adopted 102 such canons, which were approved by the Emperor Justinian, the 211 attending bishops, and other episcopal representatives, all from the Greek church. But when the emperor sent the canons to Pope Sergius I, the pope rejected them as "invalidi" (lacking authority) and said they contained "novel errors." The Orthodox churches consider the canons to be part of the Fifth and Sixth

Ecumenical Councils and hence authoritative, but the Catholic church never accepted the Council of Trullo as ecumenical.[46]

Council of Tribur in Germany (895)

Canon 41 (Mansi, 18:152D–153A; referenced at CT, VI, 412.31–37, 420.23, 424.33; IX, 646.5–6, 658.10):

If anyone marries a legitimate wife and is hindered by some kind of domestic infirmity from being able to fulfill his marital duty with her, but his brother, persuaded by the devil, being deeply loved by her, and secretly abases her and gives her back violated, they shall be completely separated and henceforth the woman shall be touched by neither of them. Therefore, the marriage which was legitimate has become defiled because of this pollution by the brother; and what had been lawful has become unlawful. Also, as Jerome says: the wife of two brothers shall not mount the nuptial bed; if she mounts it, she will be guilty of adultery. But because human weakness is liable to slip and fall, let it be strengthened in some way in order to stand. Therefore, the bishop, considering their weakness of mind, after penance is carried out by means of his instruction, shall console them with a lawful marriage if they should be unable to contain themselves, lest, while they are expected to be raised to noble deeds, they fall together into the mud.

Si quis legitimam duxerit uxorem, et inpediente quacunque domestica infirmitate, uxorium opus non valens implere cum illa: frater vero eius, suadente diabolo, adamatus ab ipsa, clanculum eam humiliaverit, et violatam reddiderit: omnimodo separentur, et a neutro ulterius eadem mulier contingatur. Igitur coniugium, quod erat legitimum, fraterna commaculatione est pollutum: et quod erat licitum, inlicitum est factum: et ut Hieronymus ait: Mulier duorum fratrum non ascendat thorum; si autem ascendit, adulterium perpetrabit. Quia vero humana fragilitas proclivis est ad labendum, aliquo modo muniatur ad standum. Idcirco episcopus considerata mentis eorum imbecillitate, post poenitentiam sua institutione peractam, si se continere non possint, legitimo consoletur matrimonio: ne, dum sperantur ad alta sublevari, corruant in coenum.

The paragraph seems to refer to an unconsummated marriage, which is not absolutely indissoluble, if this is the case, it poses no problem for the strict rendering of Western Christian teaching. It also might refer to a union that suffered from antecedent impotence, in which case, the marriage would be invalid. This

---

46. See Canons of the Council in Trullo, in NPNF-II, 14:357; also Philip Schaff, *History of the Christian Church* (New York: Charles Scribner's Sons, 1891), 4:507–9.

same chapter or canon (i.e., 41) is cited in the *Penitential of Theodore* with the title: "Illa vero, si voluerit poenitere, alium accipiat virum" (But if she wants to repent, let her receive another husband). See *Ad Poenitentiale Theodori*, which leads Pospishil to conclude that the compiler of the Penitential believed the canon referred to "any marriage in which an incestuous relationship had developed between the wife and her brother-in-law [not simply to an unconsummated union], and that he permitted remarriage to both."[47] But the Council of Tribur itself used no such title. And the editor of the 1525 edition of the *Acts and Decrees of the Council of Tribur*, Johann Cochllaeus, entitled the chapter: "Si quis duxerit uxorem, et concumbere nonvalens cum ea, frater eius clam violauerit illam" (If someone takes a wife and is unable to have intercourse with her and his brother secretly violates her), simply reproducing the details of the union under consideration within the chapter. It is also well known that the compiler of the *Penitental of Theodore* permitted divorce and remarriage according to the practices of the civil legislation of the Eastern Empire.[48]

Canon 46 (quoted from Mansi, 18:154AD; referenced at CT, VI, 424.33):

If his wife is defiled, the husband certainly may not in any way remarry for as long as his wife lives.

Si cuius uxor constuprata fuerit.... Maritus vero quamdiu ipsa vivat nullo modo alteram ducat.)

Canon 24 (referenced at CT, VI, 412.38–40):

If anyone sleeps with his stepmother, neither he nor she is able to attain marriage; but if the stepmother's husband cannot restrain himself, he is permitted, if he wishes, to remarry.

Si quis cum noverca sua dormierit, neuter potest ad coniugium pervenire; sed vir eius potest, si vult, aliam accipere, si se continere non potest.[49]

Canon 19 (quoted from and referenced at CT, VI, 413.1–3, 425.7–8):

Regarding a wife who slept with her husband's brother: it is decreed that the adulterers may never be joined by marriage. Yet to him whose wife was defiled, lawful marriages should not be denied.

47. Pospishil, *Divorce and Remarriage*, 94. See PL 99:1151.
48. See Joyce, *Christian Marriage*, 338, 360.
49. The *Acta* has this listed as canon 24 of the Council of Tribur. It actually belongs to the Council of Verberie (756), canon 10. The same canon with slightly different wording is recorded in a chapter of Verberie titled "Pepin the King": "Si filius cum noverca sua uxore patris sui dormierit, nec ille nec illa possunt ad conjugium pervenire. Sed ille vir, si vult, potest aliam uxorem habere. Sed melius est abstinere" (Mansi, 12:116C).

Quedam cum fratre viri sui dormivit: decretum est, ut adulteri numquam coniugio copulentur. Illi vero, cuius uxor stuprata est, licita coniugia non negentur.[50]

Lateran III (1179)

Appendix, part 6, no. 16 (Mansi, 22:252B; referenced at CT, IX, 419.22–24):

If anyone takes another wife while his first wife is still living, or gives her a promise regarding marrying her, she ought to be forever forbidden from his fellowship.

Si quis uxore vivente aliam acceperit, vel de ea ducenda ei fidem dederit: ab eius consortio perpetuo debet prohiberi.

Lateran IV (1215)

Constitution 52 (DEC, 1:259.26–28) [addressing the problem of hearsay evidence submitted at a matrimonial suit, the Council teaches]:

It is preferable to leave alone some people who have been united contrary to human decrees than to separate, contrary to the Lord's decrees, persons who have been joined together legitimately.

Tolerabilius est enim aliquos contra statuta hominum copulatos dimittere, quam coniunctos legitime contra statuta Domini separare.

Council of Constance (1415)

Condemned Article 16 attributed to John Wyclif (referenced at CT, VI, 110.3–4; English translation from DEC, 1:423.27–31):

The words, *I will take you as wife*, are more suitable for the marriage contract than, *I take you as wife*. And the first words ought not to be annulled by the second words about the present, when someone contracts with one wife in the words referring to the future and afterwards with another wife in those referring to the present.

---

50. The origin of this canon is uncertain. A similar canon is found in the *Capitulari of Pepin,* cap. 8: "Si quis homo habet mulierem legitimam, et frater eius adulteravit cum ea, ille frater vel illa femina qui adulterium perpetraverunt, interim quo vivunt nunquam habeant conjugium. Ille cuius uxor fuit, si vult, potestatem habet accipere aliam" (Mansi, 12:130C).

Haec verba: *Accipiam te in uxorem*, eligibiliora sunt in contractu matrimoniali, quam ista: *Ego te accipio in uxorem*. Et quod contrahendo cum una per haec verba de futuro, et post cum alia, per haec verba de praesenti, non debent frustrari verba prima per verba secundaria de praesenti.

Council of Florence (1439)

Exultate Deo (Bull of Union with the Armenians, no. 16) (referenced at CT, VI, 110.4, 420n1; IX, 411.28, 418.24, 658.9; English translation from DEC, 1:550.24–29):

And although separation of bed is lawful on account of *fornicationem*, it is not lawful to contract another marriage, since the bond of a legitimately contracted marriage is perpetual.

Quamvis autem ex causa fornicationis liceat thori separationem facere, non tamen aliud matrimonium contrahere fas est, cum matrimonii vinculum legitime contracti perpetuum sit.

APPENDIX B

RECORDED STATEMENTS OF THE GENERAL CONGREGATION ON INDISSOLUBILITY FROM 1563

Appendix B includes two parts and nine tables. Part 1 provides the full text in English and Latin of the intervention of the Venetian delegation on the second formulation of the canon on adultery from August 11, 1563. Part 2 provides in English and Latin the preliminary and three successive formulations of the doctrinal preface that precedes the canons on the sacrament of marriage. In both parts, the Latin is taken from the *Acta* as recorded in *Concilium Tridentinum*, Tom 9. English translations are supplied.

Tables B-1 to B-9 represent excerpts from the *Acta*'s recorded statements of the members of the General Congregation (i.e., those holding the status of voting prelate) on the four successive formulations of the canons on marriage that took place from July to December 1563. The statements in tables B-1 to B-8 were all made during session 23, which began on July 15 and ended on November 10, 1563. The comments and votes documented in table 9 were recorded on November 11, 1563, the opening day of session 24.

There are two types of tables. The first type (nos. B-1, B-3, B-5, B-7, B-9) *record* the remarks of the fathers on the successive formulations. These can be used as cross-references with the material in chapter 3 in which the discussions of the General Congregation from 1563 are analyzed in more detail. The second type (nos. B-2, B-4, B-6, B-8), in the form of graphs with columns, *categorize* the remarks according to whether the fathers registered a "placet," "non placet," generally approved the set of canons without specifically mentioning the canon on adultery, approved the canon with recommended emendations, or registered no opposition. The columns are all totaled to give an idea of the consensus opinion of the fathers through the course of the debates on the four successive formulations of the canon on adultery. Since they record the names of influential fathers as well as the prelates who followed those fathers' opinions, these tables can give an idea of the influence of certain fathers over the discussions on marriage.

PART 1: INTERVENTION OF THE VENETIAN DELEGATION, AUGUST 11, 1563[1]

Translation

Petition to speak of the Republic of Venice on the canon on the sacraments of marriage:

We do not think it can be doubted, most illustrious presidents and most holy Fathers, that our most noble republic always has been most devoted to the holy Apostolic See and to the ecumenical synods gathered together by its authority; and no one should doubt that the republic has embraced with a whole heart the decrees, canons, and sanctions which emanate from it, as that which always promote the glory of God, the salvation of souls and the tranquility and peace of the Christian people. Yet since there are several things in the currently circulated canon 7 on marriage, which unless moderated in some way could excite not a little scandal in the Eastern church and especially in our domains on the islands of Crete, Cyprus, Corfu, Zakynthos, Cephalonia, and many others, not only to the detriment of public tranquility, but also to the Catholic church, it seemed to us fitting to briefly mention and explain our most just desire. Everyone knows that although the church of the Greeks dissents from elements of the Roman church in some ways, yet she is not considered so lost that we cannot expect better from her [literally "promise ourselves better regarding her"], especially since in the aforementioned places and in other lands under our dominion, although Greek Christians live by their own *ritus*, yet they are obedient to the prelates of the church appointed by the Apostolic See. Wherefore, reason does not permit, and it would not befit our office if we permitted, them to be burdened with such an anathema and consequently to make occasion that they might raise a tumult and might thoroughly cut themselves off from the Apostolic See itself. The Greek custom to dismiss an adulterous wife and marry another, by following, as they say, the most ancient *ritus* of their fathers, has indeed been [long] established. And even though the *ritus* itself was always well known to the Roman Catholic church, they have never been condemned on account of this at any ecumenical council or struck with anathema. Therefore we think it is our responsibility to ask and beseech you, most Holy Fathers, in the best way we can, thus to moderate the words of this canon so that there is no disadvantage to the Greeks, especially by placing them under pain of anathema. We do not doubt

1. CT, IX, 686.

that this can be done, not only without damage to the Catholic church, but also, perhaps, with veneration to the many holy doctors [who hold contrary opinions]. Consequently, in our opinion this can be done consistent with the intentions of the holy synod and in a way that is satisfactory to our most noble authority by revising the canon as follows: *If anyone says that the holy Roman catholic and apostolic church, which is the teacher of all the others, has erred or errs, when she has taught and teaches that on account of the adultery of one of the spouses, the marriage cannot be dissolved, and that both of the spouses, or at least the innocent party who did not commit adultery* [lit. was not the cause of the adultery], *should not contract another marriage while the other spouse is living, and that he commits adultery who dismisses an adulteress and remarries, and she commits adultery who dismisses an adulterer and remarries: let him be anathema.* Whereby we ask you, most holy fathers, that your right honorable lordships deign to accommodate our most noble republic in this matter, either in the way we have proposed, or in a better way (in accordance with whatever seems best to your most prudent judgment) consistent with the words of our delegation, which was and always will be most obedient to the holy Apostolic See.

Original

Petitio oratorum rei publicae Venetiarum circa canones de sacramento matrimonii:
 Neminem dubitare posse arbitramur, I^{mi} praesidentes et Patres Sanct^{mi}, Ser^{mam} rem publicam nostrum semper addictissimam fuisse sacrosanctae Ap^{cae} Sedi et illius auctoritate congregatis oecumenicis synodis, quin et toto pectore amplexatam esse ac omni devotione prosecutam, quae inde emanaverunt decreta, canones et sanctiones, ut quae semper promovent Dei gloriam, animarum salutem et Christiani populi tranquillitatem et pacem. Verum cum aliqua sint in 7. canone de matrimonio, qui circumfertur, quae (nisi aliquo moderentur pacto) possent non modicum scandalum in orientali ecclesia et praecipue nostris in regnis et insulis Cretae, Cypri, Corcyrae, Hiacynthi, Cephaloniae et aliarum plurium excitare, non solum in praeiudicium tranquillitatis publicae, sed et catholicae ecclesiae: visum nobis est, paucis attingere nostrumque iustissimum desiderium explicare. Notum est, Graecorum ecclesiam etsi aliqua ex parte a Romana dissentiat, non tamen adeo deploratam esse, ut non possimus de illa nobis melius polliceri, praesertim cum in locis praedictis aliisque ditioni nostrae subiectis, licet suo ritu vivant, obediunt [!] tamen praesulibus ecclesiasticis a Sede Ap^{ca} assumptis. Quare non patitur ratio, nec foret nostri muneris, si permitteremus, illos tali anathemate gravari et inde occasionem accipere, ut tumultuari possent ac penitus ab ipsa Sede Ap^{ca} desciscere. Exploratum quidem est, consuevisse Graecos, fornicariam uxorem dimittere et aliam ducere, sequendo (ut dicunt) antiquissimum ritum suorum patrum; nec in aliquo oecumenico concilio fuerunt ob hoc condemnati aut aliquo anathemate percussi, quamvis ritus ipse fuisset Romanae et

catholicae ecclesiae semper notissimus. Quare nostrarum partium esse cognoscimus, petere et instare omni meliori modo quo possumus, a vobis, Sanct^{mi} Patres, ut verba illius canonis ita moderentur, ut Graecis (sub anathemate praesertim) non fiat praeiudicium. Quod et fieri posse non dubitamus, non solum sine iactura ecclesiae catholicae, sed et forsan cum plurimorum doctorum veneratione. Posset itaque nostro iudicio fieri, ut sancta synodus haberet intentum, et Ser^{mo} Dominio nostro esset satisfactum, reformando canonem in hunc qui sequitur modum: *Si quis dixerit, sacrosanctam Romanam catholicam et apostolicam ecclesiam, quae est aliarum omnium magistra, errasse vel errare, quando propter adulterium alterius coniugum docuit et docet, matrimonium non posse dissolvi, et utrumque coniugum, vel saltem innocentem, qui causam adulterio non dederit, non debere, altero coniuge vivente, aliud matrimonium contrahere, et moechari eum, qui dimissa adultera aliam duxerit, et eam, quae dimisso adultero alii nupserit: anathema sit.* Quamobrem rogamus vos, Sanct^{mi} Patres, ut dignentur ampl^{mae} D^{nes} V^{rae} vel eo modo, quo diximus, vel meliori (prout videbitur prudentissimo iudicio suo) hac in re morem genere Ser^{mae} rei publicae nostrae, quae semper obsequentissima exstitit et in posterum exsistet sacrosanctae Ap^{eae} Sedi.

PART 2: PRELIMINARY, FIRST, SECOND, AND THIRD FORMULATIONS OF THE "PRAEFATIO"

In July 1563, more than twenty-five voting prelates requested that the Council add a doctrinal introduction preceding the canons, which would allow truths regarding the sacrament of marriage to be set down in positive form before condemning what is contrary to them in the canons that follow. On August 7, the *deputatio* proposed for the first time a brief introductory statement.[2] The statement was completely revised and expanded into a doctrinal preface ("praefatio") and re-presented to the General Congregation on September 5. The *praefatio* underwent two revisions before its final promulgation on November 11. The differences between the first and second formulations of the *praefatio* are quite significant and can be easily identified. Between the second and third, they are minor. All four versions of the introductory statement are recorded here in Latin and English.

---

2. For discussion of the "titulus," see chap. 4, 113–14 and 101–2.

Preliminary: August 7, 1563[3]

Translation

The Most Holy Ecumenical Council of Trent etc., after deciding on six sacraments of the church one by one and also specifically, and condemning very many heresies and false doctrines, which had crept into the church in this our time while the enemy of the human race was inciting them, endeavors to expel for the future too those principal and rather notorious errors and heresies, which have been stirred up or contrived in these our times by the servants of Satan surrounding the sacrament of marriage; it therefore determines and decrees these conclusions.

Original

Sacrosancta oecumenica Tridentina synodus etc. post absolutam de sex ecclesiae sacramentis sigillatim atque in specie diffinitionem damnatasque plurimas haereses et falsa dogmata, quae humani generis hoste suggerente hac nostra tempestate in ecclesiam irrepserant: quod reliquum est, illos etiam praecipuos ac insigniores errores atque haereses exterminare intendens, quae circa matrimonii sacramentum a satanae ministris his nostris temporibus suscitatae aut inventae sunt, haec diffinit ac statuit.

First: September 5, 1563[4]

English

Inspired by the Holy Spirit, the forefather of the human race pronounced marriage to be a perpetual and indissoluble bond when he said: *This at last is bone of my bones and flesh of my flesh. Therefore a man shall leave his father and mother and cleave to his wife, and the two shall become one flesh.* Christ clearly explained that the couple is joined as by a yoke when he interpreted those last words [of the quotation] as spoken by God himself: *And they shall be two in one flesh.* And he immediately confirmed the same bond's lasting nature, previously only preached by Adam, when he said: *What God has joined, let no man separate.*

Moreover, St. Paul taught that holiness, the perfecter of that natural love, had been imparted more richly to this bond through the law of the Gospel, in these words: *Husbands love your wives, as Christ also loved the church*, adding shortly after: *This is a great mystery, but I mean: in Christ and the church*, implying, surely, that the mutual joining of husband and wife not only represents the union of Christ and the church, but also refers to the effective grace of Christ

---

3. CT, IX, 682.1–6.
4. CT, IX, 761.6–22.

which joins the spouses themselves, and that bears witness and yields that such grace is efficacious.

Since therefore the stability of inviolable marriage has been more completely made known by Christ, and holiness, unknown to the old law, has been added by the new law: the holy Council, justly desiring to root out the more glaring errors and heresies of the schismatics, has decreed against these very heresiarchs and their followers the anathemas that follow.

Original

Matrimonii perpetuum inviolabilemque nexum primus humani generis parens divini Spiritus instinctu pronuntiavit, cum dixit: *Os nunc ex ossibus meis et caro ex carne mea; quam ob rem relinquet homo patrem suum et matrem suam, et adhaerebit uxori suae, et erunt duo in carne una.* Duorum velut iugum esse diserte explicavit Christus, cum postrema illa verba tamquam ab ipso Deo pronuntiata interpretatus est: *Et erunt duo in carne una.* Statimque eiusdem nexus firmitatem ab Adamo tantum antea praedictam confirmavit: *Quod Deus coniunxerit, homo non separet*, inquit.

Sanctitatem porro huic lege evangelica uberius infusam, naturalis illius caritatis perfectricem, docuit in haec verba Paulus: *Viri, diligite uxores vestras, sicut et Christus dilexit ecclesiam,* et mox subdidit: *Sacramentum hoc magnum est; ego autem dico: In Christo et ecclesia,* id sc. innuens, quod mutua viri et mulieris coniunctio non solum Christi et ecclesiae coniunctionem repraesentet, sed et non otiosam Christi ipsos coniuges iungentis referat gratiam, praesentemque testetur et sufficiat.

Cum igitur matrimonii firmitas inviolabilis a Christo magis sit explicata, sanctitasque, veteri legi incognita, nova lege eidem accesserit: merito insigniores schismaticorum haereses erroresque exterminare cupiens sancta synodus, hos in ipsos haeresiarchas eorumque sectatores decrevit anathematismos.

Second: October 13, 1563[5]

Translation

Inspired by the Holy Spirit, the forefather of the human race pronounced marriage to be a perpetual and indissoluble bond when he said: *This at last is bone of my bones and flesh of my flesh. Therefore a man shall leave his father and his mother and cleave to his wife, and the two shall become one flesh.*

And Christ our Lord taught more clearly that the two are to be coupled and joined only by this bond when referring to those last words [of the quotation] as spoken by God, he said: *So they are no longer two, but one flesh,* and went on at

---

5. CT, IX, 888.22–889.2.

once to confirm the lasting nature of the same bond, declared by Adam so much earlier, with these words, *What therefore God has joined, let no man separate.*

And the grace that would perfect that natural love, strengthen the indissoluble unity, and sanctify the spouses themselves, the same Christ, the instituter and perfecter of the venerable sacraments, merited for us by his passion. The apostle Paul implied this, saying: *Husbands love your wives, just as Christ loved the church and gave himself up for her*, adding shortly after: *This is a great mystery; but I mean, in Christ and the church.*

Since therefore marriage in the law of the Gospel exceeds the old marriages by means of grace through Christ, our holy fathers, and councils, and the universal tradition of the church have always taught that marriage is rightly to be numbered among the sacraments of the new law. Against this tradition, impious and senseless men of this age have not only thought falsely about this venerable sacrament, but introducing the license of the flesh as is their habit under pretext of the Gospel, they have said and written many things that are inconsistent with the understanding of the Catholic church and with custom approved from apostolic times, causing great damage to the Christian faithful. Desiring to confront their temerity, the holy and universal Council has decided that the more glaring errors and heresies of the aforementioned schismatics must be rooted out, lest more people be drawn to their deadly contagion, decreeing against these very errors and heresiarchs the following anathemas:

Original

Matrimonii perpetuum inviolabilemque nexum primus humani generis parens divini Spiritus instinctu pronuntiavit, cum dixit: *Hoc nunc os ex ossibus meis, et caro ex carne mea. Quamobrem relinquet homo patrem suum et matrem suam, et adhaerebit uxori suae, et erunt duo in carne una.*

Hoc autem vinculo duos tantummodo copulari et coniungi, Christus Dominus apertius docuit, cum postrema illa verba tamquam a Deo prolata referens dixit: *Itaque iam non sunt duo, sed una caro*, statimque eiusdem nexus firmitatem ab Adamo tanto ante pronuntiatam his verbis confirmavit: *Quod ergo Deus coniunxit, homo non separet.*

Gratiam vero, quae naturalem illum amorem perficeret, in indissolubilem unitatem confirmaret (ipsosque coniuges) sanctificaret: idem Christus, venerabilium sacramentorum institutor atque perfector, sua nobis passione promeruit. Quod Paulus apostolus innuit dicens: *Viri, diligite uxores vestras, sicut Christus dilexit ecclesiam, et se ipsum tradidit pro ea*, mox subiungens: *Sacramentum hoc magnum est; ego autem dico, in Christo et in ecclesia.*

Cum igitur matrimonium in lege evangelica veteribus connubiis per Christum gratia praestet: merito inter novae legis sacramenta connumerandum sancti patres nostri, concilia, et universalis ecclesiae traditio semper docuerunt. Adversus quam impii homines huius saeculi insanientes non solum perperam de hoc venerabili sacramento senserunt, sed de more suo praetextu Evangelii libertatem carnis introducentes, multa ab ecclesiae catholicae sensu et ab apostolorum temporibus probata consuetudine aliena scripto et verbo asseruerunt, non sine magna Christifidelium iactura. Quorum temeritati sancta et universalis synodus cupiens occurrere: insigniores praefatorum schismaticorum errores et haereses, ne plures ad se trahat perniciosa eorum contagio, exterminandos duxit, hos in ipsos (errores et haeresiarchas) decernens anathematismos:

Third and Final: November 11, 1563[6]
Translation

Inspired by the Holy Spirit, the forefather of the human race pronounced marriage to be a perpetual and indissoluble bond when he said: *This at last is bone of my bones and flesh of my flesh. Therefore a man shall leave his father and mother and cleave to his wife, and the two shall become one flesh.*

Christ our Lord taught more clearly that the two are to be coupled and joined only by this bond when, referring to the words just quoted as spoken by God, he said: *So they are no longer two, but one flesh,* and went on at once to confirm the lasting nature of the same bond, declared by Adam so much earlier, with these words, *What therefore God has joined, let no man separate.*

And the grace that would perfect that natural love, strengthen the indissoluble unity, and sanctify the spouses, Christ himself—the instituter and perfecter of the venerable sacraments—merited for us by his passion. The apostle Paul implied this, saying: *Husbands love your wives, just as Christ loved the church and gave himself up for her,* adding shortly after: *This is a great mystery; but I mean, in Christ and the church.*

Since therefore marriage in the law of the Gospel exceeds the old marriages by means of grace through Christ, our holy fathers, and councils, and the universal tradition of the church have always taught that marriage is rightly to be numbered among the sacraments of the new law. Against this tradition, impious and senseless men of this age have not only thought falsely about this venerable sacrament, but introducing the license of the flesh as is their habit under pretext of the Gospel, they have said and written many things that are inconsistent with the understanding of the Catholic church and with custom approved from apostolic times, causing great damage to the Christian faithful. Desiring to confront their temerity, the holy and universal Council has decided that the more glaring heresies and errors of the aforementioned schismatics must be rooted out, lest more people be drawn to their deadly contagion, decreeing against these heretics themselves and their errors the following anathemas:

6. CT, IX, 966.28–967.15.

Original

Matrimonii perpetuum inviolabilemque nexum primus humani generis parens divini Spiritus instinctu pronuntiavit, cum dixit: *Hoc nunc os ex ossibus meis, et caro de carne mea. Quamobrem relinquet homo patrem suum et matrem et adhaerebit uxori suae, et erunt duo in carne una.*

Hoc autem vinculo duos tantummodo copulari et coniungi, Christus Dominus apertius docuit, cum postrema illa verba, tamquam a Deo prolata, referens dixit: *Itaque iam non sunt duo, sed una caro,* statimque eiusdem nexus firmitatem, ab Adamo tanto ante pronuntiatam, his verbis confirmavit: *Quod ergo Deus coniunxit, homo non separet.*

Gratiam vero, quae naturalem illum amorem perficeret, et indissolubilem unitatem confirmaret coniugesque sanctificaret: ipse Christus, venerabilium sacramentorum institutor atque perfector, sua nobis passione promeruit. Quod Paulus apostolus innuit, dicens: *Viri, diligite uxores vestras, sicut Christus dilexit ecclesiam, et se ipsum tradidit pro ea,* mox subiungens: *Sacramentum hoc magnum est; ego autem dico, in Christo et in ecclesia.*

Cum igitur matrimonium in lege evangelica veteribus connubiis per Christum gratia praestet: merito inter novae legis sacramenta annumerandum sancti patres nostri, concilia et universalis ecclesiae traditio semper docuerunt; adversus quam impii homines huius saeculi insanientes, non solum perperam de hoc venerabili sacramento senserunt, sed de more suo, praetextu Evangelii libertatem carnis introducentes, multa ab ecclesiae catholicae sensu et ab apostolorum temporibus probata consuetudine aliena, scripto et verbo asseruerunt, non sine magna Christifidelium iactura. Quorum temeritati sancta et universalis synodus cupiens occurrere, insigniores praedictorum schismaticorum haereses et errores, ne plures ad se trahat perniciosa eorum contagio, exterminandos duxit, hos in ipsos haereticos eorumque errores decernens anathematismos.

TABLE B-I. Remarks of the General Congregation on the First Formulation of the Canons on Matrimony (July 24–31, 1513)

C. 6: Si quis dixerit, propter adulterium alterius coniugum posse matrimonium dissolvi, et utrique coniugum vel saltem innocenti, qui causam adulterio non (dederit, licere) novare coniugum, neque moechari eum, qui dimissa adultera aliam duxerit, neque eam, quae dimisso adultero alii nupserit, anathema sit.[7]

---

[7]. "If anyone says, that on account of the adultery of one of the spouses a marriage can be dissolved, and that it is licit for both spouses, or at least the innocent spouse who gave no cause for adultery, to remarry, and that he does not commit adultery who dismisses an adulteress

The opinions of two hundred Council fathers are recorded on the first formulation (c. 6).[8] The remarks are concise, many including no more than a simple approval ("placet") or disapproval ("non placet") of the canon or a simple reference to the opinions of another bishop. In the following summary, when a bishop explicitly approves canon 6, I write "placet"; if he specifically notes that the canon should be published *as is* with no emendations, I write "placet as is"; if he adds some note to the approval, I summarize it. If he approves the canon on the condition than some emendation is made, I write "placet as amended" and note the recommended emendation. If he explicitly approves the canon while referencing—so as to concur with—the emendations of another bishop, I write "placet following [the bishop's Latin name, e.g.,] Lotharingus." If he does not explicitly mention canon 6, but says generally that he approves the canons, I write "general approval." If he generally approves the canons while adopting the emendations of another bishop, I write "general approval following [e.g.] Lotharingus." If he references multiple bishops, I note only the names of bishops who commented on canon 6. If he makes no reference to canon 6 at all, I infer that he does not oppose the canon and write "no opposition." If he disapproves of the canon's formulation I write "non placet"; if he notes reasons for the disapproval, I summarize them.

In the following list, I identify members of the *deputatio* charged with drafting the canons with the notation [X] after the name.

Office	Name	Comments/Judgments on Canon 6
Cardinal	Lotharingus	general approval; recommends adding a canon condemning three propositions of Calvin: viz., that marriage is dissolved on account of disparity of cult, hostility in communication between the spouses, and prolonged absence ("dirimatur matrimonium propter disparitatem cultus, propter non convenientiam in conversatione et propter longam absentiam," 642.25–28); Trent eventually does add a canon closely to this effect, canon 5 (see CT, IX, 967.27–28)
	Madrutius	general approval ("ceteri canones placent," 643.22); requests that the canons be expanded and made fuller, or that a concise but comprehensive doctrinal introduction be added ("compendiosam doctrinam," 643.20–21)
Patriarch	Aquilegiensis	general approval ("placent omnes canones," 643.30)
	Venetiarum	general approval ("probat omnes canones," 643.35)
	Hierosolymitanus	placet as amended: replace "novare" with "aliam ducere" (666.32); follows Lotharingus: add new canon (30–31)

(table continues)

---

and marries another, nor she commit adultery who dismisses an adulterer and marries another, let him be anathema." CT, IX, 640.

8. CT, IX, 642–79.

APPENDIX B: RECORDED STATEMENTS

Office	Name	Comments/Judgments on Canon 6
Archbishop	Cretensis	**non placet** because of the opinions of the Greeks and pseudo-Ambrose ("quia ferit Graecos et Ambrosium," 644.2)
	Hydruntinus	**placet as amended**: retain clause saying a husband may not remarry, but eliminate the clause saying a wife cannot remarry, since this is not in doubt (644.7–8)
	Granatensis [X]	**placet** ("defendit 6. canonem," 644.14)
	Florentinus	**general approval** following Hydruntinus ("quoad reliquos canones approbat annotate... Hydruntinum," 644.33–34)
	Verallus	**placet as amended**: publish as a "decree," without anathema, lest it attack Ambrose ("ne feriatur Ambrosius," 644.36)
	Antibarensis	**general approval** following recommended annotations of Lotharingus, Cretensis, Hydruntinus, and Verallus (644.40–41); he does not specify what recommendations of those bishops he intends to follow; obviously he does not follow Crete's non placet
	S. Severinae	**no opposition** (645)
	Iadrensis	**non placet** following Cretensis ("In 6. et 7. sequitur Cretensem," 645.13–14)
	Rossanensis [X]	**placet as amended**; expresses concern ("In 6 animadvertendum censeo," 645.37) saying the canon appears to condemn Ambrose and other authorities; he says even Augustine was doubtful about the gravity of the wrong done by the man who remarries after his wife's adultery, judging it himself (i.e., Augustine) to be merely venially sinful: Rossanensis disagrees with the contrary authorities and adduces twenty-four other authorities in defense of the traditional view that the bond of marriage is not dissolved on account of adultery ("vinculum matrimonii non dissolvatur per fornicationem...", 649.4–27), and recommends that the canon be formulated so as to avoid scandal that might arise because of the views of contrary authors; follows Lotharingus in proposing a new canon against the errors of Calvin (645.19–20)[1]
	Materanus	**general approval** following Hydruntinus (650.15–16)
	Bracarensis [X]	**non placet** following Cretensis (650.20)

(table continues)

1. "Immo credo, esse erroneam, et contrariam esse verissimam, quam, si opus esset, probare possum multis auctoritatibus, quas hic habeo in quadam cedula usque ad numerum 24; sed brevitatis causa non refero. Haec autem dixi, ut advertant patres sapientissimi, an canon iste sub anathemate tradendus sit, an vero alio modo declaranda sit veritas, vel saltem (quod magis placeret) aliqua expositio statim post canonem ad Ambrosii et aliorum dicta sit addenda, (ita ut) doceantur legentes et tamen scandalum non patiantur ex tantorum auctorum contradictione." CT, IX, 646.12–18.

APPENDIX B: RECORDED STATEMENTS   211

Office	Name	Comments/Judgments on Canon 6
	Genuensis	**non placet** (no explantation) (650.35)
	Ebredunensis	**general approval** following Lotharingus (651.1)
	Senensis	**no opposition** (651)
	Tarentinus [X]	**general approval** following Lotharingus and Hydruntinus; criticizes Rossanensis's interpretation of Augustine (651.6–7)
	Rheginus	**placet as amended**: publish without anathema (651.16–17)
	Amalphitanus	**general approval** following Lotharingus (651)
	Pragensis	**placet** (651.30)
	Messanensis	**no opposition** (651)
	Lancianensis	**placet as amended**; without anathema (651.38–39)
	Panormitanus	**general approval** following Verallus, Rossanensis, and Tarentinus (651.48–49)
	Naxiensis	**placet as amended**; without anathema (652.2–3)
	Barensis	**no opposition** (652)
	Senonensis	**placet as amended**; without anathema (652.32); approves Lotharingus's recommendation for a new canon; says to publish a canon saying "if anyone says that the willful absence of either spouse, or etc." ("Si quis dixerit, affectatam utriusque coniugis absentiam, aut etc," 652.29–30)
Bishop	Cavensis	**non placet** following Cretensem and no anathema following Verallus (652.9–10)
	Pientinus	**placet** following Verallus (652.16)
	Milopotamensis (first intervention)	**placet as amended**: without anathema (652.20–21)
	Milopotamensis (second intervention)	**Follow Cretensis in all things** ("secundus remittit se Cretensi in omnibus," 662.5). (Cretensis: "**non placet**, opinions of the Greeks and pseudo-Ambrose," 644.2)
	Ebroicensis	**no opposition**; follows Lotharingus in proposing a new canon (653.8–9)
	Lectorensis	**placet** (653.15)
	Bellicensis	**general approval** ("ceteri placent," 653.16)
	Cathaniensis	**no opposition** (653)
	Caiacensis	**general approval** (653)
	Civitatis Castellanae	**general approval** following Lotharingus ("canones omnes probat," 653.24)
	Tarvisinus	**placet as amended**: without anathema (653.28)
	Thermularum	**no opposition** (653)

(table continues)

212   APPENDIX B: RECORDED STATEMENTS

Office	Name	Comments/Judgments on Canon 6
	Marsicensis	**no opposition** (653)
	Minerbiensis	**no opposition** (653)
	Andegavensis	**no opposition** (653)
	Philadelphiensis	**general approval** (653)
	Britonoriensis	**placet as amended**: without anathema (653.43); follows Lotharingus in proposing a new canon (44)
	Ierapetrensis	**placet as amended**: without anathema (654.4)
	Castrensis	**non placet** following Cretensis (654)
	Oscensis	**general approval** (654)
	Castellanetensis	**non placet** following Cavensus who follows Cretensis and Verallus (654.12)
	Iustinopolitanus	**placet**; says that it should be published as is; it does not matter if it attacks (pseudo) Ambrose because particular doctors are capable error ("etiamsi feriatur Ambrosius, parum refert, quia quilibet particularis doctor potesterrare," 654.16–17)
	Sagiensis [X]	**general approval** (654)
	Colimbriensis	**placet** following Lotharingus and Hydruntinus (655.1–2)
	Recanatensis	**general approval** ("Ceteri canones placent," 655.23)
	Clugiensis	**placet**; says the canon's content derives from the Gospel ("In 6. declaretur scriptura evangelii, quae de hoc loquitur," 655.41–42); follows Lotharingus in proposing a new canon (42)
	Interamnensis	**placet**; says the canon should be published with anathema because it is "from the statements of scripture and St. Paul" (655.43–44)
	Cenetensis	**general approval** (656); follows Lotharingus in proposing a new canon (8–9)
	Sulmonensis	**placet**; publish with anathema ("6. Canonem approbat cum anathemate," 656.11–12); follows Lotharingus: add new canon (12)
	Brugnatensis	**no opposition** (656)
	Umbriaticensis	**general approval** following Hydruntinus (656)
	Tortonensis	**no opposition** (656); follows Lotharingus: add new canon (27)
	Segobiensis	**placet as amended**: says he approves the canon's content ("materiam"), but not the way it is formulated ("dispositionem," 656.41–42); says that Church Fathers such as (pseudo) Ambrose understood the Gospel of Matthew to permit a separation of bond (656.42–657.1); he proposes the following indirect formulation: "Dicatur ergo: *Si quis dixerit, ecclesiam errasse dicentem, non dissolvi matrimonium quoad vinculum per fornicationem: anathema sit*" (657.4–6)

(*table continues*)

APPENDIX B: RECORDED STATEMENTS 213

Office	Name	Comments/Judgments on Canon 6
	Virdunensis	**placet**: says "matrimonium" should read "vinculum matrimonii"; contradicting Segobiensis he says that Ambrose and Origen both say a husband cannot dismiss his wife and that remarriage constitutes adultery (657.26–29); follows Lotharingus on adding a new canon (25); recommends adding a doctrinal introduction ("doctrina") (19)
	Pactensis	**placet**; recommends publishing the canon so as not to obstruct the "ritu Graecorum et auctoritate Ambrosii" (658.8)
	Niciensis	**no opposition** (658); follows Lotharingus: add new canon (12–13); recommends adding a "doctrina" (11)
	Parisiensis	**placet** following Virdunensis (who contradicts Segobiensis) (658.18–19)
	Feretranus	**general approval** (658); follows Lotharingus: add new canon (27–28)
	Bovensis	**general approval** (658); follows Lotharingus: add new canon (29–30)
	Chironensis	**placet as amended**; without anathema (658.33); follows Lotharingus: add new canon (33–34)
	Sanctonensis	**general approval** (658)
	Catthacensis[1]	**general approval** following Rheginus (658.40–41)
	Auxerensis	**no opposition** (658); follows Lotharingus: add new canon (43)
	Mutinensis	**placet as amended**; he says the canon should also condemn those who say the church cannot prohibit remarriage after adultery ("damnari eos, qui dicunt, ecclesiam non posse id prohibere, videl. ob fornicationem non ducendam aliam uxorem," 658.47–48); he also proposes that a prefatory "titulus" be placed before the canons (45); he follows Lotharingus in his proposal for a new canon (46)
	Calamonensis	**placet** following Segobiensis's formulation or formulate without anathema (659.17–18); follows Lotharingus: add new canon (19–20); recommends adding a doctrinal introduction ("doctrina aut prooemium aut titulus") (15)
	Cauriensis	**general approval** (659); proposes adding a "brevis doctrina" (23)
	Asculanus	**general approval** following Lotharingus and Hydruntinus (659.26)

(table continues)

1. Rheginus recommends publishing without anathema; it is unclear whether Catthacensis follows him in this specificity since all he says is "in reliquis Rheginum" (reliquis referring to canons 4–11).

214   APPENDIX B: RECORDED STATEMENTS

Office	Name	Comments/Judgments on Canon 6
	Segninus	general approval (659.29); following Lotharingus: including in his recommendation to add new canon (29–30)
	Fesulanus	no opposition; says he remits (refers) the canon's content to the *deputatio* ("6. remittit se deputatis," 658.35)
	Lesinensis	general approval (659)
	Laguedonensis	placet following Segobiensis (659.46–47).
	Aurelianensis	placet following Mutinensis (660.7); proposes the addition of a doctrinal introduction ("doctrina," 3–4)
	Insulanus	non placet; "6 tollatur," "should be removed"; no explanation (660.20)
	Vulturariensis	general approval following Segobiensis, Mutinensis and doctors of the "deputorum" (660.22–23); follows Lotharingus: add new canon (25)
	Aquinatensis	non placet; "5.6. et tollatantur" (660.29)
	Montismarani	placet following recommendations on form by Segobiensis (660.34); follows Lotharingus: add new canon (34)
	Maceratensis	non placet following Cretensis (660.38)
	Lucerinus	general approval (660)
	Meldensis	general approval following Lotharingus and Hydruntinus (661)
	Leriensis	placet as is ("6. placet ut iacet," 661.7)
	Grossetanus	general approval following Mutinensis (661.22–23)
	Tiburtinus	general approval following Lotharingus and Tarentinus (661.24)
	Albinganensis	general approval (661.26–27)
	Ilcinensis	non placet following Bracarensis (follows Crete) (661.30)
	Assisiensis	general approval following Mutinensis (661.32)
	Atrebatensis	no opposition (661)
	Esinus	general approval following Lotharingus (661)
	Casertanus	placet following Segobiensis (661.49)
	Adriensis	general approval following Mutinensis (661.52)
	Alexanensis	general approval following Mutinensis (662.1)
	Asturicensis	general approval (662)
	Cathalonensis	placet following Lotharingus (662.10)
	Assaphaensis	placet as amended: without anathema (662.14); follows Lotharingus: add new canon (15)

(*table continues*)

APPENDIX B: RECORDED STATEMENTS 215

Office	Name	Comments/Judgments on Canon 6
	Larinensis	**placet as is** ("6. maneat, ut iacet," 662.18); recommends adding a doctrinal preface ("doctrina," 17)
	S. Leonis	**general approval** following Tarentinus (662.25)
	Metensis [X]	**no opposition** (662); follows Lotharingus: add new canon (29)
	Montisfalisci	**placet as amended**: without anathema (662.42)
	Gerundensis	**general approval** (663); follows Lotharingus: add new canon (13); recommends adding a preface to the canons ("praefatio") (12)
	Auriensis	**placet**; proposes the addition of a ("doctrina") (663.16); says canon 6 should be published in the "doctrina"; but if that is not possible, then propose it *as is* (18–19)
	Gebennensis	**general approval** (663.32); follows Lotharingus: add new canon (31)
	Cenomanensis	**no opposition** (663)
	Theanensis	**general approval** (663–64); follows Lotharingus: add new canon (43)
	Augustensis [X]	**general approval** (664)
	Mazariensis [X]	**no opposition** (664); follows Lotharingus: add new canon (11)
	Arianensis	**general approval** following Granatensis ("defendit 6. canonem") and Segobiensi (664.12); follows Lotharingus: add new canon (13)
	Vaurensis	**placet as is** ("6. placet ut iacet," 664.15)
	Sibinicensis[2]	**non placet** following Cretensis (664.20)
	Venetensis	**general approval** following Granatensis and Bracarensis (665.1)
	Suessionensis	**placet** (665.6); follows Lotharingus: add new canon (7)
	Quinqueecclesiensis [X]	**placet as is**; replies to the problem of (pseudo) Ambrose with the maxim of Vincent of Lerins: "we should follow the common judgment of the fathers, but not the judgment of some particular saint"; he says that in Canons of the Apostles 48, men who dismiss their wives and remarry are excommunicated, and adds, somewhat obscurely, that "in Hungary, a husband kills an adulterous wife and the wife of an adulterous husband" (665.9–13)
	Cotronensis	**general approval** (665)
	Legionensis [X]	**placet**; he defends canon 6 for "many reasons" ("Defenditque 6. canonem pluribus rationibus," 665.34); follows Lotharingus: add new canon (21)

(table continues)

2. Does not state "non placet" but states that he follows Crete, who registers a non placet.

APPENDIX B: RECORDED STATEMENTS

Office	Name	Comments/Judgments on Canon 6
	Almeriensis	placet (665.36)
	Ilerdensis	placet; publish with anathema ("ponatur sub anathemate," 666.15); recommends adding a "praefatio" (13)
	Buduensis	general approval following Almeriensis (666.22–23)
	Vicensis (Italy)	placet with anathema ("cum anathemate," 666.24–25)
	Aquensis	general approval following Mutinensis (666.39); follows Lotharingus: add new canon (38)
	Ostunensis	placet following Ilerdensi (publish with anathema) (667.2)
	Elnensis	general approval following Legionensis (667.9)
	Vestanus [X]	general approval (667.13)
	Clusinus	no opposition (667)
	Dolensis	general approval (667.25)
	Nivernensis	no opposition (667)
	Uxentinus	placet following Segobiensis and Mutinensis (667.37–38)
	Nemausensis	general approval following Mutinensis (667.41)
	Brixiensis	placet following Mutinensis (668.7–8); recommends adding a "praefatio brevis" (6)
	Comensis	general approval (668.13); follows Lotharingus: add new canon (13–14)
	Tutellensis	placet (668.20)
	Feltrensis	general approval following Hierosolymitanus (668.23)
	Calaguritanus	placet as amended; replace *novare* with *contrahere* (669.25–26)
	Civitatensis	placet as is ("6. non mutetur," 668.30)
	Isclanus	general approval following Mutinensis (668.45)
	Acerrensis	general approval (668.47)
	Civitatis Castelli	placet (669.3); follows Lotharingus: add new canon (5)
	Hyprensis	placet as is (669.24); proposes a doctrinal introduction or short preface ("doctrina vel praefatiuncula") (21)
	Namurcensis	no opposition; proposes a preface or doctrinal statement ("praefatio aut doctrina") as recommended by Mutinensis (669.40)
	Venciensis	general approval following Lotharingus and Mutinensis (670.15–16); follows Lotharingus: add new canon (16); proposes a short preface ("praefatiunculam," 15)
	Massaelubrensis	general approval following Panormitanus and Mutinensis (670.19); follows Lotharingus: add new canon (19–20)

(table continues)

APPENDIX B: RECORDED STATEMENTS 217

Office	Name	Comments/Judgments on Canon 6
	Anglonensis	**placet** (670.24); follows Lotharingus: add new canon (25); proposes "praefatio aut doctrina" (22)
	Parmensis	**general approval** following Lotharingus, Hydrutinus, and Mutinensis (670.29)
	Nimosiensis	**placet as amended**: without anathema (670.36); follows Lotharingus: add new canon (36–37)
	Barcinonensis	**placet as is** (ut iacet 670.40); proposes the addition of "doctrina aut praefatio" (ln 38)
	Dertusensis	**placet** with anathema (671.4–5); recommends that the form and the matter of the sacrament be clarified ("Et expedit, ut declaretur, quae sit forma et quae materia huis sacramenti," 671.1–2)
	Calvensis	**placet as is** (671.24)
	Niochensis	**placet as amended**; says a doctrinal introduction ("doctrina") should be added and that canon 6 should be a part of it (671.34, 36–37); follows Lotharingus: add new canon (36)
	Troianus	**placet as amended**; without anathema (671.47–48); proposes the addition of a short preface ("praefatiuncula," 46); he follows Lotharingus: add new canon (48)
	Guadiscensis	**non placet**; says Ambrose and other authorities argue that if a woman has an infirmity that prevents her from rendering the debt, the husband may remarry; Gregory II argues that if a man catches his wife in a conspiracy on his life, he may remarry if he cannot contain himself, but she must remain unmarried; ends saying the canon should be published without an anathema (672.5–12): proposes the addition of a "doctrina" (1)
	Papiensis	**placet as is** (672.21)
	Corosopitanus	**placet as is**; replies to those who say that Trent should follow Florence and withhold using an anathema by saying the reason Florence withheld it was because it never used any anathema ("nec mirum, quod in Florentino concilio non adducitur anathema, quia illud concilium nullibi utitur anathemate"); follows Lotharigum in recommending a new canon (672.28–30)
	Salamantinus	**general approval** (673.9)
	Columbriensis	**placet as is** (with anathema); says this is because of a corresponding decree of the Council of Mileve, which, holds the authority of a general council (673.12–14); he follows Lotharingus in recommending the addition of a new canon (14)
	Liciensis	**no opposition** (673)
	Nucerinus	**non placet**, no explanation (673.25)
	Sarzanensis	**placet** (673.30)

(table continues)

Office	Name	Comments/Judgments on Canon 6
	Oppidensis	**no opposition** (673)
	Pisauriensis	**general approval** following Mutinensis (673.41)
	Pennensis	**no opposition**; follows Lotharingus in recommending the addition of a new canon (673.46)
	Pampilonensis	**general approval** following Lotharingus (673.51)
	Lucensis	**placet** following Segobiensis (674.6); follows Lotharingus: add new canon (15–16)
	Senecensis	**general approval** following Mutinensis (674.37); he follows Lotharingus: add new canon (37)
	Aliphanus	**non placet**; says the church only uses an anathema when something is contrary to the common consensus of Catholics ("est contrarium communi consensui Catholicorum," 675.16); says Christ mitigated Deuteronomy's punishment against an adulteress, saying she should not be killed but rather repudiated ("eas non interficiendas, sed repudiandas," 675.17); says that in Origen's time a man could take a second wife after his first wife's adultery ("Tempore Origenis propter adulterium poterat duci alia," 675.17–18); notes seven authorities that he thinks defend this position, including (pseudo) Ambrose (675.18–21); also proposes a doctrinal preface ("doctrina") that can explicate what should be understood to be according to divine law and human law, and what is the matter, form and minister of the sacrament (674.44–675.1); ends saying the canon should follow Segobiensis and Lucensis (675.22–23); follows Lotharingus: add new canon (675.11)
	Aemoniensis	**placet** following Mutinensis (675.27); follows Lotharingus: add new canon (28); add "doctrina" (25)
	Soranus	**general approval** following Lotharingus and Mutinensis (675.33–34); follows Lotharingus: add new canon (39)
	Monopolitanus	**placet as amended**: without anathema (675.40); follows Lotharingus: add new canon (39)
	Ventimiliensis	**general approval** ("canones placent," 676.3)
	Rossensis	**placet as amended**: without anathema (676.6); follows Lotharingus: add new canon (7)
	Bobiensis	**general approval** following Mutinensis and Auriensis (676.10–11)
	Achadensis	**placet as is** (with anathema) (676.13)
	Rapotensis	**no opposition** (676)
	Faventinus	**no opposition** (676); recommends doctrina brevis (18); follows Lotharingus: add new canon (22)

(table continues)

APPENDIX B: RECORDED STATEMENTS 219

Office	Name	Comments/Judgments on Canon 6
	Urbevetanus	**general approval** (676); he says "a consummated marriage is indissoluble, because it signifies the union of the divine nature with the human, which is indissoluble" ("matrimonium est consummatum et est indissolubile, quia significant unionem divinae naturae cum humana, quae indissolubilis est," 676.39–41)
	Guardiensis	**general approval** following Hierosolymitanus and Calvensis (677.5)
	Marsicanus	**no opposition**; following Mutinensis, he recommends a "praefatio" (677.7)
	Trivicanus [X]	**general approval** (677.11)
	Sagonensis	**no opposition**; recommends adding a short preface ("praefatiuncula," 677.18)
	S. Marci	**general approval** following Mutinensis (677.21)
	Amerinus	**general approval** (677.24)
	Usellensis	**placet as is** (with anathema) (677.34); recommends a "doctrina" (25)
	Cortonensis	**general approval** following Lotharingus (677.35)
	Torcellanus	**general approval** (677.37)
	Minorensis	**general approval** following Urbevetanus (677.39)
Abbot	Claravallensis	**no opposition** (678)
	Euticius	**no opposition** (678)
	Augustinus	**placet** (678.13); recommends a "praefatiuncula" to clarify the matter, form and minister of the sacrament (10–11)
	Cassinensis	**placet**; defends the canon with the authority of Augustine, Jerome, Ambrose, and Basil (678.17–18)
	Lunaevillae	**placet as is** (678.22)
Generals	Dominicans	**general approval**; following Mutinensis, recommends adding a doctrinal preface ("titulus," 678.31–32); follows Lotharingus: add new canon (32)
	Franciscans	**placet** following Mutinensis (679.13–14)
	Augustinians	**placet** (679.31); recommends a "praefatiuncula" so that doctrine may be taught more fully (25–26)
	Servites	**placet as is**; follows Lotharingus: add new canon (679.41)
	Carmelites	**no opposition** (679)
	Jesuits	**no opposition** (679)

Table B-2. First Formulation of the Canon on Adultery (Canon 6) Using a Direct Formulation

Col. 1: *Placet*	Col. 2: *Placet as amended (P-A)* with no substantive recommendation	Col. 3: *P-A* with condemnation of those who say the church cannot prohibit remarriage	Col. 4: *P-A* without anathema	Col. 5: *P-A* with avoid offending contrary authorities	Col. 6: *General Approval*	Col. 7: *Non Placet* because of the Greeks and/or (pseudo) Ambrose	Col. 8: *Non Placet* with no explanation given	Col. 9: *No Opposition*
Granatensis 644	Hierosolymitanus 666	Mutinensis 658; add "titulus"	Verallus 644	Rossanensis 645	Lotharingus (Lorraine) 642; proposes new canon	Cretensis 644	Genuensis 650	S. Severinae 645
Pragensis 651	Hydruntinus 644	Aurelianensis 660; add "doctrina"	Rheginus 651	Segobiensis 656; agrees with content, not form, and proposes indirect formulation	Madrutius (Madruzzi) 643; add "doctrina"	Iadrensis 645; follow Cretensis	Insulanus 660	Senensis 651
Lectorensis 653	Colimbriensis 655	Brixiensis 668; add "praefatio brevis"	Lancianensis 651	Pactensis 658	Aquilegiensis 643	Bracarensis 650; follow Cretensis	Aquinatensis 660	Messanensis 651
Iustinopolitanus 654; (pseudo) Ambrose could have erred	Feltrensis 668	Aemoniensis 675; add "doctrina"	Panormitanus 651	Calamonensis 659; add "doctrina"	Venetiarum 643	Cavensis 652; follow Cretensis and Verallus	Nucerinus 673	Barensis 652
Clugiensis 655; contained in revelation	Calaguritanus 669	Franciscans 679	Naxiensis 652	Laguedonensis 659	Florentinus 644	Castrensis 654; follow Cretensis		Ebroicensis 653

Interamnensis 655; contained in revelation, with anathema	Parmensis 670	The remaining names in column 3 say generally that they follow Mutinensis in his remarks on the canons but do not mention canon 6	Pientinus 652	Vulturariensis 660; add "doctrina"	Antibarensis 644	Castellanetensis 654; follow Cavensis	Cathaniensis 653
Sulmonensis 656; with anathema		Grossetanus 661; "in reliquis Mutinensem"	Senonensis 652	Montismarani 660	Materanus 650	Maceratensis 660; follow Cretensis	Thermularum 653
Virdunensis 657; add "vinculum," add "doctrina"; the contrary opinion contradicts the ordinary reading of Ambrose and Origen		Assisiensis 661; "canones placent cum annotationibus Mutinensis"	Milopotamensis (first intervention) 652	Casertanus 661	Ebredunensis follow hotharingus 651	Ilcinensis 661; generally follow Bracarensis	Marsicensis 653
Parisicensis 658; follow Virdunensis		Adriensis 661; "subscribit sententiae Mutinensis"	Tarvisinus 653	Uxentinus 667	Tarentinus 651	Sibinicensis 664; follow Cretensis	Minerbiensis 653
						Milopotamensis (second intervention) 662: follow Cretensis	

(table continues)

Col. 1: Placet	Col. 2: Placet as amended (P-A) with no substantive recommendation	Col. 3: P-A with condemnation of those who say the church cannot prohibit remarriage	Col. 4: P-A without anathema	Col. 5: P-A with avoid of-fending contrary authorities	Col. 6: General Approval	Col. 7: Non Placet because of the Greeks and/or (pseudo) Ambrose	Col. 8: Non Placet with no explanation given	Col. 9: No Opposition
Leriensis 661		Alexanensis 662; "remittit se in omnibus Mutinensi"	Britonoriensis 653	Lucensis 674	Amalphitanus 651	Guadiscensis 672; add "doctrina"		Andegavensis 653
Cathalonensis 662		Aquensis 666; "In reliquis sequitur Mutinensem"	Ierapetrensis 654		Bellicensis 653	Aliphanus 675; add "doctrina"		Brugnatensis 656
Larinensis 662; "as is," add "doctrina"		Nemausensis 667; "in reliquis Mutinesem"	Chironensis 658		Caiacensis 653			Tortonensis 656
Auriensis 663; add "doctrina," canon 6 in "doctrina" or "as is"		Isclanus 668; "approbat in omnibus sententiam D. Mutinsensis"	Carthacensis 658		Civitatis Castellanae 653			Niciensis 658; add "doctrina"
Vaurensis 664; "as is"		Venciensis 670; add "praefatiunculam"	Assaphaensis 662		Philadelphiensis 653			Auxerensis 658

Suessionensis 665	Pisauriensis 673	Montisfalisci 662	Oscensis 654		Fesulanus 658
Quinqueecclesiensis 665; "as is"	Senecensis 674	Massaelubrensis 670	Sagiensis 654		Arrebatensis 661
Legionensis 665; "for many reasons"	Soranus 675	Nimosiensis 670	Recanatensis 655		Metensis 662
Almeriensis 665	Bobiensis 676	Niochensis 671; add "doctrina"	Cenetensis 656		Cenomanensis 663
Ilerdensis 666; "sub anathemate"	S. Marci 677	Troianus 671; add "praefatiuncula"	Umbriaticensis 656		Mazariensis 664
Buduensis 666; follow Almeriensis		Monopolitanus 675	Feretranus 658		Clusinus 667
Vicensis (Italy) 666; "with anathema"		Rossensis 676	Bovensis 658		Nivernensis 667

(*table continues*)

Col. 1: Placet	Col. 2: Placet as amended (P-A) with no substantive recommendation	Col. 3: P-A with condemnation of those who say the church cannot prohibit remarriage	Col. 4: P-A without anathema	Col. 5: P-A with avoid offending contrary authorities	Col. 6: General Approval	Col. 7: Non Placet because of the Greeks and/or (pseudo) Ambrose	Col. 8: Non Placet with no explanation given	Col. 9: No Opposition
Ostunensis 667					Sanctonensis 658			Namurcensis 669; add "doctrina"
Tutellensis 668								Liciensis 673
Civitatensis 668; "do not alter"					Cauriensis 659; add "doctrina"			
Civitatis Castelli 669					Asculanus 659			Oppidensis 673
Hyprensis 669; "as is," add "doctrina"					Segninus 659			Pennensis 673
Anglonensis 670; add "doctrina"					Lesinensis 659			
Barcinonensis 670; "as is," add "doctrina"					Lucerinus 660			Raporensis 676
Dertusensis 671; "with anathema"					Meldensis 661			Faventinus 676; add "doctrina"
					Tiburtinus 661			Marsicanus 677; add "praefatio"

Calvensis 671; "as is," no "doctrina"	Albinganensis 661	Sagonensis 677; add "praefatiuncula"
Papiensis 672; "as is"	Esinus 661	Claravallensis 678
Corosopitanus 672; "as is"	Asturicensis 662	Euticius 678
Columbriensis 673; "as is," "with anathema"	S. Leonis 662	Carmelites 679
Sarzanensis 673	Gerundensis 663; add "praefatio"	Jesuits 679
Achadensis 676; "with anathema"	Gebennensis 663	
Usellensis 677; "with anathema," add "doctrina"	Theanensis 663–64	
Augustinus 678; add "praefatiuncula"	Augustensis 664	
Cassinensis 678	Arianensis 664	

(*table continues*)

Col. 1: Placet	Col. 2: Placet as amended (P-A) with no substantive recommendation	Col. 3: P-A with condemnation of those who say the church cannot prohibit remarriage	Col. 4: P-A without anathema	Col. 5: P-A with avoid of fending contrary authorities	Col. 6: General Approval	Col. 7: Non Placet because of the Greeks and/or (pseudo) Ambrose	Col. 8: Non Placet with no explanation given	Col. 9: No Opposition
Lunaevillae 678; "as is"					Venetensis 665			
Augustinians 679; add "praefatiuncula"					Cotronensis 665			
Servites 679; "as is"					Elnensis 667			
					Vestanus 667			
					Dolensis 667			
					Comensis 668			
					Acerrensis 668			
					Salamantino 673			
					Pampilonensis 673			
					Ventimiliensis 676			

Convent	Total
Urbevetanus 676	41 fathers (21%)
Guardiensis 677	6 fathers (3%)
Trivicanus 677	5 fathers direct, 13 fathers indirect / 21 fathers (10%) (9%)
Amerinus 677	10 fathers (5%)
Cortonensis 677	56 fathers (28%)
Torcellanus 677	12 fathers (5%)
Minorensis 677	4 fathers (2%)
Dominicans 678	33 fathers (17%)

Table B-3. Remarks of the General Congregation on the Second Formulation (August 7–23)

C. 7 (August 7, 1563): Si quis dixerit, propter adulterium alterius coniugum posse matrimonium dissolvi, et utrique coniugum vel saltem innocenti, qui causam adulterio non dederit, licere, altero coniuge vivente, aliud matrimonium contrahere, neque moechari eum, qui dimissa adultera aliam duxerit, neque eum, quae dimisso adultero alii nupserit: anathema sit.[9]

C. 7, indirect formulation proposed by the Venetian delegation (August 11, 1563): Si quis dixerit, sacrosanctam Romanam catholicam et apostolicam ecclesiam, quae est aliarum omnium magistra, errasse vel errare, quando propter adulterium alterius coniugum docuit et docet, matrimonium non posse dissolvi, et utrumque coniugum, vel saltem innocentem, qui causam adulterio non dederit, non debere, altero coniuge vivente, aliud matrimonium contrahere, et moechari eum, qui dimissa adultera aliam duxerit, et eam, quae dimisso adultero alii nupserit: anathema sit.[10]

C. 5 (August 7, 1563): Si quis dixerit, propter haeresim aut molestam cohabitationem aut affectatam absentiam a coniuge dissolve posse matrimonii vinculum: anathema sit.[11]

The opinions of 193 Council fathers are recorded on the second formulation. This table also reproduces the indirect formulation proposed by the Venetian delegation on August 11. We find for the first time a formulation of canon 5 condemning the denial of indissolubility in three cases other than adultery in accordance with (but not identical to) the proposal of the cardinal of Lorraine (Lotharingus) from July 24.[12] In the following summary, most fathers explicitly approve the formulation of the Venetian delegation, but many follow the proposal of Lotharingus. The cardinal approves the Venetian proposal with the ad-

---

9. "If anyone says, that on account of the adultery of one of the spouses a marriage can be dissolved, and that it is licit for both spouses, or at least the innocent spouse who gave no cause for adultery, to remarry while the other spouse is living, and that he does not commit adultery who dismisses an adulteress and marries another, nor she commit adultery who dismisses an adulterer and marries another, let him be anathema." CT, IX, 682.21–24.

10. "If anyone says that the holy Roman catholic and apostolic church, which is the teacher of all the others, has erred or errs, when she has taught and teaches that on account of the adultery of one of the spouses, the marriage cannot be dissolved, and that both of the spouses, or at least the innocent one who gave no cause for adultery, should not contract another marriage while the other spouse is living, and that he commits adultery who dismisses an adulteress and remarries, and she commits adultery who dismisses an adulterer and remarries: let him be anathema." CT, IX, 686.28–33.

11. "If anyone says the bond of matrimony can be dissolved on account of heresy, or irksome cohabitation, or the willful desertion of one of the spouses: let him be anathema." CT, IX, 682.17–18.

12. See CT, IX, 642.26–28.

APPENDIX B: RECORDED STATEMENTS

dition of the words "iuxta scripturas." If a father follows Lorraine without explicitly mentioning the words "iuxta scripturas," I presume he follows him both in his proposal for an indirect formulation and in the addition of the words "iuxta scripturas." Some fathers, however (a small number), follow Lorraine only so far as the indirect formulation, explicitly rejecting the words "iuxta Scripturas" (or similar words). If a father generally follows Lorraine in his comments on the canons but does not explicitly mention canon 7, I write "generally follows Lotharingus." Members of the *deputatio* are designated with an [X] after the name.

Office	Name	Comments/Judgments on Canon 7
Cardinal	Lotharingus	approves the Venetian formula ("Canon 7 should be adapted to read: *If anyone says that the Catholic church erred or errs when on account of adultery* etc., as was said in the canon proposed by the orators," CT, IX, 687.7–9); recommends that the words "iuxta Scripturas" (in accordance with the scriptures) be added to the canon (9)
	Madrutius	follows Lotharingus on the formulation of the canon ("Quoad 7. approbat canonem Lotharingi," 687.20–21)
Patriarch	Hierosolymitanus	follows Lotharingus; recommends adding to the canon the words "from the words of sacred Scripture" (687.45–46)
	Aquilegiensis	follows Lotharingus; says to not add the words "iuxta Scripturas" (688.13–15)
	Venetus	approves the Venetian formula (688.24)
Archbishop	Cretensis	approves the Venetian formula; says that for many reasons, canon 7 should not be published as is (688.26–27)
	Hydruntinus	approves the Venetian formula (688.30–31)
	Granatensis [X]	approves the Venetian formula; but says to not add the words "secundum Scripturas"; says that although he believes canon 7 is true, nevertheless scripture only leads us to conclude that remarriage after adultery is illicit, not impossible, since not everything that is prohibited causes invalidity; so we can conclude that Christ prohibited remarriage after adultery, but it does not follow that he invalidated the new marriage. He references several church authorities, including (pseudo) Ambrose, who argue that remarriage after adultery is licit, at least for innocent husbands whose wives committed adultery; consequently, he disapproves of the direct formulation "quod sancti doctores damnentur" (689.15). He proposes as a possible formulation: "if anyone says that a marriage contracted by those who on account of adultery dismiss their wives is not invalid [irrita], a.s." He says it could also read: "If anyone says the Catholic church erred by teaching the prohibition that on account of adultery spouses should not remarry, a.s." (688.50–689.1–4; 689.15–20).
	Florentinus	approves the Venetian formula (690.10–11)
	Verallus	publish without anathema; publish as a "decree" (690.13)

(*table continues*)

APPENDIX B: RECORDED STATEMENTS

Office	Name	Comments/Judgments on Canon 7
	Antibarensis	approves the Venetian formula (690.18)
	Rossanensis [X]	approves the Venetian formula (690.21–22)
	S. Severinae	approves the Venetian formula (690.142–43)
	Iadrensis	approves the Venetian formula (690.52)
	Bracarensis [X]	follows Lotharingus; says to not add the words "secundum scripturas" (697.15–16)
	Genuensis	follows Granatensis, who approves Venice (697.40)
	Ebredunensis	approves the Venetian formula (698.1–2)
	Senensis	no opposition (698)
	Tarentinus [X]	placet as is or as amended by Lotharingus (698.22–23)
	Pragensis	follows Lotharingus (698.26–27)
	Messanensis	follows Granatansis (698.34)
	Lancianensis	approves the Venetian formula (699.1–2)
	Panormitanus	approves the Venetian formula (699.23–24)
	Senonensis	approves the Venetian formula; where the canon says "cannot" ("non potest"), it should say "ought not" ("non debet," 699.31)
	Rheginus	approves the Venetian formula (700.15–16)
	Naxiensis	approves the Venetian formula (700.32–33)
	Barensis	publish without anathema (701.7)
Bishop	Cavensis	approves the Venetian formula (701.20)
	Cattarensis	approves the Venetian formula (701.43–44)
	Pientinus	approves the Venetian formula (701.51–52)
	Milopotamensis	approves the Venetian formula in support of the Greeks (702.11–12)
	Ebroicensis	follows Lotharingus (702.19)
	Lectorensis	generally follows Lotharingus (702.27)
	Cathaniensis	approves the Venetian formula (702.30–31)
	Caiacensis	generally follows Lotharingus (702.37)
	Civitatis Castellanae	approves the Venetian formula (702.46)
	Thermularum	generally follows Lancianensis, who approves the Venetian formula (702.51)
	Minerbiensis	approves the Venetian formula (702.52–53)
	Andegavensis	approves the Venetian formula (703.5–6)
	Philadelphiensis	agrees with the "majority of the fathers" ("subscribit maiori parti partum," 703.19–20)
	Britonoriensis	approves the Venetian formula (703.29)
	Castrensis	approves the Venetian formula (703.37)

(table continues)

APPENDIX B: RECORDED STATEMENTS 231

Office	Name	Comments/Judgments on Canon 7
	Oscensis	generally follows Lotharingus (703.44)
	Clodiensis	approves the Venetian formula (704.3)
	Castellanetensis	approves the Venetian formula (704.38)
	Sagiensis	approves the Venetian formula; do not add *ex Scripturis* (704.47–48)
	Colimbriensis	follows Lotharingus (705.6)
	Ierapetrensis	follows Lotharingus (706.3)
	Iustinopolitanus	approves the Venetian formula (706.16)
	Recanatensis	approves the Venetian formula (707.4)
	Interamnensis	no opposition (707)
	Cenetensis	approves the Venetian formula (707.29–30)
	Sulmonensis	follows Lotharingus (707.37)
	Brugnatensis	approves the Venetian formula (708.4)
	Umbriaticensis	approves the Venetian formula (708.16–17)
	Tortonensis	follows Lotharingus (708.24–25)
	Segobiensis	approves the Venetian formula; says that some fathers assert that marriage can be dissolved for minor causes other than adultery (709.1–3)
	Virdunensis	follows Lotharingus (709.21–22)
	Pactensis	placet as is (710.3–4)
	Niciensis	approves the Venetian formula (710.8–9)
	Parisiensis	follows Lotharingus (710.15)
	Feretranus	approves the Venetian formula (710.23–24)
	Bovensis	approves the Venetian formula (710.27–28)
	Chironensis	follows Lotharingus (710.32–33)
	Sanctonensis	follows Lotharingus (710.39–40)
	Cathacensis	follows Lotharingus (710.43–44)
	Mutinensis	generally follows Lotharingus (710.46)
	Marsicensis	generally follows **Hydruntinus**, who approves Venetian formula (711.30)
	Calamonensis	approves the Venetian formula; he adds the words "ecclesiam catholicam" (711.35–36)
	Cauriensis	placet as is (712.8)
	Asculanus	approves the Venetian formula (712.18–19)
	Segniensis	approves the Venetian formula (712.21–22)
	Insulanus	approves the Venetian formula (712.24)
	Fesulanus	approves the Venetian formula (712.27–28)

(*table continues*)

232   APPENDIX B: RECORDED STATEMENTS

Office	Name	Comments/Judgments on Canon 7
	Lesinensis	approves the Venetian formula (712.43)
	Laguedonensis	follows Lotharingus, and says to add "ex Scripturis" (713.9)
	Leriensis	approves the Venetian formula (713.20)
	Aurelianensis	approves the Venetian formula (714.8–9)
	Vulturariensis	approves the Venetian formula (714.24–25)
	Aquinatensis	no opposition (714)
	Montis Marani	approves the Venetian formula (714.37–38)
	Maceratensis	approves the Venetian formula (715.9–10)
	Lucerinus	approves the Venetian formula (715.15–16)
	Aprutinus	general approval "with the annotations of the fathers especially Hydruntinus" (715.19–20), who approves Venetian formula
	Meldensis	no opposition (715)
	Grossetanus	no opposition (715)
	Tiburtinus	approves the Venetian formula (715.27–28)
	Albinganensis	approves the Venetian formula (715.30–31)
	Ilcinensis	generally follows Lotharingus and Hydruntinus (715.35)
	Assisiensis	generally follows Lotharingus and Mutinensis (715.38)
	Atrebatensis	generally follows Lotharingus, Madrutius and Mutinensis (715.41)
	Casertanus	approves the Venetian formula (716.15–16)
	Adriensis	approves the Venetian formula (716.19–20)
	Alexanensis	no opposition (716)
	Cathalonensis	generally follows Lotharingus (716.28)
	Asturicensis	placet as is "with anathema" (716.35)
	Asaphaensis	generally follows Lotharingus (716.41)
	Larinensis	placet as is "sub anathemate" (717.4)
	Milopotamensis	follows Cretensis "in everything" (717.15)
	S. Leonis	approves the Venetian formula (717.17)
	Metensis [X]	generally follows Lotharingus (717.20)
	Montisfalisci	approves the Venetian formula (718.2)
	Gerundensis	placet as is "sub anathemate"; cites many authorities in defense of the direct formulation of the canon; says that Ambrose held that remarriage is never licit for a divorced husband or a wife; says "contrary authorities are fictitious and not truly the opinions of the saints" ("auctoritates contrariae esse fictitias et non esse vere illorum sanctorum," 718.6–9)

(*table continues*)

APPENDIX B: RECORDED STATEMENTS 233

Office	Name	Comments/Judgments on Canon 7
	Auriensis	approves the Venetian formula; remove the word "posse" (718.16–17)
	Massalubrensis	no opposition (719)
	Vicensis (Spain)	approves the Venetian formula (719.15–16)
	Gebennensis	agrees with the "majority of the fathers" (719.28–29)
	Cenomanensis	generally follows Lotharingus (719.34)
	Theanensis	generally follows Lotharingus (719.37)
	Augustensis [X]	no opposition (720)
	Arianensis	general approval (720.19)
	Vaurensis	approves the Venetian formula (720.23)
	Sibinicensis	approves the Venetian formula (720.33)
	Venetensis	follows Vaurensis "in everything" (720.35)
	Suessionensis	approves the Venetian formula (720.37–38)
	Cotronensis	approves the Venetian formula (720.42–43)
	Legionensis [X]	placet as is "with anathema"; says many authorities actually oppose the Greeks by arguing that Basil teaches that one who dismisses his wife for adultery may *not* marry another, but should be reconciled to his wife; says Clement of Alexandria says the same; admits that John Chrysostom and Ambrose appear to concede the man can marry another, but he "believes that these alleged texts of the fathers are falsely attributed, or at least it can be said that they err" ("credit, textum, qui allegatur, esse falsum, vel potest dici, quod erraverit," 721.2–6, 8–9)
	Quinqueecclesiensis [X]	agrees with the "majority of the fathers" (721.26)
	Almeriensis	placet as is; "lest it give the impression that this is only a matter of church law, but not divine law" ("ne innuatur, hoc esse iuris ecclesiastici tantum, non autem divini," 721.30–31)
	Ilerdensis	placet as is; says Basil, Tertullian, Chrysostom, Hillary, Ambrose and Epiphanius seem to hold contrary opinions; but this should not be taken as an impediment to this canon; for those who adduce contrary opinions refer to the ambiguous text that apparently says that an adulterous wife cannot remarry, but which says nothing about the husband (thus apparently suggesting that the fathers think it licit for the husband to remarry); says "the holy Synod should urge the Venetians and others not to permit the Greeks to speak in opposition to the Holy See" ("Moneat sancta synodus D^{nos} Venetos et alios, ut non permittant Graecos loqui contra Sedem Ap$^{cam\cdot}$," 722.27–33)
	Buduensis	approves the Venetian formula (723.19)
	Vicensis (Italy)	approves the Venetian formula (723.22–23)

(table continues)

APPENDIX B: RECORDED STATEMENTS

Office	Name	Comments/Judgments on Canon 7
	Aquensis	approves the Venetian formula "if it does not conflict with the authority of the church" (723.26–27)
	Ostunensis	approves the Venetian formula; says this is not only on account of the Greeks, but also because of the authority of the "sanctorum"; for this "ritus Graecorum" did not begin with the schismatics, but when the Greeks were united with the Apostolic See (723.40–43)
	Elnensis	placet as is (724.27)
	Vestanus [X]	placet as is (724.32)
	Clusinus	approves the Venetian formula "if possible" (725.1–2)
	Dolensis	generally follows Lotharingus (725.19)
	Nivernensis	placet as is (725.22)
	Ugentinus	approves the Venetian formula (725.39–40)
	Nemausensis	generally follows Lotharingus; add the words "with the tradition of the ancient fathers" (725.44–45)
	Brixiensis	approves the Venetian formula; adds that the canon should be published in such as way as to make clear that a dispensation to remarry after adultery is impossible ("sed ita, ut non remaneat via (posse dispensari) de altera ducenda in causa fornicaitons," 726.29–30)
	Comensis	approves the Venetian formula (726.40–41)
	Tutellensis	approves the Venetian formula (727.4)
	Feltrensis	no opposition (727)
	Calaguritanus	approves the Venetian formula (727.15)
	Civitatensis	follows Lotharingus "provided that Scripture is mentioned" (727.30–31)
	Isclanus	no opposition (728)
	Acerrensis	generally follows Lotharingus (728.26)
	Civitatis Castellanae	generally follows Auriensis, who follows Venice (728.29)
	Hyprensis	approves the Venetian formula (729.25)
	Namurcensis	generally follows Lotharingus, Mutinensis, Civitatensis (730.3–4)
	Venciensis	generally follows Lotharingus (730.26)
	Anglonensis	approves the Venetian formula (730.32–33)
	Parmensis	follows Vestanus, who says publish as is (730.42)
	Nimosiensis	approves the Venetian formula (730.45)
	Barcinonensis	placet as is "if possible so as to satisfy the Venetian orators without concealing the truth" (731.1–2)
	Salamantinus	no opposition (731)

(*table continues*)

APPENDIX B: RECORDED STATEMENTS 235

Office	Name	Comments/Judgments on Canon 7
	Calvensis	approves the Venetian formula (731.20–21)
	Niochensis	**placet as is** (731.35)
	Troianus	approves the Venetian formula (731.36)
	Guadiscensis	**publish without anathema** (732.3)
	Papiensis	approves the Venetian formula (732.14–15)
	Columbriensis	**placet as is** (732.19)
	Liciensis	generally follows Hydruntinus, who follows Venice (732.28–29)
	Nucerinus	agrees with the "majority of the fathers" (732.30)
	Lavellinus	follows Legionensis, who says publish as is (732.34)
	Oppidensis	no opposition (732)
	Pisauriensis	follows Legionensis, who says publish as is (733.1)
	Sarzanensis	agrees with the "majority of the fathers" (733.7–8)
	Pennensis	approves the Venetian formula (733.9)
	Pampilonensis	**placet as is** (733.17)
	Lucensis	amend to read; "if anyone says the church errs by understanding the word of Matthew etc." (733.22–23)
	Senecensis	approves the Venetian formula (734.4–5)
	Aliphanus	**publish without anathema**; says Origen, Basil, Hillary, Lactantius, and many others hold a contrary position, and so do the Greeks from the time of the apostles until our time (734.9–11)
	Vabrensis	generally follows Lotharingus (734.24)
	Ventimiliensis	approves the Venetian formula (734.25)
	Rossensis	approves the Venetian formula (734.30)
	Bobiensis	approves the Venetian formula (734.34)
	Achadensis	**placet as is** (734.39)
	Rapotensis	no opposition (734)
	Guardiensis	follows Legionensis, who says publish as is (734.45)
	Marsicanus	generally follows Lotharingus (735.1)
	Trivicanus [X]	no opposition (735)
	Soranus	**placet as is** "lest we may be seen as approving the errors of the Greeks" (735.11–12)
	Faventinus	**placet as is "sub anathemate"**; he says the canon should show that the Church teaches this doctrine from the Scriptures ("ex Scripturis"), as Lotharingus said; or it should say "according to the evangelical and apostolic teaching" ("secundum evangelicam et apostolicam doctrinam"); replace "is not licit" with "is wrong" ("Ubi dicitur *non licere*, dicatur *nefas esse*," 735.20–22)

(table continues)

APPENDIX B: RECORDED STATEMENTS

Office	Name	Comments/Judgments on Canon 7
	Urbevetanus	generally follows Lotharingus and Hydruntinus (735.38)
	Sagonensis	follows Vestanus who says "placet as is" (736.31)
	S. Marci	agrees with the "majority of the fathers" (736.35)
	Amerinus	agrees with the "majority of the fathers" (736.38–39)
	Usellensis	placet as is "with anathema" (737.21)
	Cortonensis	agrees with the "majority of the fathers" (737.24)
	Torcellanus	approves the Venetian formula (737.26–27)
	Minorensis	no opposition (737)
	Monopolitanus	approves the Venetian formula (738.48)
Abbot	Cassinensis 1, 2, 3	approves the Venetian formula "if it can be done without concealment to the truth of the Gospel" (737.39, 41–42)
	Lunaevillae	follows Lotharingus (738.4–5)
Generals	Dominicans	approves the Venetian formula (738.13)
	Franciscans (observant)	placet as is (738.25)
	Franciscans (conventual)	placet as is (738.34–35)
	Augustinians	publish without anathema (740.9)
	Carmelites	approves the Venetian formula (740.20)
	Jesuits	placet as is (740.28)

TABLE B-4. Second Formulation of Canon 7

Col. 1: Approve Venetian Formula	Col. 2: Follow Lotharingus (either specifically in his comments on canon 7 or more generally in his comments on the set of canons)	Col. 3: Follow Granata, Lancianensis, Cretensis, et al., who approve Venetian formula	Col. 4: Publish without anathema	Col. 5: Publish as is	Col. 6: No opposition	Col. 7: Follow "the majority of the fathers" or similar general approvals
Lotharingus (687)	Madrutius (687)	Genuensis (697)	Verallus (690)	Tarentinus [X] (698)	Senensis (698)	Philadelphiensis (703)
Venetus (688)	Hierosolymitanus (688)	Messanensis (698)	Barensis (701)	Pactensis (710)	Interamnensis (707)	Aprutinus (715)
Cretensis (688)	Aquilegiensis (688)	Thermularum (702)	Guadiscensis (732)	Cauriensis (712)	Aquinatensis (714)	Gebennensis (719)
Hydruntinus (688)	Bracarensis [X] (697)	Marsicensis (711)	Aliphanus (734)	Asturicensis (716)	Meldensis (715)	Arianensis (720)
Granatensis [X] (688)	Pragensis (698)	Milopotamensis (717)	Augustinians (740)	Larinensis (717)	Grossetanus (715)	Quinqueecclesiensis [X] (721)
Florentinus (690)	Ebroicensis (702)	Venetensis (720)		Gerundensis (718)	Alexanensis (716)	Nucerinus (732)
Antibarensis (690)	Lectorensis (702)	Civitatis Castellanae (728)		Legionensis [X] (721)	Massalubrensis (719)	Sarzanensis (733)
Rossanensis [X] (690)	Caiacensis (702)	Liciensis (732)		Almeriensis (721)	Augustensis [X] (720)	S. Marci (736)
S. Severinae (690)	Oscensis (703)	*Lucensis (733)		Ilerdensis (722)	Feltrensis (727)	Amerinus (736)
Iadrensis (690)	Colimbriensis (705)			Elnensis (724)	Isclanus (728)	Cortonensis (737)
Ebredunensis (698)	Ierapetrensis (706)			Vestanus [X] (724)	Salamantinus (731)	
Lancianensis (699)	Sulmonensis (707)			Nivernensis (725)	Oppidensis (732)	
Panormitanus (699)	Tortonensis (708)			Parmensis (730)	Rapotensis (734)	
Senonensis (699)	Virdunensis (709)			Barcinonensis (731)	Trivicanus [X] (735)	
Rheginus (700)	Parisiensis (710)			Niochensis (731)	Minorensis (737)	
Naxiensis (700)	Chironensis (710)			Columbriensis (732)		
Cavensis (701)	Sanctonensis (710)			Lavellinus (732)		
Catarensis (701)	Cathacensis (710)			Pisauriensis (733)		
Pientinus (701)	Mutinensis (710)			Pampilonensis (733)		
Milopotamensis (702)	Laguedonensis (713)			Achadensis (734)		
Cathaniensis (702)	Ilcinensis (715)			Guardiensis (734)		
Civ. Castellanae (702)	Assisiensis (715)			Soranus (735)		
Minerbiensis (702)	Arrebatensis (715)			Faventinus (735)		
				Sagonensis (736)		

(table continues)

Col. 1: Approve Venetian Formula	Col. 2: Follow Lotharingus (either specifically in his comments on canon 7 or more generally in his comments on the set of canons)	Col. 3: Follow Granata, Lancianensis, Cretensis, et al., who approve Venetian formula	Col. 4: Publish without anathema	Col. 5: Publish as is	Col. 6: No opposition	Col. 7: Follow "the majority of the fathers" or similar general approvals
Andegavensis (703)	Cathalonensis (716)			Usellensis (737)		
Britonoriensis (703)	Asaphaensis (716)			Franciscans observ. (738)		
Castrensis (703)	Metensis [X] (717)			Franciscans convent. (738)		
Clodiensis (704)	Cenomanensis (719)			Jesuits (740)		
Castellanetensis (704)	Theanensis (719)					
Sagiensis (704)	Dolensis (725)					
Iustinopolitanus (706)	Nemausensis (725)					
Recanatensis (707)	Civitatensis (727)					
Cenetensis (707)	Acerrensis (728)					
Brugnatensis (708)	Namurcensis (730)					
Umbriaticensis (708)	Venciensis (730)					
Segobiensis (709)	Vabrensis (734)					
Niciensis (710)	Marsicanus (735)					
Feretranus (710)	Urbevetanus (735)					
Bovensis (710)	Lunaevillae (738)					
Calamonensis (711)						
Asculanus (712)						
Segniensis (712)						
Insulanus (712)						
Fesulanus (712)						
Lesinensis (712)						
Leriensis (713)						
Aurelianensis (714)						
Vulturariensis (714)						
Montis Marani (714)						
Maceratensis (715)						
Lucerino (715)						
Tiburtinus (715)						
Albinganensis (715)						
Casertanus (716)						
Adriensis (716)						
S. Leonis (717)						
Montisfalisci (718)						

	Total 38 fathers (20%)	Total 9 fathers (5%)	Total 5 fathers (2%)	Total 28 fathers (14%)	Total 15 fathers (8%)	Total 10 fathers (5%)
Auriensis (718)						
Vicensis (Sp) (719)						
Vaurensis (720)						
Sibinicensis (720)						
Suessionensis (720)						
Cotronensis (720)						
Buduensis (723)						
Vicensis (It) (723)						
Aquensis (723)						
Ostunensis (723)						
Clusinus (725)						
Ugentinus (725)						
Brixiensis (726)						
Comensis (726)						
Tutellensis (727)						
Calaguritanus (727)						
Hyprensis (729)						
Angloncnsis (730)						
Nimosicnsis (730)						
Calvensis (731)						
Troianus (731)						
Papiensis (732)						
Pennensis (733)						
Senecensis (734)						
Ventimiliensis (734)						
Rossensis (734)						
Bobiensis (734)						
Torcellanus (737)						
Monopolitanus (737)						
Cassinensis (737)						
Dominicans (738)						
Carmelites (740)						
Total 88 fathers (46%)						

* Bishop Lucensis proposes the following clause and nothing more: "if anyone says the church errs by understanding the word of Matthew etc." (733)

Table B-5. Remarks of the General Congregation on the Third Formulation (September 7–10, 1563)

Si quis dixerit, ecclesiam errare, quod iuxta evangelicam et apostolicam doctrinam propter adulterium alterius coniugum matrimonium non posse dissolvi docuit, et utrumque vel etiam innocentem, qui causam adulterio non dedit, non posse, altero coniuge vivente, aliud matrimonium contrahere, moecharique eum, qui dimissa adultera aliam duxerit, et eam, quae dimisso adultero alii nupserit: anathema sit.[13]

The opinions of 203 Council fathers are recorded on the third formulation. Members of the *deputatio* are designated with an [X] after the name.

Office	Name	Comments/Judgments on Canon 7
Cardinal	Lotharingus	**amend as follows**; add "bond of marriage" and "taught and teaches" ("In 7. dicatur *matrimonii vinculum*, et *docuit et docet*," CT, IX, 779.23–24); prefers the new preface to the old one (20)
	Madrutius	**follows Lotharingus** ("In 5. et 7. et 8. sequitur Lotharingum," 779.36); prefers the new preface, but also thinks it should be expanded ("uberior") (33)
Patriarch	Hierosolymitanus	**approves canon** 7 provided it is acceptable to the Venetian orators ("Canones placent excepto 7, nisi is placuerit oratoribus Venetis," 780.9); approves the new preface (9)
	Aquilegiensis	**no comment on canon** 7; approves new preface (780.12)
	Venetiarum	**no comment on canon** 7; approves new preface (780.16)
Archbishop	Hydruntinus	**approves canon** 7 if it pleases the Venetian orators (780.26); prefers old preface (23)
	Granatensis [X]	**non placet**, not only because of the Greeks, but also because it condemns many holy fathers ("7. canon non placet, non tantum propter Graecos, sed quia damnantur etiam plures sancti patres," 780.51–52); prefers new preface (52)
	Florentinus	**general approval** following Lotharingus ("in 5. et reliquis Lotharingum," 781.19)
	Verallus	**general approval as is** ("Ceteros probat ut iacent," 781.25); prefers old preface (23)
	Antibarensis	**general approval** ("omnia placent," 781.31)

13. "If anyone says the church errs because she taught that in accordance with the evangelical and apostolic doctrine, marriage cannot be dissolved on account of the adultery of a spouse, and that neither spouse, even the innocent one, who gave no cause for adultery, can contract another marriage while the other spouse is living, and that he commits adultery who dismisses an adulterous wife and marries another, and she commits adultery who dismisses an adulterous husband and marries another; let him be anathema." CT, IX, 760.21–25.

APPENDIX B: RECORDED STATEMENTS   241

Office	Name	Comments/Judgments on Canon 7
	Rossanensis [X]	**follows Lotharingus** ("in 5. ad 8. [sequitur] Lotharingum," 781.33); prefers new preface (32)
	S. Severinae	**no comment on canon 7**; approves new preface (782.1–2)[1]
	Iadrensis	**no comment on canon 7**; approves new preface following Madrutius, who follows Lotharingus (782.5)
	Materanus	**no comment on canon 7**; approves new preface following Madrutius (782.9)
	Callaritanus	**no comment on canon 7** (782)
	Bracarensis [X]	**general approval** following Lotharingus; approves both prefaces (782.18–19)
	Genuensis	**general approval** following Lotharingus ("In canonibus sequitur Lotharingum"); prefers old preface to new one (782.27)
	Nicosiensis	**amend to include** that "marriage is by divine law indissoluble" ("In 7. dicatur, matrimonium divino iure esse indissolubile," 782.31); prefers new preface (30)
	Ebredunensis	**general approval** following Lotharingus, including his recommendations for the preface (782.35–36)
	Senensis	**general approval** following Lotharingus; prefers new preface (782.37)
	Tarentinus [X]	**no comment on canon 7**; approves new preface (782.40)
	Messanensis	**no comment on canon 7**; approves new preface (782.45)
	Lancianensis	**no comment on canon 7** (782)
	Panormitanus	**general approval** following Madrutius, who follows Lotharingus (783.2–3); prefers new preface (782.50)
	Senonensis	**general approval** following Lotharingus; prefers new preface (782.5)
	Naxiensis	**no comment on canon 7**
	Barensis	**general approval** following Lotharingus; prefers new preface (783.13–14)
Bishop	Cavensis	**no comment on canon 7**; prefers old preface (783.16)
	Cattarensis	**no comment on canon 7**; prefers new preface (783.21)
	Pientinus	**no comment on canon 7**; prefers old preface (783.23)
	Milopotamensis	**no comment on canon 7** (783)
	Bellicensis	**general approval** following Lotharingus in everything (783.30)
	Catanensis	**no comment on canon 7**; approves both prefaces (783.31)

(*table continues*)

1. The bishop refers to annotations to the preface submitted "in writing by the secretary," Angelo Massarelli (782.1–2).

APPENDIX B: RECORDED STATEMENTS

Office	Name	Comments/Judgments on Canon 7
	Reginus[2]	**approve as amended**; replace "matrimonium" with "vinculum matrimonii"; approves both prefaces (783.36–38)
	Caiacensis	**general approval**; approves both prefaces (784.1)
	Tarvisinus	**no comment on canon 7**; approves both prefaces (784.3)
	Thermularum	**no comment on canon 7**; approves both prefaces following Tarvisinus ("in omnibus sequitur Tarvisinum," 784.5)
	Civitatis Castellanae	**no comment on canon 7** following Thermularum (784.6)
	Viglevenensis	**general approval** following Lotharingus; approves both prefaces (784.8–9)
	Marsicensis	**general approval** following Hydruntinus, who approves canon 7 if it pleases the Venetian orators (784.13)
	Minerbiensis	**general approval** following Hydruntinus (784.14–15)
	Philadelphiensis	**no comment on canon 7**; prefers new preface (784.17)
	Britonoriensis	**no comment on canon 7**; prefers new preface following Madrutius, who says the preface should be expanded (784.19)
	Ierapetrensis	**no comment on canon 7**; prefers new preface (784.27)
	Castrensis	**general approval** following Lotharingus (784.32)
	Oscensis	**no comment on canon 7**; prefers old preface (784.33)
	Clugiensis	**satisfied with Venetian formulation** with the annotations of Lotharingus ("In 7. placebat canon propositus a Venetis, et nunc etiam placet cum annotatione Lotharingi"); prefers new preface (784.35, 37–38)
	Castellanetensis	**general approval** following Madrutius, who follows Lotharingus (784.42)
	Iustinopolitanus	**satisfied with Venetian formulation** (784.43–44)
	Sagiensis [X]	**no comment on canon 7** (784)
	Recanatensis	**no comment on canon 7** (784)
	Interamnensis	**no comment on canon 7** (784)
	Cenetensis	**satisfied with Venetian formulation** (785.6–7)
	Sulmonensis	**no comment on canon 7**; approves new preface (785.10)
	Brugnatensis	**no comment on canon 7**; approves both prefaces with anathemas ("cum anathematismatibus," 785.15)
	Umbriaticensis	**no comment on canon 7**; prefers old preface (785.18)
	Virdunensis	**general approval** following Lotharingus in everything (785.19)
	Pactensis	**no comment on canon 7**; approves new preface (785.22)

(*table continues*)

2. Spoke as a substitute for the archbishop of Rheginus.

APPENDIX B: RECORDED STATEMENTS 243

Office	Name	Comments/Judgments on Canon 7
	Niciensis	satisfied with Venetian formulation; prefers old preface (785.25)
	Segobiensis	non placet; says the canon detracts from the Eastern churches and fathers of old ("derogat orientali ecclesiae et patribus antiquis," 785.33); says that it's unclear when the canon says the dogma is held from the scriptures ("ex Scripturis"); say rather, if anyone says that the church errs and goes beyond or against the divine Scriptures, etc. ("*Si quis dixerit, ecclesiam errare et praeter aut contra divinas Scripturas* etc.," 785.33–35); says it is necessary to place a "doctrina" before the canons and to say explicitly ("quae proposita est") that it is not sufficient ("necessarium esse doctrinam his canonibus [praeponere], et quae proposita est, non est sufficiens," 785.30–31)
	Naulensis	follow Segobiensis in everything (786.11)
	Parisiensis	follow Lotharingus in everything (786.12)
	Feretranus	no comment on canon 7; approves new preface (786.15)
	Bovensis	no comment on canon 7 (786)
	Chironensis	satisfied with Venetian formulation (786.20)
	Sanctonensis	general approval following Lotharingus (786.22–23)
	Catthacensis	no comment on canon 7 (786)
	Auxerensis	satisfied with Venetian formulation (786.25–26)
	Aleriensis	no comment on canon 7 (786)
	Mutinensis	canon 7 should be published without anathema *or* according to the recommendations of Lotharingus; approves both prefaces, but prefers new one (786.29, 33–34)[3]
	Calamonensis	follow Segobiensis on canon 7; approves both prefaces (786.38–39)
	Asculanus	general approval following Lotharingus (786.43)
	Segninus	general approval following Lotharingus (786.45)
	Insulanus	no comment on canon 7 (786)
	Fesulanus	general approval following Lotharingus; but adds that no changes should be made to canon 7; prefers the new preface (786.48–50)
	Lesinensis	no comment on canon 7; prefers old preface (787.7)
	Laguedoniensis	no comment on canon 7; prefers old preface (787.11)
	Leriensis	general approval following Lotharingus ("In reliquis sequitur Lotharingum," 787.23)
	Vulturariensis	no comment on canon 7; approves new preface following Segobiensis (787.24)

(table continues)

3. In the text, these remarks are referred to canon 6, but the editor, Stephanus Ehses, believes they should be referred to canon 7; see 786n1.

APPENDIX B: RECORDED STATEMENTS

Office	Name	Comments/Judgments on Canon 7
	Aquinatensis	**general approval** following Lotharingus; approves both prefaces, but suggests that the two be combined into one with the annotations of Lotharingus (787.29–30)
	Montismarani	**unclear**; follows Lotharingus, Granatensis, and Clugiensis (Lotharingus approves with two terminological emendations; Granatensis disapproves because the canon condemns Church Fathers; and Clugiensis is satisfied with the Venetian formula) (787.34); approves the new preface following Segobiensis (33)
	Maceratensis	**no comment on canon 7**; approves new preface following Segobiensis (787.38)
	Lucerinus	**general approval**; prefers new preface (787.41–42)
	Aprutinus	**no comment on canon 7** (787)
	Meldensis	**general approval** following Lotharingus (787.50–51)
	Grossetanus	**no comment on canon 7** (788)
	Tiburtinus	**no comment on canon 7** (788)
	Albinganensis	**general approval** following Lotharingus; approves new preface (788.4)
	Ilcinensis	**no comment on canon 7** (788)
	Vicensis (Spain)	**general approval** ("Cetera placent," 788.16)
	Assisiensis	**no comment on canon 7** (788)
	Atrebatensis	**no comment on canon 7**; approves new preface following Lotharingus, Granatensis, and Segobiensis (788.18–19).
	Casertanus	**no comment on canon 7**; prefers old preface (788.20)
	Alessanensis	**follow Mutinensis** in everything (who says canon 7 should be published without anathema *or* according to the recommendations of Lotharingus (788.22)
	Asturicensis	**no comment on canon 7** (788)
	Assaphaensis	**general approval** following Lotharingus; prefers old preface (788.25–26)
	Larinensis	**no comment on canon 7**; prefers new preface, but also thinks it should be expanded ("uberior," 788.27)
	S. Leonis	**general approval** following Lotharingus and Madrutius (788.33)
	Metensis [X]	**general approval** following Lotharingus; approves new preface (788.35)
	Montisfalisci	**general approval** following the majority of the fathers ("maiorem partem"), approves both prefaces, but prefers that the two be combined into one (788.39–40, 43)
	Gerundensis	**no comment on canon 7**; prefers the new preface following Lotharingus (788.44)

(table continues)

APPENDIX B: RECORDED STATEMENTS 245

Office	Name	Comments/Judgments on Canon 7
	Auriensis	no comment on canon 7; prefers new preface (789.1)
	Gebennensis	no comment on canon 7; prefers new preface following Segobiensis (789.5)
	Cenomanensis	**general approval** following Lotharingus and Mutinensis (789.7)
	Theanensis	**general approval** following Lotharingus and Mutinensis (789.7)
	Augustensis [X]	**non placet**; says the prior (direct) formulation of the canon should be restored ("Septimus canon non placet, sed restituatur, qui prius propositus fuerat," 789.8–9)
	Arianensis	**general approval** following Lotharingus, including in approving the new preface (789.13–14)
	Vabrensis (Vaurensis)	no comment on canon 7; prefers new preface following Segobiensis (who says the Council should publish a "doctrina") and Lariensis (who says preface should be expanded) (789.16–17)
	Sibinicensis	no comment on canon 7; prefers new preface following Segobiensis (789.19–20)
	Venetensis	**general approval** following Lotharingus (789.22)
	Suessionensis	**general approval** following Lotharingus (789.23)
	Cotronensis	no comment on canon 7 (789)
	Legionensis [X]	**non placet**; publish the original formulation of the canon; or if not, let it read "If anyone says the church has erred when she taught and teaches the evangelical doctrine" ("7. ponatur qui erat in principio, vel; *Si quis dixerit, ecclesiam errasse, cum evangelicam doctrinam docuit et docet*," 789.26–28)
	Almeriensis	**non placet**; says the older formulation of the canon should be restored ("7. non placet, sed restituatur canon ablatus," 789.29–30)
	Ilerdensis	**approve canon 7** with addition of "matrimonii vinculum"; prefers the old preface (789.33–35)
	Buduensis	**satisfied with Venetian formulation**; prefers the new preface, but says it should be expanded ("plenior," 789.40–41)
	Vicensis (Italy)	no comment on canon 7 (789)
	Aquensis	**general approval** following Mutinensis (publish without anathema or follow Lotharingus) and Clugiensis (follow Venetians) (789.45)
	Quinqueecclesiensis [X]	**general approval** following Lotharingus (790.4)
	Ostunensis	**non placet**; desires that the canon say that this teaching is held from tradition ("In 7. desideraret dici, hoc haberi ex traditione," 790.8–9); prefers new preface with annotations of Segobiensis; but notes that in the old law, marriage had a kind of holiness (aliquam sanctitatem)(5–6)

(table continues)

246   APPENDIX B: RECORDED STATEMENTS

Office	Name	Comments/Judgments on Canon 7
	Vestanus [X]	**no comment on canon 7**; prefers old preface (790.14)
	Clusinus	**general approval** following Lotharingus; approves both prefaces, but prefers that they be combined into one (790.18–20)
	Dolensis	**general approval** following Lotharingus (790.23)
	Nivernensis	**general approval** following Lotharingus (790.23)
	Uxentinus	**non placet** following Segobiensis; prefers new preface (790.24)
	Nemausensis	**general approval** following Lotharingus; prefers new preface following Segobiensis (790.29–30)
	Brixiensis	**general approval** following the "majority" of the fathers; approves new canon with annotations of the fathers ("cum annotationibus partum," 790.37–38)
	Comensis	**no comment on canon 7** (790)
	Tutellensis	**general approval** following Lotharingus; approves new preface following Segobiensis (790.45–46)
	Feltrensis	**general approval** following Hierosolymitanus and Venetus, who say it should be acceptable to the Venetians (791.1–2)
	Calaguritanus	**unclear**; says he follows Lotharingus [who approved of canon 7 as amended] and Granatensis [who disapproved of canon 7]; approves of both prefaces (791.7–8)
	Civitatensis	**general approval** ("Reliqua in canonibus anathematismatum et reformationum placent"); prefers the new preface (791.10, 13–14)
	Isclanus	**no comment on canon 7**; prefers new preface, but requests that it be expanded (791.19)
	Acerrensis	**no comment on canon 7** (791)
	Civitatis Castelli	**approves canon 7** following Lotharingus; prefers old preface (791.22)
	Caprulanus	**in canon 7, holds the reasoning of the Venetian delegation** ("In 7. habeatur ratio petitionis oratorum"); prefers new preface (791.29–31)
	Hyprensis	**no comment on canon 7**; approves new preface following Lotharingus (791.32)
	Namurcensis	**unclear**; says he follows Lotharingus (who approves canon 7 with emendations) and Segobiensis and Mutinensis (both of whom express concern about publishing the anathema) (791.42)
	Hyacinthanus	**no comment on canon 7** (791)
	Massaelubrensis	**follows Mutinensis in everything** (who says canon 7 should be published without anathema *or* according to the recommendations of Lotharingus) (791.46–47)

(*table continues*)

APPENDIX B: RECORDED STATEMENTS 247

Office	Name	Comments/Judgments on Canon 7
	Anglonensis	**general approval** following Lotharingus in everything (791.48)
	Parmensis	**no comment on canon 7** ("in 7 can. sequitur Vestanum"; Vestanum says nothing about canon 7) (791.49)
	Abricensis	**general approval** following Lotharingus (791.52); recommends that the following be added to canon 5: the impediment of sterility ("impedimentum sterilitas"); sickness ("morbus"); loss of fortune ("error fortunae"); found to be guilty of misconduct ("de corrupta inventa," 51–52)
	Nimosiensis	**no comment on canon 7**; prefers new preface (792.1)
	Barcinonensis	**no comment on canon 7**; prefers new preface (792.3)
	Calvensis	**no comment on canon 7** (792)
	Troianus	**general approval** following Hydruntinus (who says he approves canon 7 if it pleases the Venetian orators); approves new preface (792.9, 11–12)
	Guadiscensis	**no comment on canon 7**; prefers new preface, but requests that it be expanded (792.13)
	Papiensis	**no comment on canon 7** following Hyprensis (792.17)
	Columbriensis	**non placet** following Legionensis (who said the canon should be restored to the original formulation or read: "If anyone says the church has erred when with the evangelical doctrine she taught and teaches") (792.19)
	Liciensis	**unclear**; he generally follows Lotharingus (placet) and Segobiensis (non placet); prefers new preface following Ostunensis (who said that the teaching is held from tradition) (792.22, 24)
	Lavellinus	**follow Lotharingus in everything** (792.25)
	Sarzanensis	**no comment on canon 7** (792)
	Pisauriensis	**follow the majority of the fathers** (792.28)
	Pampilonensis	**follow Lotharingus in everything** (792.29)
	Lucensis	**follow Granatensis in everything** (792.30)
	Senecensis	**follow Lotharingus in everything** (792.31)
	Vabrensis	**follow Lotharingus in everything** (792.31)
	Monopolitanus	**no comment on canon 7** (792)
	Bobiensis	**no comment on canon 7** (792)
	Rossensis	**no comment on canon 7** (792)
	Ventimiliensis	**no comment on canon 7** (792)
	Achadensis	**no comment on canon 7** (792)
	Rapotensis	**approve everything** ("omnia placent," 792.41)
	Faventinus	**general approval** following Lotharingus (792.43)

(*table continues*)

248 APPENDIX B: RECORDED STATEMENTS

Office	Name	Comments/Judgments on Canon 7
	Guardiensis	no comment on canon 7 (792)
	Marsicanus	**general approval** following Lotharingus (792.47)
	Trivicanus [X]	**approve everything** ("placent omnia," 792.48)
	Sagonensis	**follow Madrutius in everything** (in canon 7, Madrutius follows Lotharingus) (792.49)
	S. Marci	no comment on canon 7 (792)
	Amerinus	no comment on canon 7 ("follow Hyprensis"); approves old preface (792.51)
	Paphensis	no comment on canon 7 (793)
	Torcellanus	no comment on canon 7 (793)
	Cretensis	no comment on canon 7; prefers new preface (793.6)
	Milopotamensis	no comment on canon 7; prefers new preface ("follow Cretensis in everything," 793.9)
	Praemisliensis	**non placet**; publish without anathema ("7. ponatur sine anathemate," 793.14)
	Oppidensis	no comment on canon 7 (793)
	Pennensis	no comment on canon 7 (793)
	Aliphanus	**non placet**; says he approves the proposal of the Venetian orators, or it should read: "*If anyone says that it is against the evangelical and apostolic doctrine* etc." ("7. canon non placet, sed placet propositus ab oratoribus Venetis, vel dicatur: *Si quis dixerit, esse contra evangelicam et apostolicam doctrinam* etc.," 793.31–33); he asks the Council to commend this disputed question to a subcommittee of fathers for discussion and for the committee to prepare a response ("Petit a legatis et a synodo, ut committatur aliquibus patribus, ut hoc disputent, et ipse est paratus respondere," 33–34); disapproves of the new preface because its content is deficient ("diminuta"); says it should be expanded (793.29–30)
	Soranus	no comment on canon 7; prefers old preface (793.35)
	Urbevetanus	**general approval** following the fathers; prefers the old preface (793.36, 38)
	Usellensis	**approves canon 7** following Lotharingus's recommendation to add "*matrimonii vinculum*"; proposes a new preface [not recorded] (794.3–4)
	Minorensis	no comment on canon 7 (794)
Abbot	Claravallensis	**general approval** following Lotharingus (794.9–10)
	(First Ab.) Cassinensis	no comment on canon 7; prefers the old preface (794.11)
	(Second and Third Ab.) Cassinensis	**follow first abbot of Cassinensis** (794.14)
	Lunaevillae	**general approval** following Lotharingus (794.16)

(*table continues*)

APPENDIX B: RECORDED STATEMENTS 249

Office	Name	Comments/Judgments on Canon 7
Generals	Dominicans	no comment on canon 7 (794)
	Franciscans (observant)	**general approval** following Lotharingus (794.20–21)
	Franciscans (conventual)	no comment on canon 7 (794)
	Augustinians	no comment on canon 7; prefers old preface (794.25)
	Servites	no comment on canon 7 (794)
	Carmelites	**general approval** following Lotharingus (794.28)
	Jesuits	**non placet**; canon should be formulated as it was formerly ("canon ponatur, ut prius erat"); prefers old preface (794.30, 34)
Bishop	Salamantinus	no comment on canon 7; prefers new preface (794.40)
	Elnensis	**general approval** following Lotharingus (794.43–44)
	Andegavensis	**general approval** following Lotharingus (794.43–44)
	Lectorensis	**general approval** following Lotharingus (794.43–44)
	Cathalonensis	**general approval** following Lotharingus (794.43–44)
	Cauriensis	**follow Granatensis in everything** (who disapproves of canon 7 because of the Greeks and many holy fathers) (794.45)
Archbishop	Pragensis	no comment on canon 7; approves new preface (794.46)
Bishop	Cortonensis	no comment on canon 7; approves new preface (794.48)
	Niochensis	no comment on canon 7; approves new preface (794.50)

TABLE B-6. Third Formulation of Canon 7

Col. 1: Approval of canon 7 (either mentioning the canon, or implicitly approving it by generally approving "all the canons" or "the remaining canons")	Col. 2: Approval following Lotharingus	Col. 3: Approve with emendations	Col. 4: Disapprove (*contra* practices of the Greeks, opinions of the Church Fathers, publish without anathema, etc.)	Col. 5: Approve if consistent with Venetian formulation	Col. 6: Non placet: return to a direct formulation of canon 7	Col. 7: No comment on canon 7
Verallus (781)	Madrutius (779)	Lotharingus (779)	Granatensis (780)		Augustensis (789)	Aquilegiensis (780)
Antibarensis (781)	Florentinus (781)	Nicosiensis (782)	Segobiensis (785)		Legionensis (789)	Venetus (780)
Naxiensis (783)	Rossanensis (781)	Reginus (783)	Naulensis (786)		Almeriensis (789)	S. Severinae (782)
Caiacensis (784)	Bracarensis (782)	Ilerdensis (789)	Mutinensis (786)		Columbriensis (792)	Iadrensis (782)
Lucerinus (787)	Genuensis (782)		Calamonensis (786)		Jesuits (794)	Materanus (782)
Vicensis (Sp) (788)	Ebredunensis (782)		Alessanensis (788)			Callaritanus (782)
Montisfalisci (788)	Senensis (782)		Aquensis (789)			Tarentinus (781)
Brixiensis (790)	Panormitanus (782)		Ostunensis (790)			Messanensis (782)
Civitatensis (791)	Senonensis (782)		Uxentinus (790)			Lanciancensis (782)
Pisauriensis (792)	Barensis (783)		Massaelubrensis (791)			Cavensis (783)
Rapotensis (792)	Bellicensis (783)					Cattarensis (783)
Trivicanus (792)	Viglevenensis (784)					Pientinus (783)
Urbevetanus (793)	Castrensis (784)					Milopotamensis (783)
	Castellanetensis (784)					Catanensis (783)
	Virdunensis (785)					Tarvisinus (784)
	Parisiensis (786)					Thermularum (784)
	Sanctonensis (786)					Civ. Castellanae (784)
	Asculanus (786)					Philadelphiensis (784)
	Segninus (786)					Britonoriensis (784)
	Fesulanus (786)					Ierapetrensis (784)
	Leriensis (787)					Oscensis (784)
	Aquinatensis (787)					Sagiensis (784)
	Meldensis (787)					Recanatensis (784)

Albinganensis (788)
Assaphaensis (788)
S. Leonis (788)
Cenomanensis (789)
Theanensis (789)
Arianensis (789)
Venetensis (789)
Suessionensis (789)
Quinqueecclesiensis (790)
Clusinus (790)
Dolensis (790)
Nivernensis (790)
Nemausensis (790)
Tutellensis (790)
Civitatis Castelli (791)
Anglonensis (791)
Abricensis (791)
Lavellinus (792)
Pampilonensis (792)
Senecensis (792)
Vabrensis (792)
Faventinus (792)
Marsicanus (792)
Sagonensis (792)
Usellensis (794)
Claravallensis (794)
Lunaevillae (794)
Obs.Franciscans (794)
Carmelites (794)
Elnensis (794)
Andegavensis (794)
Lectorensis (794)
Cathalonensis (794)

Interamnensis (784)
Sulmonensis (785)
Brugnatensis (785)
Umbriaticensis (785)
Pactensis (785)
Feretranus (786)
Bovensis (786)
Carthacensis (786)
Aleriensis (786)
Insulanus (786)
Lesinensis (787)
Laguedoniensis (787)
Vulturariensis (787)
Maceratensis (787)
Aprutinus (787)
Grossetanus (788)
Tiburtinus (788)
Ilcinensis (788)
Assisiensis (788)
Atrebatensis (788)
Casertanus (788)
Asturicensis (788)
Larinensis (788)
Gerundensis (788)
Auriensis (789)
Gebennensis (789)
Vabrensis (789)
Sibinicensis (789)
Cotronensis (789)
Vicensis (It) (789)
Vestanus (790)
Comensis (790)
Isclanus (791)
Accerrensis (791)

(table continues)

251

Col. 1: Approval of canon 7 (either mentioning the canon, or implicitly approving it by generally approving "all the canons" or "the remaining canons")	Col. 2: Approval following Lotharingus	Col. 3: Approve with emendations	Col. 4: Disapprove (*contra* practices of the Greeks, opinions of the Church Fathers, publish without anathema, etc.)	Col. 5: Approve if consistent with Venetian formulation	Col. 6: Non placet: return to a direct formulation of canon 7	Col. 7: No comment on canon 7
	Albinganensis (788)		Lucensis (792) Praemisliensis (793) Cauriensis (794)	Hierosolymitanus (780)		Hyprensis (791)
	Assaphaensis (788)			Hydruntinus (780)		Hyacinthanus (791)
	S. Leonis (788)			Marsicensis (784)		Parmensis (791)
	Cenomanensis (789)			Minerbiensis (784)		Nimosiensis (792)
	Theanensis (789)			Clugiensis (784)		Barcinonensis (792)
	Arianensis (789)			Iustinopolitanus (784)		Calvensis (792)
	Venetensis (789)			Cenetensis (785)		Guadiscensis (792)
	Suessionensis (789)			Niciensis (785)		Papiensis (792)
	Quinqueecclesiensis (790)			Chironensis (786)		Sarzanensis (792)
	Clusinus (790)			Auxerensis (786)		Monopolitanus (792)
	Dolensis (790)			Buduensis (789)		Bobiensis (792)
	Nivernensis (790)			Feltrensis (791)		Rossensis (792)
	Nemausensis (790)			Caprulanus (791)		Ventimiliensis (792)
	Tutellensis (790)			Troianus (792)		Achadensis (792)
	Civitatis Castelli (791)			Aliphanus (793)		Guardiensis (792)
	Anglonensis (791)					S. Marci (792)
	Abricensis (791)					Amerinus (792)
	Lavellinus (792)					Paphensis (793)
	Pampilonensis (792)					Torcellanus (793)
	Senecensis (792)					Cretensis (793)
	Vabrensis (792)					Milopotamensis (793)
	Faventinus (792)					Oppidensis (793)
	Marsicanus (792)					Pennensis (793)
	Sagonensis (792)					Soranus (793)
	Usellensis (794)					Minorensis (794)
						1.Cassinensis (794)

	Claravallensis (794) Lunaevillae (794) Obs.Franciscans (794) Carmelites (794) Elnensis (794) Andegavensis (794) Lectorensis (794) Cathalonensis (794)					2.Cassinensis (794) 3.Cassinensis (794) Dominicans (794) Conv. Franciscans (794) Augustinians (794) Servites (794) Salamantinus (794) Pragensis (794) Cortonensis (794) Niochensis (794)
Total 13 fathers (6%)	Total 56 fathers (28%)	Total 4 fathers (2%)	Total 13 fathers (6%)	Total 15 fathers (7%)	Total 5 fathers (3%)	Total 93 fathers (46%)

Unclear: Montismarani (787); Calaguritanus (791); Namurcensis (791); Liciensis (792) (total: 4 fathers, 2%)

TABLE B-7. Remarks of the General Congregation on the Fourth
Formulation (October 26–27, 1563)

Si quis dixerit, ecclesiam errare (quod iuxta evangelicam et apostolicam doctrinam propter adulterium alterius coniugum matrimonii vinculum non posse dissolvi docuit et docet), et utrumque, vel etiam innocentem, qui causam adulterio non dedit, non posse, altero coniuge vivente, aliud matrimonium contrahere, moecharique eum, qui dimissa adultera aliam duxerit, et eam, quae dimisso adultero alii nupserit: anathema sit.[1]

The opinions of 163 Council fathers are recorded on the fourth formulation. In the following remarks, "general approval" means the Council father implicitly approves canon 7 with comments such as "omnia placent" or "ceteri canones placent" (in which canon 7 is one of the "other" canons). The words "generally following *so and so*" means he follows *so and so*, but says nothing regarding whether he approves or disapproves of the canons. "Non placet following *so and so*" means he explicitly follows *so and so* on canon 7 (where *so and so* disapproves). "No comment on Canon 7" means he says nothing relevant to the canon. If he approves or disapproves of canon 7 by way of following the opinions of another (e.g., "in 7. sequitur *so and so*"), I note in parentheses the opinion of the other. If he only *generally* follows another (e.g., "in canonibus, sequitur *so and so*"), I do not note the opinion of the other. These comments are sometimes conflicting and therefore can be unreliable guides as to a father's precise opinion on canon 7. For example, without mentioning canon 7, Barensis (CT, IX, 900) says generally "sequitur Madrutium et Hydruntinum" (i.e., he generally follows Madrutius and Hydruntinus). But Madrutius says he disapprove of canon 7 ("7. canon non placet") and Hydruntinus indicates he approves of it ("ceteri canones placent"). The extent to which Barensis intends to follow the others is therefore unclear. As above, members of the *deputatio* are designated with an [X] after the name.

---

1. "If anyone says the church erroneously taught and teaches, in accordance with the evangelical and apostolic doctrine, that the bond of marriage cannot be dissolved on account of the adultery of a spouse, and that neither spouse, even the innocent one, who gave no cause for adultery, can contract another marriage while the other spouse is living, and that he commits adultery who dismisses an adulterous wife and marries another, and she commits adultery who dismisses an adulterous husband and marries another; let him be anathema" (CT, IX, 889.14–18).

APPENDIX B: RECORDED STATEMENTS 255

Office	Name	Comments/Judgments on Canon 7
Cardinal	Madrutius	non placet: "has taught" ("docuisse") should replace "taught and teaches" ("7. canon non placet, sed dicatur, ecclesiam iuxta evangelicam et apostolicam doctrinam docuisse," CT, IX, 898.42–43); in the *doctrina*, he disapproves of the words: "two only are to be coupled by this bond"; delete them and replace with the words of Paul, where "Christ is said to have loved the church" ("In doctrina non placet quod dicitur, hoc vinculo duos tantum copulari, et ideo deleatur, et ponantur verba Pauli, quibus Christus dicitur dilexisse ecclesiam [Eph. 5:25]," 898.37–39); also, refer to the authority of John, because Christ attended the wedding feast at Cana ("Item ponatur auctoritas Ioannis, quod Christus interfuit nuptiis [Jn. 2:2]," 898.39–40)
Patriarch	Hierosolymitanus	generally follow Madrutius (899.1)
	Venetus (Venetiarum)	no comment on canon 7; in *doctrina*, follows Madrutius (899.4)
Archbishop	Cretensis	general approval ("omnia placent," 899.8)
	Hydruntinus	general approval (899.11)
	Granatensis [X]	non placet, because it condemns the opinions of many saints ("quia eo damnatur sententia multorum sanctorum," 899.15–16)
	Verallus	general approval (899.18)
	Antibarensis	general approval; follows Madrutius on the *doctrina* (899.19)
	Rossanensis [X]	generally follow Madrutius; including on the *doctrina* (899.20–21)
	S. Severinae	no comment on canon 7; says the *doctrina* should note the "two effects" of the sacrament that were proposed by Evaristus, namely, that a married couple is "pleasing to the Lord and that they have children" ("In doctrina addantur duo effectus huius sacramenti positi ab Evaristo, videl. ut Domino placeant et soboles habeant," 899.22–23)
	Iadrensis	general approval (899.28)
	Materanus	general approval following Hydruntinus (general approval) (899.30)
	Callarensis (-itanus)	non placet following Granatensis (opinions of the saints) (899.31)
	Corcyrensis	generally follow the majority ("maiorem partem," 899.34); in *doctrina*, he recommends that "Paul indicates" ("*Paulus innuit*") be changed to Paul "testifies" ("*testator*," 33)
	Senensis	general approval (899.35)
	Rheginus	non placet following Madrutius ("docuisse," 899.37)

(*table continues*)

256   APPENDIX B: RECORDED STATEMENTS

Office	Name	Comments/Judgments on Canon 7
	Pragensis	non placet following Madrutius ("docuisse"); also in *doctrina* (899.41)
	Messanensis	general approval (900.3)
	Lancianensis	general approval (900.5)
	Panormitanus	approval with reservations; says canon 7 should be made clearer ("6. et 7. lucidiores fiant," 900.7–8)
	Senonensis	non placet following Madrutius ("docuisse"); also in *doctrina* (900.11–12)
	Naxiensis	general approval (900.17)
	Barensis	generally follow Madrutius and Hydruntinus (900.18)
Bishop	Cavensis	generally follow Madrutius (900.19)
	Pientinus	generally follow Hydruntinus (900.21)
	Bellicensis	generally follow Madrutius; also in *doctrina* (900.22)
	Catanensis	no comment on canon 7 (900)
	Camerinensis	no comment on canon 7 (900)
	Caiacensis	general approval (900.27)
	Tarvisinus	general approval (900.27)
	Civitatis Castellanae	no comment on canon 7 (900)
	Viglevenensis	generally follows the majority (900.29)
	Marsicensis	generally follow Madrutius (900.30)
	Minerbiensis	generally follow Madrutius (900.30)
	Britonoriensis	generally follow Madrutius (900.31)
	Castrensis	no comment on canon 7 (900)
	Oscensis	general approval (900.35)
	Clugiensis	general approval (900.36)
	Iustinopolitanus	no comment on canon 7 (900)
	Colimbriensis	generally follow Madrutius; also on preface (900.40)
	Recanatensis	general approval (900.42)
	Interamnensis	generally follow Madrutius and Hydruntinus (900.45–46)
	Sulmonensis	general approval (900.47)
	Brugnatensis	general approval (901.1)
	Umbriaticensis	general approval following Hydruntinus (general approval) (901.3)
	Segobiensis	general approval (901.6)

(*table continues*)

APPENDIX B: RECORDED STATEMENTS 257

Office	Name	Comments/Judgments on Canon 7
	Verdunensis	approve as amended; move the words "taught and teaches" to the beginning or end of the canon ("*docuit et docet* ponatur aut in principio aut in fine"); in *doctrina*, change the word "perpetual" ("*perpetuum*") to "stable" ("*firmum*"); also change the word "connubium" (does not say to what it should be changed; 901.14–16)
	Ariminensis	no comment on canon 7 (901)
	Pactensis	non placet following Madrutius ("docuisse"); follow M. also in *doctrina* (901.23)
	Niciensis	no comment on canon 7 (901)
	Naulensis	general approval (901.29)
	Carinolensis	generally follow Hydruntinus (901.30)
	Feretranus	general approval (901.31)
	Bovensis	no comment on canon 7 (901)
	Chironensis	general approval (901.34)
	Catacensis	general approval (901.34)
	Xantonensis	general approval; but follows annotations of Senonensis (who follows Madrutius) (901.35)
	Mutinensis	general approval (901.36)
	Calamonensis	general approval (901.40)
	Cauriensis	general approval (901.41)
	Asculanus	general approval (901.42)
	Insulanus	general approval (901.42)
	Segninus	no comment on canon 7 (901)
	Fesulanus	general approval (901.44)
	Lesinensis	generally follow Madrutius (901.45)
	Laquedoniensis	approve as amended do not add "docuit et docet" (901.46–47)
	Aquinatensis	general approval (902.1)
	Milopotamensis	general approval (902.3)
	Niochensis	general approval (902.4)
	Castellanetensis	general approval (902.36)
	Montismarani	non placet following Granatensis (opinions of the saints) (902.37)
	Lucerinus	no comment on canon 7 (902.40)
	Grossetanus	general approval (903.1)
	Tiburtinus	general approval (903.3)
	Albinganensis	no comment on canon 7 (903)

(*table continues*)

258   APPENDIX B: RECORDED STATEMENTS

Office	Name	Comments/Judgments on Canon 7
	Ilcinensis	no comment on canon 7 (903)
	Vicensis (Spain)	generally follow Granatensis and Segobiensem (903.7–8)
	Atrebatensis	non placet following Madrutius ("docuisse"); publish without anathema (903.11)
	Casertanus	general approval (903.15)
	Asturicensis	general approval (903.15)
	Alexanensis	generally follow Mutinensis (903.16)
	Assaphaensis	approve as amended; publish without anathema (903.17)
	Larinensis	no comment on canon 7 (903)
	S. Leonis	no comment on canon 7 (903)
	Montisfalisci	no comment on canon 7 (903)
	Gerundensis	non placet; should return to the first formulation ("restituatur septimus primo propositus"). The text is unclear as to whether he means the first formulation of the indirect canon 7 from September 5, or the first formulation from session 23, i.e., canon 6 from July 20 (see 903n3). We infer from his approval of canon 6 in the first formulation (663) and his comments on the second formulation, that he disapproves of the indirect formulation; see 718.6–9 (903.24).
	Auriensis	no comment on canon 7; follows Verdunensis on *doctrina* (change "perpetual" to "stable"; change "connubium," 903.27)
	Gebennensis	general approval (903.34)
	Mazariensis [X]	generally follow majority (903.36)
	Arianensis	general approval (903.37)
	Sibinicensis	general approval (903.38)
	Quinqueecclesiensis [X]	non placet indirect formulation ("In 7. non placet, ut dicatur: *Si quis dixerit, ecclesiam errare*," 903.39–40)
	Cotronensis	general approval (903.41)
	Legionensis [X]	non placet; let the canon be restored to the first formulation (see his earlier comments at 789.26–28) ("7. non placet, sed maneat (primus canon prius positus)," 903.42–43)
	Almeriensis	non placet; no explanation, but we infer from his comments on the third formulation (789.29–30) that he disapproves of the indirect formulation (903.44)
	Ilerdensis	general approval (903.48)
	Buduensis	general approval (903.49)
	Vicensis (Italy)	general approval (904.2–3)
	Aquensis	generally follow Mutinensis (general approval) (904.4)

(*table continues*)

APPENDIX B: RECORDED STATEMENTS 259

Office	Name	Comments/Judgments on Canon 7
	Ostunensis	generally follow Segobiensis and Mutinensis (904.5)
	Elnensis	generally follow Segobiensis and Mutinensis (904.6)
	Vestanus [X]	general approval (904.7)
	Clusinus	non placet following Quinqueecclesiensis (who disapproves of the indirect formulation) (904.8–9)
	Nivernensis	general approval; following annotations of Segobiensis and Senonensis (904.11)
	Ugentinus	generally follow Mutinensis (general approval) (904.12)
	Nemausensis	generally follow Senonensem and Rheginus (who follows Madrutius) (904.14)
	Comensis	no comment on canon 7 (904)
	Nimiosensis	general approval (904.17)
	Calaguritanus	generally follow Granatensis and Pragensis (904.21)
	Civitatensis	general approval (904.23)
	Isclanus	general approval (904.24)
	Neocastrensis	non placet following Quinqueecclesiensis (disapproves of the indirect formulation); in *doctrina*, follows Madrutius (904.25–26)
	Acerrensis	general approval (904.31)
	CivitatisCastelli	**approval with reservations**; says the canon should be conceived more clearly ("clarius concipiatur," 904.33); in *doctrina*, follows Madrutius (32)
	Caprulanus	non placet following Madrutius ("docuisse," 904.36–37)
	Hyprensis	non placet following Gerundensis (return to first formulation) (904.39)[1]
	Namurcensis	generally follow Hyprensis (905.1)
	Cremonensis [X]	general approval (905.2–3)
	Massanus	general approval (905.2–3)
	Hyacinthanus	general approval (905.2–3)
	Massaelubrensis	general approval (905.2–3)
	Anglonensis	general approval (905.2–3)
	Papiensis	general approval (905.2–3)
	Calvensis	no comment on canon 7 (905)
	Praemisliensis	non placet: publish without anathema; in *doctrina*, follows Madrutius (905.5–6)

(table continues)

1. See 904n3 explaining that the clause reading "7 non placet ut ponatur sub anathemate" seems to be referring to canon 6.

APPENDIX B: RECORDED STATEMENTS

Office	Name	Comments/Judgments on Canon 7
	Troianus	general approval (905.8)
	Guadiscensis	non placet following Granatensis (opinions of the saints); publish without anathema (905.9–10)
	Columbriensis	non placet; no explanation, but we infer from his comments on the third formulation (792.19) that he disapproves of the indirect formulation (905.12)
	Liciensis	general approval (905.15)[2]
	Famagustanus	general approval (905.17)
	Lavellinus	general approval (905.18)
	Sarzanensis	general approval (905.18)
	Oppidensis	non placet; publish without anathema (905.20)
	Pisauriensis	general approval (905.21)
	Pennensis	non placet following Quinqueecclesiensis (disapproves of the indirect formulation) (905.23)
	Pampilonensis	generally follow Almariensis (non placet) (905.26)
	Lucensis	general approval; says the *doctrina* should be expanded (905.28)
	Aliphanus	generally follow Segobiensis; says the *doctrina* should be expanded (905.32–33)
	Monopolitanus	non placet following Quinqueecclesiensis; in doctrina, follow Madrutius (905.35–36)
	Imolensis	no comment on canon 7 (905)
	Rossensis	non placet following Madrutius ("docuisse," 905.43)
	Bobiensis	non placet following Granatensis (opinions of the saints) (905.44)
	Achadensis	non placet following Quinqueecclesiensis (905.47)
	Faventinus	approves following Civitatis Castelli; says canon 7 is more clearly conceived (905.48)
	Guardiensis	approves following Civitatis Castelli; says canon 7 is more clearly conceived (905.48)
	S.Marci	approves following Civitatis Castelli; says canon 7 is more clearly conceived (905.48)
	Trivicanus [X]	general approval (905.49)
	Amerinus	no comment on Canon 7 (905)
	Usellensis	non placet following Legionensis (return to the first formulation); in *doctrina*, not only condemn the heresiarchs, but also their followers ("non solum anathematizenter haeresiarchae, sed et reliqui," 906.1–3)

(*table continues*)

2. See 905nc.

APPENDIX B: RECORDED STATEMENTS 261

Office	Name	Comments/Judgments on Canon 7
	Cortonensis	general approval (906.7)
	Torcellanus	general approval (906.7)
	Paphensis	no comment on canon 7 (906)
	Minorensis	generally follow Madrutius (906.9)
Abbot	Stephanus	non placet following Quinqueecclesiensis (906.10)
	Augustinus	general approval (906.12)
	Eutitius (Cassinensis)	non placet following Quinqueecclesiensis (906.14)
Generals	Dominicans	general approval (906.16–17)
	Franciscans (observant)	general approval (906.16–17)
	Franciscans (conventual)	general approval (906.16–17)
	Augustinians	general approval (906.16–17)
	Servites	no comment on canon 7; in *doctrina*, replace the words "the same Christ" ("idem Christus") with "Christ himself" ("ipse Christus," 906.18–19)
	Jesuits	general approval (906.23)
Vice general	Carmelites	general approval (906.22)

TABLE B-8. Fourth Formulation of Canon 7

Col. 1: Placet, explicit approval of canon 7 with minor emendations or with reservations	Col. 2: Placet, general approval of canon 7	Col. 3: Non placet, disapproval of the indirect formulation	Col. 4: Non placet, condemns opinions of saints, publish without anathema	Col. 5: Non placet, "docuisse" (has taught) should replace "taught and teaches"	Col. 6: Generally follows one or more Council fathers; position is uncertain	Col. 7: No comment relevant to canon 7
Panormitanus (900)	Cretensis (899)	Gerundensis (903)	Granatensis (899)	Madrutius (898)	Hierosolymitanus (899)	Venetus (899)
Verdunensis (901)	Hydruntinus (899)	Quinqueecclesiensis (903)	Callarensis (899)	Rheginus (899)	Rossanensis (899)	S. Severinae (899)
Laquedoniensis (901)	Verallus (899)	Legionensis (903)	Montismarani (902)	Pragensis (899)	Corcyrensis (899)	Catanensis (900)
Civitatis Castelli (904)	Antibarensis (899)	Almeriensis (903)	Assaphaensis (903)	Senonensis (900)	Barensis (900)	Camerinensis (900)
Faventinus (905)	Iadrensis (899)	Clusinus (904)	Praemisliensis (905)	Pactensis (901)	Picentinus (900)	Civitatis Castellanae (900)
Guardiensis (905)	Materanus (899)	Neocastrensis (904)	Guadiscensis (905)	Atrebatensis (903)	Cavensis (900)	Castrensis (900)
S. Marci (905)	Senensis (899)	Hyprensis (904)	Oppidensis (905)	Caprulanus (904)	Bellicensis (900)	Iustinopolitanus (900)
	Messanensis (900)	Namurcensis (905)	Bobiensis (905)	Rossensis (905)	Viglevenensis (900)	Ariminensis (901)
	Lancianensis (900)	Columbriensis (905)			Marsicensis (900)	Niciensis (901)
	Naxiensis (900)	Pennensis (905)			Minerbiensis (900)	Bovensis (901)
	Caiacensis (900)	Pampilonensis (905)			Britonoricensis (900)	Segninus (901)
	Tarvisinus (900)	Monopolitanus (905)			Colimbriensis (900)	Lucerinus (902)
	Oscensis (900)	Achadensis (905)			Interamnensis (900)	Albinganensis (903)
	Clugiensis (900)	Usellensis (906)			Carinolensis (901)	Ilcinensis (903)
	Recanatensis (900)	Stephanus (906)			Lesinensis (901)	Larinensis (903)
	Sulmonensis (900)	Euritius (906)			Vicensis (Sp) (903)	S. Leonis (903)
	Brugnatensis (901)				Alexanensis (903)	Montisfalisci (903)
	Umbriaticensis (901)				Mazariensis (903)	Auriensis (903)
	Segobiensis (901)				Aquensis (904)	
	Naulensis (901)				Ostunensis (904)	
	Feretranus (901)				Elnensis (904)	
	Chironensis (901)				Ugentinus (904)	
	Catacensis (901)				Nemausensis (904)	
	Xantonensis (901)				Calaguritanus (904)	
	Mutinensis (901)				Aliphanus (905)	
	Calamonensis (901)				Minorensis (906)	

Cauriensis (901)
Asculanus (901)
Insulanus (901)
Fesulanus (901)
Aquinatensis (902)
Milopotamensis (902)
Niochensis (902)
Castellanetensis (902)
Grossetanus (903)
Tiburtinus (903)
Casertanus (903)
Asturicensis (903)
Gebennensis (903)
Arianensis (903)
Sibinicensis (903)
Cotronensis (903)
Ilerdensis (903)
Buduensis (903)
Vicensis (It) (904)
Vestanus (904)
Nivernensis (904)
Nimiosensis (904)
Civitatensis (904)
Isclanus (904)
Accerrensis (904)
Cremonensis (905)
Massanus (905)
Hyacinthanus (905)
Massaelubrensis (905)
Anglonensis (905)
Papiensis (905)
Troianus (905)
Liciensis (905)

Comensis (904)
Calvensis (905)
Imolensis (905)
Amerinus (905)
Paphensis (906)
Servites (906)

(table continues)

Col. 1: Placet, explicit approval of canon 7 with minor emendations or with reservations	Col. 2: Placet, general approval of canon 7	Col. 3: Non placet, disapproval of the indirect formulation	Col. 4: Non placet, condemns opinions of saints, publish without anathema	Col. 5: Non placet, "docuisse" (has taught) should replace "taught and teaches"	Col. 6: Generally follows one or more Council fathers; position is uncertain	Col. 7: No comment relevant to canon 7
	Famagustanus (905) Lavellinus (905) Sarzanensis (905) Pisauriensis (905) Lucensis (905) Trivicanus (905) Cortonensis (906) Torcellanus (906) Augustinus (906) Dominicans (906) Franciscans (obs.) (906) Franciscans (conv.) (906) Augustinians (906) Jesuits (906) Carmelites (906)					
Total 7 fathers (4%)	*Total* 74 fathers (46%)	*Total* 16 fathers (10%)	*Total* 8 fathers (5%)	*Total* 8 fathers (5%)	*Total* 26 fathers (16%)	*Total* 4 fathers (14%)

Table B-9. Final *Vota* of the Council Fathers on the Final Formulation (November 11, 1563)

Si quis dixerit, ecclesiam errare, cum docuit et docet, iuxta evangelicam et apostolicam doctrinam, propter adulterium alterius coniugum matrimonii vinculum non posse dissolvi, et utrumque, vel etiam innocentem, qui causam adulterio non dedit, non posse, altero coniuge vivente, aliud matrimonium contrahere, moecharique eum, qui dimissa adultera aliam duxerit, et eam, quae dimisso adultero alii nupserit: anathema sit.[1]

The final votes of 200 Council fathers on the fourth formulation are recorded here. The council secretary, Angelo Massarelli, assisted by two Council notaries, questioned the fathers and recorded their replies. Each father was asked to approve or disapprove of the *doctrina*, the twelve canons on marriage, and the ten reform canons. Recorded here are only comments relevant to the *doctrina* and canon 7.

Office	Name	"Votum" on *Doctrina* and Canon 7
Cardinal	Moronus: papal legate, first Council president	No comment (971)
	Varmiensis: papal legate, Council president	No comment (971; see also 1007–1008, no. 343)
	Simonetta: papal legate, Council president	Placent (971.31)
	Navagerius: papal legate, Council president	Placent (971.34)
	Lotharingus	Placent (971.42)
	Madrutius	Placent (972.3)
Patriarch	Hierosolymitanus	Placent (972.5–6)
	Aquilegiensis	Placent (972.16)
	Venetus (Venetiarum)	Placent (972.17)
Archbishop	Cretensis	Placent (972.26)
	Hydruntinus	Placent (972.27)
	Granatensis	Placent (972.28)

(table continues)

1. "If anyone says the church errs, when she taught and teaches, in accordance with the evangelical and apostolic doctrine, that the bond of marriage cannot be dissolved on account of the adultery of a spouse, and that neither spouse, even the innocent one, who gave no cause for adultery, can contract another marriage while the other spouse is living, and that he commits adultery who dismisses an adulterous wife and marries another, and she commits adultery who dismisses an adulterous husband and marries another; let him be anathema." CT, IX, 967.31–35.

APPENDIX B: RECORDED STATEMENTS

Office	Name	"Votum" on *Doctrina* and Canon 7
	Caputaquensis	Placent (972.30)
	Antibarensis	Placent (972.31)
	Rossanensis	Placent (972.32)
	S. Severinae	Placent (972.39)
	Iadrensis	Placent (972.39)
	Bracarensis	Placent (972.39)
	Genuensis	Placent (972.39)
	Materanus	Placent (972.40)
	Callarensis (-itanus)	Placent (972.41)
	Nicosiensis	Placent (972.43); asks that an excerpt from a letter published in the proceedings of a provincial council at Cyprus in 1340 be printed under his name. Following a lengthy introduction asserting the fidelity of Greek, Maronite, and Armenian bishops to the teachings set forth by that assembly, the excerpt reads: "We humbly ask, that they be permitted to remain in their rites, which are not contrary to the faith, and we entreat the said lord Archbishop to deign to make known to the Supreme Lord Pontiff their devotion" (*"Petentes humiliter, quod eis liceret, in suis ritibus, fidei non contrariis, permanere, ac deprecantes dictum D. archiepiscopum, ut devotionem eorum intimare D. Summo Pontifici dignaretur,"* 973.3–20)
	Corcyrensis	Placent (973.21)
	Senensis	Placent (973.21)
	Tarentinus	Placent (973.21)
	Rheginus	Placent (973.22)
	Amalphitanus	Placent (973.34)
	Pragensis	Placent (973.35)
	Messanensis	Placent (973.35)
	Lancianensis	Placent (973.35)
	Panormitanus	Placent (973.37)
	Senonensis	Placent: "follows the majority" (973.38)
	Naxiensis	Placent (973.40)
	Barensis	Placent (973.41)
Bishop	Cavensis	Placent (973.44)
	Cattarensis	Placent (973.47)
	Pientinus	Placent (973.48)
	Milopotamensis	Placent (973.53)

(*table continues*)

APPENDIX B: RECORDED STATEMENTS 267

Office	Name	"Votum" on *Doctrina* and Canon 7
	Lectorinsis	Placent (973.54–55)
	Bellicensis	Placent (973.54–55)
	Caiacensis	Placent (973.54–55)
	Tarvisinus	Placent (973.54–55)
	Viglevenensis	Placent (973.54–55)
	Camerinensis	Placent (973.56)
	Cathaniensis	Placent (974.1)
	Marsicensis	Placent (974.3)
	Minerbiensis	Placent (974.4)
	Britonoriensis	Placent (974.7–8)
	Cavensis Casella	Placent: "follows the majority" (974.9–10)
	Hierapetrensis	Placent (974.14)
	Oscensis	Placent (974.14)
	Clodiensis	Placent (974.14)
	Castrensis	Placent (974.15)
	Castellanetensis	Placent (974.16)
	Iustinopolitanus	Placent (974.17)
	Sulmonensis	Placent (974.17)
	Brugnatensis	Placent (974.17)
	Colimbriensis	Placent (974.18)
	Interamnensis	Placent (974.18)
	Umbriaticensis	Placent (974.20)
	Ariminensis	Placent (974.20)
	Virdunensis	Placent (974.22)
	Pactensis	Placent (974.23)
	Naulensis	Placent (974.23)
	Feretranus	Placent (974.23)
	Niciensis	Placent (974.24)
	Carinolensis	Placent (974.25)
	Bovensis	Placent (974.27)
	Chironensis	Placent (974.28–29)
	Sanctonensis	Placent (974.28–29)
	Cattacensis	Placent (974.28–29)
	Auxerensis	Placent (974.28–29)
	Aleriensis	Placent (974.28–29)
	Mutinensis	Placent (974.28–29)

(*table continues*)

APPENDIX B: RECORDED STATEMENTS

Office	Name	"Votum" on *Doctrina* and Canon 7
	Calamonensis	Placent (974.28–29)
	Cauriensis	Placent (974.28–29)
	Asculanus	Placent (974.28–29)
	Insulanus	Placent (974.28–29)
	Segninus	Placent (974.30)
	Fesulanus	Placent (974.31)
	Lesinensis	Placent (974.32)
	Laquedoniensis	Placent (974.36)
	Montismarani	Placent (974.36)
	Maceratensis	Placent (974.36)
	Aquinatensis	Placent (974.37)
	Lucerinus	Placent (974.38)
	Meldensis	Placent (974.47)
	Grossetanus	Placent (974.47)
	Tiburtinus	Placent (974.47)
	Albinganensis	Placent (974.47)
	Atrebatensis	Placent (974.48)
	Ilcinensis	Placent (974.51)
	Casertanus	Placent (974.52–53)
	Adriensis	Placent (974.52–53)
	Alexanus	Placent (974.52–53)
	Catalonensis	Placent (974.52–53)
	Asturicensis	Placent (974.52–53)
	Assaphensis	Placent (974.52–53)
	Larinensis	Placent (974.54)
	Senogalliensis	Placent (975.1)
	Milopotamensis (junior)	Placent (975.2)
	S. Leonis	Placent (975.2)
	Campaniensis	Placent (975.2)
	Montisfalisci	Placent (975.3)
	Auriensis	Placent (975.18–19)
	Theanensis	Placent (975.18–19)
	Mazariensis	Placent (975.18–19)
	Arianensis	Placent (975.18–19)
	Sibinicensis	Placent (975.18–19)
	Suessionensis	Placent (975.18–19)

(*table continues*)

APPENDIX B: RECORDED STATEMENTS 269

Office	Name	"Votum" on *Doctrina* and Canon 7
	Gebennensis	Placent (975.20)
	Augustensis	Placent (975.23)
	Vaurensis	Placent (975.24)
	Quinqueecclesiensis	**Canon 7 non placet** "because of the added clause *the Church errs*, since the canon remains most reliable and true and catholic even without this [clause]" ("7. canon non placet propter adiectam clausulam *ecclesiam errare*, quia etiam absque eo canon verissimus est et catholicus," 975.26–27)
	Cotronensis	Placent (975.28–29)
	Legionensis	Placent (975.28–29)
	Almeriensis	Placent (975.28–29)
	Ilerdensis	Placent (975.28–29)
	Thelesinus	Placent (975.28–29)
	Dolensis	Placent (975.28–29)
	Vicensis (Italy)	Placent (975.28–29)
	Buduensis	Placent (975.30)
	Aquensis	Placent (975.34–35)
	Ostunensis	Placent (975.34–35)
	Elnensis	Placent (975.34–35)
	Nivernensis	Placent (975.34–35)
	Uxentinus	Placent (975.34–35)
	Brixiensis	Placent (975.34–35)
	Vestanus	Placent (975.37)
	Clusinus	Placent (975.39)
	Nemausensis	Placent (975.40)
	Comensis	Placent (975.41)
	Tutellensis	Placent (975.44)
	Feltrensis	Placent (976.6)
	Calaguritanus	Placent (976.7)
	Civitatensis	Placent (976.7)
	Isclanus	Placent (976.7)
	Acerrensis	Placent (976.7)
	Neocastrensis	Placent (976.8)
	Civitatis Castelli	Placent (976.9)
	Caprulanus	Placent (976.38)
	Iprensis	No comment (976)

(table continues)

Office	Name	"Votum" on *Doctrina* and Canon 7
	Cremonensis	Placent (976.41–42)
	Massaelubrensis	Placent (976.41–42)
	Iacinthensis	Placent (976.41–42)
	Anglonensis	Placent (976.41–42)
	Bergomensis	Placent (976.41–42)
	Verulanus	Placent (976.41–42)
	Salamantinus	Placent (976.41–42)
	Massanus	Placent (976.43)
	Parmensis	Placent (976.44)
	Nemosiensis	Placent (976.46)
	Barcinonensis	Placent (976.48)
	Calvensis	Placent (976.49)
	Liciensis	Placent (976.49)
	Praemisliensis	Canon 7 non placet: disapproves of the anathema ("6. et 7. can., quod illis canonibus sit appositum anathema, non placet," 976.50–51)
	Niochensis	Placent (976.52)
	Papiensis	Placent (976.52)
	Columbriensis	Placent (976.52)
	Nucerinus	Placent (976.52)
	Troianus	Placent (977.1)
	Famagustanus	Placent (977.3); he adds that he follows Nicosiensis in his request on behalf of the Greeks ("sed petit, quod petiit D. Nicosiensis quoad Graecos," 3–4)
	Lavellinus	Placent (977.5–6)
	Sarzanensis	Placent (977.5–6)
	Oppidensis	Placent (977.5–6)
	Pisauriensis	Placent (977.5–6)
	Emoniensis	Placent (977.5–6)
	Pennensis	Placent: "follow majority" (977.8)
	Pampilonensis	Canon 7 non placet; no explanation (977.9)
	Lucensis	Placent (977.10)
	Monopolitanus	Placent (977.11)
	Bobiensis	Placent (977.11)
	Achadensis	Placent (977.11)
	Rapotensis	Placent (977.11)

(*table continues*)

APPENDIX B: RECORDED STATEMENTS

Office	Name	"Votum" on *Doctrina* and Canon 7
	Imolensis	Placent (977.14)
	Rossensis	Placent (977.15)
	Faventinus	Placent (977.16)
	Urbevetanus	Placent (977.17)
	Guardiensis	Placent (977.19)
	Sagonensis	Placent (977.21)
	S. Marci	Placent (977.22)
	Amerinus	Placent (977.29)
	Usellensis	Placent (977.30–31)
	Cortonensis	Placent (977.30–31)
	Torcellanus	Placent (977.30–31)
	Trivicanus	Placent (977.30–31)
	Argolicensis	Placent (977.30–31)
	Paphensis	Placent (977.32); says he approves what Nicosiensis says concerning the Greeks ("approbat ea, quae dixit Nicosiensis quoad Graecos," 32)
	Mercanensis	Placent: follow majority (977.34)
Abbot	Lunaevillanus	Placent (977.36)
	Villaebertranus	Placent (977.38)
	Eutichius	Placent (977.39)
	Augustinus	Placent (977.40–41)
	Stephanus	Placent (977.40–41)
Generals	Dominicans	Placent (977.40–41)
	(conventual) Franciscans	Placent (977.40–41)
	Augustinians (Eremitarum)	Placent (977.40–41)
	Servites	Placent (977.40–41)
	Carmelites	Placent (977.42)
	Jesuits	Placent (977.43)

Cardinal Moroni announced at the conclusion of the voting session:

"The *doctrina* and canons on the sacrament of marriage were approved by all; in some instances, however, they desired things to be added or subtracted." (Doctrina et canones de sacramento matrimonii approvata fuere ab omnibus; aliqui tamen in nonnullis desiderarent quaedam adiici et detrahi.) 977.47–49.

APPENDIX C

SCHEDULE OF THE COUNCIL OF TRENT

Pope Paul III summoned an ecumenical council on May 22, 1542, with his bull *Initio nostri huius pontificati* (known as the "Bull of the Convocation"). The Council formally opened in Trent on December 13, 1545. Its purpose as stated in the bull was "to condemn certain widespread errors, remove abuses, and restore among Christian people the peace that they needed if they were to defend themselves against the Turks."[1] The Council's proceedings occurred in three phases (relevant decrees are indicated within parentheses).

PHASE ONE, 1545–48 (PAUL III, 1534–49)
Trent, 1545–47

Summons: May 22, 1542 (Bull of Convocation, Paul III)
Session 1: December 13, 1545 (Opening of the Council)
Session 2: January 7, 1546 (Matters to be Observed)
Session 3: February 4, 1546 (Symbol of Faith)
Session 4: April 8, 1546 (Canonical Scriptures)
Session 5: June 17, 1546 (Original Sin)
Session 6: January 13, 1547 (Justification)
Session 7: March 3, 1547 (Septenarium of the Sacraments)
Session 8: March 11, 1547 (Transfer of the Council to Bologna)

---

1. Jedin, *Crisis and Closure of the Council of Trent*, 5.

Bologna, 1547–48

Session 9: April 21, 1547 (Temporary discontinuation of the session)
[first discussion on marriage in April-June]
Session 10: June 2, 1547 (Temporary discontinuation of the session)
[second discussion on marriage in June–September]
[third discussion on marriage in September–December]

PHASE TWO, 1551–52 (JULIUS III, 1550–55)
Trent

Session 11: May 1, 1551 (Resumption of the Council)
Session 12: September 1, 1551 (Temporary discontinuation of the session)
Session 13: October 11, 1551 (Eucharist)
Session 14: November 25, 1551 (Penance and Extreme Unction)
Session 15: January 25, 1552 (Temporary discontinuation of the session)
Session 16: April 28, 1552 (Suspending the Council)

Pope Julius was succeeded by Marcellus II, who reigned for less than a month; he was succeeded by Paul IV [1555–59], who was succeeded by Pius IV.

PHASE THREE, 1562–63 (PIUS IV, 1560–65)
Trent

Session 17: January 18, 1562 (Celebration of the Council)
Session 18: February 26, 1562 (Choice of Books)
Session 19: May 14, 1562 (Temporary discontinuation of the session)
Session 20: June 4, 1562 (Temporary discontinuation of the session)
Session 21: July 16, 1562 (Communion under Both Kinds)
Session 22: September 17, 1562 (Sacrifice of the Mass)
Session 23: July 15, 1563 (Order)
[Formal debates on canons on marriage]
[July 24–31, on first reform: first direct formulation of canon 6/7]
[August 7–23, on second reform: second direct formulation of canon 7]
[August 11, Venetian delegation intervention]
[September 7–10, on third reform: first indirect formulation of canon 7]
[October 26–27, on fourth reform: second indirect formulation of canon 7]
Session 24: November 11, 1563 (Decree on Matrimony)
Session 25: December 3–4, 1563 (Close of the Council)
Oration: December 4, 1563 (Oration at Close of the Council)
Bull: December 4, 1563 (Ten Rules Concerning Prohibited Books)
Bull: January 26, 1564 (Confirmation of the Council)

SELECTED BIBLIOGRAPHY

Adrian VI, Pope. *De Sacramentis*. Rome, 1522.
Alexander III, Pope. *De divortiis*. CIC 2.
Ambrose of Milan. *De patriarcha Abraham*. PL 14.
———. *De Virginitate*. PL 16.
———. *Expositio Evangelii secundum Lucam*. PL 15.
Ambrosiaster. *Commentary on 1 Cor. 7*. PL 17.
Aquinas, Thomas. "Commentary on the Sentences of Peter Lombard." *Opera Omnia*, tom. 7. Parma, 1858.
———. *Summa Theologiae*. Edited by Fathers of the English Dominican Province. London: Benziger, 1948.
Augustine. *De Adulterinis Conjugiis ad Pollentium* (On Adulterous Marriages). In *Marriage and Virginity (Works of St. Augustine: A Translation for the 21st Century)*, edited by John Rotelle, OSA. Hyde Park, N.Y.: New City, 2000.
———. *De Bono Conjugali*. PL 40. FOTC 27.
———. *De Fide et Operibus*. PL 40.
———. *De Genesi Ad Litteram Libri Duodecim*. PL 34. FOTC 84.
———. *De Nuptiis et Concupiscentia*. PL 44. NPNF-I 5.
———. *De Sermone Domini in Monte*. PL 34.
Basil the Great. *Canonical Epistle 188, to Amphilochius: Canon 9*. PG 32.
———. *Canonical Epistle 199, to Amphilochius 2, Caput 48*. PG 32.
———. *Moralia*. PG 31. FOTC 9.
Batz, Johann Joseph. *Harmonie der neuesten Baierischen Ehescheidungs-Gesetze mit Schrift und Tradition*. Bamberg: Joseph Anton Goebhardt, 1809.
Beal, John P. "Commentary on Art. 1, Ch. IX, Title VII: Marriage." In *New Commentary on the Code of Canon Law*, edited by John P. Beal, James A. Coriden, and Thomas J. Green, 1359–62. New York: Paulist Press, 2000.
Bede. *Commentary on Mark 10*. PL 92.
Bede (Pseudo-). *Commentary on 1 Cor. 10, Venerabilis Bedae Operum*, tom. VI. *In Omnes Divi Pauli Epistolas*. Coloniae Agrippinae, 1688.
Benedict XIV, Pope. *Constituion Nuper ad Nos* (Profession of Faith Prescribed for the Orientals [i.e., Maronites]). March 16, 1743. Denz., no. 1470.
Benedict XVI, Pope. *Sacramentum Caritatis* (On the Eucharist as the Source and Summit of the Church's Life and Mission). Apostolic Exhortation. February 22, 2007. Available at www.vatican.va.

Bevilacqua, Anthony. "The History of the Indissolubility of Marriage." *Proceedings of the Catholic Theological Society of America* 22 (1967): 253–308.
Biblia Sacra Iuxta Vulgatam Versionem. Edited by Robert Weber, OSB. Stuttgart: Deutsche Bibelgesellschaft, 1969.
Bintherim. *Collectio dissert. sing. de matrimonio*. Dusseldorf, 1807.
Braun, J. Adamus. *Dissertatio utrum matrimonii vinculum, et in casu adulterii alterius conjugum, juxta Tridentini can: VII. sess: XXIV jure divino an solum ecclesiastico insolubile sit*. Moguntiae, 1787.
Bressan, Luigi. *Il Canone Tridentino Sul Divorzio Per Adulterio e L'interpretazione Degli Autori*. Rome: Università Gregoriana Editrice, 1973.
———. *Il divorzio nelle Chiese orientali: ricerca storica sull'atteggiamento cattolico*. Bologna: Edizione Dehoniane Bologna, 1976.
Brugger, E. Christian. "Damnatio Memoria? The Council of Trent and Catholic Teaching on Divorce." *La Chiesa*, October 17, 2014. Available at http://chiesa.espresso.repubblica.it/articolo/1350897?eng=y.
Brundage, James A. *Law, Sex, and Christian Society in Medieval Europe*. Chicago: The University of Chicago Press, 1987.
Bungener, L. F. *History of the Council of Trent*. New York: Harper and Brothers, 1855.
Cajetan, Cardinal. *Commentary on Matthew*. In Thomae de Vio (Cardinalis Cajetan), *Opera omnia quotquot in Sacrae Scripturae expositions reperiuntur*. 5 vols. Lyon, 1639.
Calvin, John. "Commentary on Matthew 5:31." In *Commentary on a Harmony of the Evangelists, Matthew, Mark, and Luke*, vol. 1, translated by William Pringle. Edinburgh: The Calvin Translation Society, 1845.
———. "Commentary on Matthew 19:3–9." In *Commentary on a Harmony of the Evangelists, Matthew, Mark, and Luke*, vol. 2, translated by William Pringle. Edinburgh: The Calvin Translation Society, 1845.
———. *Commentary on St. Paul's First Epistle to the Corinthians*. Translated by John King. Altenmünster: Jazzybee Verlag, 2012.
———. *Institutes of the Christian Religion*. Translated by Henry Beveridge. Grand Rapids, Mich.: Eerdmans, 2001.
———. "Les Ordonnances Ecclesiastiques De 1561." *Opera Quae Supersunt Omnia*, vol. 10. Edited by Guilielmus Baum, Eduardus Cumtz, and Eduardüs Reüss. Brunsvigae: C. A. Sohwetsohke and Son, 1871.
Canisius, Peter, SJ. *A Summe of Christian Doctrine*. St. Omer, 1622. Available at *https://archive.org/details/ASumOfChristianDoctrine_830*.
Canons of the Apostles. "Canon 47." In *Constitutiones Apostolorum*, edited by F. X. Funk. Paderborn: In Libraria Ferdinandi Schoeningh, 1905.
Cappello, Felix. *De Matrimonio*. Rome: Marietti, 1961.
Catechism of the Catholic Church. 1997. Available at www.vatican.va.
Cayré, F. "Le divorce au IV siècle dans la loi civile et les canons de saint Basile." *Échos d'Orient* 19 (1920): 295–321.
Chrysostom, John. *De Libello Repudii, II*. PG 51.
———. *De Virginitate, 28*. PG 48.
———. *In epistolam primam (I) ad Corinthios: Hom. 19.3*. PG 61.
———. *In Matt. Homil. 17*. PG 57.
———. *In Matt. Homil. 62*. PG 58.

Concilium Tridentinum: diariorum, ectorum, epistularum tractatuum nova collectio, Societas Goerresiana. Tomus VI, vol. 1. Edited by Theobald Freudenberger. Freiburg im Breisgau: Herder, 1964.

Concilium Tridentinum: diariorum, ectorum, epistularum tractatuum nova collectio, Societas Goerresiana. Tomus IX. Edited by Stephen Ehses. Freiburg im Breisgau: Herder, 1965.

Congregation for the Doctrine of the Faith. "*Instruction Donum Veritatis*" (On the Ecclesial Vocation of the Theologian). 1990. Available at www.vatican.va.

Conway, Bertrand L., CSP. "Original Diaries of the Council of Trent." In his *Studies in Church History*. 2nd ed. London: Herder, 1916.

Corpus Iuris Canonici. Vol. 1. Edited by Aemilius Friedberg. Graz: Druck, 1959.

Council of Arles I. *Cap. 10.* Mansi, vol. 2.

Council of Carthage VII. *Canon 69.* Mansi, vol. 3.

Council of Constance. *Condemned Article 16 attributed to John Wyclif.* In DEC, 1:405–51.

Council of Elvira. *Canons 8–10.* Mansi, vol. 2.

Council of Florence. *Cantate Domino (Bull of Union with the Copts).* In *DEC*, 1:567–82.

———. *Exultate Deo (Bull of Union with the Armenians).* In *DEC*, 1:534–59.

Council Lateran III. *Appendix, part 6, no. 16.* Mansi, vol. 22.

Council Lateran IV. *Constitution 52.* In *DEC*, 1:259.26–28.

Council of Mileve (Milevitanum) II. *Canon 17.* Mansi, vol. 3.

Council of Tribur. *Canons 24, 41, 46.* Mansi, vol. 18.

Council of Trullo (The Quinisext Council). *Canon 87.* NPNFC-II 14. Mansi, vol. 11.

Council Vatican II. *Dei Verbum.* November 18, 1965. In *DEC*, 2:971–81.

———. *Gaudium et Spes.* December 7, 1965. In *DEC*, 2:1069–1135.

———. *Lumen Gentium.* November 21, 1964. In *DEC*, 2:849–98.

Council of Venice. *Cap. 2 (can. 2).* Mansi, vol. 7.

Crouzel, Henri. *L'Église primitive face au divorce: Du premier au cinquième siècle.* Paris: Beauchesne, 1971.

Curran, Charles E. *Faithful Dissent.* London: Sheed and Ward, 1986.

D. Bartholomaei a Martyribus, Venerabilis Servi Dei. "Summa Conciliorum Omnium: tam generalium, quam provincialium." *Opera Omnia*, tom 1. Rome: Jerome Mainardi at Monte Citatorio Square, 1734.

Dacquino, Pietro. *Storia del matrimonio cristiano alla luce della Bibbia. 2. Inseparabilità e monogamia.* Leumann: Elle Di Ci, 1988.

Denzinger, Heinrich. *Enchiridion Symbolorum.* 43rd ed. Edited and translated by Peter Hünermann. San Francisco: Ignatius, 2012.

Du Plessis d'Argentré, Charles. *Collectio Judiciorum de novis erroribus qui ab initio saec. XII [to 1735] in Ecclesia proscripti.* Lutetiae Parisiorum, 1728.

Erasmus of Rotterdam. *In novum testamentum annotationes, in priorem ad Corinth. c. 7.* Basel, 1555.

———. "Paraphrases in Novum Tetamentum, In Marcum 10." In *Opera Omnia*. Leiden: Lugduni Batavorum, 1706.

Erickson, John H. "Eastern Orthodox Perspectives on Divorce and Remarriage." In *Divorce and Remarriage: Religious and Psychological Perspectives*, edited by William P. Roberts, 15–26. Kansas City, Mo.: Sheed and Ward, 1990.

Fahrner, Ignaz. *Geschichte des Unauflöslichkeitsprinzips und der vollkommenen Scheidung der Ehe im kanonischen Recht*, vol. 1: *Geschichte der Ehescheidung im kanonischen Recht*. Freiburg im Breisgau: Herder, 1903.

Feldbrugge, Ferdinand. *Law in Medieval Russia*. Leiden: Koninklijke Brill NV, 2009.

Fransen, Piet, SJ. *De indissolubilitate Matrimonii christiani in casu fornicationis. De canone septimo Sessionis XXIV Concilii Tridentini (Jul.–Nov. 1563)*. Rome: Pont. Univ. Gregoriana, 1947.

———. "Divorce on the Ground of Adultery—The Council of Tent (1563)." In *Concilium: The Future of Marriage as Institution*, edited by Franz Böckle, 89–100. New York: Herder and Herder, 1970.

———. "Echtscheiding na echtbreuk van een van de gehuwden. Het kerkrechterlijk dossier van Trente (1563)." *Bijdragen* 14 (1953): 363–87.

———. "Ehescheidung bei Ehebruch: Die endgültige Fassung des 7. Kanons auf der 24. Sitzung des Trienter Konzils in ihren theologischen und geschichtlichen Hintergründen (August bis November 1563)." In *Hermeneutics of the Councils*, edited by Mertens and de Graeve, 181–97.

———. "Ehescheidung bei Ehebruch: Die theologischen und geschichtlichen Hintergründe der ersten Stellungnahme zum 7. Kanon in der 24 Sitzung des Trienter Konzils (Juli 1563)." In *Hermeneutics of the Councils*, edited by Mertens and de Graeve, 157–80.

———. "Ehescheidung Im Falle Von Ehebruch: Der fundamentaltheologisch-dogmatische Ertrag der Bologneser Verhandlungen (1547)." In *Hermeneutics of the Councils*, edited by Mertens and de Graeve, 126–56.

———. "Réflexions sur l'anathème au Concile de Trente (Bologne, 10–24 septembre 1547)." *Ephemerides Theologicae Louvanienses* 29 (1953): 657–72.

———. "The Sacramental Character at the Council of Tent (17 January–3 March 1547)." *Bijdragen* 32 (1971): 2–33.

Gallagher, Clarence. *Church Law and Church Order in Rome and Byzantium: A Comparative Study*. Cornwall: Ashgate, 2002.

Gigot, Francis E. *Christ's Teaching Concerning Divorce in the New Testament: An Exegetical Study*. New York: Benziger, 1912.

Goyau, G. "Versailles." *The Catholic Encyclopedia*. New York: Robert Appleton, 1912. Available at http://www.newadvent.org/cathen/15366a.htm.

Gratian. *Decretum Gratiani*. PL 187.

Gregory II, Pope. *Letter to Boniface*. CT, VI, 413.8–12.

———. *Letter to the Legates of Bavaria*. PL 89.

Gregory XVI, Pope. *Mirari Vos*. August 15, 1832. Available at https://www.ewtn.com/library/ENCYC/G16MIRAR.HTM.

Hefele, Karl Joseph von. *Histoire Des Conciles D'Après Les Documents Originaux*. Paris: Letouzey et Ané, 1908.

Himes, Kenneth R., OFM, and James A. Coriden. "The Indissolubility of Marriage: Reasons to Reconsider." *Theological Studies* 65, no. 3 (2004): 453–99.

Hilary of Poitiers. *Commentary on Matthew 5:31*. PL 9. FOTC 22.

Hofmann, G. "Wie stand es mit der Frage der Kircheneinheit auf Kreta im XV. Jahrhundert?" *Orientalia Christiana Periodica* 10 (1944): 91–115.

Hunter, David G. "The Paradise of Patriarchy: Ambrosiaster on Women as (Not) God's Image." *Journal of Theological Studies* 43 (1992): 447–69.

———. "Ambrosiaster." *Dictionary of Major Biblical Interpreters*. Edited by Donald K. McKim. Downers Grove, Ill.: InterVarsity Press, 2007.
Innocent I, Pope. *Epistle to Exsuperius*. PL 20.
———. *Epistle to Probus (no. 36)*. PL 20.
———. *Second Epistle to Victricius*. PL 20.
Innocent III, Pope. *Quanto*. CIC 2:723.
International Theological Commission. "Propositions on the Doctrine of Christian Marriage." *Origins* 8 (1978): 235–39.
Jedin, Hubert. *Ecumenical Councils of the Catholic Church: An Historical Outline*. London: Herder and Herder, 1960.
———. *A History of the Council of Trent*, vol. 2. St. Louis, Mo.: B. Herder, 1961.
———. *Crisis and Closure of the Council of Trent*. New York: Sheed and Ward, 1967.
———. *Geschichte des Konzil von Trent IV/2*. Freiburg: Herder, 1975.
Jerome. *Adversus Jovinianum*. PL 23.
———. *Commentary on Matthew, 19:9*. PL 26. FOTC 117.
———. *Epist. 55 (ad Amandum)*. PL 22. NPNF-II 6.
———. *Epist. 77*. PL 22. NPNF-II 6.
John Paul II, Pope. "Homily on the Occasion of the Closure of the Sixth Synod of Bishops." October 25, 1980. Available at www.vatican.va.
———. *Familiaris Consortio*. Apostolic Exhortation. November 22, 1981. Available at www.vatican.va.
———. *Gratissimam Sane*. Apostolic Letter. February 2, 1994. Available at www.vatican.va.
———. "Address to the Tribunal of the Roman Rota." January 21, 2000. Available at www.vatican.va.
———. "Address to the Prelate Auditors, Officials and Advocates of the Tribunal of the Roman Rota." January 28, 2002. Available at www.vatican.va.
Joyce, George Hayward, SJ. *Christian Marriage: An Historical and Doctrinal Study*. London: Sheed and Ward, 1933.
Justinian. "Novel 22, Preface." *Corpus Iuris Civilis*. Cambridge: Cambridge University Press, 2014.
Kampowski, Stephan, and Juan José Pérez-Soba. *The Gospel of the Family: Going Beyond Cardinal Kasper's Proposal in the Debate on Marriage, Civil Re-Marriage and Communion in the Church*. San Francisco: Ignatius Press, 2014.
Kasper, Walter. *Theology of Christian Marriage*. New York: Crossroad, 1981. Originally published as *Zur Theologie der christlichen Ehe*. Mainz: Matthias-Grünwald-Verlag, 1977.
———. *The Gospel of the Family*. Mahwah, N.J.: Paulist Press, 2014.
Kingdon, Robert M. *Adultery and Divorce in Calvin's Geneva*. Cambridge, Mass.: Harvard University Press, 1995.
L'Huillier, Peter. "The Indissolubility of Marriage in Orthodox Law and Practice." In *Catholic Divorce: The Deception of Annulments*, edited by Pierre Hegy and Joseph Martos, 108–26. New York: Continuum, 2000.
Lactantius. *Divine Institutes*. PL 6.
Launoy, Johannes. *Regia in Matrimonium Potestas*. Paris: Edmundi Martini, 1674.
Le Courayer, Pierre François. *Histoire du Concile de Trente*. Amsterdam, 1750.

Lehmann, Karl. "Zur Sakramentalität der Ehe." In *Ehe und Ehescheidung: Diskussion Unter Christen*, edited by Franz Henrich and Volker Eid, 57–74. München: Kösel, 1972.
———. *Gegenwart des Glaubens*. Mainz: Matthias-Grünwald-Verlag, 1974.
Leo I, Pope. *Epist. 159 ad Nicetam Episcopum Aquileiensem*. PL 54.
Leo XIII, Pope. *Arcanum Divinae (On Christian Marriage)*. Encyclical Letter. February 10, 1880. In AAS 12 (1879–80): 400. Available at www.vatican.va.
Luther, Martin. "Commentary on 1 Corinthians 7." In *Luther's Works*, vol. 28. Edited by Hilton C. Oswald. St. Louis, Mo.: Concordia, 1973.
———. "Epithalamium." In *D. Martin Luthers Werke*, vol. 12. Weimar: Hermann Böhlau, 1891.
———. "Estate of Marriage." In *Luther's Works*, vol. 45, edited by Walther I. Brandt. Philadelphia: Muhlenberg Press, 1962.
———. "On Marriage Matters." *Luther's Works*, vol. 46, edited by Robert C. Schultz. Philadelphia: Fortress Press, 1967.
———. "On the Babylonian Captivity of the Church." In *Luther's Works*, vol. 36, edited by Abdel R. Wentz. Philadelphia: Fortress Press, 1959.
———. "The Sermon on the Mount." In *Luther's Works*, vol. 21, edited by Jaroslav Pelikan. St. Louis, Mo.: Concordia, 1956.
Mackin, Theodore, SJ. *Divorce and Remarriage*. New York: Paulist Press, 1984.
Mansi, Giovanni Domenico. *Sacrorum Conciliorum Nova et Amplissima Collectio*. Florence and Venice, 1759–98; reprinted in Paris: H. Welter, 1901–27.
Meier, John P. "The Historical Jesus and the Historical Law: Some Problems within the Problem." *Catholic Biblical Quarterly* 65 (2003): 52–79.
Mertens, H. E., and F. de Graeve, eds. *Hermeneutics of the Councils and Other Studies*. Leuven: Leuven University Press, 1985.
Meyendorff, John. *Marriage: An Orthodox Perspective*. Crestwood, N.Y.: St. Vladimir's Seminary Press, 1978.
———. *Byzantine Theology: Historical Trends and Doctrinal Themes*. New York: Fordham University Press, 1979.
———. "Christian Marriage in Byzantium: The Canonical and Liturgical Tradition." *Dumbarton Oaks Papers* 44 (1990): 102–3.
Migne, J.-P., ed. Patrologiae Cursus Completus, Series Graeca. Paris, 1857–66.
———. Patrologiae Cursus Completus, Series Latina. Paris, 1841–55.
Origen. *Comment. In Matthaeum 19*. PG 13.
Pallavicino, Pietro Sforza. *Istoria del Concilio di Trento* (History of the Council of Trent). 1656–57.
———. "Letter to Marchese Durazzo." *littere del Pallavicino*. Venice, 1669.
Palmieri, Dominico. *Tractatus de Matrimonio Christiano*. Rome, 1880.
Pani, Giancarlo, SJ. "Matrimonio E 'Seconde Nozze' Al Concilio Di Trento." *La Civiltà Cattolica* IV, no. 1 (2014): 3–104.
Pelland, Giles, SJ. "Did the Church Treat the Divorced and Remarried More Leniently in Antiquity than Today?" *L'Osservatore Romano* 5 (February 2, 2000): 9.
Perrone, Johannes. *De Matrimonio Christiano*, vol. 3. Liege: Dessain, 1861.
Photius, Patriarch of Constantinople. "Nomokanon 13." In *Opera Omnia*. PG 104:1210.
Pius V, Pope. *Catechism of the Council of Trent for Parish Priests* (1566). Translated by John A. McHugh, OP, and Charles J. Callan, OP. London: Herder, 1934.

Pius VI, Pope. *Rescript. ad Episc. Agriens* (Official Reply to the Bishop of Agria). July 11, 1789.

Pius VII, Pope. "The Indissolubility of Marriage." Letter to Charles of Dalberg, archbishop of Mainz. November 8, 1803. Denz., nos. 1600–1601.

Pius IX, Pope. *Ad Apostolicae sedis fastigium.* Apostolic Letter. August 22, 1851.

———. *Allocution Acerbissimum vobiscum.* September 27, 1852. Denz., no. 1640.

———. *Casti Connubii.* Encyclical Letter. December 31, 1930. In AAS 22 (1930): 552. Available at www.vatican.va.

———. *Syllabus Errorum* (Syllabus of Errors). December 8, 1864. Available at www.vatican.va.

———. *Verbis exprimere* (to the Bishops of the province of Fogaras and Weissenburg). August 15, 1859. In *Papal Teaching on Matrimony*, edited by the Benedictine monks of Solesmes, translated by Michael J. Byrnes, 111–12. Boston: St. Paul Editions, 1963.

Pius XII, Pope. ———. "Address to the Tribunal of the Sacred Roman Rota." October 3, 1941. In AAS 33 (1941): 424–25. Available at www.vatican.va.

———. "Address to Newlyweds." April 22, 1942. In *Pope Pius XII Speaks to Married Couples: Dear Newlyweds*, translated by James Murray Jr. and Bianca Murray, 86–89. Kansas City, Mo.: Sarto House, 2001.

———. "Address to Newlyweds." April 29, 1942. In *Pope Pius XII Speaks to Married Couples*, 89–91.

Pontifical Council for Legislative Texts. *Declaration Concerning the Admission to Holy Communion of Faithful Who Are Divorced and Remarried.* June 24, 2000. Available at www.vatican.va.

Pospishil, Victor J. *Divorce and Remarriage.* New York: Herder and Herder, 1967.

Ratzinger, Joseph. "Zur Frage nach der Unauflöslichkeit der Ehe: Bemerkungen zum dogmengeschichtlichen Befund und zu seiner gegenwärtigen Bedeutung." In *Ehe und Ehescheidung: Diskussion Unter Christen*, edited by Franz Henrich and Volker Eid, 35–56. München: Kösel, 1972.

Ratzinger, Joseph, and the Congregation for the Doctrine of the Faith. *Letter to the Bishops of The Catholic Church Concerning the Reception of Holy Communion by the Divorced and Remarried Members of the Faithful.* 1994. Available at www.vatican.va.

———. *Concerning Some Objections to the Church's Teaching on the Reception of Holy Communion by Divorced and Remarried Members of the Faithful.* 1998. Available at www.vatican.va.

Rist, John. "Divorce and Remarriage in the Early Church: Some Historical and Cultural Reflections." In *Remaining in the Truth of Christ: Marriage and Communion in the Catholic Church*, edited by Robert Dodaro, OSA, 64–92. San Francisco: Ignatius Press, 2014.

Roskovány, Augustinus de. *De Matrimonio in Ecclesia Catholica.* Augsburg: Charles Hollmann, 1840.

Rupert of Deutz. *De trinitate et operibus eius, in Gen. Lib. II.* PL 167.

Ryan, Peter F., SJ, and Germain Grisez. "Indissoluble Marriage: A Reply to Kenneth Himes and James Coriden." *Theological Studies* 72 (2011): 369–415.

Sarpi, Paolo. *Istoria del Concilio Tridentino.* London, 1619. Translated into English as *History of the Council of Trent.* London, 1676.

Schaff, Philip. *History of the Christian Church*, vol. 4. New York: Charles Scribner's Sons, 1891.

Schaff, Philip, ed. *Nicene and Post-Nicene Fathers, First Series*. Peabody, Mass.: Hendrickson, 1994.

Schaff, Philip, and Henry Wace, eds. *Nicene and Post-Nicene Fathers, Second Series*. Peabody, Mass.: Hendrickson, 1994.

Snuth, David L. "Divorce and Remarriage from the Early Church to John Wesley." *Trinity Journal* 11, no. 2 (Fall 1990): 131–42.

Soto, Domingo de. *In quartum Sententiarum*, vol. 2. Venice, 1584.

Sullivan, Francis A. *Creative Fidelity: Weighing and Interpreting Documents of the Magisterium*. New York: Paulist Press, 1996.

Tanner, N., SJ, and G. Alberigo, eds. *Decrees of the Ecumenical Councils*. 2 vols. London: Sheed and Ward, 1990.

Tertullian. *Adversus Marcionem*. PL 2.

Theodore. *Penitential*. PL 99.

Tixeront, J. *History of Dogmas*, vol. 2. St. Louis, Mo.: Herder, 1914.

Vacant, A., and E. Mangenot. "Divorce." *Dictionnaire de théologie catholique*, vol. 4. Paris: Librairie Letouzey et Ané, 1924.

Vasil', Archbishop Cyril, SJ. "Separation, Divorce, Dissolution of the Bond, and Remarriage: Theological and Practical Approaches of the Orthodox Churches." In *Remaining in the Truth of Christ*, edited by Robert Dodaro, OSA. San Francisco: Ignatius Press, 2014.

Wenham, Gordon, and William Heth. *Jesus and Divorce*. Eugene, Ore.: Wipf and Stock, 2010.

Witte Jr., John, and Robert M. Kingdon. *Sex, Marriage, and Family in John Calvin's Geneva*, vol. 1: "Courtship, Engagement, and Marriage." Grand Rapids, Mich.: Eerdmans, 2005.

Zachary, Pope. "Concubuisti." Quoted in *Decretorum Liber Decimus Nonus of Burchardi, Bishop of Worms*. PL 140.

INDEX

Abricensis, 247, 251, 252
Abrincensis, 83
Acerrensis, 216, 226, 234, 238, 246, 251, 259, 263, 269
Achadensis, 97n30, 118n129, 118n131, 218, 225, 235, 237, 247, 252, 260, 262, 263, 270
Aciensis, 73, 75–76, 80n111, 82
Acts, 81
Adam, 121, 126, 127, 204, 206, 207
Adrian VI, Pope, 7n27
Adriensis, 214, 221, 232, 238, 268
Adultera, 8n30, 9n31, 29n34, 30n36, 30n37, 48n52, 48n54, 55n14, 63n55, 64n60, 72n83, 74n95, 77n105, 78n106, 95n26, 103n61, 105n70, 110n99, 112n101, 116n122, 120n144, 132n15, 152, 169–70, 177, 182, 183, 186, 187, 190, 195, 203, 208, 228, 240, 254, 265
Adulterium, 8n30, 9n31, 48n52, 48n54, 56n20, 68n71, 79n109, 93n14, 95n26, 103n61, 105n70, 110n99, 112n101, 116n122, 120n144, 132n15, 151, 158, 161, 162, 165, 166–67, 176, 179, 180, 184, 185, 196, 198n50, 203, 208, 218, 228, 240, 254, 265
Adultery. in Ambrose, 153, 155, 156; in Ambrosiaster, 157; in Aquinas, 158; in Augustine, 3–4, 158–61, 163–66, 168; in Basil the Great, 168–70; in Bede the Venerable, 172–73; in Bologna Sessions, 53–54, 54–55; in Calvin, 27n25; Chris and, in Greek church, 46; divorce and, 3–4, 3n12; in Erasmus, 175, 176; in Fransen, 14; in General Congregation, 67–77; in Greek church, 46–48; in Gregory the Great, 186; in Innocent I, 186–87; in Jerome, 181–82; in John Chrysostom, 177–78; in Lactantius, 183; in Luke, 152; in Luther, 24–26, 25n11; in Mark, 151; in Matthew, 4, 150–51; in Origen, 183–84; in Pseudo-Bede, 173–74; remarriage and, 14n50, 18; in Rupert of Deutz, 185; in Tertullian, 185; in Zachary, 190–91. *See also* Sui fecit copiam
Adversus Jovinianum (Jerome), 181
Adversus Marcionem (Tertullian), 185
Aemoniensis, 102n58, 218, 220
Affectatam absentiam, 8, 46n48, 98, 98n37, 104n65, 129n6, 130, 131, 228
Alatrinus, 80n114
Albinganensis, 214, 224, 232, 238, 244, 251, 252, 257, 262, 268
Alciato, Terenzio, 10
Aleriensis, 243, 251, 267
Alessanensis, 115n119, 115n121, 244, 250
Alexander III, Pope, 66, 70, 70n80, 92, 185–86
Alexanensis, 214, 221, 232, 237, 258, 262, 263
Alexanus, 268
Alexius I, 44–45
Aliam ducere, 53n8, 55n18, 73n92, 74n95, 79n109, 92n11, 92n12, 94n23, 123n157, 168, 202, 209
Aliphanus, 35n7, 100n49, 102n58, 108n89, 109n95, 120n141, 218, 235, 237, 248, 252, 260, 262, 263

283

Almeriensis, 111n100, 115n114, 118n129, 216, 223, 233, 237, 245, 250, 258, 263, 269
Alyphanus, 72, 72n88, 80, 80n114
Amalphitanus, 211, 221, 266
Ambrose, 35n7, 57, 92, 108, 109, 153–57
Ambrosiaster, 3n12, 57, 57n27, 58n27, 66n66, 70n80, 90n2, 99, 108, 157, 157n10
Ameaux, Benoite, 27n25
Ameaux, Pierre, 27n25
Amerino, 227
Amerins, 219
Amerinus, 236, 237, 248, 252, 260, 263, 271
Andegavensis, 212, 221, 230, 238, 249, 251, 253
Anglonensis, 217, 224, 234, 239, 247, 251, 252, 259, 263, 270
Anniversary Council of Hierarchs of the Russian Orthodox Church (ACHROC), 45n46
Antibarensis, 210, 221, 230, 237, 240, 250, 255, 262, 266
Aprutinus, 78n107, 79n109, 80n114, 81, 232, 237, 244, 251
Aquensis, 79n109, 80n114, 115n119, 115n121, 216, 222, 234, 239, 245, 250, 258, 262, 263, 269
Aquensis Vorstius, 69, 78n109, 80
Aquilegiensis, 106n76, 209, 220, 229, 237, 240, 250, 265
Aquinas, 62n50, 67n67, 68–69, 71, 80n111, 127, 158, ix, ix–n5
Aquinatensis, 80n111, 82, 214, 220, 232, 237, 244, 250, 257, 263, 268
Argolicensis, 271
Arianensis, 215, 225, 233, 237, 245, 251, 252, 258, 263, 268
Ariminensis, 257, 262, 267
Aristenes, 45
Armacanus, 63, 78n109
Armenian Orthodox Christians, 36, 36n9, 68n68, 123. *See also* Greek church
Articles of heresy, 29, 30, 53, 64–65, 74–76, 90
Asculanus, 213, 224, 231, 238, 243, 250, 257, 263, 268

Assaphensis, 117–18, 117n127, 119, 214, 222, 232, 238, 244, 251, 252, 258, 262, 263, 268
Assisiensis, 214, 221, 232, 237, 244, 251
Asturicensis, 214, 225, 232, 237, 244, 251, 258, 263, 268
Atrebatensis, 117n126, 214, 223, 237, 244, 251, 258, 262, 263, 268
Augustensis, 95n25, 115n114, 215, 225, 233, 237, 245, 250, 269
Augustine, 3–4, 57, 58, 58n29, 60, 66, 71n80, 78n109, 92, 94, 158–68
Augustinians, 53n6, 219, 226, 236, 237, 261, 264, 271
Augustinus, 102n58, 219, 225, 261, 264, 271
Aurelianensis, 102n57, 214, 220, 232, 238
Auriensis, 102n58, 215, 222, 233, 239, 245, 251, 258, 262, 268
Auxerensis, 213, 222, 243, 252, 267

Babylonian Captivity (Luther), 7, 7n28, 23, 26, 29, 30, 33, 53–54, 53n7, 53n8, 55
Balsamon, 45
Barba, John James. *See* Aprutinus
Barcinonensis, 217, 224, 234, 237, 247, 252, 270
Barensis, 211, 220, 230, 237, 241, 254, 256, 262, 263
Barletano, Padua, 57, 57n24
Basil the Great, 35, 35n7, 99, 168–72
Batz, Johann Joseph, 11n37
Bede the Venerable, 66, 172–73
Bellicastrensis, 69
Bellicensis, 211, 241, 250, 256, 262, 263, 267
Bene, Bernardo del. *See* Nemausensis
Benedict XVI, Pope, x–xi. *See also* Ratzinger, Joseph
Bergoglio, Jorge, x. *See also* Pope Francis
Bergomensis, 270
Bernerius, John, 56n22
Bèze, Théodore de, 97
Bituntinus, 78n109, 80
Bobiensis, 118n128, 218, 223, 235, 239, 247, 252, 260, 262, 263, 270
"Bologna Sessions," 51–86
Bond, of marriage, 126–27, 134
Bononiensis, 72–73, 80n111, 82

Bovensis, 213, 223, 231, 238, 243, 251, 257, 262, 267
Bracarensis, 95n25, 106n76, 112n103, 210, 220, 230, 237, 241, 250, 266
Brandmüller, Walter, 36n9
Braun, J. Adamus, 11n37
Bressan, Luigi, 7n27, 47, 55, 98–99, 103, 108, 108n88, 135
Britonoriensis, 79n109, 80n114, 212, 221, 230, 238, 242, 250, 256, 262, 263, 267
Brixiensis, 216, 220, 234, 239, 250, 269
Brugnatensis, 212, 222, 231, 238, 242, 251, 256, 262, 267
Buduensis, 216, 223, 233, 239, 245, 252, 258, 263, 269
Byzantine law, 3, 40–45

Caiacensis, 211, 230, 237, 242, 250, 262, 267
Cajetan, Cardinal, 7n27, 73, 73n92, 92, 174
Calaguritanus, 216, 220, 234, 239, 246, 259, 262, 263, 269
Calamonensis, 100n49, 102n58, 115n119, 213, 220, 231, 238, 243, 250, 257, 262, 268
Callarensis, 117n127, 255, 262, 263, 266
Callaritanus, 241, 250
Calvensis, 79n109, 217, 224, 235, 239, 247, 252, 259, 263, 270
Calvin, Antoine, 27n25, 31n41
Calvin, John, 7, 27–28, 27n25, 31–32, 97, 104, 129, 130–31, 131n111
Camerinensis, 78n109, 80n114, 262, 267
Campaniensis, 106n76, 268
Campeggio, Giovanni. *See* Parentinus
Campegius, Alexander. *See* Bononiensis
Canisius, Peter, 59, 59n34
Canonical Epistle 199 (Basil the Great), 170–72
Canon law: adultery in, 25; Luther and, 25; Pauline Privilege in, 5
Canons of the Apostles, 41n29, 57, 57n23, 66, 92, 174, 190, 215
Caporella, Peter Paul, 59, 61–62, 62n50
Caprulanus, 69, 79n110, 82, 117n126, 246, 252, 259, 262, 263, 269
Caputaquensis, 266
Carinolensis, 257, 262, 263, 267

Carmelites, 219, 225, 236, 239, 249, 251, 253, 261, 264, 271
Casertanus, 100n49, 214, 221, 232, 238, 244, 251, 258, 263, 268
Cassinensis, 35n7, 109, 219, 225, 236, 239, 248, 249, 252, 253
Castagna, Giovanni Battista. *See* Rossanensis; Urban VII, Pope
Castellanetensis, 231, 238, 242, 250, 257, 263, 267
Castrensis, 212, 220, 230, 238, 242, 250, 256, 262, 267
Catacensis, 257, 262, 267
Catalonensis, 268
Catanensis, 241, 250, 256, 262
Cathacensis, 231, 237, 267
Cathalonensis, 214, 222, 232, 238, 249, 251, 253
Cathaniensis, 211, 221, 230, 237
Catharinus, Ambrogio, 7n27
Cattarensis, 230, 237, 241, 266
Catthacensis, 213, 222, 243, 251
Cauriensis, 102n58, 115n119, 213, 223, 231, 237, 249, 252, 257, 263, 268
Cavensis, 211, 220, 230, 237, 241, 250, 256, 262, 263, 266
Cavensis Casella, 267
Cenetensis, 212, 223, 231, 238, 242, 252
Cenoma, Richard, 57
Cenomanensis, 215, 223, 233, 238, 245, 251, 252
Cenomani, 64
Cervini, Marcello, 51, 63, 64, 71, 83–84
Charles V, Emperor, 51, 78n107
Cherubim of Cassia, 60
Chironensis, 69, 78n109, 83, 213, 222, 231, 237, 243, 252, 257, 262, 267
Christian Marriage (Joyce), 12–13
Chrysostom, 35, 35n7, 58, 58n29, 66, 94, 176–80
Civitatensis, 97n30, 107, 216, 224, 234, 238, 246, 250, 259, 263, 269
Civitatis Castellane, 211, 230, 234, 237, 242, 250, 256, 262
Civitatis Castelli, 117n126, 216, 224, 246, 251, 252, 259, 262, 263, 269

Claravallensis, 219, 225, 248, 251, 253
Clement of Alexandria, 38, 92, 233
Clodiensis, 231, 238, 267
Clugiensis, 212, 220, 242, 252, 256, 262
Clusinus, 118n129, 118n131, 216, 223, 234, 239, 246, 251, 252, 259, 263, 269
Cochllaeus, Johann, 197
Colimbriensis, 212, 220, 231, 237, 256, 263, 267
Colloquy of Poissy, 97–98, 129
Columbriensis, 97n30, 112, 115n114, 118n129, 217, 225, 235, 237, 247, 250, 260, 262, 263, 270
Comensis, 216, 226, 234, 239, 246, 251, 259, 263, 269
Commentary on a Harmony of the Evangelists (Calvin), 27–28
Commentary on I Corinthians (Ambrosiaster), 57, 70n80, 157
Commentary on I Corinthians (Calvin), 28
Commentary on I Corinthians (Pseudo-Bede), 173–74
Commentary on I Corinthians 7 (Luther), 24–25
Commentary on Mark 10 (Bede the Venerable), 172–73
Commentary on Matthew 5:32 (Cardinal Cajetan), 174
Commentary on Matthew 5:32 (Hilary of Poitiers), 180
Commentary on Matthew 19:9 (Cardinal Cajetan), 174
Commentary on Matthew 19:9 (Jerome), 182
Comment. In Matthaeum (Origen), 183–84
Concubuisti (Zachary), 190–91
Congregatio theologorum, 56–63
Consilium, John, 57–58, 57n27, 58–59, 64
Consistory, 32n41
Constantine, 3n11
Consummation: Adrian VI on, 7n27; bond and, 134; in Council of Tribur, 66, 196–97; defined, 6n24; dissolution and, 16, 17n58; in Gregory U, 189; indissolubility and, 1–2, 6, 7, 85, 127, 144–45;

ratification vs., 6n14; in Second Vatican Council, 2
Contarini, Francesco. *See* Paphensis
Corcyrensis, 120n141, 255, 262, 263, 266
Coriden, James, ix
Corinthians. *See* I Corinthians; II Corinthians
Corosopitanus, 217, 225
Cortonensis, 219, 227, 236, 237, 245, 249, 253, 261, 264, 271
Cotronensis, 215, 226, 233, 239, 251, 258, 263, 269
Council at Bologna, 26
Council of Arles I, 66, 66n66, 68–69, 193
Council of Carthage, 66, 112n103
Council of Constance, 60, 198–99
Council of Elvira, 57, 66, 71n80, 77n105, 92, 193
Council of Florence, 2, 36–37, 36n9, 45, 60, 68, 68n68, 82, 84, 84n137, 92, 94, 142n42, 199
Council of Mileve, 57, 58, 66, 77n105, 82, 84, 84n138, 92, 94, 112–13, 112n103
Council of Tribur in Germany, 66, 66n66, 69, 196–98
Council of Trullo, 42, 43, 195–96
Council of Venice, 66, 66n66, 69, 195
Cremonensis, 95n25, 259, 263, 270
Crete, 104, 104n68
Cretensis, 108n89, 210, 220, 229, 237, 248, 252, 255, 262, 265
Crouzel, Henri, 38–39, 38n17, 39n19
Cuesta, Andres. *See* Legionensis
Curran, Charles, 15n53, 17, 34–35

Damasus I, Pope, 57n27
De Adulterinis Conjugiis ad Pollentium (Augustine), 58, 165–68
Death penalty, 24
De Bono Conjugali (Augustine), 160–62
De captivitate babylonica (Luther), 7, 7n28, 23, 26, 29, 30, 33, 53–54, 53n7, 53n8, 55
Decree with Armenians, 36n9
Decretum Gratiani, 32n42
De divortiis (Alexander III), 185–86
De Fide et Operibus (Augustine), 162–63

De Genesi Ad Litteram Libri Duodecim (Augustine), 163
De Libello Repudii (John Chrysostom), 178–79
De Matrimonio Christiano (Perrone), 11
Demochares, Antonius, 92, 96
De Nuptiis et Concupiscentia (Augustine), 163–64
De patriarcha Abraham (Ambrose), 153
Deputatio, 48, 95, 96, 101–3, 112–13, 115, 116, 118, 125, 135, 203, 209, 213, 229, 254
Dertusensis, 97n30, 102n58, 217, 224
De Sermone Domini in Monte (Augustine), 158–60
de Soto, Domingo, 7n27
De trinitate et operibus eius (Rupert of Deutz), 185
De Virginitate (John Chrysostom), 179–80
Dictionnaire de théologie catholique, 12
Didacus of Leon. *See* Columbriensis
Diet of Spires, 25
Dimissa, 8n30, 9n31, 29n34, 30n36, 30n37, 48n52, 48n54, 55n14, 63n55, 64n60, 70n77, 70n78, 74n95, 77n105, 78n106, 79n109, 95n26, 103n61, 105n70, 110n99, 112n101, 116n122, 120n144, 132n15, 163, 166–67, 168, 181, 194, 203, 208, 228
Dissolvere, 68n71, 158
Divine Institutes (Lactantius), 183
Divorce. adultery and, 3–4, 3n12; in Alexander III, 185–86; in Ambrose, 153; in Augustine, 160–63, 168; in Basil the Great, 168–70, 170–72; in Bologna Sessions, 53–54, 54–55, 79–81; in Cajetan, 174; in Calvin, 27–28; in Erasmus, 175, 176; in General Congregation, 67–77; in Greek church, 3, 22, 34–35, 35–49, 45–49, 47n49, 115–16, 123, 139–40; in Gregory II, 188–89; in Hilary of Poitiers, 180; infallibility and, 17n58; in Innocent I, 187; in John Chrysostom, 178, 179–80; Justinian I and, 39–40, 40–41; legislation, 39; "legitimating cause" for, 40–45; in Luke, 152; Luther and, 21–22, 22–23, 23–27;

in Mark, 151; in Matthew, 150–51; Pauline Privilege and, 4–5; Petrine Privilege and, 5; Protestants and, 3, 47, 48; in Roman law, 3n11, 47; in Russian Orthodox church, 45n46; in Scholastikos, 41–42; in Second Vatican Council, 2; through history, 2–3. *See also* Indissolubility
Divortio/divortium, 2n6, 29n33, 30n35, 30n36, 30n37, 53, 53n7, 53n8, 54n13, 55n15, 55n18, 56n19, 59n32, 63n54, 63n56, 64n60, 68n71, 74n96, 79n109, 90n1, 91n3, 96n27, 153, 161, 164, 175, 188
Doctrina, 35, 48, 88, 101–2, 102n58, 120, 120n141, 122–24, 126–28, 133–34, 139, 141, 144, 145–47, 213, 214, 215, 216, 217, 218, 219, 220, 221, 222, 223, 224, 225, 243, 245, 255, 256, 257, 258, 259, 260, 261, 265–71
Dolensis, 216, 226, 234, 238, 246, 251, 252, 269
Dominicans, 219, 227, 236, 239, 249, 253, 261, 264, 271
Draskovic, George. *See* Quinqueecclesiensis
Durantibus, Vincent de, 82

Eastern church. *See* Greek church
Ebredunensis, 211, 221, 230, 237, 241, 250
Ebroicensis, 211, 220, 230, 237
Ecclesiam errare, 9n31, 23, 48n54, 112n101, 116n122, 118, 118n130, 120n144, 122n149, 124, 132n15, 135, 135n24, 240, 243, 254, 258, 265, 269
"Ecclesiastical Ordinances" (Calvin), 28
Economia, 13n50, 14n50, 17, 35, 45–46, 45n46, 75, 142, 142n41, 143
Elnensis, 216, 226, 234, 237, 249, 251, 253, 259, 262, 263, 269
Emoniensis, 270
Ephesians, 94
Epistle to Exsuperius (Innocent I), 57, 187
Epistle to Probus (Innocent I), 187–88
Epithalamium. *See* Commentary on I Corinthians 7 (Luther)

Erasmus, 7n27, 56, 56n19, 57n27, 58–59, 59n32, 62, 62n51, 175–76, 176n25
Esinus, 214, 225
Estate of Marriage (Luther), 23
Eugenius IV, Pope, 36, 45
Eutichius, 271
Euticius, 219, 225
Eutitius, 118n129, 118n131, 261, 262, 263
Evdokimov, Paul, 46n46
Ex causa fornicationis, 31n39, 68n68, 71n83, 84n136, 84n137, 85n141, 86n146, 94n21, 96n28, 156, 157, 199
Exceptio, 67n67, 69, 69n76, 71n82, 74n94, 93n14, 94n23, 158
Exceptive clause, 4, 18, 23, 27–28, 27n25, 47, 92–93, 129, 134, 138, 138n31
Exposito Evangeli secundum Lucam (Ambrose), 153–56

Falsetta, Egidius. *See* Caprulanus
Famagustanus, 122–23, 123n153, 260, 264, 270
Faventinus, 102n58, 106, 218, 224, 235, 237, 247, 251, 252, 260, 262, 263, 271
Feltrensis, 69, 78n109, 216, 220, 234, 237, 246, 252, 269
Feretranus, 213, 223, 231, 238, 243, 251, 257, 262, 267
Ferretti, Giovanni Pietro. *See* Mylonensis Ferrettus
Fesulanus, 214, 222, 238, 243, 250, 257, 263, 268
I Corinthians, 4–5, 60, 68, 70, 71, 76, 88, 91–92, 94, 152, 168. *See also* Commentary on I Corinthians; Paul
Florentinus, 210, 220, 229, 237, 240, 250
Fornicationem, 4, 31n38, 53, 57n25, 60n39, 60n42, 62n51, 64n60, 67n67, 68n68, 70n77, 73n92, 74n95, 74n97, 76n101, 77n104, 78n109, 79n109, 79n110, 80n111, 84n135, 85n139, 85n143, 93n14, 93n18, 94n23, 95n23, 99n47, 100n52, 151, 156, 167, 169, 173, 178, 179, 199, 210, 212, 213
Foscarari, Egidio. *See* Mutinensis
Fragi, Peter. *See* Usellensis

Francis, Pope, 16n55, x
Franciscans, 219, 220, 236, 238, 249, 251, 253, 261, 264, 271
Frankish church, divorce in, 3n11
Fransen, Piet F., 14, 14n52, 18n62, 32n42, 62n50, 74–75, 84n138, 85–86, 98, 99–100, 99n42, 107n85, 110, 119, 124, 135
Freudenberger, Theobald, 55, 58n29, 85n143

Gagliego, Arias. *See* Gerundensis
Gebennensis, 215, 225, 233, 237, 245, 251, 258, 263, 269
General Congregation, 15, 20, 30, 51, 64, 67–78, 74, 83, 87, 111, 113, 115n120, 117n127
Generalis Praedicatoru, 80n111
Genesis, 69–70, 72, 114, 150
Genuensis, 106n76, 211, 220, 230, 237, 241, 266
Gerundensis, 102n58, 118n129, 119, 119n136, 215, 225, 232, 237, 244, 251, 258, 262, 263
Godvellus, Thomas. *See* Assaphensis
Gonzaga, Don Ferrante, 78n107
Görres-Gesellschaft, 12
Gospel of Luke, 58, 73, 76, 81, 88, 91–92, 94, 152
Gospel of Mark, 58, 60, 68, 71, 73, 76, 88, 91–92, 94, 151
Gospel of Matthew, 4, 18, 23, 25, 26, 27n25, 47, 58–59, 60, 66, 68, 70, 71, 73, 76, 80n111, 81–84, 90, 91–92, 92–93, 94, 109, 114, 129, 134, 135, 138, 138n31, 139–40, 150–51, 156
Grace, 115–16, 127
Granatensis, 95n25, 106n76, 109n95, 115, 115n119, 117, 117n127, 210, 220, 229, 237, 240, 250, 255, 262, 263, 265
Grandis, Nicolas, 64, 77n105
Gratian, 70n80
Greek church: adultery in, 46–48; Byzantine law and, 40–45; Council of Florence and, 36–37, 36n9; divorce in, 3, 22, 34–35, 35–49, 45–49, 47n49, 115–16, 123, 139–40; *economia* in, 35, 45–46;

INDEX

exceptive clause and, 47; indissolubility and, 45–49; *Nomokanon* and, 44; Quinisext Council and, 42; remarriage and, 18–19, 35–49; *ritus* in, 45–49; Roman law and marriage in, 37–40; in Venice, 34
Gregory I, Pope, 66, 92
Gregory II, Pope, 66, 66n66, 188–90
Gregory III, Pope, 92
Gregory the Great, Pope, 99, 186
Grisez, Germain, x
Grossetanus, 214, 221, 232, 237, 244, 251, 257, 263, 268
Guadiscensis, 102n58, 108n89, 117n127, 217, 235, 237, 247, 248, 252, 260, 262, 263
Guarde Alvaro de la. *See* Venusinus
Guardiensis, 219, 226, 235, 237, 252, 260, 262, 263, 271
Gueron, Anthony. *See* Almeriensis
Guerra, Matthew, 93–94, 96
Guerrero, Pedro. *See* Granatensis
Guise, Charles de, 27. *See also* Lotharingus

Heresy, 29, 30, 53, 56, 64–65, 74–76, 90, 191
Hervetus, Gentianus, 60
Hierapetrensis, 267
Hierosolymitanus, 209, 220, 229, 237, 240, 252, 255, 262, 263, 265
Hilary of Poitiers, 58, 58n29, 99, 180
Hugo, Jacob, 92, 96
Hyacinthanus, 246, 252, 259, 263
Hydruntinus, 106n76, 210, 220, 229, 237, 240, 252, 254, 255, 262, 265
Hyprensis, 97n30, 102n58, 107, 118n129, 119, 119n136, 216, 224, 234, 239, 246, 252, 259, 262, 263

Iacinthensis, 270
Iadrensis, 210, 220, 230, 237, 241, 250, 255, 262, 266
Ierapetrensis, 212, 222, 231, 237, 242, 250
Ilcinensis, 214, 232, 237, 244, 251, 258, 262, 268
Ilerdensis, 97n30, 109, 109n95, 115, 216, 223, 233, 237, 245, 250, 258, 263, 269

Imolensis, 260, 263, 271
In Bavariam Ablegatis (Gregory II), 188–89
Indissolubility, 125–47; in Ambrose, 156; in Bologna Sessions, 55; changing of teaching on, 6; consummation and, 1–2, 6, 7, 85, 127, 144–45; as continuing principle, 2–3; in Council of Trent, 7–8, 9–12; defense of, 127–28; divorce and, 3–4, 3n12; extrinsic, 5–6; and grace of Christ, 115–16; Greek church and, 45–49; intrinsic, 5–6; in Paul, 4–5; in Second Vatican Council, 2. *See also* Divorce
In epistolam primam (I) ad Corinthios: Hom. 19.3 (John Chrysostom), 177–78
Infallibility, 6n16, 12, 17n58, 147
Initio nostri huius pontificati (Paul III), 50n1, 272
In Matt. Homil. 17, 4 (John Chrysostom), 176
In Matt. Homil. 62 (John Chrysostom), 176–77
Innocent I, Pope, 57, 66, 92, 186–87
Innocent III, Pope, 5n18, 66, 92, 191
Innocent X, Pope, 10
In quartum Sententiarum (Tapper), 7n27
Institutes of the Christian Religion (Calvin), 27–28, 27n25
Insulanus, 214, 220, 231, 238, 243, 251, 257, 263, 268
Interamnensis, 212, 221, 231, 237, 242, 251, 256, 262, 263, 267
International Theological Commission (ITC), 140
Iprensis, 122n152, 269
Isclanus, 216, 222, 234, 237, 246, 251, 259, 263, 269
Istoria del Concilio Tridentino (Sarpi), 9, 9n32, 9n33, 10n34
Iustinopolitanus, 108n86, 109, 109n91, 212, 220, 231, 238, 242, 252, 256, 262, 267
Iuxta evangelicam et apostolicam doctrinam, 9n31, 48n54, 112, 112n110, 113, 116n122, 120n144, 132, 132n15, 133, 194, 240, 254, 255, 265

Jedin, Hubert, 130n9
Jerome, 57, 58, 66, 71n80, 94, 181–82
Jesuits, 115n114, 219, 225, 236, 238, 249, 250, 261, 264, 271
Jesus Christ: adultery and, 46; grace of, indissolubility and, 115–16; inferring will of, 52; on marriage, 1–2. *See also* Gospels
John, 120n141
John Chrysostom, 35, 35n7, 58, 58n29, 66, 94, 176–80
John Paul II, Pope, 17n58
John Scholastikos, 41–42, 41n29
Joyce, George H., 12–13
Julius III, Pope, 273
Justinian I, 39–41, 41n26
Justinian II, 42

Kasper, Walter, 13, 13n50, 14, 17, 142, 142n41, 184, x–xi

Lactantius, 183
Laguedonensis, 100n49, 214, 220, 232, 237, 243, 251
Lancianensis, 211, 230, 237, 241, 250, 256, 262, 266
Laquedoniensis, 257, 262, 263, 268
Larinensis, 97n30, 102n58, 215, 222, 232, 237, 244, 251, 258, 262, 268
Lateran III, 94, 198
Lateran IV, 60, 198
Launoy, Jean de, 10–11, 12
Lavellanus, 78n107, 80, 80n114
Lavellinus, 69–70, 235, 237, 247, 251, 252, 260, 264, 270
Law: Roman law: adultery and, 46; in Ambrose, 57n26, 153, 155; in Ambrosiaster, 157; in Augustine, 164; in Bede the Venerable, 173; Byzantine, 3, 40–45; in Cajetan, 174; in Chrysostom, 176, 178, 179, 180; civil with ecclesiastical, 42; in Council of Mileve, 194; divorce and, 3; in Erasmus, 176; Gospels and, 81–82; in Hilary of Poitiers, 180; indissolubility and, 84–86, 114; in Innocent I, 188; in Jerome, 182; John and, 42; in Justin-
ian, 42; natural, 56, 59, 63, 78n109; in *Nomokanon,* 44; in Origen, 183, 184; in Paul, 152; polygamy and, 61; in *Synagoge,* 42; in Zachary, 190. *See also* Canon law
Law of Moses, 25, 26, 93
Leccavella de Chio, Sebastiano. *See* Naxiensis
Le Courayer, Pierre François, 11n37, 12
Lectorensis, 211, 220, 230, 237, 249, 251, 253, 267
Le Fert, Anne, 27n25
Legionensis, 35n7, 95n25, 109, 115, 115n114, 118–19, 118n129, 215, 223, 233, 237, 245, 250, 258, 262, 263, 269
Lehmann, Karl, 14
Leo the Great, Pope, 58, 58n29, 66, 191–92
Leo VI, Emperor, 44
Leo XIII, Pope, 12
Leriensis, 214, 221, 232, 238, 243, 250
Lesinensis, 214, 224, 232, 238, 243, 251, 257, 262, 263, 268
Letter to Boniface (Gregory II), 189–90
Letter to the Legates of Bavaria (Gregory II), 188–89
Leviticus, 26
Liciensis, 217, 223, 235, 237, 247, 260, 263, 270
Lili, Thomas. *See* Soranus
Lippomani, Luigi. *See* Veronensis
Li vero (Gregory the Great), 186
Lombard, Peter, 62n50, 68, ix–n5
Los Mártyres, Bartolomé de. *See* Bracarensis
Lotharingus, 46n48, 97, 97n34, 104, 105, 110–11, 118n130, 129, 129n5, 130–31, 133n17, 209, 220, 228–29, 237, 240, 250, 265
Lucensis, 100n49, 115n119, 120n141, 218, 221, 235, 237, 247, 252, 260, 264, 270
Lucerino, 238
Lucerinus, 214, 224, 232, 244, 250, 257, 262, 268
Luke. *See* Gospel of Luke
Lunaevillae, 107, 219, 225, 236, 238, 248, 251, 253

INDEX

Lunaevillanus, 271
Luther, Martin, 3, 7, 21–22, 23–27, 25n11, 32–33, 50, 53–54, 53n7, 53n8, 55–56, 65–66, 87, 91, 91n3, 100, 134–35, 136
Lympus, Balthasar. *See* Portuensis

Maceratensis, 78n107, 79n109, 80n114, 214, 232, 238, 244, 251, 268
Mackin, Theodore, 13, 13n47, 140–41
Madrutius, 117n126, 209, 220, 229, 237, 240, 250, 254, 255, 262, 263, 265
Maioricensis, 79n110, 82
Mantua, 50
Mark. *See* Gospel of Mark
Maronites, 123
Marriage Ordinance (Calvin, 1546), 130–31
Marsicanus, 102n58, 219, 224, 235, 238, 248, 251, 252
Marsicensis, 212, 221, 231, 237, 242, 252, 256, 262, 263, 267
Massaelubrensis, 115n119, 115n121, 216, 223, 233, 237, 246, 250, 263, 270
Massanus, 259, 263, 270
Massarelli, Angelo, 10, 29, 29n31, 53, 55, 62, 64, 66, 74, 76, 77, 91n3
Massarelli, August, 77n105
Materanus, 67n67, 68–69, 78n109, 210, 221, 241, 250, 255, 262, 266
Matthew. *See* Gospel of Matthew
Mazariensis, 95n25, 215, 223, 258, 262, 263, 268
Mechari/moechari/moechandi, 8n30, 30n36, 30n37, 48n52, 63n56, 64n60, 71n83, 72n83, 77n105, 78n106, 78n109, 79n109, 79n110, 80n111, 82, 83, 83n130, 83n133, 83n134, 85, 93n14, 95n26, 103n61, 105n70, 110n99, 151, 167, 203, 208, 228
Mechatur, 74n96, 79n109, 80
Medici, Giovanni Angelo. *See* Pius IV, Pope
Melanchthon, Philip, 53, 91n3
Meldensis, 214, 224, 232, 237, 244, 250, 268
Mercanensis, 271

Messanensis, 106n76, 211, 230, 237, 241, 250, 256, 262, 266
Metensis, 95n25, 215, 223, 232, 238, 244
Meyendorff, John, 46n46, 47n49
Milevitanum, 194
Milopotamensis, 248, 250, 252, 257, 263, 266, 268
Milopotamensis (first), 211, 221, 230, 232, 237, 241
Milopotamensis (second), 211
Minerbiensis, 212, 221, 230, 237, 242, 252, 256, 262, 263, 267
Minorensis, 83, 83n134, 219, 227, 236, 237, 248, 252, 261, 262, 263
Minoriensis, 73–74, 73n93, 76, 79n109, 80–81, 80n114
Mocenicos, Filippo. *See* Nicosiensis
Moncalvius, John Baptist Vastinius, 60
Monopolitanus, 118n129, 118n131, 218, 223, 236, 239, 247, 252, 260, 262, 263, 270
Monte, Giovanni del, 51, 64, 67, 73n92
Montealcino, Augustine, 59
Montisfalisci, 215, 222, 232, 238, 244, 250, 258, 262, 268
Montismarani, 100n49, 117n127, 214, 221, 232, 238, 244, 257, 262, 263, 268
Moralia (Basil the Great), 168–70
Moronus, 122n152, 265
Moses, 25, 26, 93
Motulanus, 69, 70
Musso, Cornelio. *See* Bituntinus
Mutinensis, 100, 102n58, 103, 115n119, 115n121, 213, 220, 221, 231, 237, 243, 257, 262, 267
Mylensis, 69
Mylonensis Ferrettus, 78n109, 80
Mylonensis Graecus, 79n109

Namurcensis, 102n58, 118n129, 216, 223, 234, 238, 246, 259, 262
Natural law, 56, 59, 63, 78n109
Naulensis, 115n119, 243, 250, 257, 262, 267
Navagerius, 265
Naxiensis, 69, 79n111, 82, 82n126, 211, 230, 237, 241, 250, 256, 262, 266

Nemausensis, 106, 216, 222, 238, 246, 251, 252, 259, 262, 263, 269
Nemosiensis, 270
Neocastrensis, 118n129, 118n131, 259, 262, 263, 269
Niciensis, 102n58, 213, 222, 231, 238, 243, 252, 257, 262, 267
Nicosiensis, 115, 122, 124, 241, 250, 266
Nimiosensis, 259, 263
Nimosiensis, 217, 223, 234, 239, 247, 252
Niochensis, 102n58, 217, 223, 235, 237, 249, 253, 257, 263, 270
Nivernensis, 216, 223, 234, 237, 246, 251, 252, 259, 263, 269
Nobili, Benedetto de. *See* Aciensis
Nomokanon in XIV Titles, 44
Non debere, 48n52, 105n70, 110–11, 113, 181, 203, 228
Non licere, 70n77, 89, 93n18, 96, 169, 235
Non posse dissolvi, 9n31, 48n52, 48n54, 96, 105n70, 110n99, 112n101, 116n122, 120n144, 132n15, 132n16, 203, 228, 240, 254, 265
Non rumpit vinculum, 67n67, 68n67, 71n83, 74, 74n98, 78n109, 79n109
Non separat vinculum, 79n109
Novellae (Justinian I), 40–41, 40n22, 40n23, 41n26
Nucerinus, 217, 220, 235, 237, 270

Oikonomia. *See* Economia
On Marriage Matters (Luther), 25
Opera Omnia (Erasmus), 56n19, 175–76, 176n25
Oppidensis, 117n127, 118n128, 218, 224, 235, 237, 248, 252, 260, 262, 263, 270
Origen, 35, 35n7, 58, 58n29, 66, 92, 183–84
Oscensis, 212, 222, 231, 237, 242, 250, 256, 262, 267
Ostunensis, 109n95, 115n119, 216, 223, 234, 239, 245, 250, 259, 262, 263, 269

Pactensis, 108n89, 109n90, 117n126, 213, 220, 231, 238, 242, 251, 257, 262, 263, 267
Pallavicino, Pietro Sforza, 10, 10n34
Palmieri, Domenico, 12, 12n42, 132n16

Pampilonensis, 118n129, 122, 218, 235, 237, 247, 251, 252, 260, 262, 263, 270
Panormitanus, 117n126, 211, 230, 237, 241, 250, 256, 262, 263, 266
Pan-Russian Council, 45
Paphensis, 123, 248, 252, 261, 263, 271
Papiensis, 217, 225, 235, 239, 247, 252, 259, 263, 270
Parentinus, 69, 70, 79n110, 82
Paris condemnation, 56, 56n20
Parisiensis, 97n30, 107, 108n86, 213, 221, 231, 237, 243, 250
Parmensis, 217, 234, 237, 247, 252, 270
Paschalis, Angelus. *See* Motulanus
Paul, 59, 60, 61–62, 68, 69, 70, 76, 79n109, 81, 82, 88, 120n141, 152–53. *See also* I Corinthians; Romans
Paul III, Pope, 50, 50n1, 78n107, 272–73
Pauline Privilege, 4–5
Paul V, Pope, 9
Paul VI, Pope, 143–44
Pelargi, Ambrose, 63, 64
Pelikan, Jaroslav, 25n15
Pelland, Gilles, 156–57, 170
Pelleve, Nicolaus de. *See* Senonensis
Pennensis, 118n129, 118n131, 218, 224, 235, 239, 248, 252, 260, 262, 263, 270
Peretti, Felice, 56n22
Pérez de Ayala, Martin. *See* Segobiensis
Permanence, of marriage, 1–2
Perrone, Giovanni, 11–12, 11n37
Petrine Privilege, 5
Philadelphiensis, 212, 230, 237, 242, 250
Photian Schism, 43
Pientinus, 211, 221, 230, 237, 241, 250, 256, 262, 263, 266
Pighino, Sebastiano. *See* Alyphanus
Pisauriensis, 218, 222, 235, 237, 247, 250, 260, 264, 270
Pistoriensis, 78n107, 79n109, 80n114
Pius IV, Pope, 90, 95, 273
Placentia, Vincent, 59–60
Pole, Reginald, 51n2
Polito, Catharinus. *See* Minoriensis
Polygamy, 61, 62, 62n50
Pope Adrian VI, 7n27

INDEX

Pope Alexander III, 66, 70, 70n80, 92, 185–86
Pope Benedict XVI, x–xi. *See also* Ratzinger, Joseph
Pope Damasus I, 57n27
Pope Eugenius IV, 36, 45
Pope Francis, 16n55, x
Pope Gregory I, 66, 92
Pope Gregory II, 66, 66n66, 188–90
Pope Gregory III, 92
Pope Gregory the Great, 99, 186
Pope Innocent I, 57, 66, 92, 186–87, 191
Pope Innocent III, 5n18, 66, 92, 191
Pope Innocent X, 10
Pope John Paul II, 17n58
Pope Julius III, 273
Pope Leo the Great, 58, 58n29, 66, 191–92
Pope Leo XIII, 12
Pope Paul III, 50, 50n1, 78n107, 272–73
Pope Paul V, 9
Pope Paul VI, 143–44
Pope Pius IV, 90, 95, 273
Pope Sixtus V, 56n22
Pope Urban VII, 99, 114
Pope Zachary, 66, 66n66, 190–91
Popishil, Victor, 13, 13n46
Portuensis, 79n109, 81–82
Praefatio, 101, 102, 102n58, 113, 116, 121–22, 125–26, 203–8, 215, 216, 218, 220, 224, 225
Praemisliensis, 115n119, 115n121, 122, 248, 270
Pragensis, 117n126, 211, 220, 230, 237, 249, 253, 256, 262, 263, 266
Protestants, 22–32, 51; anathema to, 11–12; divorce and, 3, 47, 48. *See also* Luther, Martin
Psaulme, Nicolas. *See* Virdunensis
Pseudo-Ambrose, 3n12, 18, 57, 66, 90n2, 99, 101, 108, 157, 157n10
Pseudo-Bede, 173–74

Quanto (Innocent III), 191
Quinisext Council, 42, 43, 66, 195–96
Quinqueecclesiensis, 95n25, 97n30, 109, 109n91, 118, 118n129, 118n130, 215, 223, 233, 237, 245, 251, 252, 258, 262, 263, 269

Ragazzonus, Girolam. *See* Famagustanus
Ramirez, John, 92–93, 96
Rapotensis, 218, 224, 235, 237, 247, 250, 270
Ratified marriage, 6
Ratzinger, Joseph, 14, 14n53, 17, 142n40. *See also* Benedict XVI, Pope
Recanatensis, 212, 223, 231, 238, 242, 250, 256, 262
Reginus, 115, 115n113, 242, 250
Remarriage: adultery and, 14n50, 18; in Ambrosiaster, 157; in Augustine, 158–60, 161–64, 165–66; in Basil the Great, 170–72; in Bede the Venerable, 172–73; in Bologna Sessions, 54–55, 79–81; in Calvin, 27–28; in de Sotto, 91–92; exceptive clause and, 18; in Greek church, 3; Greek church and, 18–19, 35–49; in Gregory II, 189; in Gregory the Great, 186; in Hilary of Poitiers, 180; in I Corinthians, 152; in Innocent I, 186–87; in Innocent III, 191; in Jerome, 181–82; in John Chrysostom, 178; Justinian and, 40–41; in Kasper, 13n50; in Lactantius, 183; in Luther, 21, 23–27; in Matthew, 22; in Origen, 183–84; in Paul, 152; Petrine Privilege and, 5; in Pseudo-Bede, 173–74; in Roman law, 3n11; in Tertullian, 185. *See also Aliam ducere*
Republic of Venice, 34, 104–10, 141–42, 201–3
Rheginus, 117n126, 211, 237, 255, 263, 266
Rithovius, Martin, 119
Ritus, 45–49, 86
Roman law: divorce in, 3n11, 47; Greco-Christian marriage legislation and, 37–40
Romans, 71, 76, 88, 91–92, 94, 152. *See also* Paul
Romeus, Franciscus, 82, 84–86
Roskovány, Augustinus de, 11n37
Rossanensis, 95n25, 99, 108n89, 114, 210, 220, 230, 237, 241, 250, 255, 262, 263, 266
Rossensis, 117n126, 218, 223, 235, 239, 247, 252, 260, 262, 263, 271
Rupert of Deutz, 66, 185

Russian Orthodox church, 45. *See also* Greek church
Ryan, Peter F., x

Sagiensis, 95n25, 212, 223, 242, 250
Sagonensis, 102n58, 219, 224, 236, 237, 248, 251, 252, 271
Salamantino, 226
Salamantinus, 217, 234, 237, 249, 253, 270
Salazar, Francis, 60, 64
Salutiarum, 78n109
Sanctonensis, 213, 223, 231, 237, 243, 250, 267
Saraceni, Giovanni Michele. *See* Materanus
Sarpi, Paolo, 9–10, 9n33, 12
Sarra, Diego de, 94–95
Sarsinensis, 79n109, 80n114
Sarzanensis, 217, 225, 235, 237, 247, 252, 260, 264, 270
Scholastikos, John, 41–42, 41n29
Scripture, in Council of Trent, 150–53
Sebastensis, 69
Second Council of Mileve, 128n4, 194
Second Epistle to Victricius (Innocent I), 186–87
II Corinthians, 59, 153
Second Vatican Council, 2, 90, 143–44, 144–45, ix
Sed tantum thorus, 68n67, 73n92, 78n109, 79n109, 93n18
Segniensis, 231, 238, 262
Segninus, 214, 224, 243, 250, 257, 268
Segobiensis, 99–100, 108n89, 109n95, 115, 115n119, 212, 220, 231, 238, 243, 250, 256, 262
Segovia, 35n7
Senecensis, 218, 223, 235, 239, 247, 251, 252
Senensis, 211, 230, 237, 241, 250, 255, 262, 266
Senogalliensis, 95n25, 268
Senonensis, 98, 98n36, 117n126, 211, 221, 230, 237, 241, 250, 256, 262, 263, 266
Separationem, 31n38, 31n39, 67n67, 68n68, 74n97, 76n101, 76n103, 77n104, 84n136, 84n137, 86n146, 88n147, 92n11, 94n21, 96n28, 135n24, 199

Separatio tori, non vinculi, 69
Seripando, Girolamo, 53n6, 79n109, 80n114, 83
Servites, 120n141, 121n146, 219, 226, 249, 253, 261, 263, 271
Seventh Council of Carthage, 192
Sibinicensis, 69, 78n109, 80n114, 215, 233, 239, 245, 251, 258, 263, 268
Sighicelli, Giovanni Battista, 106
Simonetta, 265
Sixtus V, Pope, 56n22
S. Leonis, 215, 225, 232, 238, 244, 251, 252, 258
S.Leonis, 262
S. Leonis, 268
S. Marci, 219, 223, 236, 237, 248, 252, 260, 262, 263, 271
Soranus, 106, 218, 223, 235, 237, 248, 252
Sotto, Peter de, 91–92, 96
S. Severinae, 120n141, 210, 230, 237, 241, 250, 255, 262, 266
Stella, Thomas. *See* Iustinopolitanus
Stella, Tommaso. *See* Lavellinus
Stephanus, 118n129, 118n131, 261, 262, 263, 271
Suessionensis, 215, 222, 233, 245, 251, 252, 268
Sui fecit copiam, 29, 29n33, 30n36, 30n37, 54n13, 56, 56n19, 63n54, 64n60, 175
Sullivan, Francis, 14
Sulmonensis, 108, 212, 221, 231, 237, 242, 251, 256, 262, 267
Summa Theologiae (Aquinas), 158
Synagoge (Scholastikos), 41–42
Synod of Constantinople, 44

Tapper, Ruard, 7n27
Tarentinus, 95n25, 211, 221, 230, 237, 241, 250, 266
Tarvisinus, 211, 221, 242, 250, 256, 262, 267
Tertullian, 66, 92, 185
Theanensis, 215, 225, 233, 238, 245, 251, 252
Thelesinus, 269
Thermularum, 211, 221, 230, 237, 242, 250
Thomas Aquinas, 62n50, 67n67, 68–69, 71, 80n111, 127, 158, ix, ix–n5

Tiburtinus, 214, 224, 232, 238, 244, 251, 257, 263, 268
Torcellanus, 219, 227, 236, 239, 248, 252, 261, 264, 271
Tortonensis, 212, 222, 231, 237
Tractatus de Matrimonio Christiano (Palmieri), 12n42
Trivicanensis, 95n25
Trivicanus, 219, 227, 235, 237, 248, 250, 260, 264, 271
Troianus, 102n58, 217, 223, 235, 239, 247, 252, 260, 263, 270
Tutellensis, 216, 223, 234, 239, 246, 251, 252, 269

Ugentinus, 234, 239, 259, 262, 263
Umbriaticensis, 212, 223, 231, 238, 242, 251, 256, 262, 267
Upsalensis, 78n109
Urban VII, Pope, 99, 114
Urbevetanus, 219, 226, 235, 238, 248, 250, 271
Usellensis, 97n30, 102n58, 118n129, 119, 119n136, 120n141, 219, 225, 236, 238, 248, 251, 252, 260, 262, 263, 271
Uxentinus, 100n49, 115n119, 216, 221, 246, 250, 269
Uxor, 29n33, 30n37, 54n13, 56n19, 62n51, 64n60, 67n67, 70n79, 72n85, 72n88, 79n109, 82n121, 92n11, 92n13, 93n14, 93n19, 151, 156, 159, 168, 173, 175, 176, 178, 182, 190, 197, 198, 198n50

Vabrensis, 235, 238, 245, 247, 251, 252
Vacant, Alfred, 12
Valentia, Gaspar de, 60
Varmiensis, 122n152, 265
Vatican II. *See* Second Vatican Council
Vaurensis, 97n30, 215, 222, 233, 239, 269
Venciensis, 216, 222, 234, 238
Venerable Bede, 66, 172–73
Venetensis, 215, 225, 233, 237, 245, 251, 252
Venetiarum, 209, 220

Venetus, 229, 237, 250, 255, 262, 265
Venice, 8–9, 34, 104–10, 141–42, 201–3. *See also* Council of Venice
Ventimiliensis, 109n96, 218, 226, 235, 239, 247, 252
Venusinus, 74, 76, 80n111, 82
Verallus, 108n89, 109n90, 210, 229, 237, 240, 250, 255, 262
Verdunensis, 120n141, 257, 262, 263
Verona, 69
Veronensis, 70–71, 80n114
Verulanus, 270
Vestanus, 95n25, 216, 226, 234, 237, 246, 251, 259, 263, 269
Vicecom, Charles. *See* Ventimiliensis
Vicensis, 108, 216, 223, 233, 239, 244, 245, 250, 251, 258, 262, 263, 269
Viglevenensis, 242, 250, 256, 262, 263, 267
Vigorniensis, 78n109
Villaebertranus, 271
Vir, 57n26, 68n71, 70n77, 72n88, 82n121, 93n19, 152, 156, 157, 159, 160, 162, 168, 169, 173, 176, 178, 179, 181, 182, 183, 186, 197, 197n49
Virdunensis, 97n30, 100n50, 101–2, 102n58, 107, 108n86, 109, 109n91, 213, 231, 237, 242, 250, 267
Vorst, Peter van der. *See* Aquensis Vorstius
Vosmediano, Melchior a, 117
Vows, 1
Vulturariensis, 100n50, 102n58, 214, 221, 232, 238, 243, 251

Ware, Kallistos, 46n46
Wauchope, Robert, 63, 72

Xantonensis, 257, 262

Yprensis. *See* Hyprensis

Zachary, Pope, 66, 66n66, 190–91
Zanettini, Dionisio de. *See* Chironensis
Zonaras, 45

The Indissolubility of Marriage & the Council of Trent was designed and typeset in Garamond Premier by Kachergis Book Design of Pittsboro, North Carolina. It was printed on 60-pound Sebago IV B18 Cream, and bound by Maple Press of York, Pennsylvania.

www.ingramcontent.com/pod-product-compliance
Lightning Source LLC
Chambersburg PA
CBHW020316010526
44107CB00054B/1860